ORTHODOX CHRISTIANS AND THE RIGHTS REVOLUTION IN AMERICA

ORTHODOX CHRISTIANITY AND CONTEMPORARY THOUGHT

SERIES EDITORS
Aristotle Papanikolaou and Ashley M. Purpura

This series consists of books that seek to bring Orthodox Christianity into an engagement with contemporary forms of thought. Its goal is to promote (1) historical studies in Orthodox Christianity that are interdisciplinary, employ a variety of methods, and speak to contemporary issues; and (2) constructive theological arguments in conversation with patristic sources and that focus on contemporary questions ranging from the traditional theological and philosophical themes of God and human identity to cultural, political, economic, and ethical concerns. The books in the series explore both the relevancy of Orthodox Christianity to contemporary challenges and the impact of contemporary modes of thought on Orthodox self-understandings.

ORTHODOX CHRISTIANS AND THE RIGHTS REVOLUTION IN AMERICA

A. G. ROEBER

FORDHAM UNIVERSITY PRESS
New York • *2024*

Visit us online at www.fordhampress.com.

Library of Congress Cataloging-in-Publication Data available online at https://catalog.loc .gov.

Printed in the United States of America

26 25 24   5 4 3 2 1

First edition

to the suffering church and all citizens of the sovereign
nation-state of Ukraine

CONTENTS

Prologue: A Rights Primer   1

Introduction   21

1   Deferential Society and Church? Protestant to Orthodox Social Ethos   34

2   The Nineteenth-Century Orthodox Confrontation with Rights   67

3   Pluralism and the Rights of Freedom of Speech and Expression   89

4   Rights of and for a Self-Governed American Orthodox Church   116

5   "Greek" North American Orthodox Rights   146

6   The Orthodox, Sex, and Marriage before the Rights Revolution   173

7   The Orthodox, Gender, and Sexuality and the Rights Revolution   205

8   Human Rights Claims and the Orthodox in America   239

Conclusion   287

Bibliography   313

Index   357

ORTHODOX CHRISTIANS AND THE RIGHTS REVOLUTION IN AMERICA

PROLOGUE: A RIGHTS PRIMER

Orthodox Christians have encountered a variety of terms involving rights in the North American context. But they are also heirs of terms that might be thought of as relating to "rights" developed over centuries in historically Orthodox cultures and regimes. It will prove useful for the reader to have at hand a short historical primer of such rights claims, which sometimes overlap, and have changed in meaning and significance over time. Martti Koskenniemi concludes that even "if rights cannot be grounded on faith or philosophy, we might at least think of them historically, as part of the normative organization of a period . . . there are serious interpretive questions about the meaning and relations of 'natural rights,' 'individual rights,' 'subjective rights,' and 'human rights' in different periods."[1]

I. Remote Origins

According to some historians, ancient Stoic philosophers contributed to an understanding of rights, but what the word "rights" meant both in the late ancient world and in its later impact on rights history continues to produce different, and sometimes opposing, assessments. Stoic philosophy

---

1. Martti Koskenniemi, "Rights, History, Critique," in *Human Rights: Moral or Political?*, Adam Etinson, ed. (Oxford: Oxford University Press, 2018), 41–60, at 42–43.

1

placed a heavy emphasis on the importance of justice and equity, based on an appeal to a belief that all humans were bound together by their "nature," an insight developed at length by Cicero.[2] But historians of ancient Rome, while acknowledging the importance of the Stoic tradition, nonetheless conclude that the Stoics, despite their respect for the dignity of humans, did not develop a universal understanding of dignity or "dignitary rights" in the sense that such language is used currently.[3] At least for some historians, the universal understanding of dignity and rights had to await the rise of Christianity. Roman law under the republic had long-established notions of "personality" and "status" before Christianity emerged as a new religious movement at the dawn of the Empire. When Roman jurists wrote of "personality" they addressed how the law of the republic applied to Roman citizens, not to "outsiders." "Status" in that tradition defined free males; full citizens; and then the conditions created by family, marriage, and minority age. This "law of status" allowed Romans "to deal with the rights and duties of different types of persons within the group without the need to create elaborate social mechanisms and legal enforcement to install and perpetuate order" because for the most part "status was determined at birth" and changed only as one passed from child to adult, entered marriage, (and in the case of women) entered a new "natural family."[4] It is accurate to say that Roman law recognized the person or "natural personality," but one cannot argue that a "right" existed for the "subject" in ways that would later inform the growth of "subjective human right." Both philosophers of law and historians concur that *jus* in the Roman context meant "just" or a kind of power that could be attributed to a thing or person—and had little to do with what much later came to be

2. John A. McGuckin, *The Ascent of Christian Law: Patristic and Byzantine Formulations of a New Civilization* (Yonkers, NY: St. Vladimir's Seminary Press, 2012), 54.

3. Kyle Harper, "Christianity and the Roots of Human Dignity in Late Antiquity," in *Christianity and Freedom: Vol. I: Historical Perspectives*, ed. T. Shah and A. Hertzke (Cambridge: Cambridge University Press, 2016), 123–148, at 127–30.

4. William J. Curran, "An Historical Perspective on the Law of Personality and Status with Special Regard to the Human Fetus and the Rights of Women," *Milbank Memorial Fund Quarterly/Health and Society* 61, no. 1 (1983): 58–75, at 58–59.

understood as "subjective right" if we understand that word to imply the capacity or "faculty" of claiming. Thus, it is both correct to say that ancient Romans spoke of "subjective right" meaning *jus*—right and just—but also to assert that they had little sense of "rights-claiming."

Charles Donahue took issue with the argument of some scholars that subjective right is a concept that emerged only in a Western Christian medieval context. Instead, he pointed out, "the notion of subjective right . . . was, in fact, quite fundamental to Roman law. Because the idea of subjective right was quite fundamental to Roman law, there was nothing particularly original about the canonists' and civilians' use of the idea in the twelfth and thirteenth centuries. What was original was the development of the idea of subjective natural right."[5] Unfortunately, the later development of distinctions between "subjective versus objective" rights, especially in the work of G.W.F. Hegel, threatens to bleed back into the ancient to early-modern discussions that had little to do with his assertions. For those earlier generations, a distinction between right as "what is right" and right as a "sphere of authority" perhaps best expresses their worldview. Moreover, they would have insisted that authority to make choices and decisions did not release one from moral obligations.[6]

But a long argument has emerged since the 1970s about where to locate a "divide" between ancient Roman understanding of subjective right, the medieval Western Christian development of natural rights, and then, modern claims for individual rights. Moreover, in attempting to trace the origins of rights concepts, alternative readings of the evidence continue to

5. Charles Donahue, Jr., "*Ius* in the subjective sense in Roman law. Reflections on Villey and Tierney," in *A Ennio Cortese*, ed. Domenico Maffei et al., 3 vols. (Rome: Il Cigno Galileo Galilei, 2001), 1:506–535, at 506; Fabian Wittreck, *Christentum und Menschenrechte* (Tübingen: Mohr Siebeck, 2013), 6–9. See also Tony Honore, *Ulpian: Pioneer of Human Rights*, 2nd ed. (Oxford: Oxford University Press, 2002). For important explorations of the pre-Christian and Christian explorations of the "self as individual" see Alexis Torrance and Johannes Zachhuber, eds., *Individuality in Late Antiquity* (Farnham, UK: Ashgate, 2014).

6. I am indebted to Philip Hamburger for pointing out this danger. On Hegel's views, see Steven B. Smith, "What is "Right" in Hegel's Philosophy of Right," *American Political Science Review* 83:1 (March, 1989), 3–18; David James, "Subjective Freedom and Necessity in Hegel's *Philosophy of Right*," *Theoria: A Journal of Social and Political Theory* 59:131 (June, 2012), 41–63.

produce different conclusions that bear on how, and to what degree, Orthodox Christians can reconcile such modern claims to their own theological convictions. Rather than attempting an analysis of each participant's point of view, or rehearsing the vast literature on these topics, we need to focus on those elements that bear directly on how the experience of rights claims created the particular version in the North American context with which the Orthodox had to contend.[7] Scholars who have pondered the origins of the concept of the "self" have continued to offer different assessments of the importance of interior experience that emerged from the Franciscan thought of the fourteenth century, and they have built upon the profound influence of Augustine of Hippo's explorations. Even if expressed at times in Aristotelian categories, this focus on interior experience led most people in the West to a rejection of nominalism and to locate both sensation and reflection in the mystery of cognition.[8] In that development remote figures once regarded as avatars of a secular vision of rights, such as the Italian Renaissance figure Pico della Mirandola, have now received a closer reading, revealing how deeply even such controversial figures maintained their loyalty to a Christian perspective on God and his relationship to human affairs.[9]

Brian Tierney, Francis Oakley, and other scholars have probed the legacy of ancient Roman law and the Western theological debates that broke

---

7. The summaries below draw upon the following: Siegfried Van Duffel, "From Objective Right to Subjective Rights: The Franciscans and the Interest and Will Conceptions of Rights," in *The Nature of Rights: Moral and Political Rights in Late Medieval and Early Modern Philosophy*, ed. Virpi Mäkinen (Helsinki: The Philosophical Society of Finland, 2010), 63–92; Thomas Mautner, "How Rights Became 'Subjective,'" *Ratio Juris* 26, no. 1 (March 2013): 111–132.

8. Christian Rode, *Zugänge zum Selbst: Innere Erfahrung in spätmittelalter und früher Neuzeit* (Münster: Aschendorff Verlag, 2016), 399–476, at 467.

9. On Pico della Mirandola's 1486 oration and his decidedly non-Kantian Christology and focus on mystical union with God, see the entry in the *Stanford Encyclopedia of Philosophy*: Brian Copenhaver, "Giovanni Pico della Mirandola," *The Stanford Encyclopedia of Philosophy* (Fall 2016). http://plato.stanford.edu /entries/pico-della-mirandola/ (accessed July 31, 2014); M.V. Doughtery, "Three Precursors to Pico della Mirandola's Roman Disputation and the Question of Human Nature in the *Oratio*," in *Pico della Mirandola: New Essays,* Doughtery, ed. (Cambridge: Cambridge University Press, 2008), 114–151, especially at 132–146.

out in the twelfth century. Far from confining the concept of "right" to corporate bodies, a small but influential group of theologians argued that, based on biblical precedent, and even, in a limited fashion, on aspects of ancient, pre-Christian Roman law, rights emanated from the principle of consent and from within the Church—as well as from secular concepts and forms of concern for property rights, worldly privilege, and human dignity.[10] Charles Donahue insists that "the idea of subjective right was quite fundamental to Roman law," and the thirteenth-century decretalists built on this to develop "the idea of subjective natural right." Granted that the Roman term *ius* was quite ambiguous, nonetheless it encompassed "not only a body of normative rules, a legal order, and . . . a right of an individual . . . but also an objective situation that was right. . . ."[11] By the mid-1200s, scholars in the West had focused increasingly on William of Ockham's claims about rights, at least insofar as those discussions shaped events on the Western European continent. But Tierney in particular has shown that the tendencies scholars, such as Michel Villey, identified in Ockham were already developing in the twelfth century. Whether Ockham's claims contributed to the specifically English political debates about rights versus the role of law, deserves more elaborate consideration that we must undertake shortly. But what we can say immediately is that the thirteenth-century decretalists developed various synonyms "when they wished to provide substitutes for the word *ius* used subjectively." "When we speak of rights in the Church we do not speak of an alien or a strictly secular concept . . . rather, we are making use of a set of concepts that was given its early shape and definition by the canon lawyers of the twelfth and thirteenth centuries. A rights vocabulary is accordingly an integral part of

10. Brian Tierney, *The Idea of Natural Rights: Studies on Natural Rights, Natural Law and Church Law 1150-1625* (Atlanta: Scholars Press, 1997), 13–77; James H. Hutson, "The Emergence of the Modern Concept of a Right in America: The Contribution of Michel Villey," *The American Journal of Jurisprudence* 39 (1994): 185–224; for the warning that for Ockham, a "human right . . . is a right, all things being equal, to (take steps for one's own) survival based on mentally competent personhood, and which may only be activated in times of extreme need, or in an environment not subject to conventional human positive law;" Jonathan Robinson, *William of Ockham's Early Theory of Property Rights in Context* (Leiden: Brill, 2013), 4.

11. Donahue, "*Ius* in the subjective sense," 506, 507.

the Church's tradition."[12] Endorsers of Tierney's accomplishment point to his central claim that "rights may be seen as a web of doctrines which transcends the present, has deep roots in the past, and has a universal validity and applicability . . . [and] if Tierney is right . . . subjective rights are not the creation of a selfish, individualistic, capitalistic society. Rather, they have long been a part of Western thought. The concept of rights arose in societies whose spirits were far more communitarian than ours today and whose laws were not as closely identified with the will of the nation-state."[13] The disagreements between Tierney and Villey may come down to this, that Villey claimed that the "new conception of rights was the first step on the downhill road to modernity, individualism, egoism, and neglect of social solidarity and the common good" divorced from the "overall objective and just order which was given a classical statement by Thomas Aquinas."[14] Tierney does not cast the medieval debates in this light. Some Orthodox do; others, as we will see, do not.

Arguments about how the belief in natural rights grew from medieval to early modern Christian societies also depend upon a contested reading of Paul's letter to the Romans, especially Chapter 5 verse 12 where the apostle addresses the question of whether there is a kind of "law written on the heart"—which, if one accepts the assertion—has provided the basis for further claims that a "law of nature" exists, understood as a kind of reasoning that free persons can deploy to identify and choose that which is deemed to be good from that understood to be evil. Whatever the Apostle Paul believed to be the case, his scholarly contemporaries in Second Temple Judaism were not of one mind as to whether a basic set of "Noachic" laws

---

12. Charles J. Reid, Jr., "Thirteenth-Century Canon Law and Rights: The Word *ius* and Its Range of Subjective Meanings," *Studia canonica* 30 (1996): 295–342, at 299, 342.

13. Kenneth Pennington, "Review Essay: The History of Rights in Western Thought," *Emory Law Journal* 47 (1998): 237–252, at 238, 240.

14. Mautner, "How Rights Became 'Subjective'," 125. The claim that seventeenth-century notions of natural rights stemmed from individuals and their entry into civil social compacts is advanced by C.B. MacPherson, *The Political Theory of Possessive Individualism* (Oxford: Oxford University Press, 1962); Ian Shapiro, *The Evolution of Rights in Liberal Theory* (Cambridge: Cambridge University Press, 1986) traces the later (and in his argument, negative) consequences of how the seventeenth-century theorists were subsequently used.

applied universally to humans outside the Covenant. For Christians who accepted Paul's teaching, the most one can say is that as long as one confines one's understanding of "natural law" to this limited view—that people are actually in a position to reason their way to choosing what appears to be good versus a choice that results in evil consequences—one can understand why late-ancient and early medieval Christian theologians assumed that conscience existed, and operated in this fashion. Beyond this limited understanding, however, Orthodox theologians were not inclined to push the argument any further. Rather, aside from some scattered comments, Eastern Orthodox writers devoted little attention to teasing out what was meant by "nature" other than concluding that the word designated what a person or object "was."[15] The quite different historical contexts and lived experiences with forces of nature, warfare, political institutions, and understandings of the Church itself guaranteed the absence of Eastern Orthodox participants in the developing Western Christian understanding of natural law and natural rights.[16]

Because it was the legacy of English political and legal thought and experience that shaped the later debates over rights in the North American context far more than continental philosophy or the impact of Roman law, one important dimension of those debates cannot be overlooked—the role of property and the natural rights claims that were made on its behalf. Nowhere were the claims of William of Ockham repudiated as sharply as they were in England. Himself born in Surrey, England, Ockham is justly remembered for his contribution to medieval political thought by insisting

15. For the literature on Noachic law and varying interpretations, see A.G. Roeber, "'What the Law Requires Is Written on Their Hearts': Noachic and Natural Law among German-Speakers in Early Modern North America," *William and Mary Quarterly*, 3rd Series 58, no. 4 (October, 2001): 883–912, at 884–89. For a deeply skeptical assessment of the possibility of reconciling "natural law" theory to Orthodox understanding of the human person see David Bentley Hart, "Is, Ought, and Nature's Laws," *First Things*, March, 2013, http://www.firstthings.com/article/2013/03/is-ought-and-natures-laws.

16. For explorations of the claim that Orthodox concerns for personhood are not bound up with a concern for "nature" but instead should be understood in terms of existential, phenomenological and personalist insights, see Doru Costache, Darren Cranshaw, and James Harrison, eds., *Wellbeing, Personal Wholeness and the Social Fabric*, (Newcastle on Tyne: Cambridge Scholars Publishing, 2017).

on the separation of power and authority exercised by throne and altar. But his thought has also been identified with those looking to justify a near-absolute right or prerogative to power on the part of sovereigns. His reflections on the nature of Franciscan poverty, shared with other members of his order, came to an end in his own country between his death in 1347 and the renewed drive toward a vigorous exercise of royal prerogative undertaken by the Tudor and Stuart dynasties beginning in 1485. Scholars who have probed his arguments agree that in regard to his use of the word *jus,* "depending on the context, we translate this word into either 'right" or 'law", although it is not always clear which meaning was (primarily) intended." Adding to the difficulties, the Franciscans apparently believed that "having a (legal) right . . . involved having some kind of normative power . . . the rights under consideration were those that can give rise to legal proceedings." It appears that for Ockham as well as many of his contemporaries, "legal rights were often implicitly seen as arising from the exercise of natural rights."[17] Ockham had argued on the basis of a "tertiary natural law" that the rights of a monastic corporation to elect its prior or to decide to sell property owned in common were not inalienable, but alienable rights.[18] While England's canon lawyers may have doubted that property could be located in natural law, suggesting that the law of nations was an example of positive law only, England's common law commentators interpreted the matter differently.[19]

By 1765, Sir William Blackstone's *Commentaries on the Laws of England* summed up a century and a half of refutation of such claims. The "absolute rights" grounded in "immutable laws of nature," Blackstone concluded, had originally been the rights of all humans, but now had become the special preserve and characteristic summation of the "rights of Englishmen." No individual could entirely alienate his rights. A limited alienation was possible but subject to qualifications such as those made by the philosopher John Locke—i.e. short of creating a tyranny. Stopping short of that, government could regulate how limited alienations were worked out in concrete

17. Jonathan Robinson, *William of Ockham's Early Theory of Property Rights in Context,* 65; Van Duffel, "From Objective Right to Subjective Rights," 7.

18. See Tierney, *Idea of Natural Rights,* 170–94.

19. Edward S. Corwin, *The 'Higher Law' Background of American Constitutional Law* (Ithaca: Cornell University Press, 195), 15–23, 21n.62.

terms. None of those qualifications were thought to grant to government an unlimited power to alienate the rights to personal security, personal liberty, and private property. That conviction crossed the Atlantic with British subjects who, in the wake of a revolution, relied heavily on a carefully edited version of Blackstone for their proof that private property was an unalienable right, and rooted in the laws of nature.[20] The seventeenth and eighteenth-century continental philosophical elaborations of novel claims that justice could be derived without indebtedness to ancient and medieval understanding of a right order, cosmic in nature, had little impact on North American discussions of rights. Few North American thinkers probed the threats of the "'pretend' theism of Descartes, and, lurking in the background, the 'atheism' or pantheism of Spinoza . . . [or] Cartesianism, at least as it was imagined by its enemies, [that] was insidious in that it appeared to concede [the existence of God] but, by denying the doctrine of final causes, in fact denied [divine providence]."[21] The sources that shaped American understandings of rights would come instead from the Scottish Common Sense philosophers and North American colonists' indebtedness to a peculiar reading of English history and its defense of the "rights of Englishmen,"[22] both strains of Western philosophical, legal, and theological reflection alien to the Eastern Orthodox.

20. William Blackstone, *Commentaries on the Laws of England: A Facsimile of the First Edition of 1765–1769*, introduction by Stanley N. Katz, 4 vols. (Chicago: University of Chicago Press, 1979), 1:120–41 at 122. Blackstone nonetheless held that no appeal to a higher law could vitiate a statute of Parliament, whose supremacy he defended so strenuously that American admirers had to edit his work in an adaptation and modification of his commentaries. For some details, A. G. Roeber, *Faithful Magistrates and Republican Lawyers: Creators of Virginia Legal Culture, 1680–1810* (Chapel Hill: University of North Carolina Press, 1981), 164, 236, 237, 246.

21. Brian W. Ogilvie, "Natural History, Ethics, and Physico-Theology," in *"Historia": Empiricism and Erudition in Early Modern Europe*, ed. Gianna Pomata and Nancy G. Sirensi (Cambridge and London: MIT Press, 2015), 75–103, at 96. For a further survey of the shift from natural law to natural rights language among political philosophers, see Pauline C. Westerman, *The Disintegration of Natural Law Theory: Aquinas to Finnis* (Leiden: Brill, 1998).

22. On the importance of the Common Sense philosophers see Chapter One and again, Chapter Eight.

II. Origins of Episcopal Rights, Privileges, and Authority

Some might be tempted to argue that we should avoid using the term "rights" altogether when translating words from the Greek that have to do with honor, privilege, and the pre-eminence of bishops in the governance of the Orthodox Church. Unfortunately, in some of the disputes that we examine in the chapters that follow, "rights" is the term that was invoked by disputants. There is no exact equivalent in Orthodox Christianity to "canon law" as that term developed in Roman Catholic or some Protestant communities. The canons, or pastoral measures adopted in local and eventually universal councils, do provide an institutional framework for the bishops of the Church by which they both safeguard the received Tradition of the Orthodox and try to adjust its teachings, beliefs and practices to sometimes difficult and challenging cases.[23] Canons fall into three categories: those that instruct on how dogmatic statements are to be implemented, and hence, are not normally open to debate or challenge; those that have ceased to be invoked because the original political, social, and ecclesial issues they addressed have vanished; and the majority that continue to be adjusted to the experience of Christian communities in contemporary life. To make those adjustments, Orthodox bishops rely on an ancient form of "managing" (*oikonomia*) of household regulations to achieve what is "right and just" (*dikaios*) as well as "condescending" or "coming to the aid or

---

23. "Tradition" in the Orthodox Church encompasses both written and unwritten practices of worship that also carry the substance of belief. Scripture cannot be seen or called Scripture outside the lens of belief in the Cross and Resurrection of Christ testified by an unbroken lived witness within the Church; Scripture and Tradition are not separate, with the latter holding a superior rank under a magisterium of the papacy, as Roman Catholic theologians eventually argued. Nor is Tradition "a possession . . . [but] also as something that receives us . . . the totality of Church's lived experience over time. . . ." (Marcus Plested, "Between Rigorism and Relativism: The Givenness of Tradition," Public Orthodoxy 25 May, 2017, 2; https://publicorthodoxy.org/2017/05/25/between-rigorism-and -relativism (accessed May 27, 2022). For a further introduction, see John Breck, *Scripture in Tradition: The Bible and its Interpretation in the Orthodox Church* (Crestwood, New York: Saint Vladimir's Seminary Press, 2001), 10–12; Anthony Roeber, "Orthodox Christians and Biblical Studies: A Historian's Perspective," *Greek Orthodox Theological Review* 63: 1 / 2 (2018), 61–95.

rescue" (*sygkatabasis*) of a difficult situation. Orthodox Christians continue to think of issues surrounding rights, privileges, authority, and accountability in case-by case terms when addressing concrete wrongs.[24]

By the time a fully developed Christian imperial law emerged in the Eastern Roman Empire, a commitment to a "rule of law, based upon notions of equity and systematic reason" had grown upon which understandings of society could be based. One took for granted that any aspect of what one might call "social contract" depended upon a belief in the "sacral nature of a society caught up in God's work of the deification of humanity. The second was that this theoretical bonding together of the sacred community . . . was made real and concrete by the supreme transnational power of the emperor, God's Vice-Gerent."[25] But the task of achieving "substantive justice" in such a society had to do primarily with "providing a symbolic framework for understanding the world and impressing and internalizing moral and metaphysical lessons—not necessarily addressing 'real' legal and political problems (although it did this too—at least occasionally)."[26] Early Christianity did not rely exclusively on this Roman law tradition but instead claimed for itself the continuation of ancient Israel and that community's sacred writings. Christians were therefore bound to ponder the implications of the teaching of Genesis 1:27: "And God made humankind according to divine image he made it; male and female he made them."[27]

24. For a more extensive discussion of the idea of *oikonomia,* the canons, and the difficulties surrounding a comparison of Orthodox and Western Christian notions of canon law, see Anthony Roeber, *Mixed Marriages,* 23–66.

25. McGuckin, *Ascent of Christian Law,* 253.

26. David F. Wagschal, *Law and Legality in the Greek East: The Byzantine Canonical Tradition, 381–883* (Oxford: Oxford University Press, 2015), 9.

27. Albert Pietersma and Benjamin G. Wright, eds., *A New English Translation of the Septuagint and the other Greek Translations traditionally included under that Title* (Oxford: Oxford University Press, 2007), 7. The translations that specify "image and likeness" rarely identify this device for what it is—*hen diadys*—"one from two" that suggests a singular, rather than a plural quality of the "image." But logically contingent, created beings cannot "be" God but can only share a "likeness" or similarity. For an introduction to the prolix literature on Orthodox "theosis" or "divinization" see Mickey L. Mattox and A.G. Roeber, *Changing Churches,* 69–111.

The Greek terms designating what is "right and just" have rough equivalents in the other languages and cultures that have been historically Orthodox. Thus, the Church Slavonic equivalent of *dikaois* is *pravednj* (i.e., that which is "right") (in modern Russian, *spravedlivyj*); Arabic Christians speak of that which is "right" *hakk (haqq)*.[28] If one looks at ancient, medieval, and early modern texts, Orthodox Christians understood notions of "prerogatives" or "privileges" (*presbeia*) that pertained to age, seniority, rank, and dignity, but such notions did not imply an individual right disconnected from the community of the one exercising such a privilege. The term has been used to convey different meanings in different contexts and thus can be potentially misleading as a guide to what is meant by "rights."[29]

The responsibility of bishops to exercise discretion in the discharge of their office had pre-Christian roots in the Greco-Roman evolution of the term and concept of *oikonomia*. That evolution bequeathed a conflicted legacy with regard to the role of the bishop, as the Church moved

---

28. In other words, "just"—not equality before the written law (*isonomia* or *zakonnyj*).

29. See John H. Erickson, "Chalcedon Canon 28: Its Continuing Significance for Discussion of Primacy in the Church," Orthodox Synaxis, https:// orthodoxsynaxis.files.wordpress.com/2018/10/erickson-chalcedon-canon-28.pdf (accessed October 2018). "If one examines texts . . . one cannot but be struck by the fluidity of terminology. Words like *presbeia, primatus, privilegia, time, honores, potestas, proteia,* and *auctoritas* are used in various combinations and almost interchangeably . . . in some cases *presbeia* may simply mean seniority or precedence, but in other cases it may mean the rights and prerogatives that go with seniority, i.e., an institutionalized position of responsibility." English translation typescript from Erickson, "Canon 28 de Calcedonia: Su permanente significado para el debate del primado en la Iglesia," in *Communio et Sacramentum: En el 70 cumpleaños del Prof. Dr. Pedro Rodriguez,* ed. Jose R. Villar (Pamplona: Universidad de Navarra, 2003), 733- 753; see also Archbishop Peter L'Huillier, *The Church of the Ancient Councils: The Disciplinary Work of the First Four Ecumenical Councils* (Crestwood, NY: St. Vladimir's Seminary Press, 1996), 291–296; Brian E. Daley, S.J., "The Meaning and Exercise of 'Primacies of Honor' in the Early Church," in *Primacy in the Church: The Office of Primate and the Authority of Councils,* ed. John Chryssavgis (Yonkers, NY: St. Vladimir's Seminary Press, 2016), 35–50; Daley, "Universal Love and Local Structure: Augustine, the Papacy, and The Church in Africa," *The Jurist* 64 (2004): 39–63.

from the condition of persecuted to tolerated to imperial religion status, and its clergy were absorbed into the "course of honors" understanding of ascending offices of responsibilities, duties, privileges, honor, and rights. Long after the memory of the Church's sometimes contentious struggles with specific emperors had vanished, the impact of these Roman legal institutions, offices, and practices persist to the present day.[30]

The only source we have on administrative hierarchy (civil and religious) (the *Notitia Dignitatum*) does not give us an actual description of offices, dignities, and privileges as they existed in the then-empire. It was, rather, a rather forlorn attempt at idealization whose purpose was "to illustrate and emphasize the unity and cohesion of the Roman Empire at a time when this unity and cohesion had all but disappeared."[31] By the early fifth century the imperial Church had also adopted the civil tradition of the *cursus honorum*, originally a Roman civic structure of offices demanding greater degrees of service from the holder, but which by the fifth century already suffered from misunderstandings in the Church that now stipulated transition from the diaconate to priesthood or episcopacy. Ambrose of Milan, Cyprian of Carthage, and finally Canon 10 (13) of the Council of Sardica (343 AD?) had already begun to equate the notion of *honorum* with "dignities" borrowed from the later understanding of this word in Roman civil administration, which no longer focused on the obligations and duties the term originally implied.[32] The clergy of the imperial church had been subsumed into the ranks of "honors" but we know little about what specific *presbeia,* the privileges, honors, jurisdictions, and obligations, such titles and offices actually meant in practice. By the time the Council of Chalcedon met in 451 (which failed to resolve Christological differences between advocates of "one" (Miaphysis) versus "two" (Dyophysis)"natures" in the "person" of Christ), the administration of the civil dioceses of the Empire had changed so much that the diocesan *vicarius* had ceased to be a person of political or administrative significance. Instead, real political and

30. For the literature and the evolution of *oikonomia*, see Roeber, *Mixed Marriages*, 52–66.

31. Michael Kulikowski, "The *Notitia Dignitatum* as a Historical Source," *Historia* 49, no. 3 (2000): 358–377, at 358.

32. Philip Zymaris, "Tonsure and Cursus Honorum up to the Photian Era," *Greek Orthodox Theological Review* 56, nos. 1–4 (2011): 321–345.

administrative decisions had already been effectively centralized and controlled by the imperial court officials at Constantinople.[33]

The late ancient understandings of *jus* never equated "right" with "law" (*lex*). But as Christianity grew in numbers and influence within the Roman Empire, its bishops gradually found themselves called upon to render judgments in concrete law cases, a process that created its own legacy for how the Church struggled to do justice within its inherited legal tradition. The first compilation of Roman law under Christian auspices, the *Codex Theodosianus*, begins with the laws of Rome in the reign of the Emperor Constantine and focuses on the imperial constitutions that had long been the actual basis for law since the time of Hadrian (76–138). That fact would be recognized by those who labored to construct Justinian's *Corpus Juris Civilis*. They began their compilation of imperial decrees with Hadrian's reign. Although experts debate the relationship of the so-called Sirmondian Constitutions to the Theodosian Code, most agree that these compilations, composed in the latter seventh century, "have to do with attempts to ally secular with ecclesiastical law, and in particular to show that privileges claimed by the Church under barbarian rulers were based on prerogatives given by the legislation of Roman emperors."[34]

The tension between the privileges that came to be associated especially with Metropolitans (who had duties and obligations to apply the canons within the largest cities and larger territories within the Empire) and reliance upon a more synodal or conciliar model of consultation with other bishops was never entirely resolved. Centralization of secular power thus found an echo in episcopal relations.

The definition of what was "orthodox" became increasingly important as bishops were called upon to discern the "wrong choice" (*airesis*) from "correct teaching" (*orthe doxa*). As bishops were integrated into Roman legal practice, they, like their civil counterparts, had to try to obey the rules of forensic practice and follow the continued elaboration of the law's meaning, despite the existence of imperial laws that appeared to prescribe the

33. Laurent Cases, "Remaking Provincial Administration: Dioceses, Vicarii and Social Change in Late Antiquity (283–395)" (PhD diss., The Pennsylvania State University, 2016).

34. John F. Matthews, *Laying Down the Law: A Study of the Theodosian Code* (New Haven: Yale University Press, 2000), 121–167, especially at 122–23.

outcome of certain kinds of cases. Thus, "even where the legal issue is technically prescribed in a formula tailor-made for the instant case, it still requires interpretation and 'handling' by forensic practitioners. What are forensic arguments in a given case today could influence the judgment of cases in court tomorrow."[35] Bishops could serve not only as judges but also as arbitrators between disputants or be called upon by civil magistrates as expert witnesses. Thus, "from the early fourth century onwards . . . the structure of the *episcopalis audientia* came increasingly to mirror that of the bureaucratic courts. . . ." Moreover, the value of real expertise meant that those men would advance in importance in the church and empire if, as was the case, "key late Roman bishops in the Eastern Church had received an education in forensic rhetoric," such as Gregory Nazianzus, Basil of Caesarea, Gregory of Nyssa, Amphilocius of Iconium, and others. Over the course of the fifth and sixth centuries, the deep involvement of bishops in the intricacies of Roman law, its procedures and complexities, guaranteed the "transformation of bishops from the fishermen of an apostolic church to the forensic orators of an imperial one."[36]

Ancient Israel's concern for doing justice, and, after 318, Roman legal procedures, shaped the development of spiritual courts. The latter development began when the emperor Constantine ordered judges of imperial courts to accept the role of bishops as judges, first in purely ecclesiastical, but gradually in civil and criminal causes. In this tradition, "a central maxim . . . was that a trial is an act that involves three persons: the judge, the actor or plaintiff, and the accused party. Nobody else needed to attend the trial. Only the accused had the right to involve and advocate . . . the judge alone was responsible for ensuring a fair and just procedure in the individual case." In sharp contrast to what developed in the English, and eventually the Anglo-American tradition, no adversarial calling of witnesses with the right of cross examination emerged in the Roman-canonical approach to judicial procedure.[37]

35. Caroline Humfress, *Orthodoxy and the Courts in Late Antiquity* (Oxford: Oxford University Press, 2007), 9–28, at 27.

36. Humfress, *Orthodoxy and the Courts*, 153–195, at 167, 180, 181–2, 272.

37. Mathias Schmoeckel, "Procedure, proof, and evidence," in *Christianity and Law: An Introduction,* ed. John Witte, Jr., and Frank S. Alexander (Cambridge, UK and NY: Cambridge University Press, 2008), 143–162, at 147, 150.

Those who have studied the surviving letters of early bishops also caution us on several fronts. First, much of the surviving corpus of letters stems from the 500s, a century that marked changes in the roles bishops played, changes that had begun during the political and religious crises of the previous century. Second, in the case of eminent and influential bishops who brought former military and civic expertise to their office, for example, from "the dynamic Ephrem, successively comes Orientis and patriarch of Antioch for eighteen years (526–544), we have not a single surviving letter documenting the tumultuous times in which he lived. . . ."[38] Bishops, by virtue of their participation in the judicial/legal structure of the Empire, may have moderated some of the Roman legal use of torture and execution, both at the level of informal dispute resolution as well as in the courtroom practice of forensics. Christian bishops could not help, however, but become increasingly identified by the late fourth century with the more feared aspects of Roman rule, and with the wealthy, the influential, and the powerful claimants of rights, even among their own flocks. The influence of Jewish law that had informed the early bishops' sense of obligation to defend the rights of the poor never vanished entirely. But in the course of the fourth and early fifth centuries, the "Judaic judicial framework was weakened to the point of obliteration by the strong resistance of the Graeco-Roman models of both personal and public patronage . . . while the Jewish model of almsgiving rested upon a precept of equal human dignity between rich and poor, the Christianization of the personal patronage model was ruthlessly hierarchical . . . the increasing aristocratization of the episcopate over the course of our two centuries" applies equally to the Eastern as well as the Western Empire.[39]

---

38. Pauline Allen and Bronwen Neil, *Crisis Management in Late Antiquity (410–590 CE): A Survey of Evidence from Episcopal Letters* (Leiden: Brill, 2013), 2, 26.

39. Allen and Neil, *Crisis Management,* 171–72. In the Jewish legal tradition that addresses rights, "what the secular world would describe as a right that is innately conferred on all individuals by virtue of their existing, Jewish law would impose on them as a duty." There are no "rights" or "entitlements" absent obligation. For more details and a survey of the literature, see Michael J. Broyde, "Human Rights in Judaism Reviewed and Renewed," in A.G. Roeber, ed., *Human v. Religious Rights? German and U.S. Exchanges and their Global Implications* (Göttingen:Vandenhoeck & Ruprecht, 2020), 59–75 at 59, 60.

Procedures followed in these late ancient and medieval episcopal courts and the kinds of cases bishops had to adjudicate also remain difficult to reconstruct. "Although the process of hearing cases according to civil law formed such a large part of the bishop's duties, we are still reasonably in the dark about the kinds of cases brought before him." Although rare exceptions have been found, "the more common impression is that bishops were very little involved in the needs of the poor and oppressed in the fourth century, and only marginally so in the fifth and sixth centuries, and then their interventions were overwhelmingly in favor of the formerly wealthy."[40] The wealthy and the powerful received a hearing much more frequently than the marginal, the poor. At the same time, Christian subjects of the Empire did expect that bishops would seek to temper justice with mercy. Bishops continued to serve both as spiritual leaders and imperial civil servants and were themselves circumscribed by the larger circles of power and influence in the Empire. "We do find in the letters of bishops creative attempts to find solutions to human suffering, but not as often as we see evidence of them using letters to wield power for ends that were less noble, at least from a modern perspective."[41]

Kevin Uhalde's examination of what Christians expected from bishops in pursuit of their quest for justice reveals both how limited the bishops were in achieving this end, and how they eventually cast themselves in the figures of humans who "judge like God." The attempt to contrast their self-portraits as persons judging according to divine precepts with discretion and discernment was intended to place their role as judges on a higher plane than the "hastier, scattershot, and always bloody inquisition of ordinary judges."[42] The "judicial culture" bishops inherited included the perennial problem of "calumny," whose persistence threatened both the empire and the Church since the term "took in whatever might threaten the judicial system and foster uncertainty over its ability to deliver justice." Bishops' courts were bound by the same secular rules of evidence in religious affairs as were demanded in civil disputes and thus these standards "limited what laypeople could expect from episcopal justice." Recognizing the

---

40. Allen and Neil, *Crisis Management*, 174, 177.

41. Allen and Neil, *Crisis Management*, 202, 203.

42. Kevin Uhalde, *Expectations of Justice in the Age of Augustine* (Philadelphia: University of Pennsylvania Press, 2007), 66.

failure of ordinary imperial legislation to curb the curse of calumny, the "oath of calumny" had been imposed before Christian times, a move that "exploited the religious force inherent within Roman law in order to bring the threat of divine revenge to bear on the perjurer. It was one of the earliest means of preventing false accusations and vexatious litigation." To that, ordinary Christians added the use of curses, spells, and prayers to the saints. And even though various canons emerged as a means for wealthier laity to proceed against bishops as well as for punishing laity falsely accusing clergy of wrong-doing, these canons addressed the rights and wrongs of powerful and wealthy persons. They remained almost exclusively concerned with disputed wills, legacies, and property matters. Not even excommunication could be wielded by bishops because the due process demands for public evidence meant that a private confession of guilt failed the evidentiary test. And if bishops' hands were tied with regard to powerful and wealthy lay offenders, even less so could the marginally well-off or the poor expect to see justice speedily—or even, eventually, done.[43] The demand for order and the avoidance of chaos—commonly understood as the preconditions for the exercise of Christian virtue—also led by the sixth century to both imperial and episcopal determination to impose, by force if necessary, correct Christian doctrine and practice. This primary concern of the bishops also brought with it demands for more ascetically inclined episcopal candidates. Thus arose the popularity of the monk-bishop who, whatever his personal virtues, was by definition a person even more disconnected to the everyday concerns of the Christians living "in the world."[44]

Bishops themselves conceded that they were somewhat hapless—"representing divine justice while administering worldly justice, dealing in timeless truth and absolute categories of salvation while neck deep in the treachery of human society, bishops could not do everything their occupation required with uniform success."[45] After initial attempts

---

43. Uhalde, *Expectations of Justice*, 19–37, at 19, 20, 22, 32, 36–7.

44. This conclusion can be followed in detail in Claudia Rapp, *Holy Bishops in Late Antiquity: The Nature of Christian Leadership in an Age of Transition* (Berkeley: University of California Press, 2003); Andrea Sterk, *Renouncing the World Yet Leading the Church: The Monk-Bishop in Late Antiquity* (Cambridge, MA: Harvard University Press, 2004).

45. Uhalde, *Expectations of Justice*, 137.

during the 530s to reconcile Dyo- and Mia-physite Christians in his Empire, Justinian by the 550s turned to military force to suppress his subjects who refused to accept the teachings agreed upon by the majority of bishops attending the 451 Council of Chalcedon.[46] Among the most implacable of his episcopal allies the emperor counted the former military commander and now Patriarch of Antioch Ephrem who, even before Justinian's shift in tactics, used military force to suppress Miaphysites in his Patriarchate, a violent strategy that had been pioneered by the anti-Chalcedonians themselves in their murder of Bishop Stephen in 479.[47] Although such incidents can and should be judged in the context of their times, the legacy of the Orthodox episcopal claim to the right of personal discretion and authority has fostered a corresponding unwillingness to acknowledge the tendency toward an authoritarian understanding of episcopal office that has cast a long shadow over discussions of the rights not only of bishops singly and as a body, but of others. Denial of this tendency has led to embarrassing instances where Orthodox bishops have asserted that "there was nothing for which Orthodoxy had to ask pardon," and that the Orthodox have never "exploited the civil authorities to achieve its aims. . . ." despite unimpeachable evidence that "when it had the power of the Byzantine Empire behind it, the Orthodox Church rammed itself down the throats of others without scruple (if you do not believe that, you have never talked to a Copt or an Armenian.")[48] Moreover, between the tenth and the seventeenth century, as the Eastern Roman Empire itself began its long collapse, bishops acquired the vestments, symbols, and privileges of the Imperial court itself, leading to an

46. For the shift in Justinian's objectives and tactics, John Behr, ed. and trans., *The Case against Diodore and Theodore: Texts and their Contexts* (Oxford: Oxford University Press, 2011), 105–129.

47. Allen and Neil, *Crisis Management*, 74–5, 106.

48. Robert F. Taft, S.J., "Perceptions and Realities in Orthodox-Catholic Relations Today: Reflections on the Past, Prospects for the Future," in *Orthodox Constructions of the West*, ed. George E. Demacopoulos and Aristotle Papanikolaou (New York: Fordham University Press, 2013), 23–44 at 33. For further reflections on this turn toward "ecclesiastical colonialism," see Stephen J. Davis, *The Early Coptic Papacy: The Egyptian Church and its Leadership in Late Antiquity* (Cairo: The American University in Cairo Press, 2017), 85–128 at 87.

even more elaborate identification of the "rights" of the episcopacy with those of monarchy.[49]

With these compressed summaries of ancient to early modern contributions to the variety of rights terms and claims, we turn specifically to the North American context. We begin with an introduction, which explains where this book fits into the larger questions scholars of law and religion in North America have now put to Orthodox Christians. Those people find themselves forced to reconcile the wide variety of inherited understandings of rights that come from their own late ancient to early modern experiences with a profoundly different North American heritage of rights language and the consequent vision of what a society should look like.[50]

49. Vassa Larin, "The Hierarchal Liturgy in Late Byzantium and After: Toward a Liturgical Ecclesiology," *St. Vladimir's Theological Quarterly* 55:1 (2011), 5–26, and more extensively, Larin, *The Byzantine Hierarchal Divine Liturgy in Arsenij Suxanov's Proskinitarij* (Rome, Italy: Pontificio Instituto Orientale; *Orientalia Christiana Analecta* 286, 2010).

50. Unless a particular case or controversy calls for more discussion, I do not discuss in detail "moral rights," e.g., rights having to do with intellectual property issues. Nor do I attempt to assess the debate between Lon Fuller and H.L.A. Hart on the separation of law and morals (H.L.A. Hart, "Positivism and the Separation of Law and Morals," *Harvard Law Review* 71 (1958): 593–629 and Lon Fuller, *The Morality of Law: Revised Edition* (New Haven: Yale University Press, 1964), 187–242). I do touch on moral rights because the topic has arisen as part of the discussion of human rights. I assume the kind of ascending scale of rights Kyle Harper suggests, that rights are usually legal but civil rights "are the just powers and immunities immanent in citizenship and promised in equal measure to all citizens." Constitutional rights serve as a guarantor of civil and political rights, the latter two related and the result of legislation on the part of a state authority. Political rights emphasize procedural fairness in law, including the rights of redress, assembly, petition, and voting. Legal rights pertain to claims recognized and enforceable. Civil rights differ from civil liberties since the latter involve the restraints placed on authority by citizens or subjects, whether in the form of a written or unwritten constitution of a particular polity. But natural rights like human rights claims are regarded as "above, beyond, outside, or prior to any institution." (See Harper, "Christianity and the Roots of Human Dignity," 124–25.) I assess different generations of human rights and claims about their origins with respect to Orthodox perspectives in Chapter Eight.

INTRODUCTION

This book investigates how Orthodox Christians in the United States have selectively embraced, but also rejected an increasing and sometimes bewildering variety of "rights languages." Orthodox engagements with rights claims involve issues both internal and external to the Church. The Orthodox, along with other Christians, struggle with the manner in which rights claims have exploded since the 1960s, the period identified by commentators foreign and domestic as the beginning of the "rights revolution."[1] Sociologists, most famously James Davison Hunter, located the division that we might argue has driven the expansion of rights claims. That division became manifest in the 1960s between those who continue to defer to a religious text, ancient philosophy, political theory, or religious tradition as authoritative versus those who view institutions and authoritative claims of the past with suspicion. The latter have championed the cause of political liberty, individual conscience, and freedom of choice and expression.[2] On the surface, given the history of their Orthodox homelands where deference to tradition, age, and authority were taken for granted, the Orthodox in

1. For example, Charles R. Epp, *The Rights Revolution: Lawyers, Activists, and Supreme Courts in Comparative Perspective* (Chicago: University of Chicago Press, 1998); Michael Ignatieff, *The Rights Revolution (CBC Massey Lecture)*, 2nd ed. (Toronto: House of Anansi Press, 2007).

2. James Davison Hunter, *Culture Wars: The Struggle to Define America: Making Sense of the Battles over the Family, Art, Education, Law and Politics* (New York: Basic Books, 1991).

North America seem to be denizens of the first group. In fact, they have become sometimes uneasy converts to the second. Moreover, they struggle with loyalty to each position. The late theologian John Meyendorff recognized the willingness of at least some Orthodox "to celebrate the burial of Christian empires and states." But he wondered if endorsement of the values of liberty of conscience, choice, and expression might not lead to a version of Christianity not altogether different from its ancient and early modern past. Might it not be the case, he queried, that Christians would end up being tempted to "solve the problems of this world . . . and practically, to use secular means to attain a goal which has been set by others."[3]

Because of changes in how Americans have come to make claims about "natural rights," "legal rights," "civil rights," "religious rights," "contractual rights," and "moral rights," even citizens not familiar with the history of American law cannot avoid noting controversies that have erupted regarding religious rights and freedoms that appear to pit claims to privacy and individual rights against historic religious bodies and teachings. Secular critics have demanded reassessment of long-standing court inclinations to protect religious rights under notions of "accommodation," "ministerial privilege," "neutral principles," and "deference." Experts will argue about the details, but the claim to a "right" to privacy, for example, has thrown into sharp relief the difference between constitutional "originalists," all of whom are also "textualists," and opponents who believe that in order for the U.S. Constitution to guard "life, liberty, and the pursuit of happiness" declared by the Declaration of Independence to be "unalienable rights," it must address the lived experience of citizens. Americans, such opponents argue, cannot rest content on a supposed recovery of what the authors of that distant past intended and what meaning they gave to a text. To a far lesser extent, but no less controversially, similar quarrels have arisen surrounding the historical texts that have shaped the governance of the Orthodox Church.

Faced with such a maelstrom of rights claims, one is tempted to abandon any attempt at a coherent narrative of how the Orthodox navigated the changes in rights languages. Historians of an older generation (including this author) probably read Isaiah Berlin's famous 1953 essay *The Hedgehog and the Fox* less as a clarification of the scholar's understanding of history than as a

---

3. John Meyendorff, *Living Tradition: Orthodox Witness in the Contemporary World* (Crestwood, NY: St. Vladimir's Seminary Press, 1978), 143.

description of how they go about their own work.[4] Is one the hedgehog, expert on a single, carefully identified idea, concept, or phenomenon? Or do one's writings reveal the fox-like curiosity about many things? The present essay follows the fox partly out of necessity, given the conflation of various "rights languages", partly because of the author's own inclinations. Whether following the fox along the trails of such rights language results in at least some degree of satisfaction, the reader will have to judge. To provide some markers around the pursuit, the historical method this essay follows begins with the advice of two eminent scholars of law and religion in the United States. The chapters of the book devote attention to their queries.

In their collection of essays, *The Teachings of Modern Christianity*, John Witte Jr. and Frank S. Alexander ask how the Orthodox in the United States address the following questions: What do the Orthodox deem essential "to the regime of human rights"? How do they "reconstruct Christian theories of society"? What is the "meaning of freedom of speech and expression"? How do the Orthodox understand "the meaning of gender equality"?[5] Because this book is a history, and because Orthodox engagement with the "regime of human rights" began quite recently, we postpone examining that question until the very end of the book. We begin with the examination not just of theories of Christian societies, but very specifically, the lived experience of the Orthodox in American society and various Christian claims about it. A reader will recognize right away that these questions overlap with one another, and for the sake of avoiding repetition I choose to address the questions in a narrative from early modern to late modern, saving for the very end, where I ask whether the terms "post-modern" and "post-secular" help or hinder the Orthodox engagement with rights claims.

The Eastern and Oriental Orthodox in North America have grown since the nineteenth century into a complex body composed of First Peoples, immigrants from traditionally Orthodox parts of the world, converts from other Christian traditions, and those from non-religious backgrounds. The time, place, and character of Orthodox Christianity's presence in North

---

4. Isaiah Berlin, *The Hedgehog and the Fox: An Essay on Tolstoy's View of History*, ed. Henry Hardy, 2nd ed. (Princeton: Princeton University Press, 2013).

5. John Witte, Jr., and Frank S. Alexander, eds. *The Teachings of Modern Christianity on Law, Politics, and Human Nature*, 2 vols. (New York: Columbia University Press, 2006). 1:xxxi-xxxii.

America deserve attention because they all had profound impact upon how the Orthodox would encounter various rights claims. The Orthodox remain a very small group in the overall population of the United States (less than 2 percent) among a global population of the Orthodox estimated at about 260 million. Strictly speaking, before the schism that separated the Orthodox from the Latin West (between 1054 and the 1200s) one could have legitimately identified the first Orthodox in North America with the Norse settlements in Greenland (980 to the fifteenth century) or the brief (1021) Newfoundland attempt at settlement at L'Anse aux Meadows. But a lasting presence of the Orthodox did not take root on the Atlantic coast of North America. Rather, in 1794, with the arrival of monastics in Alaska (following their cross-continental journey on foot from the Valaam monastery in Karelia on the far northwestern edge of the Russian Empire to the voyage across the Bering Sea), the Orthodox became a permanent part of the larger story of Christianity in North America. The purpose of that missionary endeavor focused on the conversion of First Peoples of America to Orthodox Christianity. Only subsequently, with the arrival of a bishop and the work of both Russian and Creole converts, did the mission expand by the 1840s to serve Russian speakers from Alaska southward to Fort Ross and Russian sailors and settlers in San Francisco. The acquisition of Alaska by the United States in 1867 triggered the first intense debates over "rights" between the Orthodox and arriving Presbyterians. And only with the surge in migration from East-Central Europe, Russia, the Balkans, and the Middle East did the Russian Mission shift its headquarters to San Francisco in 1872 and finally to New York by 1905, turning its attention to the arrivals and away from its original missionary purpose. By that time, both the First Peoples converts and the Slavic- and Arabic-speaking arrivals had become a minority among the Orthodox following a massive arrival of Greek speakers, who probably constituted the majority of the Eastern Orthodox in North America at the outbreak of World War I and remain so today. Thus, adoption and affirmation of various kinds of rights claims by the Orthodox was never uniform, nor concerned solely with how rights have come to be understood in the social and political arena but included debates over the rights and privileges of laity, clergy, and hierarchy within the Orthodox Church itself.[6]

6. For more details, see https://www.pewresearch.org/religion/2017/11/08 /orthodox-christianity-in-the-21st-century/; Thomas E. Fitzgerald, *The Orthodox*

The privileges, honor, and rights of the late-arriving Orthodox bishops sparked repeated clashes over property and contract rights claimed by the laity that challenged the age-old culture of deference to hierarchs. Considerable tension emerged—and has never been entirely resolved—between those who rely upon the legacy of ancient Roman law's emphasis on the authority, duties, rights and privileges of the magistrate (and by extension the monarchical bishop) versus those who point to a medieval natural rights tradition that argued, among other significant claims, that the consent of the governed—initially a very small and privileged group of laity in a variety of ethnic parishes—had to be obtained in order to guard liberties wedded to a Protestant understanding of an ancient and never-ending contest against the pretensions of monarchs, hierarchs, and lay aristocrats.

Because various kinds of rights continue to be invoked, even the history of some of the specific rights terms remains contested ground. The prologue provides a survey of both the terms and the arguments among scholars about origins, historical meanings, and present-day implications. Chapter One then examines the social and cultural ethos of the late eighteenth and the nineteenth century in North America into which the Orthodox appeared by the 1790s—albeit in then Russian-held Alaska. By the time of their arrival, the Orthodox lay members of a fur trading company remained untouched by the rejection of deference to a Christian monarch and the aristocratic societies of Europe where the clergy comprised one of the "estates." But the social-cultural vision of the newly created United States did not result in the abandonment of deference. Propertied, white, and increasingly young, Protestant males shaped the society of the new republic. To the profound disappointment of key personalities among the founders, those young Americans also embraced one or the other variety of revivalist and increasingly personal Protestant Christianity. By the last third of the nineteenth century, when the Orthodox clashed openly with the Presbyterian version of an American "Christian" society, the Russian clergy also took aim at the baneful legacy of what they identified as "the Enlightenment." Those criticisms shaped how

---

Church (Boston: Greenwood Press, 1995); John H. Erickson, *Orthodox Christians in America: A Short History* (New York: Oxford University Press, 2008); Mark A. Noll, *A History of Christianity in the United States and Canada* (Grand Rapids, MI: William B. Eerdmans Publishing Company, 1992), 344–48; John Anthony McGuckin, *The Eastern Orthodox Church: A New History* (New Haven and London, 2020), 181–254.

the Orthodox would struggle to reconcile social assumptions inherited from their homelands with the attempt on the part of Protestants to have the United States officially proclaimed a "Christian nation." The "Christian nation" claim that once stood for "traditional values" continues to resonate among some American Orthodox even though from an historical and doctrinal perspective, the United States was never Orthodox Christian. It only has the potential to *become* a nation whose social, cultural, and theological worship and teachings reflect an Orthodox understanding of God and what it means to be fully human. Visions of what kind of society the United States should be continued to be shaped well into the twentieth century by various forms of Reformed Protestant theology and practices, increasingly by those attached to a vague "religion of the heart." What neither the Orthodox nor their Protestant belligerents appreciated, however, was the degree to which between 1865 and 1900 a more openly and unapologetically secular social vision that relied on a pragmatic and positivist view of the law had already begun to erode the older Protestant assumptions.[7]

Chapter Two takes up those conflicts in the nineteenth century context. Chapter Three then examines the central problem of how the Orthodox understand pluralism as the context for asking questions about "freedom of speech and expression." Disputes about this topic emerged as a primary characteristic of American social and political life in the late nineteenth century at the very time Orthodox Christians began a rapid expansion of their numbers, overwhelmingly among the laity first, with a small number of parish priests following, and finally, bishops. For some Orthodox critics of American pluralism, there persists the ongoing allure of a social and political order shaped and enforced by an Orthodox willingness to rely upon the power and authority of a state to achieve such an end. That approach is most obvious in the stance of the Patriarchate of Moscow and the Russian Orthodox Church.[8] Given this powerful and influential counter example of how the rights of others and Orthodox beliefs are accepted, American

---

7. See Steven K. Green, *Inventing a Christian America: The Myth of the Religious Founding* (Oxford: Oxford University Press, 2015); Carl H. Esbeck and Jonathan J. Den Hartog, eds., *Disestablishment and Religious Dissent: Church-State Relations in the New American States, 1776–1833* (Columbia, MO: University of Missouri Press, 2019).

8. Kristina Stoeckl, *The Russian Orthodox Church and Human Rights* (London: Routledge, 2014).

Orthodox communities—a mix of "cradle" and "convert" parishioners—differ considerably in their appreciation of or abhorrence for the pluralistic expressions of opinion and belief in North American life. By examining the prevailing assessments of American political and social life from the writings of major American Orthodox authors, we glean additional insight into how the Orthodox esteem the American socio-political experience with claims to freedom of religion and expression. Orthodox struggles with this question continued to be informed well into the 1960s by alarms raised by Protestant commentators, and subsequently in engagements with Catholic reflections on the advantages people of faith enjoyed to freely follow their convictions in a constitutionally grounded representative democracy. Chapter Four then explores how questions of rights to self-determination have become deeply controversial in the North American Orthodox context as a consequence of the Bolshevik Revolution, the policies of the Soviet Union, and the Cold War.

Chapter Five demonstrates how the struggle over the right of self-determination engulfed not just the descendants of the original Russian Mission, but by the 1980s, Greek- and Arabic- speaking Eastern Orthodox as well. Chapters Six and Seven then turn to Witte and Alexander's question about how the Orthodox have struggled with questions raised by the women's rights movement, and questions of marriage before the "rights revolution" and then to gender feminism, difficult bio-ethical questions, and sexuality. These stand among the most volatile rights debates facing the Orthodox in America. They arose in the mid- to late 1960s and appear to pit religious and civil rights claims against one another in a particularly stressful manner. These chapters assess how these questions of rights in the American legal-constitutional context shape an Orthodox response, and how the Orthodox bring to these issues insights and experiences that should in turn mold the larger American handling of these claims. The Orthodox Church confronts pleas for more attention to the lived experience of women and sexual minorities. These voices have proven as challenging as jousts with government administrators and responses to challenges to religious rights brought by aggressive secular citizens who have come to regard much of Catholic, Protestant, and Orthodox America as inimical to the rights claims made by LGBT persons.[9]

9. I choose to use the shorter abbreviation (LGBT) given the paucity of Orthodox theological commentary beyond same-sex relations and the question of gender dysphoria. See Chapter Seven.

Chapter Eight turns to North American Orthodox engagement with the shifting understandings of what constitutes "the regime of human rights." No one book on the Orthodox and the variety of rights claims in the United States can address all aspects of the questions Witte and Alexander posed. An assessment of how the Orthodox engage with major thinkers in contemporary philosophy occurs in the engagement with (for example) Catholic philosophers such as Charles Taylor and Adrian Pabst, and Protestant theologians including John Milbank and Nicholas Wolterstorff with regard to specific cases and questions, especially the critical judgment of whether "modern" notions of natural rights and human rights represent a decline and departure from the "classical" origins of those terms.[10]

Some Christians have concluded that the rise of an aggressive, individualistic secularism has made it increasingly difficult for Christians to defend their belief in the rights of all human persons grounded in the identity of humans created in the image and likeness of God. As debates about rights have intensified, the term "human rights" has been invoked by some who claim that what historically and legally were defined as civil rights should now be understood as part of human rights. But the term "human rights" played little or no role in the Orthodox discussion of rights before the end of World War II, and the meaning of that term understood in its immediate post-war context has also now changed dramatically. Religious and secular commentators alike agree on the importance of paying attention to the worth, the dignity, of the individual human person. But agreement—even about how to understand dignity—stops there. One important assessment of how "human dignity" has come to be used by judges, for example, argues that historical scrutiny of how this term developed reveals that "there are several conceptions of dignity that one can choose from, but one cannot coherently hold all of these conceptions at the same time. Dignity appears to become other than impossibly vague only when it is tethered to a coherent community of interpretation."[11] The same can be said for the variety of languages that fall under the term

---

10. My initial reflections on Taylor can be followed in Anthony Roeber, *Mixed Marriages: An Orthodox History* (Yonkers, NY: St. Vladimir's Seminary Press, 2018), 215–231.

11. Christopher McCrudden, "Human Dignity and Judicial Interpretation of Human Rights," *The European Journal of International Law* 19, no. 4 (2008): 655–724, at 723.

"rights." This has especially become the case because the understanding of what rights consist of has shifted in the United States context toward identity politics for some. For others, disenchantment with political radicalism as a way of securing any universal implications of rights has led them—whether committed to a religious view of the world or not—to prefer engagement with specific social, economic, or political wrongs. It is not only the Orthodox who have become discouraged by the difficulty that surrounds defining what we mean by human rights. But for Orthodox Christians no less than for philosophers, social scientists, and legal scholars, if individual human dignity and rights discourse cannot provide a consensus about the substantive meaning of such terms, nonetheless a language has developed by which we can "justify how [we] deal with issues such as the weight of rights, the domestication and contextualization of rights, and the generation of new or more extensive rights."[12]

The conclusion to this book has been shaped by two global crises that have intensified Orthodox concerns about rights: the COVID-19 pandemic, and the Russian invasion of Ukraine. Although no one at present can confidently predict the long-term implications of either, an historical examination of how the Orthodox have responded to these crises and the resulting focus on rights cannot be avoided.

As is always the case, I am indebted to a long list of colleagues from around the world who have instructed me, participated in conference sessions, read drafts, and responded to queries as I have attempted to frame the argument. In many respects, this book has become a kind of summary statement that draws upon work undertaken over a forty-plus year career. If there is a consistent theme to those labors, it emerges as a persistent questioning about how Christian belief has intersected with, influenced, or conflicted with legal cultural norms and expectations in different historical settings. In some respects, the present work comes full circle, concentrating as it does on religion and law questions in the context of the United States. I remain indebted to my *Doktorvater* Gordon S. Wood and to the late William G. McLoughlin, Jr. and Sumner B. Twiss, all of whom shaped

12. Ibid., 724. For a more extensive summary of the different assessments of human dignity see Christopher McCrudden, "In Pursuit of Human Dignity: An Introduction to Current Debates," in *Understanding Human Dignity*, ed. Christopher McCrudden (Oxford: Oxford University Press/The British Academy, 2013), 1–58.

my engagement with legal-constitutional questions and their intersection with religious norms and practices. My initial inquiries into the difficult processes that allowed a transplanting and transformation of English legal norms to early North America and the early American Republic continue to inform my arguments even today. Recognizing how little I knew about a large non-English population's grasp both of law and of their specific religious commitments led to a second inquiry into ideas of "liberty" and "property" in a trans-Atlantic context. A planned extension of those arguments in the 1990s came to a sudden halt because I had to re-assess my personal and professional understanding of both Catholic and Protestant debates over how God works in human societies, what legal norms emerged from those understandings, and how those debates appeared to provide unconvincing defenses against the radical critiques of Western theological anthropology. A personal and familial decision to become Orthodox Christian re-directed the trajectory of professional inquiry as well.[13]

Thus, a long-planned book on the relationship between law and Christianity in North America that began in the 1990s transmogrified into the present version. My re-reading of the history of Christianity and various forms of the law in Europe, India, and North America drew upon earlier work and reflected some revised judgments made under quite different faith

13. A.G. Roeber, *Faithful Magistrates and Republican Lawyers: Creators of Virginia Legal Culture, 1680–1810* (Chapel Hill, North Carolina: University of North Carolina Press, 1981); Roeber, *Palatines, Liberty, and Property: German Lutherans in Colonial British America* (Baltimore and London: Johns Hopkins University Press, 1993); Roeber, "The Long Road to *Vidal*: Charity Law and State Formation in Early North America," in *The Many Legalities of Early America*, Bruce Mann and Christopher Tomlins, eds. (Chapel Hill: University of North Carolina Press, 2001), 427–30; Roeber, "The Limited Horizons of Whig Religious Rights," in *The Nature of Rights at the American Founding and Beyond*, Barry Alan Shain, ed. (Charlottesville and London: University of Virginia Press, 2007), 198–229. On the crisis in western philosophy, Christos Yannaras, *On the Absence and Unknowability of God: Heidegger and the Areopagite*, ed. with and Introduction by Andrew Louth, Haralambos Ventis, trans. (London and New York: T&T Clark International, 2005); Mickey L. Mattox and A.G. Roeber, *Changing Churches: An Orthodox, Catholic, and Lutheran Theological Conversation* (Grand Rapids, MI and London: William B. Eerdmans Publishing Company, 2012).

commitments. Parts of the argument in the present book on questions of human sexuality, gender, and marriage developed from two earlier efforts written as part of those reassessments.[14]

In the development of this project, John Witte, Jr. of the Emory University Law School has been a consistently enthusiastic and generous editor, colleague, and friend. Both Aristotle Papanikolaou and George Demacopoulos at Fordham were early cheerleaders for the work. I am grateful to them and to Ashley Purpura for endorsing the book for inclusion in their series, Orthodox Christianity and Contemporary Thought. The book was supported by my participation as Senior Fellow in the Orthodoxy and Human Rights Scholars project sponsored by Fordham University's Orthodox Christian Studies Center, and generously funded by the Henry Luce Foundation and Leadership 100. I am likewise indebted to the other senior fellows of the project for reading and offering suggestions about chapters of the book. Philip Hamburger of the Columbia Law School gave the manuscript his close attention and critique and provided suggestions for clarifying the argument, as did Mark Noll. Jan Stievermann in Heidelberg, Alfons Brüning in Amsterdam with Thomas Bremer and Assaad Elias Kattan at Münster, and the members of the Oslo Coalition on Freedom of Religion or Belief and their New Directions in Orthodox Thought initiative helped me to place the American debates in a broader context. I learned again how much I had to ponder the intensifying debates about religious rights from the presenters and commentators at the 2014 Harvard Law School conference on "Considering 'Religious Accommodation.'" I am also grateful to those who took the time to respond to my queries, especially to those who received questions from a colleague they have never met, including Paul Babie of the University of Adelaide and Norman Doe of Cardiff University. Elizabeth Prodromou, Sally Gordon, John Movsesian, and Alfons Brüning agreed to participate in the 2015 session at the American Society for Church History meeting that provided additional opportunity for refining the book's argument. Scott Kenworthy and Christina Stoeckl have done much to inform my understanding of the Russian and Russian American experience in the story as have the Reverend Deacon

14. A.G. Roeber, *Hopes for Better Spouses: Protestant Marriage and Church Renewal in Early Modern Europe, India, and North America* (Grand Rapids, MI and London: William B. Eerdmans Publishing Company, 2013).

Nicholas Denysenko and Professor Gayle Woloschak on the Ukrainian Orthodox perspective. Professor Jeff Bishop of St. Louis University's theology faculty made important suggestions and observations about my handling of the marriage, sexuality, and gender chapter. I am grateful for advice on the details of canonical procedure in Orthodox ecclesiastical courts provided by His Grace, the Right Reverend Bishop Basil of the Diocese of Wichita; the Very Rev. Luke Uhl, former Chancellor of the Greek Metropolis of Denver; the Very Rev. Alexander Rentel, present Chancellor of the Orthodox Church of America; the Very Rev. John Jillions, former Chancellor of the OCA; the Very Rev. Thomas Zain, Vicar General of the Antiochian Orthodox Christian Archdiocese of North America, the Reverend Anton Vrame of the Greek Orthodox Archdiocese, and Professor Andrew Walsh. The Armenian American theologian and friend Vigen Guroian has been deeply skeptical about the possibility of integrating the present state of rights claims with an Orthodox theological and ecclesial vision, and I am indebted to him for his critical reading of an earlier version of the argument. John Inazu continues to inform my perspectives on the challenges of pluralism, the right of association, and American Christianity. The international symposium I organized in March 2017 at Penn State on "Human Rights, Religious Rights, Civil Rights in the Federal Republic of Germany and the United States since 1948" enabled me to sharpen my understanding of the American context within which to place my assessment of Orthodox grappling with these issues.[15]

Former Penn State colleagues, Philip Jenkins and Cathy Wanner have provided critical readings and suggestions to the book as it progressed. My research assistants David Bodin and Dr. Robert Olsen paved the way for the book with customary careful and quick response to requests for help in tracking down sources and amending drafts. I also acknowledge especially the staff of the Interlibrary Loan department at the Pattee-Paterno Library at Penn State, especially Eric Novotny; the administrative staff of the Department of History at Penn State; James Hutson and his staff at the Library of Congress; and the staff at The Presbyterian Historical Society in Philadelphia. Funds for research support came from the late

15. For those essays, see A.G. Roeber, ed., *Human v. Religious Rights? German and U.S. Exchanges and their Global Implications* (Göttingen: Vandenhoeck & Ruprecht, 2020).

former Dean Susan Welch's generous access to the Charles and Joyce Mathues Faculty Research Funds from the College of the Liberal Arts at Penn State. Two anonymous readers deserve my gratitude for their critiques and endorsement of the book, as do John Garza, Courtney Lee Adams, Jr., Kem Crimmins, and Eric Newman at Fordham University Press. As always, my biggest debt remains to Patricia Stutzman-Roeber who has sacrificed many a right, privilege, and honor to support this, and all my endeavors.

Pascha, 2022

St. Louis, Missouri and Yonkers, New York

1

DEFERENTIAL SOCIETY AND CHURCH?
PROTESTANT TO ORTHODOX
SOCIAL ETHOS

By the 1980s, as the rights revolution was already well underway, the Armenian American Orthodox theologian Vigen Guroian concluded that "a social ethic will exist only if Orthodox conscientiously endeavor to come to terms with their recent diaspora in the West. Though their situation is distinctive, the Orthodox will not be alone in doing social ethics from a minority perspective."[1] Our task here is not to describe an Orthodox social ethic as such, but to come to terms with the history of how the Orthodox have engaged with concrete rights claims within American society from its late eighteenth-century emergence as an independent nation state to the late nineteenth-century. The Orthodox clashed in the territory of Alaska with the predominantly Protestant claims about what a so-called Christian nation should look like. The importance of relying on historical experience in provincial governance and the defense of what had been thought of as the "rights of Englishmen" rather than articulation of a political-philosophical system that could produce a social ethos led John Dickinson of Pennsylvania at the dawn of the experiment in republican government to urge his fellow delegates at the Constitutional Convention that "experience must be our only guide. Reason may mislead us."[2] Reason,

1. Vigen Guroian, "The Problem of a Social Ethic: Diaspora Reflections," in *Incarnate Love: Essays in Orthodox Ethics*, ed. Vigen Guroian (Notre Dame: University of Notre Dame Press, 1989), 117–139 at 118.
2. The classic study of Dickinson remains Douglass Adair, "'Experience Must Be Our Only Guide': History, Democratic Theory, and the United States

however, in the eighteenth-century Atlantic world could not be divorced from discussions of nature, and potentially useful but unsettling claims about a "law of nature" upon which some continued to believe the rights of a common humanity had to depend if they were to have any meaning at all.

If we focus on concrete experiences, we must admit that it is not possible to speak of a single Orthodox social justice tradition. The interdisciplinary group of scholars who responded in 2017 to the Ecumenical Patriarch's request to produce a document on the social ethos of the Orthodox understood themselves to be providing a theological basis upon which something like the Roman Catholic tradition of social justice might go forward. They did not attempt to address concrete examples of economic policy, poverty, tensions between capitalism and labor, the nature of family life, or the role of a state authority and the Church's responsibilities on such matters. The document was intended to encourage a more optimistic outlook for the Orthodox as they come to terms with social issues in contemporary societies rather than, for example, focusing on darker warnings about the perils of contemporary social and political developments. The Russian Orthodox Church's document issued in 2000 reflected its fears about non-religious populations and their influence upon social policies and actions.[3]

Constitution," in *Fame and the Founding Fathers: Essays by Douglass Adair*, ed. Trevor Colbourn (New York: Norton/Institute of Early American History and Culture at Williamsburg, Va., 1974), 152–175. See also Peter C. Messer, *Stories of Independence: Identity, Ideology, and History in Eighteenth-Century America* (DeKalb: Northern Illinois University Press, 2005).

3. The Ecumenical Patriarchate's document: Ecumenical Patriarchate of Constantinople, Special Commission on Social Doctrine, *For the Life of the World: Toward a Social Ethos of the Orthodox Church*, John Chryssavgis, et al. Istanbul: Ecumenical Patriarchate of Constantinople, 2020, http://www.goarch.org/social -ethos ; for the Russian Patriarchate's document: Patriarchate of Moscow, *The Basis of the Social Concept of the Russian Orthodox Church*, Metropolitan Kirill of Smolensk and Kaliningrad et al. Moscow: Patriarchate of Moscow, 2001, http://mospa tusa.com/files/the-basis-of-the-social-concept.pdf, at XVI.4. For the American Orthodox participant Aristotle Papanikolaou's assessment of the 2019 document, see Charles C. Camosy, "'Orthodox Social Ethos' aims to put Eastern Church spin on social issues," *Crux: Taking the Catholic Pulse.* May 16, 2020,

To appreciate how the Orthodox in America have come to grips with the social visions that dominated American life before the rights revolution we need to understand the seventeenth and eighteenth-century legacies of conflicting claims about what was necessary to achieve a just, free, and prosperous society—and who its guardians were. The language of natural rights informed at least some of the North American concerns about what underlay those claims that remained beyond the power of those who governed to control or deny. The legal, political, and civil rights understandings of the eighteenth century at times referenced natural rights, but never in a coherent, systematic fashion. Historians who have attempted to identify just what version of natural rights informed the founding generation of American leaders still are not of one mind.[4]

From the early plantings of European settlements through the seventeenth century, "the first settlers of those jurisdictions had no acquaintance with the philosophers' idea of subjective rights . . . the great majority of the colonists were equally unacquainted with the new practice of defining rights by applying titled ownership to incorporeal objects, such as parliamentary immunities . . . as a result, libertarian language in the colonies initially had an antiquated, even medieval quality." To describe early European Americans as "individualists," thus misrepresents them, and their worlds.[5] Well into the early nineteenth century, when North Americans

---

https://cruxnow.com/interviews/2020/05/orthodox-social-ethos-aims-to-put -eastern-church-spin-on-social-issues/ (accessed October 26, 2020).

4. My own conclusions have been shaped by the investigations of David Konig, first in an unpublished paper for the American Society of Legal History's 2000 meeting at Princeton University: David Konig, "Thomas Jefferson and the Search for an American Natural Law Tradition" (paper presented at the American Society of Legal History, Princeton University, Princeton, NJ, 2000); David Konig, "Natural Rights, Bills of Rights, and the People's Rights in Virginian Constitutional Discourse, 1787–1791," in *The South's Role in the Creation of the Bill of Rights*, ed. Robert Haws (Jackson: University Press of Mississippi, 1991), 33–50; David Konig, "Regionalism and Early American Law," in *The Cambridge History of American Law, Vol I: Early America (1580–1815)*, ed. Michael Grossberg and Christopher Tomlins (Cambridge: Cambridge University Press, 2008), 144–177.

5. James H. Hutson, "The Emergence of the Modern Concept of a Right in America: The Contribution of Michel Villey," in *The Nature of Rights at the*

talked of rights they did so with an eye toward "the correlative character of rights and duties," because "a religious society, as eighteenth-century America was, opened its arms to natural or subjective rights, presented as moral power inherent to individuals. Ministers of the gospel . . . were enthusiastic proponents of subjective rights," but "subjective right was no more successful in sweeping the field of its rivals than it had been in England."[6] As one commentator has concluded, "it would not . . . be difficult to discern a theme of individualist rights in the writings of, say, Paine, Adams, Jefferson, Emerson, and Lincoln, as well as within American culture more broadly . . . [but] one could also assemble a compendium of writings by an overlapping set of prominent Americans—say, Adams, Jefferson, Marshall, Jackson, and Lincoln—showcasing a tradition of rights in which communities rather than (or in addition to) individuals are properly the bearers of rights."[7]

By the seventeenth century, the claim that the rights of Englishmen were rooted in an ancient and immemorial unwritten constitution that obligated even monarchs to respect the rights of subjects had become part of a peculiar view of history and its political language and self-concept among the English. Jurists and members of Parliament, alarmed by what they believed to be tyrannical inclinations of the Stuart monarchs, cast their opposition in such terms, including the invocation of a "higher law" to which even kings were obliged to submit. The actual historical record of the English monarchy's long-term success in subjecting medieval claims to rights to hold baronial, manorial courts and corporate bodies did not distract the defenders of the rights of subjects from insisting on the sovereignty of the common law that they claimed to be an expression of "higher law." A rich irony surrounded the transfer of such notions across the Atlantic to the collection of chartered, proprietary, and royal colonies in North America. There, for a time at least, local assemblies, governors, and eventually Parliament itself thought rights grounded in property were endangered (depending on colony and issue). When the monarchy finally emerged in the

American Founding and Beyond, ed. Barry Alan Shain (Charlottesville: University of Virginia Press, 2007), 25–63, at 42.

6. Hutson, "Emergence," 48–9.

7. Richard Primus, "An Introduction to the Nature of American Rights," in *The Nature of Rights at the American Founding and Beyond*, ed. Barry Alan Shain (Charlottesville: University of Virginia Press, 2007), 15–24, at 23.

mid-1770s as the true culprit bent on the destruction of property, liberty, and the rights of Englishmen, written constitutions emerged as the best defense of these ancient and immemorial rights from abuses by arbitrary government.[8] But Americans would continue to disagree about whether these written documents were expressions of a higher law that itself could be traced back to Christian belief and teaching. The fanciful history upon which such claims were based created an unsettled legacy when Americans tried to come to terms with the variety of rights they now had to express in language other than the that of the rights of Englishmen. As one legal historian has demonstrated, such arguments "were not contentions for law based on the proven facts of historical scholarship, but rather they sought to project current constitutional principles onto a presumed past . . . it was believed that rights were immemorial: those existing today have existed from a time before there were kings to grant them, and the only evidence to prove immemoriality was that they exist today . . . it was insignificant that the thesis could not be proven historically. What mattered was that it was a defensible statement of what the writer wanted to be current law."[9] Only a few Americans were up to the task of confronting the tension that underlay this version of the history of the rights of Englishmen. Some, "like John Rutledge and James Duane in the Continental Congress debates" recognized the "conflict between history and reason . . . and they resisted efforts to invoke the law of nature alongside the English constitution, fearful of allowing the certainty of what had been, however irrational it may

8. A prolix literature exists on these issues; for useful introductions, see Corwin, *The 'Higher Law' Background of American Constitutional Law*; J.G. A. Pocock, *The Ancient Constitution and the Feudal Law: a Study of English Historical Thought in the Seventeenth Century* (Cambridge: Cambridge University Press, 1987); Gordon S. Wood, "The History of Rights in Early America," in *The Nature of Rights at the American Founding and Beyond*, ed. Barry Alan Shain (Charlottesville: University of Virginia Press, 2007), 233–257; Roeber, *Faithful Magistrates and Republican Lawyers*, 3–31; Peter C. Hoffer, *Law and People in Colonial America* (Baltimore: Johns Hopkins University Press, 1998); John M. Murrin and A.G. Roeber, "Trial by Jury: The Virginia Paradox," in *The Bill of Rights: A Lively Heritage*, ed. Jon Kukla (Richmond: The Virginia State Library, 1987), 109–130.

9. John Phillip Reid, "The Authority of Rights at the American Founding," in *Nature of Rights at the American Founding and Beyond*, ed. Barry Shain (Charlottesville: University of Virginia Press, 2007), 67–115, at 91.

have become, to be replaced by the revolutionary vagueness of what natural reason declared should be." The most tragic case remained that of James Otis, "as well read as any American in both the English common law and the European theories of natural law." Unable to "reconcile the two laws . . . he clung stubbornly to the veracity of seventeenth-century notions of jurisprudence and parliamentary supremacy" and "to deny natural reason for the sake of historical truth."[10] Despite such disagreements, the centrality of constitution-making and the availability of printed versions of these texts persisted well into the nineteenth-century, acquiring in some circles a status close to that of holy writ. By contrast, the Declaration of Independence, "was certainly widely read and reprinted in some regions of the world but . . . it never exerted the same degree and depth of impact as the American constitution."[11]

Because Americans were not of one mind about what natural rights consisted of, "the bills of rights drafted by the new states after 1776 were a hodge-podge of every kind of libertarian language then available."[12] Those who crafted both the state and, later, the Federal documents intended to protect the rights of the states against the possibility of a Federal tyranny persisted in the older belief—even when they as individuals were not especially devout with regard to a specific form of Christianity—"that linked concepts of duty and obligation—to God first, but to kindred, society, and nation as well." Although James Madison argued for a defense of the "rights of conscience" in the debates over the adoption of the Bill of Rights, he failed. His failure can be best understood by appreciating that an appeal to interior experience and conscience had proven to be the source of religious fanaticism and political violence in England and across Europe. Convinced of what that history of unbridled conscience could produce in political turmoil, his contemporaries demurred.[13]

---

10. Gordon S. Wood, *The Creation of the American Republic, 1776–1787* (Chapel Hill: University of North Carolina Press, 1969), 9.

11. Linda Colley, *The Gun, Ship, and The Pen: Warfare, Constitutions, and the Making of the Modern World* (New York and London: Liveright Publishing Corporation, 2021), 133.

12. Hutson, "Emergence," 51.

13. Roeber, "Limited Horizons," 198–229, at 200. My assessment of Madison and the issue of conscience differs significantly from that of Jack N. Rakove,

Attempts to extend absolute protection to the judgment of private conscience failed to generate support in late eighteenth-century America. The founders shared a conviction that the rights of individual conscience could not be divorced from the obligation to defend a vague, but nonetheless real, Protestant heritage linking legal and political rights to a defense of the experiment in republican government, the sanctity of property and contract, and Protestant religious liberty. By refusing to be drawn into systematic philosophical and theological debates over the exact nature of natural rights, and "by leaving the disputes over religious rights to the states and a properly informed Protestant Christian public opinion, the founders hid behind the very Protestantism whose ecclesiastical establishment they rejected."[14] Protestants, Lockeans, classical Roman-indebted republicans and most who did not differentiate among the meanings of "virtue," "corruption," or "tyranny" contributed to the lack of consensus not only about these terms, but of what was meant by "rights", as well. Not until after the conflagration of the American Civil War did the "founders' Bill morph into what might be called a second Bill of Rights—the strong nationalist and individualistic charter celebrated by today's liberal nationalists."[15]

Most scholars now agree that there was never one Enlightenment that informed the language of rights upon which the architects of the American republican experiment had relied. The variety of forms "enlightenment" took cannot be traced solely to European origins. It has become "increasingly clear that the Enlightenment cannot simply be equated with secularization, but on the contrary was deeply embedded in religious world views." If the global history of how various enlightenments came to be referenced has a salutary lesson, it lies in the patterns of "re-articulation and reinvention, under conditions of inequalities of power, that transformed multiple claims on Enlightenment into a ubiquitous presence."[16]

Beyond Belief, Beyond Conscience: The Radical Significance of the Free Exercise of Religion (New York: Oxford University Press, 2020), 69–100.

14. Roeber, "Limited Horizons," 221.

15. Akhil Reed Amar, "Creation, Reconstruction, and Interpretation of the Bill of Rights," in *Nature of Rights at the American Founding and Beyond*, ed. Barry Shain (Charlottesville: University of Virginia Press, 2007), 163–180, at 172–73.

16. Sebastian Conrad, "Enlightenment in Global History: A Historiographical Critique," *American Historical Review* 117, no. 4 (October, 2012),: 999–1027, at

For eighteenth century North Americans, the version of a Christian Enlightenment that mattered was the work of the Scottish Common Sense philosophers whose writings found a deep reception among the privileged few who enjoyed the wealth and leisure to pursue such issues. "Americans found the Scottish philosophy useful in three ways: (1) for justifying the Revolution against Britain, (2) for outlining new principles of social order in the absence of the stability of British rule, and (3) for re-establishing the truths of Christianity in the absence of an established church."[17] The profound influence of the Scottish Common Sense moral philosophers on American life through the first half of the nineteenth century cannot be disputed. The utility of this new moral philosophy garnered quick recognition among the religious and political elite of the early republic. Uses included " a universal moral sense as the basis for personal and social ethics, inspired confidence in the existence of moral absolutes, even after traditional institutions of moral authority like God-ordained monarchy or the established church were cast aside . . . moral guidance historically offered by social elites could be retained, and even improved upon, in a much more democratic society [and] escaping the traditional influence of learning, family authority, and communal guidance did not mean a descent into moral chaos." Perhaps most important, for Americans who strove to be serious Christians, the new philosophy gave those "who for both personal and social reasons were committed to traditional faith—but who with their peers had given up the inherited props for supporting those faiths—a means to retain that allegiance with intellectual self-respect."[18]

This dominant philosophy also produced its critics at home and abroad. By the eve of, and especially in the wake of the Civil War as "republicanism drifted toward individual rights and personal liberties" memories of the French Revolution's excesses produced calls for a return to the "mixed" and "balanced" understandings of politics that did not exclude a form of aristocracy and strong executive power. Most Americans rejected such calls because the new moral philosophy had provided the basis for establishing

1004, 1005. See also Simon Grote, "Review-Essay: Religion and Enlightenment," *Journal of the History of Ideas* 75, no. 1 (January, 2014): 137–160.

17. Mark A. Noll, *A History of Christianity in the United States and Canada*, 154–57, at 154–55.

18. Mark A. Noll, *America's God: From Jonathan Edwards to Abraham Lincoln* (New York: Oxford University Press, 2002), 217.

not just an experiment in republican government, but "a vocabulary for ordinary Americans to protest against the pretensions of American elites, and not least, because it seemed so clearly to explain the nature of American social experience. . . ."[19] More important than memories of the French Revolution, the ominous implications of what occurred in Haiti drove pro-slavery partisans to defend aristocracy as abolitionists increasingly favored a strong executive as the only means short of the violence of war that could rid America of this scourge.[20]

The importance of the Common Sense tradition and its impact upon generations of religious and political leaders in North America helps to account for the fact that, "despite more spectacular gains of Baptists and Methodists, Presbyterians, together with their Congregational allies, maintained the intellectual and social leadership they had gained during the Colonial and Revolutionary eras."[21] Historians grounded in the Reformed tradition such as Noll and Marsden have issued critical complaints against the deficiencies of the Common Sense moral philosophers. Eminent political figures such as James Madison during his undergraduate years at the College of New Jersey heard John Witherspoon's moral philosophy lectures that drew upon—but also differed in many respects from—the work of Thomas Reid and Francis Hutcheson. Reid's main project "integrated the facility of reason more fully into Scottish moral philosophy, focusing on the role of rational moral judgment at the top of a perceptual pyramid." For Reid, "the faculty of reason ordered and discerned pre-rational moral perceptions, which sat at the foundation of the pyramid." Concerned to

19. Noll, *America's God,* 219, 220. For the spread of the moral philosophers and moral reasoning beyond their Reformed origins to the Methodist movement, see 348–359.

20. Colley, *The Gun, The Ship, and The Pen,* 41–55.

21. George M. Marsden, *The Evangelical Mind and the New School Presbyterian Experience: A Case Study of Thought and Theology in Nineteenth-Century America* (Eugene, OR: Wipf and Stock Publishers, 2003), Preface, xi. Marsden's first work bypassed the importance of the Common Sense philosophers and focused instead on other internal debates within the Presbyterians. He would agree, however, that after the crisis of the Civil War, the Presbyterians endured a bitter struggle over how to define "orthodox" Reformed doctrine. See his Chapter 11 "Presbyterian Reunion: A Question of Orthodoxy," 212–249. On the relationship of that controversy to the Orthodox in Alaska, see below.

refute skeptics and immaterialists, Reid insisted on the trustworthy "inter-action between primary sentiments and secondary reason."[22]

Scholars sympathetic to Reid's importance nonetheless conclude that the philosopher's "discussion of Common Sense is confusing. And not just con-fusing but confused."[23] Nicholas Wolterstorff maintains that if we wish to understand Reid's "principles of Common Sense" there are two under-standings: one, "Principles of Common Sense are shared first principles, and principles of Common Sense are what we all do and must take for granted in our lives in the everyday. " But these two understandings "don't mesh."[24] Admitting that Reid never reconciled these two principles, Wolt-erstorff argues that Reid's importance lies in the fact that, as a convinced Reformed Christian theist, he rejected any claim that humans can find causal agencies of God in nature. Instead, "what lies at the bottom of Re-ideian epistemological piety is acknowledging the darkness—or the 'mys-tery' as Reid sometimes calls it . . . Reid is not the only Enlightenment philosopher in whom one finds this theme of darkness. One finds it in Locke as well. Locke located the darkness at a different point," namely in "our inability to know the essences of substances," but such darkness could be lifted by the use of reason. "Reason, for Reid, has no such power."[25] Instead, it is "trust" that is rationally ungrounded that characterizes "the piety of all humanity. What's deepest in *Reidian* piety, is acknowledging that fact, and acknowledging the darkness which that fact implies, and not railing against the mystery but accepting it humbly and gratefully."[26]

We can only speculate on what might have occurred had the first Or-thodox missionaries arriving in Alaska in significant numbers by the 1820s encountered Reformed missionaries schooled in Reid's epistemological pi-ety and reverence for mystery. In the American context, Common Sense philosophy came to lack the sense of darkness that is unmistakable in Reid, who insisted that reason, for all its virtues, begins with axioms that can-not be demonstrated by reason itself, an anti-foundationalism American

22. Gideon Mailer, *John Witherspoon's American Revolution* (Chapel Hill: University of North Carolina Press, 2017), 85, 86, 166–67.

23. Nicholas Wolterstorff, *Thomas Reid and the Story of Epistemology* (Cambridge: Cambridge University Press, 2004), 218.

24. Wolterstorff, *Thomas Reid*, 225.

25. Wolterstorff, *Thomas Reid*, 256, 257.

26. Wolterstorff, *Thomas Reid*, 261.

Protestants chose to ignore. Orthodox teaching on the relationship of God to his creation and human access to God had by the eighteenth century developed a deep and pervasive commitment to the claim that God in his essence is unknowable, eternally shrouded in darkness and light. That did not imply that the use of human reason was to be scorned, nor that the human subject is only a passive recipient of God's grace and forgiveness with no capacity for making free rational choices—a position like Reid's own. Still, the priority in Orthodox approaches remained humility and silent openness to the possibility of drawing closer to God because of the immanent divine energies—God as humans are capable of knowing Him—that come close to the notion of sanctification as Reid would have understood this issue.[27]

At subsequent events would prove, the possibilities of that encounter had vanished by the 1860s. Reid's work reveals the persistence of a deep, theistic commitment to trust in the capacity of ordinary humans to understand enough about themselves and their world, tempered with a deep humility and acknowledgment of the mystery of the Divine, to refrain from supposing they could construct a rational, legally ordered kingdom of God and righteous society on earth. The Scottish theologians and philosophers believed that some forms of society and politics better served the proclamation of the Gospel and the practice of communal and individual virtues. But as Reformed theologians clustered within the walls of seminaries rather than shaping the collegiate institutions that produced political and social Protestant leaders, they inadvertently encouraged a non-critical complacency among those who were convinced of a "coherence between immutable ethical perception and a benevolently created divine cosmos that those perceptions seemed to corroborate." A younger generation of Americans emerged disinclined to defer to cautions advanced by theologians,

---

27. For a survey of various Orthodox understandings of the essence/energies distinction, see Alexis Torrance, "Precedents for Palamas' Essence-Energies Theology in the Cappadocian Fathers," *Vigiliae Christianae* 63 (2009): 47–70; For the pre-Christian roots of the distinction, David Bradshaw, *Aristotle East and West: Metaphysics and the Division of Christendom* (Cambridge: Cambridge University Press, 2004); for further discussion of Reformed hesitancy to endorse the notion of theosis and the distinction between Reformed and Lutheran approaches to the problem, Mickey L. Mattox and A.G. Roeber, *Changing Churches*, 38–56; 69–82.

firmly convinced that they were to be in the process of realizing an unprecedented social, economic, and political destiny.[28]

The humility and the hesitancy to issue a full-throated endorsement of a Protestant republic did not become more common, and Reid's subtle approach to the questions of confidence in human knowledge and that knowledge's relationship to the divine grew less evident in succeeding generations. Reformed Protestant criticism of the tendency to identify the experiment in republicanism as the working out of God's agency in the legal and political realm persisted, but it failed to halt more zealous and over-confident strains in the Reformed tradition by the middle of the nineteenth century. And it was the latter versions of Reformed piety and political theology that the Orthodox would encounter.[29] The Protestant ethos of those decades differed significantly from that of Reid and his contemporaries.

What few devotees of any version of Enlightenment—including Reformed theologians such as Witherspoon—contested was the continued importance of deference to qualified leaders, albeit leaders hedged about with restrictions on their temptation to abuse the rights of others. The eighteenth-century North American critics of the lawfully established churches of Europe continued to assume that claims to political, civil, and legal rights could not be divorced from obligations and responsibilities to fellow subjects or citizens. That conviction would only start to disappear in the last third of the nineteenth century. But Orthodox engagement with some strains of the European Enlightenment, when it occurred at all, focused almost exclusively on "a cohesive theoretical founding of practical ethics." When the discussion turned to "social and political theory, the Eastern church had to confront a growing insistence emanating from Enlightenment Europe on the importance of law as a social contract between

---

28. Mailer, *John Witherspoon's American Revolution*, 397. On the variety of Reformed theological, social, and philosophical strains, see Noll, *America's God*, "The Americanization of Calvinism: Explosion: 1827–1860," 293–329.

29. The best analysis of this struggle within ante-Bellum Protestantism remains Mark Y. Hanley, *Beyond a Christian Commonwealth: The Protestant Quarrel with the American Republic, 1830–1860* (Chapel Hill: University of North Carolina Press, 1994). See also my review of Hanley, A.G. Roeber, "No Bishop, No King, No Millennial Republic," *Reviews in American History* 23, no. 2 (June, 1995): 202–205.

rulers and ruled . . . [and] the hierarchical church reacted sharply against appeals for democratic or contractual thinking . . . [and] hardened its position in concert with monarchies and both Catholic and Protestant established churches, especially after the French revolutionary regicide of 1793."[30] A century after the American Revolution, when the Russian Orthodox clergy in Alaska confronted what it deemed to be the most unsavory aspects of American society, it was not only the heresy of Protestantism in its Presbyterian vesture that earned condemnation. The Russian understanding of "the Enlightenment" accounted for the errors of what Americans in their "civilizing" projects were doing, and why they were wrong in asserting what a society should look like.

In his 1901 retrospective on the Russian Orthodox Mission in Alaska, the Hieromonk Dionysius reflected on the baleful influence of American Protestant missionary work that had mixed political and cultural objectives with their intent of creating a "civilized" society among the First Peoples of Alaska. But Protestants were not the sole culprits. What too few Americans understood, he concluded, was that "European culture and civilization are by no means, as so many fancy, wholly an outgrowth of Christianity. European culture owes to Christianity only the little that is really noble and lofty in it;—if we go into particulars, we shall find that it is in direct opposition to it . . . composed of self-love, sensuality, extreme egotism, complete attachment to earth, tending wholly to man's utter enslavement to earth, by the witchery of the earthly comforts it keeps inventing . . . a mixing of spiritual with cultural aims, and, still more, a substitution of the latter for the former in a mission's work, must lead to most deplorable results." The late Archbishop Innocent, Dionysius insisted, "was strongly opposed to the propagation . . . of European culture and civilization." Mere "enlightenment" understood as "cultural instruction" would not transform the moral character of the First Peoples who remained the main object of Russian Orthodox missionary concern. Quoting at length from the bishop's 1840 reflections on his labors, Dionysius noted that Western emphases on the importance of "culture" and "civilization" had led to "intensify

---

30. Dimitrios Moschos, "The Churches of the East and the Enlightenment," in *The Oxford Handbook to Early Modern Theology,* ed. Ulrich Lehner, Richard Muller, and A.G. Roeber (Oxford: Oxford University Press, 2016), 499–516, at 510, 511, 512.

their worst vices and further, not the regeneration, but the extinction of the native races."[31]

Students familiar with the history of competing visions about the future of American society that had emerged by the 1790s agree that many of the eminent political leaders of the new Federal republic had expected a degree of deference to age and experience that would have made eminent sense to Orthodox theologians and hierarchs. But this form of conservative republicanism was hijacked by Southern proslavery advocates, alienating opponents of slavery, especially white Northerners who had been ambivalent about abolition. Those American political leaders were, in larger or smaller degrees, indebted to the more conservative, religiously-based strains in early European Enlightenment thought. But they were destined to be disappointed. John Adams believed, on the basis of close observation, that Americans were as vicious, self-centered, ambitious, and unscrupulous as any European subject of corrupt monarchies and aristocracies. "He correctly saw that no society, including America, could ever be truly egalitarian, and he attempted . . . to come to terms with this fact of social and political life." His definition of an American aristocracy "'the rich, the well-born, and the able,' with their heightened sense of avarice and ambition, were especially dangerous . . . [but] they generally represented the best society could offer in honor and wisdom."[32] Failure to confront the grim reality of what Americans at their worst could be like, Adams believed, amounted to a dismissal of what age and experience should have taught a society that exploded demographically. Young, free, white males dominated it, their raucous, violent, and alcoholic behavior demonstrating how little they were willing to defer to Adams' warnings or to the importance of traditional sources of authority.

The spread of energetic but wasteful patterns of consumption and ecological devastation accompanied the "market revolution" and the resultant society of the early nineteenth century. The American Revolution had unleashed a deep-seated habit of reliance among the free white male property holders on "private or small-scale collective actions [that] held the key

---

31. Hieromonk Dionysius, "The main Problems and the Character of the Russian Orthodox Foreign Mission work . . ." in *Alaskan Missionary Spirituality*, ed. Michael Oleksa (New York: Paulist Press, 1987), 279–284, at 280, 281, 283.

32. Wood, *The Creation of the American Republic*, 569, 577.

to getting what they wanted . . . talk of liberty and independence drifted toward a libertarian sense of the term: freedom from government more than freedom to govern well. . . . In the early American republic the logic of freedom, the language of nature and natural rights, the abundance of resources, the habits of the people to seek, demand, or take what they wanted, pulled such traditional impulses away from the collective class or village attachments and toward acquisitive individualism."[33] By the time the Orthodox encountered the descendants of these Americans in post-1867 Alaska, they agreed with the diagnosis about what ailed American society, even if the abuses of Alaska's First Peoples had begun at the hands of Russian Orthodox traders, not the late-arriving Protestant Americans.

But the cultural and social implications of the Revolution could not be confined to alterations in American political life or discussions of a society shorn of its religious experiences. Appeals to self-evident truths, inalienable rights, and the equal creation of all generated debates over whether deference was acceptable as well "for its Christian churches." Had the Orthodox been first-hand observers of what occurred in the newly constituted Protestant Episcopal Church, "the most self-consciously British of the major Protestant churches," they would have been appalled. Despite the existence of a hierarchy, "the denomination's local vestries continued to exercise the powers they had gained during the War, when clerical leadership was scarce. The church's bishops forswore the political power that had for centuries been an accepted part of a bishop's service in England. And the American bishops also yielded a great deal of power to the laity and the lower clergy of the church" where the lower house of the church's General Convention, the "House of Clerical and Lay Deputies . . . [enjoyed] the unprecedented privilege of overturning actions of the former."[34]

---

33. John L. Larson, *Laid Waste! The Culture of Exploitation in Early America* (Philadelphia: University of Pennsylvania Press, 2020), 99. For an analysis of the details of the market revolution, see Larson's *The Market Revolution in America: Liberty, Ambition, and the Eclipse of the Common Good* (New York: Cambridge University Press, 2011).

34. On the demographic explosion that changed the nature of American society in the early nineteenth century, David Hackett Fisher, *Growing Old in America* (New York: Oxford University Press, 1977); on the social impact of the Revolution on the churches, Noll, *A History of Christianity*, 148, 150.

Awareness of the emerging North American society among the seven-teenth- or eighteenth-century Orthodox subjects of the Ottoman Empire or early modern Moscovite Russia had been sporadic, and produced no re-flections on the part of any of those involved about how the Orthodox understood, accepted, or rejected the emerging Protestant vision for an American society. Orthodox theology and Church life, in their turn, only merited the attention of Protestants and Catholics in their respective po-lemical attacks on one another—for the Orthodox could sometimes be used to advantage as potential allies. By the eighteenth century, even the brief flirtations of dissident Anglicans with both Greek and Russian Or-thodox reflected a growing dissatisfaction among some English Protestants with what they perceived to be an established Church of England that had failed to live up to its own confessional heritage and obligations. In fair-ness to those who remained loyal to the Church of England, among the combination of "forces, economic, social, and intellectual, that went to un-dermine the comfortable Erastianism of the eighteenth century establish-ment none is more difficult to put into perspective than religious pluralism." The recognition that "the civil community contains more than one church" forced early modern British observers to recognize in an increasingly diverse set of religious societies, that "churches are assemblies of like-minded people, and religious freedom is the ability of a person who disapproves of the teach-ing or practice of one church to leave it and join another."[35]

This eighteenth-century development rested on much deeper principles, among the most important that of ecclesial constitutionalism that had been founded on the right of those being governed to give their consent. By the time the Orthodox entered the North American continent, an ancient third- or fourth-century Syrian practice of selecting a bishop by a "quo-rum of twelve valid electors" that reflected the fact that the "right to elect a bishop belong[ed] to the community" had long since been abandoned.[36]

---

35. Robert E. Rodes, Jr., *Law and Modernization in the Church of England: Charles II to the Welfare State* (Notre Dame: The University of Notre Dame Press, 1991), 80–149, at 80, 81. For the growing tensions between theologians and jurists over the rights of a sovereign to determine marriage legislation in a European context, see Roeber, *Hopes for Better Spouses*, 67–96.

36. Lewis J. Patsavos, *A Noble Task: Entry into the Clergy in the First Five Centuries*, transl. Norman Russell (Brookline, MA: Holy Cross Orthodox Press, 2007), 68

But in the western Christian Church, Nicholas of Cusa's eighth chapter in Book Two of his *Catholic Concordance* provided the basis for those who agreed that "the authority of councils does not depend on its head but on the common consent of all."[37] Even admitting that a principle of consent did not envision an active exercise of rights by those at the lower margins of ancient, medieval, or early modern societies, the principle of the right to give consent was no "alien importation onto ecclesial soil of secular constitutional notions . . . [but] unquestionably drew a great deal of inspiration from the essentially synodal or conciliar mode of governance that had characterized the ancient church. . . ."[38] The demographic growth of Orthodox Christians in the North American context by the end of the nineteenth century would trigger anew discussions about what ecclesial society, and not only that of the host nation-state, should look like.

Convincing arguments have been put forward to assert that the origins of what we today would call the right to religious liberty and its expression had their roots in the Christian faith that developed in the urban centers of the Roman Empire.[39] Nevertheless, even those sympathetic to this argument have also observed that the Christian defense of the rights to liberty of religious expression suffered from the influence of Roman magisterial law and "sacral" kingship that in different ways received the blessings of the bishop of Rome in the West, and the patriarchs of the East. The deep-seated suspicion of and hostility toward that development, however, manifested itself in the English Reformation's attack upon the social, economic, and political power of clergy, an attitude and reading of history that shaped the Anglo-American legal and constitutional developments of the early modern era.[40]

37. Nicholas of Cusa, *The Catholic Concordance*, ed. Paul E. Sigmund (Cambridge: Cambridge University Press, 2003), 76–80, 76.

38. Francis Oakley, "The Conciliar Heritage and the Politics of Oblivion," in *The Church, the Councils, & Reform: The Legacy of the Fifteenth Century*, ed. Gerald Christianson, Thomas M. Izbicki, and Christopher M. Bellitto (Washington, D.C.: The Catholic University of America Press, 2008), 82–97, at 91–2. See also Paul Valliere, *Conciliarism: A History of Decision-Making in the Church* (Cambridge: Cambridge University Press, 2012), 137–161.

39. Robert Louis Wilken, *Liberty in the Things of God: The Christian Origins of Religious Freedom* (New Haven: Yale University Press, 2019).

40. See Francis Oakley's review of Wilken, *Liberty in the Things of God*: Francis Oakley, "Throne & Altar: Liberty in the Things of God," *Commonweal* 31

Among privileged Anglicans who exercised their liberty of religious and rational choice in leaving the Church of England for the Orthodox faith, the colonial Maryland planter Philip Ludwell serves as an early, but unique exemplar. Scion of one of the wealthiest families in the Proprietary colony whose ruling family, the Calverts, had abandoned the Roman Catholic faith for the more politically comfortable berth of Anglicanism, Ludwell was accepted into the Orthodox Church under Russian auspices in 1762. The details of his own journey to the Orthodox faith interest us less than does the recognition that neither he nor his Russian patrons and protectors hesitated to affirm the right of choice to leave the Church of England by law established in favor of the statistically insignificant Orthodox presence in Great Britain. The story of Ludwell's conversion might have provided a case study of what social costs could be expected of Orthodox living in the kind of social and cultural isolation that Roman Catholics in Britain and in Maryland had accepted as the price for maintaining their faith commitment. But his early death after conversion postponed this vital question of engagement, or rejection by the Orthodox of the broader contours of religious liberty and its implications for American society as they were coming to be understood in the eighteenth-century Atlantic world. The Orthodox would not until much later engage the choices that Anglicanism had to confront—"the liberal view of religion as an idiosyncratic element in a homogenous culture, and the Protestant view of denomination as an idiosyncratic element in a homogenous Christianity."[41]

The first expansion of God-endowed "unalienable rights" mentioned in the Declaration of Independence used the words "human rights" and hinted at a more radical vision of what an American social ethos should entail. This occurred in the context of the abolitionist movement led by

---

(July 2019), http://commonwealmagazine.org/throne-altar (accessed February 27, 2020); a classic reflection in the early American context on these assumptions is John Adams, "Dissertation on the Canon and Feudal Law" (1765), in *The Works of John Adams, Second President of the United States*, ed. Charles Francis Adams, 9 vols. (Boston: Little, Brown, and Company, 1850–56), 3:455–57.

41. For Ludwell and the details of Orthodox relationship to the predominantly Protestant biblical culture of early North America, see A.G. Roeber, "The Orthodox Christians and the Bible," in *The Oxford Handbook of the Bible in America*, ed. Paul Gutjahr (New York: Oxford University Press, 2017), 531–545. For the assessment of Anglicanism's dilemma, Rodes, Jr., *Law and Modernization*, 149.

William Lloyd Garrison. At least "In the first issue of the *Liberator* in 1831," Garrison explicitly invoked "'the great cause of human right' based on assent to the self-evident truth" of the equality of all humans because of their creation by God—including the enslaved African Americans.[42] Crediting Garrison for this human rights claim plumbs the depths of irony, given his famous denunciation of the U.S. Constitution as a "covenant with death," and his spurning any claim that such an instrument could be thought of as being grounded in natural rights assertions about the equal rights of all humans. And yet, even in the infamous compromises over slavery and the counting of each enslaved African American as 3/5 a person in the Constitution, the founders who opposed slavery had refused to endorse what the proponents of slavery wanted: to affirm that property in human beings was a right protected by the Constitution.[43] Disagreement over that interpretation would destroy the first version of constitutional government in the United States by 1861. The passage of the Thirteenth and Fourteenth Amendments, however, did not usher in a new consensual understanding of what American society should look like, at least not where its African American citizens were concerned, nor its obligations to the First Peoples of the North American continent.

When the Orthodox encountered the language of rights in North America, they did not do so in the context of the debates over slavery, women's rights, or the animus which the Church of Jesus Christ of Latter-Day Saints provoked when this early nineteenth-century American religion dared in the 1840s to resume the practice of Old Testament polygamy. Instead, Orthodox Christians first faced a vigorous, intrusive form of Reformed Protestantism that had dominated American educational and religious life from the early nineteenth century, a dominance that would only begin to fade in the post–Civil War decades. Numerically, the Methodists and Baptists

42. Rogers M. Smith, "The Politics of Rights Talk, Then and Now," in *The Nature of Rights at the American Founding and Beyond,* ed. Barry Shain (Charlottesville: University of Virginia Press, 2007), 303–323, at 312.

43. Sean Wilentz, *No Property in Man: Slavery and Antislavery at the Nation's Founding* (Cambridge, MA: Harvard University Press, 2018); James Oakes, *The Crooked Path to Abolition: Abraham Lincoln and the Antislavery Constitution* (New York: W.W. Norton & Co., 2020). The classic study of Garrison remains John L. Thomas, *The Liberator: William Lloyd Garrison: A Biography* (New York: Little, Brown, 1963).

accounted for the largest shares of the sometimes cooperating, sometimes competing, denominations within American Protestantism. What they shared with the more confessionally defined Presbyterians was a dilemma that on the one hand insisted upon a sharp separation of the state from any form of organized religion but on the other championed a self-aware individualized Protestant faith whose specific doctrinal details were left intentionally ambiguous. Inevitably, debates erupted about the importance of deference to historical confessional statements versus a notion of a Christian society based on the supremacy of individual faith commitments and common deference to a nonsectarian King James version of scripture. That dilemma had a long and fractious history in Europe before the first successful plantings of English-speaking Europeans occurred on the shores of North America.[44]

Even the idea that an American society could be comprised of secular, autonomous individuals did not emerge in the United States until the very decades when the Orthodox in Alaska were absorbed into the territory of the United States.[45] The tensions that had arisen in the late eighteenth-century between an officially secular federal republic and the existence of a broad social vision that assumed the dominance of cultural Protestantism had shaped the social ethos of America until the catastrophe of 1861–65, and echoed in diminishing decibels until the turn of the new century.[46]

The elite generation of the Founding Fathers who had dared to hope for an enlightened understanding of religion critical for the inculcation of private virtues and a society characterized by self-sacrificing public virtue collapsed with the deaths of the last of the signers of the Declaration of Independence. By the 1830s, the full impact of the Second Great

44. Gerrit Voogt, "Primacy of Individual Conscience or Primacy of the State? The Clash between Dirck Volckertsz, Coornhert and Justus Lipsius," *Sixteenth Century Journal* 28, no. 4 (1997): 1231–1249.

45. The classic statement against equating Protestantism and American individualism is Barry Shain, *The Myth of American Individualism: The Protestant Origins of American Political Thought* (Princeton: Princeton University Press, 1996). See also his essay *Man, God and Society: An Interpretive History of Individualism* (London: University of London Institute of United States Studies, 2000).

46. For Albrecht Ritschl's "cultural Protestantism" and its impact on the interpretation of religious history in the United States, H. Richard Niebuhr, *Christ and Culture* (New York: Harper and Row, 1951), 84.

Awakening's emphasis on emotional and non-confessional Protestantism had triumphed, and the campaign against alcoholism proceeded on an odd basis. The conviction that Christianity was in some vague form part of the common law tradition still informed American jurisprudence, and hence, society. That sentiment managed to co-exist with a culturally dominant view of individualized rights to liberty of religious choice. The roots of this continued tension between historical experience and rights claims had been obvious in Thomas Jefferson's own essay "Whether Christianity is a part of the Common Law" directed against his fellow Virginian Edmund Pendleton. Whatever disagreements interrupted for a time Jefferson's friendship and correspondence with John Adams, he shared the latter's detestation of medieval Christian chicanery, "thus identifying Christianity with the ecclesiastical law of England." The corruption of genuine law founded on reason and equality had been sealed by ecclesiastics and triumphed by the reign of Charles I. In Jefferson's opinion, only a return to the simplicity of pre-eighth-century Saxon law and the distribution of property through gavel-kind would guarantee the future of a genuine republican society. This romanticized vision of history and the promised future of American society had little in common with Jefferson's own inability to face the reality of chattel slavery while invoking unalienable rights based on the claim of all men being endowed by their Creator. That failure exposed a later generation to the trauma of slaughter in the Civil War in whose aftermath the elite political, literary, and legal writers including Abraham Lincoln, Emily Dickinson, Herman Melville, Mark Twain and Oliver Wendell Holmes, Jr. abandoned faith in any connection between a Creator and rights, capable only of acknowledging a God "they found in their hearts," if they had any use for a God at all.[47]

Most American citizens of the early republic, possessed of basic literacy but neither exposed nor inclined to theological debates, devoted little time or effort to the task of thinking through how to integrate their vision of

---

47. For Jefferson's essay, see Roeber, *Faithful Magistrates*, 163–66. On the legal and social consequences of the claims for the connection between Christianity and American law, Stuart Banner, "When Christianity was Part of the Common Law," *Law and History Review* 15, no. 1 (Spring, 1998): 27–62; see also William G. McLoughlin, *Revivals, Awakenings, and Reform: An Essay on Religion and Social Change in America, 1607–1977* (Chicago: University of Chicago Press, 1978), 98–140; Noll, *America's God*, 438.

American society with obligations to a republican form of government and the role of organized churches in that society.[48] Lack of clarity continued to characterize American opinions on such subjects well into the 1830s. It had been plausible for Presidents such as James Madison to proclaim official days of prayer and at the same time to use a presidential veto to prevent the incorporation of the Episcopal Church in Alexandria inside the District of Columbia. Columbian College (originally founded by Baptists in 1819) managed to obtain incorporation only under the condition that the college could not interfere with the legal right of an individual to study there because of his religious profession. At the same time, no one protested the practice of federal money being used to support Protestant missionary efforts among the First Peoples with the objective of founding elementary schools or providing indirect financing to specific tribal groups to rebuild destroyed churches as parts of the civilizing projects dear to American understandings of what society should look like. A Protestant chaplain could preside in the House of Representatives, the Senate, and the Federal military, and regular Sunday services were conducted in the U.S. capital into the 1840s. Brief protests of the practice of Sunday delivery of the mails provoked more commotion than did disputes over the incorporation of churches, a practice that varied widely from state to state. This vague social vision that took for granted the existence of confessionally undefined Protestantism managed to satisfy the white, property-owning male voters of the republic until the 1830s, when both the condition of enslaved African Americans and the challenge of Mormon polygamy unsettled the questions of religious rights, the authority of the state, and the sources of authority within religious groups to advance policies that would guarantee the promotion of social reform.[49] But by the 1840s the Supreme Court dealt a further blow to those who tried to claim that public virtue and the social needs of the republic outweighed individual rights of a testator. Neither the objections of heirs nor a need to inculcate moral virtues for the good of social and political order in the republic through religiously affiliated

48. James S. Kabala, *Church-State Relations in the Early American Republic, 1787–1846* (London: Pickering & Chatto, 2013), 190, n. 22

49. Kabala, *Church-State Relations*, 11–44; Philip Hamburger, *Separation of Church and State* (Cambridge, MA: Harvard University Press, 2002).

institutions could be allowed to assail the sanctity of the right of disposing of one's property as the testator saw fit.[50]

Preachers of the Protestant denominations adjusted downward any expectations they once had about the claim of a denomination upon the property dispositions of a deceased member. They also could agree with one another that no official connection should bind church and state together even though the maxim that "Christianity is a part of the Common Law" continued to enjoy widespread support, especially at the state level, well into the 1840s. Social norms that included laws against the consumption of alcohol in certain states, established quiet Sundays, and prosecuted blasphemy co-existed with the conviction that none of these strictures raised questions about the fundamental principle of the rights of conscience and religious liberty. Many also agreed that natural rights claims upon which civil rights could be defended did not extend to enslaved Africans, or to the First Peoples with whom treaties were made—and violated with impunity.[51]

If the Orthodox Russians and their First Peoples converts in Alaska found inconsistency in American claims to be defenders of liberty and rights, their perceptions were accurate. The championing of the extension of democratic representative government, the extension of slavery into the West and subsequent failure to defend African American civil rights

---

50. Roeber, "The Long Road to *Vidal*," 414–47.

51. Steven K. Green, *The Second Disestablishment: Church and State in Nineteenth-Century America* (New York: Oxford University Press, 2010), 149–203. On the relationship of the late colonial governments, the early United States and Christian missionaries to First Peoples, see Jane T. Merritt, *At the Crossroads: Indians and Empires on a Mid-Atlantic Frontier, 1700–1763* (Chapel Hill: The Omohundro Institute of Early American History and Culture and University of North Carolina Press, 2003); Bernard W. Sheehan, *Seeds of Extinction: Jeffersonian Philanthropy and the American Indian* (Chapel Hill: The Omohundro Institute of Early American History and Culture and University of North Carolina Press, 1973); William G. McLoughlin, *Cherokees and Missionaries, 1789–1839* (New Haven, CT: Yale University Press, 1984); Hermann Wellenreuther and Carola Wessel, eds., *Moravian Mission among the Delaware during the American Revolution: The Diaries of David Zeisberger 1772 to 1781*, trans. Julia Weber (University Park: The Pennsylvania State University Press, 2005); A.G. Roeber, ed., *Ethnographies and Exchanges: Native Americans, Moravians, and Catholics in Early North America* (University Park: The Pennsylvania State University Press, 2008).

proceeded hand in hand with the expulsion of the First Peoples of the continent throughout the nineteenth century.[52] Furthermore, while a popular belief persisted in a supposed tie between America's constitutional tradition and some vague version of a "higher law" connected to Christianity, this was not the case among the country's judges and legal profession. Those tasked with resolving concrete disputes in cases were not much interested in "higher law" theories. "Few legal writers have believed that it was appropriate for higher law directly to trump positive law, and the Constitution has been more or less consistently understood as a form of superpositive law enacted by the sovereign people." American legal experts continued to quarrel over whether judges "discover" law—as Jefferson had insisted—or whether they "make" law. In neither case did protagonists refer back to medieval understandings of natural law and natural rights. Instead, disagreement centered on whether and to what extent one could "imply" beyond what was plainly stated "in a contract, statute, or constitution." Perhaps most striking was the shift away from the seventeenth and eighteenth-century conviction of the absolute right of property to the conclusion reached by the early twentieth century that property was created by law and that judges "make, not find the law."[53] These shifts toward endorsing the view of the pragmatic need to "make" law to fit changing social, economic, and political circumstances lay behind the difference between an older understanding of "due process" and the rise of "substantive" due process as well.[54]

52. Christina Snyder, *Great Crossings: Indians, Settlers, and Slaves in the Age of Jackson* (New York: Oxford University Press, 2017), 17.

53. Morton J. Horwitz, "Natural Law and Natural Rights," in *Rights: Concepts and Contexts*, eds. Brian H. Bix and Horacio Spector (London: Routledge, 2012), 43, 45, 44.

54. Procedural due process has been derived from the Fifth and the 14th Amendments to the Constitution to protect individuals from government threats to life, liberty, and property in both criminal and civil cases. A classic examination remains Henry J. Friendly, "Some Kind of Hearing," *University of Pennsylvania Law Review* 123 (1975): 1267–1317, https://scholarship.law.upenn.edu/cgi/viewcontent.cgi?article=5317&context=penn_law_review, April 25, 2019. For two strikingly different assessments of substantive due process, see Edward Keynes, *Liberty, Property, and Privacy: Toward a Jurisprudence of Substantive Due Process* (University Park, PA: Penn State University Press, 1996), and David E. Bernstein,

Presbyterians like James Henley Thornwall (a representative example of Southern Reformed theologians) and Charles Hodge (in the North) would not have been comfortable with claims that judges, especially those lacking in a commitment to Protestant Christianity, should be thought capable of "making" rather than "finding" the law. Both engaged the question of whether the Christian Church as an organization could, or should, address social problems and how the laws of a Christian people should shape that society. Although opinions differed on this question, nearly unanimous teaching insisted that the Christian individual was not only allowed but obligated to become engaged with what was often referred to as the "left hand" of God.[55] Non-English-speaking members of the German Reformed tradition felt compelled to remind Presbyterians that they had sharply criticized the absence of German-speaking engagement with social and ethical issues that touched directly on the rights of freedom of conscience and the sovereignty of individual liberty. In 1829 the Presbyterian *New York Observer* lamented this tendency toward passivity while their own Ezra Stile Ely in a subsequently published sermon, "The Duty of Christian Freemen to Elect Christian Rulers," outlined a posture German Reformed critics rejected by emphasizing in their own *Magazine of the German Reformed Church* that obedience to spiritual authority had nothing to do with the affairs of this world. Well into the 1850s, religious minority groups even within a distinctly Reformed theological tradition insisted upon the protection of individual religious rights to freedom of conscience above any other consideration, including the possible extension of civil and

---

"A History of 'Substantive' Due Process: It's Complicated," *Texas Law Review See Also* 95 (2016): 1–11, https://papers.ssrn.com/sol3/papers.cfn?abstract_id=2908130>. The most trenchant and important critique of the expansion of administrative law as an outgrowth of monarchical power and the threat that growth portends for contemporary American defenses of rights in an administrative state is Philip Hamburger, *Is Administrative Law Unlawful?* (Chicago: University of Chicago Press, 2014); see especially the literature and issues cited at 573n13 to 597n8. For an opposing argument, Jerry L. Mashaw, *Creating the Administrative Constitution: The Last One Hundred Years of Administrative Law* (New Haven, CT: Yale University Press, 2012).

55. David Van Drunen, *Natural Law and the Two Kingdoms: A Study in the Development of Reformed Social Thought* (Grand Rapids, MI: William B. Eerdmans Publishing Company, 2010), 256–275.

legal rights to those who historically had not been deemed capable of possessing or exercising such rights.[56]

The accommodating Lutheran theologian Samuel Simon Schmucker had been an exception to this general pattern. Professor at the Gettysburg Lutheran Seminary, Schmucker had in the 1830s joined the American Colonization Society. In 1838 in a letter to Gerrit Smith, Schmucker announced his resignation because of the Society's reluctance to call for rapid colonization of African Americans freed from slavery, and worse, against the integration of those who wished to remain in America. Schmucker denounced as "the strange anomaly in the moral government of God, that justice, which is always a duty, cannot now be done to two and a half millions of God's rational creatures in our midst, and consigns . . . [them to] grievous moral and intellectual privations . . . entirely at variance with the law of Christian love, and the principles of our holy and benevolent religion."[57]

Constitutional and legal historians have described a kind of broad consensus among social norms, the law, and the Protestant churches between the 1820s and the eve of the Civil War, in which all of the participants "harmonized the English assumption of the essential Christianity of the common law with the American state tradition of religious liberty. . . . Christianity was part of state common-law jurisprudence . . . including the permanence of marriage, the prohibition of polygamy, and the support due from a husband to his wife." Because of the history of common law and its relationship to Christian marriage, American legislators were not convinced that they had any obligation to see "religious freedom" as a cover to excuse practices such as polygamy.[58]

56. Steven M. Nolt, *Foreigners in Their Own Land: Pennsylvania Germans in the Early Republic* (University Park: The Pennsylvania State University Press, 2002), 89–108, at 93, 101–102; on the roots of debate over commitment to broader American social and political reform in the context of language, see Friederike Baer, *The Trial of Frederick Eberle: Language, Patriotism, and Citizenship in Philadelphia s German Community 1790 to 1830* (New York: New York University Press, 2008).

57. *Letters of Rev. Dr. Schmucker and Gerrit Smith, Esq.* [U.S.] [1838?] [electronic resource] Penn State University, ezaccess.libraries.psu.edu. September 18, 2014, 1.

58. Sarah Barringer Gordon, *The Mormon Question: Polygamy and Constitutional Conflict in Nineteenth Century America* (Chapel Hill: University of North

Religious rights and the freedom to express them not only clashed with but were also subordinated to what American male voters at the time believed were more basic civil rights. The two great crises of that age—slavery and the polygamy debates—led to the collapse of what had been an established consensus over the social influence of Protestant Christianity. Before the Orthodox arrived in significant numbers in the United States, the country was torn by the question of whether and in what manner that broad Protestant consensus could insist upon the intrusion of the federal government in matters of religion in order to preserve the Christian character of society. Given the long history of Reformed theology's impact upon such questions, only two possibilities presented themselves: Either one could stand on the right of liberty of conscience and religion, or one could insist that the Protestant church itself—regardless of denomination—was obliged to inform the leaders of the state where their duties lay in order to preserve true liberty and rights in the republic, and hence, to shape society. While the numerically dominant Presbyterians, Methodists, and Baptists, North and South, tore asunder their national unity in the slavery debate, as soon as the war came to an end, they united again to express the political consensus that polygamy was an un-Christian manifestation of barbarism—exactly as the opponents of slavery had identified the "peculiar institution."[59]

Thus, the pre–Civil War conviction that Christianity was part of the common law tradition of the United States with the insistence upon the sovereignty of rights to religious liberty collapsed because of the twin crises posed by slavery and the challenge of the Mormon Church in its attempt to revive polygamy as an accepted form of Christian marriage. Especially now in the realm of family law, despite the rhetoric that emphasized the religious liberty of any individual American citizen, legal protection that had grown up around traditional European Christian definitions of marriage and family were invoked to demonstrate that they could not be reconciled with Mormon—or Islamic—practices to the

---

Carolina Press, 2002), 66; Banner, "When Christianity Was Part of the Common Law," 27–62.

59. On the sacralization of the Civil War, Harry S. Stout, *Upon the Altar of the Nation: A Moral History of the American Civil War* (New York: Viking, 2006), 248–58, 457–61; Mark Noll, *The Civil War as a Theological Crisis* (Chapel Hill: University of North Carolina Press, 2006).

contrary.[60] Northern and Southern Presbyterians, Methodists, and Baptists united under the common conviction that polygamy now stood as a clear indication of an un-Christian and un-American sign of social barbarism and an attack on the sacred nature of the family perhaps even more dangerous and loathsome than what White Southerners called the "peculiar institution."[61]

Even as the carnage of the American Civil War continued, a fleeting majority of Protestant Americans, perhaps shaken by the failure of religious convictions and constitutional frameworks that were supposed to have bolstered a vision of a Christian society, flirted with a kind of "moral Constitutional thinking." Their convictions led, not long after the end of the war to the decision of the U.S. Supreme Court against the practice of polygamy among the Mormons.[62] Not only was polygamy not permissible in the United States, but those assailing the Mormons also insisted that the Constitution should be described as a "Protestant document." Even more challenging, as the Orthodox would now discover in disagreements with Presbyterian missionaries and U.S. government officials in Alaska, the individual right to self-determination was limited, and those limitations stemmed from failure to live up to a social and legal interest in promulgating appropriate sexual and domestic behavior.[63] During the latter two-thirds of the 19th century, the Supreme Court would increasingly display its conviction that its proper role in the governance of the nation was that of exercising "guardian review." Although the Court had earlier reviewed decisions of the executive and of Congress, that practice excluded "cases that would subsequently be termed 'civil rights' or 'civil liberties' cases, testing the scope of protection for the rights of individuals against government regulation of their affairs."[64] The "guardian review" posture of the Court that nonetheless would prohibit the practice of polygamy lay in the somewhat odd distinction that claimed that the Constitution protected

60. Gordon, *The Mormon Question*, 66.

61. Stout, *Upon the Altar of the Nation*, 248–58, 457–61; Noll, *The Civil War as a Theological Crisis*, 110 citing "Ohio," *Protestantische Kirchenzeitung für das evangelische Deutschland* 10, no. 32 (Aug. 10, 1861): 763–4.

62. *Reynolds v. United States* 98 U.S. 145 (1878).

63. Gordon, *The Mormon Question*, 228.

64. G. Edward White, *Law in American History, Volume II: From Reconstruction through the 1920s* (New York: Oxford University Press, 2006), 2:350.

religious belief but not "actions." The decision in *Reynolds* "unambiguously reaffirmed the role of the state in defining marriage in the late nineteenth century," and rejected polygamists' invocation of the Free Exercise Clause of the First Amendment.[65]

The older conviction that the Constitution and laws of the republic in some way mirrored its overall Protestant cultural and social norms had proven no defense against the republic's near-collapse. Despite their own discomfort in the face of growing immigration by both Orthodox and Catholics from Eastern, Central, and Southern Europe, political leaders refused to consider a drive now undertaken by some Protestant Americans that would have created an even tighter connection between Reformed Protestant visions of a Christian society and the U.S. Constitution. Petitions to Congress presented by the National Reform Association, originally founded in 1864 by an aggressive coalition of immigrant Scottish Presbyterians in Pennsylvania and Ohio, demanded that Congress craft a constitutional amendment that would identify the United States as a Christian republic. Despite earlier reservations about the dangers posed by too close an association of the federal state with any religious tradition, German and Dutch Reformed as well as some Methodists now joined the movement. Authorities at the state and federal levels, however, distanced themselves from the effort. By 1904 the Supreme Court of North Carolina repudiated the claim that a general Protestant faith was an integral part of the constitutional tradition of the United States. Against the assertion that America was a "Christian nation," the court ruled that "it is incorrect to say that Christianity is part of the common law of the land. . . ."[66]

Reformed Protestant theology managed this one last effort to cement Protestant religious beliefs about society and culture by demanding a Constitutional amendment to declare Protestant Christianity the religion of the Republic. Yet at the same time American Protestants could not relinquish their deeper republican suspicion of ecclesiastical authorities and their

---

65. White, *Law in American History* 2:220–222, at 221.

66. Green, *The Second Disestablishment*, 334–337 on the National Reform Association, and at 389; and more extensively, Gaines Foster, *Moral Reconstruction: Christian Lobbyists and the Federal Legislation of Morality, 1865–1920* (Chapel Hill, NC: University of North Carolina Press, 2002).

attachment to a nearly absolute individual right to religious liberty. To understand aright the dilemma this issue posed for arriving Orthodox as they struggled to understand the various rights claims of Americans—especially an aggressive Presbyterianism in Alaska—we need to see the broader, trans-Atlantic trajectory of these trends in the Reformed tradition that unfolded in ways that many Protestant contemporaries did not find discordant. This is especially the case because it would be with that same Reformed tradition that the Orthodox would now clash over the question of the political, legal, and civil rights of Alaskan First Peoples collectively and as individuals, and over assaults aimed at Orthodox Christianity as a whole.

Even though German-speaking Lutherans outnumbered their language cousins in the Reformed tradition in the American Protestant culture of the nineteenth century, Lutherans contributed little to the assertions about the importance of an absolute liberty and right of individual conscience and religious choice. Most insisted on deference and obedience to authority exercised by a state, regardless of religious confession. Protestant theologians in Europe had also become largely content with rather vague affirmations of their particular confessional tradition without probing the possible tensions between religious liberty and the venerable tradition that bound rights claims to duties and obligations.[67] For American Protestants,

---

67. For example, Charles Porterfield Krauth, *The Conservative Reformation and Its Theology: As Represented in the Augsburg Confession, and in the History and Literature of the Evangelical Lutheran Church* (Philadelphia: J.B. Lippincott Company, 1888); Samuel S. Schmucker, *Elements of Popular Theology, with special reference to the Doctrines of the Reformation, as avowed before the Diet at Augsburg, in MDCCC*, 2nd ed. (New York: Leavitt, Lord, Co., 1834), "On Civil Governments," 271–287: "legitimate political enactments are good works of God . . . it is lawful for Christians to hold civil offices, to pronounce judgment and decide cases according to the imperial and other existing laws; to inflict just punishment, wage just wars and serve in them; to make lawful contracts; hold property; to make oath when required by the magistrate, to marry and be married . . . had the divine Saviour prescribed any form, it would doubtless have been the republican; for such is essentially the form of government which he gave to his church. . . ." 271, 275. Schmucker criticized passive understandings of obedience to authority, championed the absolute separation of church and state in the name of individual rights to liberty of conscience without clarifying how he resolved the tension between the

Martin Luther's actual writings on liberty of conscience and the duties owed to authority were neither critically engaged nor examined until after the First World War in the context of the "Luther Renaissance" in German scholarship.[68] In the United States, theological discourse continued to be heavily marked by the inheritance of Reformed thought and developed into a notion of "one kingdom." The conviction grew into accepted teaching that the Kingdom of Christ could hallow all aspects of human society, a conviction that led the unwary into the conclusion that America stood as the teleological fulfillment of a lineally conceived history of salvation that allowed the construction of the kingdom of God on earth. By the end of the nineteenth century, this conviction finally began to collapse as the rapidly industrializing and economically expanding nation transformed the social and economic landscape and regarded such religious notions as unnecessary for justifying the role of the United States in world affairs.[69] But in the territory of Alaska, as well as in the other sparsely settled areas of the American West, older convictions persisted even in the face of theological crisis that gripped American Presbyterians by the 1890s.

It would take more than half a century for the full implications of the Protestant dilemma to manifest itself in the United States, whereas Europeans, traumatized by the brutality of the First World War, would give up much earlier on faith in the possibility of reconciling a liberal cultural

---

two positions. See Schmucker, *The American Lutheran Church, Historically, Doctrinally, and Practically Delineated in Several Occasional Discourses* (Springfield: Harbaugh & Butler, 1851; New York: The Arno Press, 1969), 230, 250–51. Citations refer to the Arno Press edition.

68. Hartmut Lehmann, "Die Lutherjubiläen 1883 und 1917 in Amerika," in *Luthergedächtnis 1817 bis 2017*, Hartmut Lehmann (Göttingen: Vandenhoeck Ruprecht, 2012), 78–93, at 93, and on the earlier understanding of Luther, see (in the same work) Lehmann, "Die Entdeckung Luthers in Amerika des frühen 19. Jahrhunderts," 35–43.

69. Annette G. Aubert, *The German Roots of Nineteenth-Century American Theology* (New York: Oxford University Press, 2013); E. Brooks Holifield, *Theology in America: Christian Thought from the Age of the Puritans to the Civil War* (New Haven, CT: Yale University Press, 2003), 291–305, 368–394; Walter H. Conser, Jr., *Church and Confession: Conservative Theologians in Germany, England, and America, 1815–1866* (Macon, GA: Mercer University Press, 1984), 217–309.

Protestant social vision with notions of reason, progress, and inevitable, if gradual, improvement of human affairs directed by an easily recognized deity.[70] Recognition of how weak this tradition had been in North America only manifested itself some 75 years later. The retrospective analysis of an American Lutheran theologian—whose own tradition had never endorsed the "one kingdom" approach of the Reformed—concluded that his own church's "two kingdoms" approach had been just as unsuccessful in creating a social ethos:

> In a strange way the liberal doctrine of the essentially private nature of religious associations and the Lutheran doctrine of two kingdoms proved to be functional equivalents under the pluralistic conditions of American life. For the "life of faith" defined a private piety; the public sphere, one affirmed implicitly at least, lay beyond the reach of the gospel. The legislative hall, the courtroom, the market, the ship, even the school, ran on their own inherent principles . . . two swords and two kingdoms had meaningful institutional referents; they existed alongside one another in organized form. But within the community we do not have church (singular) but churches—of diverse traditions, sizes, and theological persuasions. . . . [71]

By the time this recognition occurred, both Reformed and Lutheran theologians in the United States warned that such a faith focused on an individual who imagined him/herself to be living in a morally autonomous world constituted exactly what "secularism" meant, a view of God and Christian society that had little or nothing to do with any form of historic Christianity.[72] It also constituted a view that the founders of the American experiment in constitutional representative democracy would also not have

70. George Marsden, *The Twilight of the American Enlightenment: The 1950s and the Crisis of Liberal Belief* (New York: Basic Books, 2014), 132, 143, 160, 166–74, 194–204.

71. Karl H. Hertz, *Two Kingdoms and One World* (Minneapolis: Augsburg Publishing House, 1976), 328, 327.

72. For the emergence of "the modern concept of the self and of a recognizably modern regime of rights grounded in national citizenship" in the revolutionary European context, see Eric D. Weitz, "Self-Determination: How a German Enlightenment Idea Became the Slogan of National Liberation and a Human Right," *American Historical Review* 120, no. 2 (April, 2015): 462–496, at 479.

recognized. Before Orthodox Christians could confront this twentieth-century social and political ethos, they first had to respond to the last gasp of an aggressive Presbyterian assault on what the Orthodox learned quickly to identify as their "rights." That confrontation occurred in Alaska, but its echoes and repercussions would reverberate far beyond the confines of that far northwestern area of Orthodox North America.

2

THE NINETEENTH-CENTURY ORTHODOX CONFRONTATION WITH RIGHTS

T he acquisition of Alaska by the United States in 1867 set in motion decades-long conflicts between the Orthodox and Protestant missionaries who harbored no doubts about the potential for creating the right kind of society among the peoples of the territory, exemplified in the person of Presbyterian missionary Sheldon Jackson (1834–1909). Jackson's willingness to cooperate with other Protestants in Alaska rested upon one unshakeable objective, "to counteract . . . and minimize the influence of the Orthodox Church." Responsible by 1878 for helping to found the Women's Executive Committee of the Presbyterian Church and the Women's Board of the Home Missionary Society after a vigorous career of founding Presbyterian missions in Colorado and other western states, Jackson continued unrelenting attacks on the Orthodox that eventually triggered court cases. Protesting the interference of Protestants in the wishes of indigenous Orthodox converts to be buried according to the rite of the Orthodox, Orthodox clergy and their hierarchs began to regard the open support of American political leaders in the federal government for the Presbyterian efforts as an alarming sign that American claims to respect the rights of the indigenous according to the Act of Cession did not include respecting the rights of the Orthodox in Alaska to use its own understandings of culture and education to craft its own social ethos.[1]

1. For further details, see Alexander Krivonosov, "When East Meets West: A Landscape of Familiar Strangers—Missionary Alaska, 1794–1898" (Ph.D. diss.,

Jackson and some—but by no means all—of his Presbyterian associates, while seeking to minimize Orthodox influence over the peoples of Alaska, argued early on for the rights of citizenship to be extended to the "civilized" among the First Peoples. At the same time, they located their understanding of rights in a bundle of assumptions deeply rooted in the Anglo-American tradition linking liberty and rights to private property. The solution to pre-marital sexual promiscuity, to polygamy, and the susceptibility to alcoholic addiction, they argued, lay in the ability of individual male heads of houses to build their own homes and sequester their wives and children from abuses. Even indigenous tribal leaders reinforced this conviction by stating that securing the pre-marital virginity of women was an impossibility as long as entire groups of men, women, and children lived together in a large room. For that reason, the construction of saw-mills to provide sufficient lumber; the erection of individual homes; and the adoption of "civilized" behavior provided the preconditions for the exercise of citizen rights by the First Peoples of Alaska, restricted to males. That connection was made explicit in Jackson's correspondence with his co-religionists, and by 1901 John W. Kelly had concluded that on St. George Island the only solution to making the indigenous "useful citizens" lay in the removal of Russo-Aleut priests to be replaced by Orthodox clergy from the United States who "know something of our country and its institutions, and who have the country's welfare at heart. . . ." As early as 1880 an unknown correspondent had informed Jackson that "while both the Church & the State hold to individual rights & responsibilities yet the Family is regarded as the unit in each community. This unit as we understand it does not exist here. How they live in large communal houses, have but one fire etc. you know well . . . if they are to be separated into families of one man & his wife & children they must be assisted by the missionary society or the government."[2]

The Pennsylvania State University, 2008), 76–91, for the judgment about Jackson's objectives, at 80.

2. Sheldon Jackson Papers, 1855–1909 (RG 239) Series I: Correspondence, 1856–1908, Presbyterian Historical Society, Philadelphia; John W. Kelley to Jackson, December, 1901; Unknown Correspondent to Jackson, September 6, 1880. On the sawmill issue, see the Jackson Circular Letter, June 9, 1881 citing as examples the Moravians of Labrador and the London Church Mission Society in British Columbia. For an endorsement of citizenship by Jackson's colleague S. Hall Young, see Young to Jackson, November 15, 1881.

For the Orthodox who began only in the post–Civil War decades to come to grips with civil, political, and religious rights claims, the Presbyterian emphasis upon a more individualistic, autonomous sense of rights shorn from the older Christian commitment to social obligation and duty appeared ominous. The convictions of American Reformed Protestants proclaimed America to be a Christian Protestant nation whose vigorous reform-minded leaders defined "civilization" to mean nothing less than "the adoption of accepted habits of hygiene and dress, education for literacy, and the achievement of economic self-sufficiency."[3] It was within this context and plan for a social reform of the "uncivilized" that the Russian Mission and subsequently Orthodox immigrants from historically Orthodox parts of the Middle East and Europe had to confront questions of civil, legal, property, and religious rights.

Not long after the sale of Alaska to the United States, the then-Archbishop Innocent wrote to the Holy Synod indicating his support for the transfer since, as he put it, "I see in this event one of the ways of Providence by which Orthodoxy will penetrate the United States, (where even now people have begun to pay serious attention to it)." To further the success of the Orthodox mission beyond its initial focus on North America's First Peoples, Innocent encouraged making San Francisco the episcopal see, and urged a new bishop to be appointed "from among those who know the English language." The new bishop's clergy and staff should come from "converts to Orthodoxy from among American citizens who accept all its institutions and customs."[4]

The importance of understanding the "institutions and customs" including their civil, religious, and property rights in this new order proved a daunting task. The Treaty of Cession had guaranteed to any Russian individual the right of return to Russia. But Article III stated that those choosing to remain were to be "admitted to the enjoyment of all the rights, advantages, and immunities of citizens of the United States and shall be

3. This attempt to rescue Jackson's reputation, without acknowledging that his definition of civilized Christianity excluded Orthodoxy is Stephen W. Haycox, "Sheldon Jackson in Historical Perspective: Alaska Native Schools and Mission Contracts, 1885–1895," *The Pacific Historian* 28, no. 1 (1984): 18–28, at 20.

4. Letter of Innocent Venianimov to the Ober-Procurator of the Holy Synod, 1868, in Michael Oleksa, ed., *Alaskan Missionary Spirituality* (New York: Paulist Press, 1987), 251.

maintained and protected in the free enjoyment of their liberty, property, and religion." Article II declared the right over all property in Alaska to be held by the United States except for private property and with the exception of the Orthodox churches that would remain "the property of the members of the Greek Oriental Church resident in the territory, as may choose to worship therein." The "uncivilized tribes" were not included in the enumeration of rights and privileges.[5]

Conversion to Christianity had been assumed by Protestant Americans to be the bedrock upon which the civilizing project of achieving a social vision of Protestant America had been founded. Even as the United States moved beyond the pre–Civil War convictions that this was a "Christian nation," Protestant, Reformed theological Christians who had come of age before that cataclysm remained convinced of the soundness of that enterprise. In the person of Sheldon Jackson, the Orthodox met a protagonist who was impatient regarding the rights of the Orthodox to continue their religious and educational mission in Alaska. That territory's First Peoples he argued, were being misled and kept from genuine civilization by Russian Orthodox clerics.

Jackson, like most Protestant Americans of his age, shared the perspective of the authors of a chapter devoted to "The Greek Church" in a description of world religions that appeared in 1884. The Orthodox would have been scandalized to read that the Orthodox and the Roman church were one not only in doctrinal unity for eight centuries but also in "their acknowledgment of the supremacy of the Roman pontiff." Throughout the description of Orthodoxy, the repeated observation of "superstition" culminated in the judgment that "the number of ceremonies and superstitious customs among the Russians nearly equals that of the Romish Church."[6] American Presbyterian missionaries like Jackson, intent on both conversion

5. The March 30, 1867 Proclamation of the Treaty is found at the Library of Congress site: *The Treaty Concerning the Cession of the Russian Possessions in North America by his Majesty the Emperor of all the Russias to the United States of America* (Washington, D.C.: March 30, 1867), 539–543. From the Library of Congress, https://memory.loc.gov/cgi-bin/ampage?collId=llsl&fileName=015/llsl015 .db&recNum=572.

6. Albert Rawson, et al., *What the World Believes, The False and the True, embracing the People of All Races and Nations, their Peculiar Teachings, Rites, Ceremonies, from the Earliest Pagan Times to the Present, to which is added an Account*

and civilization, encountered "highly literate Christians with a longstanding tradition of native clergy. Unfortunately, it was the wrong kind of Christianity. . . ." As Orthodox schools were closed by force, the Orthodox could not help but regard the policies set in motion by Jackson as an intentional violation of protected rights and as a "campaign against Orthodox and Native culture in Alaska." Ironically, just as Jackson and his contemporaries believed that the civilizing project appeared to be making headway, others became even more convinced that "cultural and religious diversity pose problems for the spread of Western customs, beliefs and institutions," but even more still convinced that "market-driven commerce promotes the growth of democratic political institutions and the legal enforcement of human rights."[7]

The decision taken by the federal government to end tribal collective rights and identity took the form of the Dawes Act of 1887. The devastating impact of this decision reverberated through most of the First Peoples' tribal units, extended to the Cherokee in the 1890s, and remained effectively in force until the 1930s. The conflicts between Sheldon Jackson and the Russian Orthodox in Alaska during the last decades of the nineteenth and the first decade of the twentieth century can only be understood within this larger context.[8]

---

of What the World Believes Today, by Countries (New York: Gay Brothers & Co., 1884), 139–216, at 139, 179.

7. For the comparison of Jackson with the Orthodox missionary and later Bishop Ivan Veniaminov, see Richard Dauenhauer, "Two Missions to Alaska," *The Pacific Historian* 25, no. 1 (1982): 29–41, at 39, 40; and more extensively Richard Dauenhauer, "Conflicting Visions in Alaskan Education," Occasional Paper #3 (Fairbanks, Alaska: Center for Cross-Cultural Studies, University of Alaska - Fairbanks, 1980). For the deep history of the Christian "civilizing" project in Great Britain and the early United States, Sheehan, *Seeds of Extinction,* and more extensively and for the last above quotation, Joseph S. Lucas, "Conquering the Passions: Indians, Europeans, and the Idea of Cultural Change in Early American Social Thought, 1580–1830" (unpublished Ph.D. dissertation, The Pennsylvania State University, 1999) 252.

8. The indispensable starting place for assessing the policies remains Francis Paul Prucha, *American Indian Policy in Crisis: Christian Reformers and the Indian, 1865–1900* (Norman: University of Oklahoma Press, 1975); Prucha, *The Churches and the Indian Schools, 1888–1912* (Lincoln: University of Nebraska Press, 1979),

Jackson had memorialized the U.S. Congress in 1880 while still serving as the Superintendent of Presbyterian Schools in the Territories, requesting to take responsibility for the "native inhabitants" and the "Creoles of mixed blood" who for the most part "are docile, peaceful, partially civilized, apt in the mechanical arts & anxious for instruction . . .". What both groups needed above all was access to "the common branches of an English Education, the principles of a republican government, and such industrial pursuits as may seem best adapted to their circumstances."[9] A year later, Jackson was urged to push his agenda in Washington by insisting first that "the whites who are living with Indian women should be compelled to marry them & their property should go to the children. 2. These Indians should be from the first treated as American citizens—no agencies nor treaties. They should be allowed to vote as soon as they can read & write & have adopted civilized habits."[10] By 1883 Jackson pressed the Secretary of the Interior Henry M. Teller to uphold the agreements made with Russia under the 1867 Cession. Jackson pointed out that Article 3 of the Treaty stipulated that all Alaskans except for "uncivilized Indians" were to be granted all "the rights & privileges of American Citizens. This includes the Aleutes as well as Creoles. These classes number several thousand. Up to the present time this article remains unfulfilled."[11]

Jackson's lobbying for Aleut and Creole citizenship met with fierce resistance among nominally Protestant Americans arriving in Alaska who were equally opposed to Jackson's attempt to stamp out the illegal liquor

---

and Prucha, *The Great Father: The United States Government and the American Indian,* 2 vols. (Lincoln: University of Nebraska Press, 1984). For a more exhaustive account of the complex legal and constitutional issues surrounding questions of Indian sovereignty from the perspective of American Indian Studies, see David E. Wilkins and K. Tsianima Lomawaima, *Uneven Ground: American Indian Sovereignty and Federal Law* (Norman, OK: University of Oklahoma Press, 2001).

9. Sheldon Jackson Papers, 1855–1909 (RG 239) Series I: Correspondence, 1856–1908, "A Memorial to the Honourable Senate & House of Representatives . . ." February 2, 1880. Jackson would be appointed General Agent of Education for Alaska under the Department of the Interior; see copy of appointment John Eaton, Commissioner to Jackson, April 11, 1885.

10. Sheldon Jackson Papers, Hall Young to Jackson, November 15, 1881.

11. Sheldon Jackson Papers, Jackson to Teller, October 13, 1883.

trade that he identified as the source of devastation among the First Peoples of Alaska. By 1890 he received the discouraging news from the District of Alaska Governor Lyman Knapp regarding proposed legislation that "I am sorry it does not come out squarely and define the natives of Alaska as citizens."[12]

The neglect of Creole rights and violation of protected rights of the First Peoples, however, provided the impetus for both converts and Russian Orthodox commentators to appeal to the defense of the rights of individuals and not merely those of a collective group identified as "uncivilized tribes" or "creoles." In an 1897 petition the Orthodox Tlingit leadership reminded President William McKinley that upon their being moved under the protection of the United States they had not become slaves but were assured of "some rights and privileges which were later made lawful and firm by the U.S. Congress." But it was not just collective tribal rights that they demanded be respected. The clear implication of the Organic Act that set up territorial government in Alaska stipulated in Section 8 that "every Indian has a right to dispose of his own life and liberty and his own property whether it consists in personal possessions or real estate. . . ."[13] A year later, in a valedictory letter to McKinley, Bishop Nicolas of Alaska begged the President to remember that he was as obligated to protect the First Peoples of Alaska as he had done "in the name of humanity of justice and freedom" in liberating Cuba, Puerto Rico, and the Philippines "for their human rights", an obligation whose fulfillment Alaskans were still waiting, hopefully not in vain. The dubious record of the United States in respecting the rights of the peoples of the Philippines only emerged gradually; both

12. Sheldon Jackson Papers, Lyman Knapp to Jackson, December 27, 1890. Henry E. Nayden of Chicago opposed citizenship as he explained to Jackson that such a concession would destroy Protestant missionary efforts since the "influence of the Russian Priests and every member of the Greek Church, would be used against American and Protestant interests." (Nayden to Jackson, January 9, 1893); for Jackson's and other correspondents' denunciation of government complicity in the illegal liquor trade, L.M. Stevenson to Jackson, September 17, 1892; L.M. Stevenson to Jackson, September 17, 1892; Jackson to Rev. M.O. McClelland, May 12, 1899.

13. Oleska, *Alaskan Missionary Spirituality*, 323–326, at 324. The letter was first published in *Pravoslavyi amerikanskii viestnik [Russian Orthodox American Messenger]*, (February 27, 1897), 242–246.

Protestant and Catholic support for the War in the subscription of major figures to a war memorial did not include the Orthodox leadership of the United States.[14] During the late 1890s, complaints against Protestant missionaries and officials brought by Russian Orthodox or converted First Nation peoples cited the violation of principles of "American liberty" and "toleration" without invoking the language of rights. But increasingly, the editors and contributors to the *Russian Orthodox American* did not hesitate to point out that "it is an accepted opinion in Europe that in no other country can be found greater liberty of consciences and fuller guaranties of every citizen's individual rights than exist in the United States of North America." But when it came to the protection of "individual rights and immunity of property," the American leadership appeared to be unconcerned about violation of those rights in the Russian and First Peoples' instances. A Russian newspaper correspondent picked up the theme of lamenting the failure of Americans to grant to Russians and their Orthodox converts "freedom, and all the rights of citizens of the Republic: special protection for the Orthodox religion," among them.[15] By the time the priest-monastic Anatolius arrived in Sitka, he confronted so much disorder among the indigenous that he founded the "Orthodox Indian Temperance and Mutual Aid Society" with the blessing of Bishop Nicolas. In

14. "Nicolas to McKinley, 5 October 1898" in Oleksa, *Alaskan Missionary Spirituality*, 326–328, at 327. Sheldon Jackson, the Presbyterian protagonist of the Orthodox in Alaska was a member of the "National Monument Committee for the Erection of a National Memorial to the Dead Heroes of the Cuban Battlefields and the Martyrs of the Main" that included the Roman Catholic Archbishop Michael Corrigan of New York and James Cardinal Gibbons of Baltimore. See Sheldon Jackson Papers, 1855–1909 (RG 239) Series I: Correspondence, 1856–1908, September 27, 1898. On the controversy over the War with Spain, see Edward Beisner, *Twelve Against Empire: The Anti-Imperialists, 1898–1900* (New York: McGraw Hill, 1968); and on general support for the war on the part of American religious leaders, Richard E. Welch, Jr., *Response to Imperialism: The United States and the Philippine-American War, 1899–1902* (Chapel Hill: University of North Carolina Press, 1978), Chapter 6, "The Response of Organized Religion and the Missionary Impulse," 89–100. I have found no evidence that the Orthodox bishop of the Russian Mission was approached to solicit his support.

15. *Russian Orthodox American Messenger*, December, 1896, 111–112; February 13, 1897, 196; 204–05.

his reflections published eighteen months later, Anatolius criticized American government indifference to the plague of alcoholism but went on to target tribal chieftains who continued to attempt to demand absolute subjection from tribal members. "The American Government does not recognize his rights . . ." to such power, Anatolius noted, but did nothing to curb a leader's violation of individual rights. Despite the claims of the Treaty, he concluded, an individual member of the First Peoples had no way to actually "own personal property in the strict sense of the phrase. All property belongs to the family or clan. . . ." Worse yet, he believed, "Indians elude legal marriage, whether civil or religious" and as a result of these ills, "there is no such thing as law for the Indians and non-Americans generally in Alaska."[16]

The adjustment of the Russian Mission to rapidly changing social and political conditions in Alaska in the late 1860s occurred at a time when novel rights claims were also being advanced in two of the most unlikely locations where Orthodox Christians were far more numerous than they were on the North American continent: Russia and the Ottoman Empire. Yet by the end of the nineteenth century, disputes over rights claims would find their way from Eastern Europe into the North American Orthodox world.

Imperial Russia had abolished the slave trade in 1842, but it was the emancipation of the serfs first advocated under Tsar Alexander II in 1856 and accomplished by 1861 that appeared utterly at odds with the political, religious, and social ethos of that empire. The most plausible explanation for the Tsar's willingness to contemplate what at first glance appeared to be a move toward a very different society can be found in the humiliation of Russia in the Crimean War of 1853–56. The complicated process of emancipation in stages and under different regional rules meant that "the peasants were to be freed not individually, but collectively." The fear that social control would be lost provoked an increasingly reactionary attitude among both landlords and many in Imperial government service alike. They correctly divined that the implications of emancipation would result in an "uncomfortable impetus toward the horizontal equalities and protected rights of citizens of a nation."[17] Whatever the abolition of slavery

16. Anatolius' remarks begin in the May 15, 1897 issue of the *Messenger*, 367 and conclude in August, 1897, 395–6.

17. Valerie A. Kivelson and Ronald Grigor Suny, *Russia's Empires* (New York and Oxford: Oxford University Press, 2017), 185–94, at 189, 191.

and the emancipation of the serfs portended for Imperial Russia, neither produced an understanding, much less an embracing, of the notion of "rights" beyond that of collective identities.

A parallel development with equally unsettling results was developing for the Orthodox within the bounds of a weakening, and for Christians, increasingly dangerous, Ottoman Empire. Those events would have a direct impact upon the Orthodox in North America once a flood of emigration from Eastern and Southern Europe and the Middle East began in the late 1880s that relegated Russia's original Alaska mission to a secondary field of endeavor. Historically, Orthodox Christians had once been defined by Ottoman law as one people, the Christian *millet*, regardless of their language, geographic location, or folk cultures. This arrangement now collapsed in the rise of nationalist identity that looked to speech itself—*ethne*—as the basis for understanding the identity and meaning of what it meant to be Orthodox. Discontented with the treatment they received at the hands of the Phanariot Greek clergy of the Ecumenical Patriarchate in the Ottoman Empire, the Bulgarian Orthodox successfully petitioned the Grand Porte for permission to create their own, independent Orthodox Church that would include all dioceses where two-thirds of the population was ethnically Bulgarian. Refusing the innovation (as he saw it) in the evolution of a self-governing Orthodox Church, the Ecumenical Patriarch called a pan-Orthodox Synod, which met in 1872. In Article 1 of its decrees, it condemned as heretical "the doctrine of phyletism, or the difference of races and national diversity in the bosom of the Church of Christ."[18]

The specter of a social future that might be based on racial and ethnic idolatry had caught the attention of the Ecumenical Patriarchate at least a decade before the Bulgarian incident. But it was the Civil War in the United States, not growing unrest in Bulgaria, which first provoked Patriarch

---

18. On the controverted question of the Ecumenical Patriarch's role as primate, see the canonical and historical survey provided by Lewis Patsavos, "The Primacy of the See of Constantinople in Theory and Practice," Panorthodox Synod, September 13, 2018, https://www.goarch.org/-/the-primacy-of-the-see-of -constantinople-in-theory-and-practice-. The unsettled atmosphere surrounding the issues of nationalism and the reactions of the Ottoman Empire can be seen in the deposition and restoration of the Patriarchs Joachim II (1860–63) (1873–78); Gregory VI Constantine (1867–71); Anthimus VI (1871–73), the last-named the Patriarch who presided over the 1872 Pan-Orthodox Synod.

Joachim II's concerns. His retrospective letter on the events of the year 1862 appeared in the December 31 edition of the *Anatolikos Aster (Star of Anatolia)* published in Constantinople. The paper could express only those views and opinions that were consonant with the specific rights and protections granted to the Orthodox Christian *millet* in the Empire whose sole connection to the Grand Porte was the Patriarch. In his reflections, the Patriarch commented on the outbreak of the American Civil War and made clear that the Union, and not the Confederacy, was "guided by true reason and evangelical principles. . . . ." More realistically than Americans who still hoped for an early end to the war, Joachim predicted a long and vicious conflict. But he also believed, he wrote, that "those who contend so nobly for the most unquestionable and humane rights, will, God helping them, reach the object of their desires."

Joachim's invocation of the existence of unquestionable "humane rights" (*tes anthropotos dichaiomaton*) did not imply an awareness or endorsement of an embryonic form of human rights as that term would come to be understood in the twentieth century. But his choice of words carried significance, nonetheless, as did his condemnation of the South's blind pursuit of "material interest," in which expansion the Confederate leaders "obstinately and anti-Christianly seek the perpetuation of slavery."[19] Since so

19. This English language translation account appeared in the April 24, 1863 issue of the abolitionist newspaper *The Liberator* where the Patriarch's remarks, reproduced from *The Presbyterian and Theological Review,* in contrast to his British counterpart's "studied aloofness," reported favorably on Joachim II's observations. See: "The Greek Church," *The Liberator,* April 24, 1863, www.theliberatorfiles.com /wp-content/uploads/2015/10/The-Liberator-1863–04-24-Page-2.png. The original Greek (printed in the *Ανατοληκός Αστήρ*) is available in digitized form from the Parliament of Greece. I am indebted to the Rev. Dr. Joachim Cotsonis, librarian of the Hellenic College/Holy Cross Greek Orthodox School of Theology for alerting me to the digitized version. http://srv-web1.parliament.gr/display_doc.asp?item =43669&seg=10768 (accessed July 6, 2016). Mr. Matthew Namee first drew attention to the incident in his remarks "Ecumenical Patriarch Opposes American Slavery in 1862," Orthodox History, April 27, 2015, https://orthodoxhistory.org /2015/04/27/ecumenical-patriarch-opposes-american-slavery-in-1862/. The use of the word "humane" as opposed to "human" poses problems. Although the former spelling did mean "human" for many centuries, this was no longer true by the late eighteenth century. It remains unclear, therefore, whether the translators in Britain intentionally invoked an archaic spelling, or whether they intended to suggest that

little is known of Joachim's own life, we can only speculate that he chose to portray the struggle over "humane rights" in the United States because of the ongoing and controversial *Tanzimat* reforms underway in the Otto-man Empire. His condemnation of "material interest" reflected a long-standing denunciation of greed and indifference to the suffering of the poor that had produced a sermon literature emerging in the fourth century in the writings of Orthodox hierarchs such as Basil of Caesarea and John Chrysostom. Yet unlike those ancient authors, Joachim was willing to denounce slavery itself as incompatible with a Christian ethos of a just society.[20]

Beginning in 1839, Ottoman reformers had struggled to protect the Em-pire from threats from Muslims such as the Egyptian vassal Mehmet Ali Pasha Kavalah. They also intended to incorporate non-Muslims as actual citizens into an Empire that had to attempt to reconcile traditional cate-gories of persons, privileges, and obligations with emerging economic and social challenges coming from increased contact with non-Ottoman, and non-Muslim states. However the Muslim population of the Empire was inclined to regard the reforms—and most appeared to be hostile—leaders of the non-Muslim *millets* at first were inclined to see the changes as an affirmation that they also had a legal right to equality in the eyes of the Ottoman Empire and its laws that would have social and economic consequences.

But by the time the 1876 Fundamental Law of the Sultanate, adopted two years before Joachim II's death, was formally proclaimed, the Greek Orthodox *millet* opposed the reforms. Western observers who read the doc-ument in translation tended to dismiss the effort, their cynicism con-firmed when the deputies of the representative parliamentary Chamber began criticizing the Sultan and the powerful ruling families, resulting in the suppression of the Chamber by the Sultan.[21] The Greek Orthodox

---

"to be humane is human," a use contemporary to the Patriarch's observations. See OED 1345 column 3.

20. For an introduction to that literature, see *On Social Justice: St. Basil the Great* transl., with introduction and commentary by C. Paul Schroeder (Crestwood, NY: St. Vladimir's Seminary Press, 2009).

21. Robert Devereux, *The First Ottoman Constitutional Period: A Study of the Midhat Constitution and Parliament* (Baltimore: Johns Hopkins University Press, 1963), 60–90; 254–56.

opposed the reforms in part because the reforms appeared to dislodge them from their favored status and put them on the same footing with other, smaller *millets,* including obligatory military service now expected of them (though not actually imposed until 1910). The prospect of so-called crypto-Christians now claiming they could legitimately leave Islam jockeyed with non-Muslim complaints of forced conversions to Islam. Most significantly, the creation of secular peoples' assemblies intensified ethnic identity even if a claim to legal, political, and social equality for all Ottoman subject/citizens could be teased out of the Ottoman conviction that all subjects, since regardless of religious belief enjoyed standing as "children of God."[22] Much as in the rival Russian Empire, the Ottomans had constructed a kind of umbrella law that applied to the entire population but at the same time had attempted to use a modified version of legal pluralism "to assimilate non-Muslims into a hegemonic Islamic court system while keeping interreligious peace and tolerance."[23]

By the nineteenth century, the accepted ways of maintaining the boundaries among the different non-Muslim communities had frayed to such an extent that novel forms of economic and legal mechanisms undercut universal claims for Ottoman law and, "fatefully, new forms of ethnic and national self-understanding."[24] Despite reformist efforts within Greek Orthodox circles to push the Orthodox clergy into support for the Tanzimat reforms, those efforts came to nothing. By tarring reform efforts as "innovative," opponents within the hierarchy could identify such calls with a putative "Western" attack upon the Orthodox faith. They also opposed lay participation in the governance of the *Rum millet* as an infringement upon clerical rights and privileges, a position encouraged by the opposition of the Greek government to the reforms. Joachim himself would not

22. Wajih Kawtharani, "The Ottoman *Tanzimat* and the Constitution (Research Paper)" *Tabayyun* 3 (Winter, 2013), 7–22; Berdal Aral, "The Idea of Human Rights as Perceived in the Ottoman Empire," *Human Rights Quarterly* 26, no. 2 (May, 2004): 454–482, at 467–8; on the problems of conversion and apostasy, see Selim Deringil, *Conversion and Apostasy in the Late Ottoman Empire* (Cambridge: Cambridge University Press, 2012), 28–66, 111–155.

23. Karen Barkey, "Aspects of Legal Pluralism in the Ottoman Empire," in *Legal Pluralism and Empires, 1500–1800,* ed. Lauren A. Benton and Richard Jeffrey Ross (New York: New York University Press, 2013) 83–107, at 84.

24. Barkey, "Aspects of Legal Pluralism," 103.

survive these internal struggles over rights and privileges, and he was re-moved in 1863 for apparently consenting to the Romanian government's confiscation of monastic properties in Moldovlachia.[25]

Joachim's condemnation of American slavery even in the face of accel-erating uprisings of non-Muslims in the Ottoman Empire had outstripped that of the Orthodox Church's former sister Church. Pope Gregory XVI condemned the slave trade in his 1839 *In supremo Apostolatus fastigio* but refrained from forming the condemnation in terms of natural law, stig-matizing the trade as "'inhuman' without developing an argument." More-over, despite Leo XIII's encyclical of 1888 (*In plurimis*) that congratulated Brazil for abolishing slavery, Rome even then could not bring itself to spell out the implications for a more just social order even though the terms "human dignity" and "divine likeness" found their way into the letter. Nei-ther the letter nor subsequent teaching would be "read by the moral theo-logians as a radical rejection of an institution accepted for over eighteen hundred years. Leo labeled the institution 'base' and 'cruel' He did not condemn it as intrinsically evil."[26]

In the aftermath of the American Civil War, the abolition of slavery, and the repudiation of Mormon polygamy, religious conflicts in the United States found a new focus. Assumptions about the rights of property and contract and their relationship to religious organizations found their way into court cases that would also come to affect the Orthodox. In 1871, the U.S. Supreme Court heard arguments regarding the dispute over the prop-erty of the Walnut Street Presbyterian Church in Louisville, Kentucky. Founded in 1842 and incorporated in 1854, the Walnut Street Church had always been identified as part of the Presbyterian Church of the United

---

25. Dimitris Stamatopoulos, "Holy Canons or General Regulations? The Ecumenical Patriarchate *vis-à-vis* the Challenge of Secularization in the Nineteenth Century," in *Innovation in the Orthodox Christian Tradition? The Question of Change in Greek Orthodox Thought and Practice,* ed. Trine Stauning Willert and Lina Molokotos-Liederman (Farnham, UK: Ashgate Publishing, 2012), 143–162.

26. John T. Noonan, Jr., *A Church That Can and Cannot Change: The Development of Catholic Moral Teaching* (Notre Dame, IN: University of Notre Dame Press, 2005), 107 on Gregory XVI's condemnation and 110–188, at 113. On *In Plurimis.* For the text of the encyclical, Pope Leo XIII, *In Plurimis,* Papal Encyclicals Online (May 5, 1888), www.papalencyclicals.net/Leo13/l13abl.htm>, accessed June 17, 2016.

States. Because of internal disputes and disagreements about the congregation's assessment of the slavery issue, a fight over the right of possession erupted at the end of the war. But rather than become entangled in the internal controversies over correct doctrine or disputes over the standing of elders and members, the court insisted that what it was hearing was a property dispute case—in its words, "strictly one of identity and of lawful organic succession" in the question of who exercised authority over the property. In its final decision, the court laid down principles that would affect all religious groups, including the Orthodox in the United States, although the impact would not be felt for nearly another century. Secular courts, the justices ruled in *Watson v. Jones*, cannot rule on the correctness of religious teachings in any religious body; secular courts must defer to any prior, clear decisions made internally by a religious body; secular courts must defer to the majority of a specific congregation if condition number two does not exist. If the body in question is hierarchical—and considerable ambiguity surrounded the agreed-upon definition of what this word meant for a religious group—the civil courts defer to the prevailing hierarchical opinion about the rights to property claimed by the contesting parties.[27] Whatever discussion of the rights of possession the court could entertain, those rights were held by an identifiable structure of authority and did not involve claims to individual rights—of conscience or correctness of belief.

Concerns about the rights of possession did not begin among the Orthodox solely because of the events that unfolded in Alaska or the *Watson* decision. Nor did the reform efforts among subjects "in a free Ottoman Empire" preoccupy Greek-speakers in the declining Ottoman world. Over the course of centuries under various Islamic rulers, the former Syriac and now Arabic-speaking Christians of the Middle East had declined in numbers and social standing to such a degree that by the early modern period, in the opinion of some scholars, "the first half-century of Ottoman rule . . . continued the inertia of cultural decline that engulfed the Christian East during the Mamluk period . . . nor was knowledge of canon law up to standard . . . exemplified by the opinion of the Patriarch of Alexandria to his counterpart

---

27. *Watson v. Jones* 80 U.S. 679 (1871). For the later implications of this case upon the Orthodox dispute over right of possession to St. Nicholas Cathedral in New York, see below.

in Antioch that the First Ecumenical Council of Nicaea had adopted only 21 canons as opposed to the 42 the Antiochian presumed to cite."[28]

Although a brief "Melkite Renaissance" temporarily rejuvenated Middle Eastern Orthodoxy in the seventeenth century, on balance, the period up to 1800 was characterized by "high points of cultural creativity and political activity . . . followed by decades of torpor." Both the willingness of Ottoman rulers to be alternatively tolerant and manipulative as they juggled competing Latin, Orthodox, Armenian, and Coptic rights of possession claims to the pilgrimage sites in Jerusalem, coupled with the inability of the Arab Orthodox to compete energetically in an increasingly plural and aggressive world, contributed to the malaise.[29] These tendencies accelerated in the nineteenth century and left a bitter legacy of multiple Orthodox Christian groups fighting with varying degrees of success for collective rights and identity, a conflict that would spill over into North America as emigration from the region began in earnest in the latter part of an increasingly violent late nineteenth-century.

Nothing illustrates these Orthodox debates over rights of possession as eloquently as the negative exchanges that erupted between the Greek Orthodox who enjoyed preferential treatment by the Ottomans and the Slavic and Arabic Orthodox in the Empire. In a searing attack levelled against the corrupt practices of the Greek-speaking "Brotherhood of the Holy Sepulcher" written in 1893, two years before his arrival in North America, the Arabic Christian priest Raphael Hawaweeny invoked the language of the protected legal rights of Orthodox Christians under the Empire that had in theory, been strengthened by the *Tanzimat* reforms.[30]

The Brotherhood, founded in 1534 by the Greek monastic Germanus the Peloponnesian, gradually wrested control of the Patriarchate of Jerusalem away from Arabic-speaking clergy, replacing them with Greek-speakers

---

28. Constantine A. Panchenko, *Arab Orthodox Christians Under the Ottomans 1516–1831,* Brittany Pheiffer Noble and Samuel Noble, trans. (Jordanville, NY: Holy Trinity Seminary Press, 2016), 439. For the 20 canons and commentary see Peter L'Huillier, *The Church of the Ancient Councils: The Disciplinary Work of the First Four Ecumenical Councils,* 17–100.

29. Panchenko, *Arab Orthodox Christians,* 497.

30. Page numbers in what follows are from Raphael Hawaweeny, *An Historical Glance at the Brotherhood of the Holy Sepulcher,* trans. Archpriest Michel Najim (Torrance, CA: Oakwood Publications, 1996), at 41.

and forbidding the ordination of Arabic Christians to the ranks of the clergy or as members of the monastic community. Hawaweeny, in his indictment of the Brotherhood, detailed the financial corruption, bribery, influence-peddling and lawsuits against the Arabic Christians that over time destroyed the original "right of predominance" over the Christian pilgrimage sites given by Caliph Omar Ibn al-Khatab to the Jerusalem Patriarch Sophronios in 637. Despite the later attempts of Greek-speakers to claim that the Caliph had granted this right to Greeks, Hawaweeny argued that "only the indigenous people possess the right to have legal authority over Jerusalem," and the prejudices of Greek speakers to the contrary, "their Arabic language does not deprive them of the right to manage" what the Caliph had granted their forebears. That right had been confirmed in 1250 by the Mamluk Sultan El Zaher, who had expelled the Latin Christians from Jerusalem and "secured the right of the indigenous Orthodox people over the Holy Places." The Greek monastics, Hawaweeny concluded, had "no right to take possession of the Holy Land which is the right of the native children of Jerusalem."[31]

Hawaweeny, serving first at the Patriarchate of Antioch and subsequently at the Antiochian Patriarchate's *metochion* (ecclesiastical embassy church) in Moscow, had been demoted to teaching at a school in Kazan by a furious Greek-speaking occupant of the Antiochian Patriarchate. Hawaweeny was recruited by bishop Nikolai Ziorov to begin serving Arabic-speaking Orthodox in the Russian Church's American mission. What Hawaweeny encountered in the United States was an Orthodox community that had moved its headquarters from Sitka, Alaska, to San Francisco, and eventually New York City. Faced with their own adjustments to American society, the members of ethnically defined churches relied on their places of worship as places of refuge where social customs of language, food, and worship could be maintained. These immigrants were "totally unaware of the history of the Alaskan Church" and "despite the expansion and acceleration of many of the mission's activities, most of the news from Alaska was not good."[32] Yet if Hawaweeny remained largely isolated from events in Alaska, he was still aware of Protestant theologians' arguments directed

31. Hawaweeny, *An Historical Glance*, 9, 18, 19, 20, 27.
32. Michael J. Oleksa, *Orthodox Alaska: A Theology of Mission* (Crestwood, NY: St. Vladimir's Seminary Press, 1992), 168.

against Roman Catholic claims for subordinating political authority and the construction of a Christian society to papal authority. Orthodox reaction was filtered through already-existing Protestant theological positions that went largely unacknowledged. The main objections of the Orthodox were predictable: "refusal of excessive forms of primacy, the rejection of infallibility, and the repudiation of the claim that faith in papal primacy is a prerequisite for salvation." Orthodox theologians did not actually read the documents in Latin that emanated from Vatican I. For example, Hawaweeny, who would later become the first Orthodox bishop ordained in the United States, composed his response to Vatican I and acknowledged that "he was relying on Protestant material translated from German into Russian. Yet, while he explicitly refers to Harnack's *Dogmengeschichte* in a Russian translation," the future bishop never subjected Adolph von Harnack's own perspectives on the sensitive issues of the relationship between political authority and the Church to Orthodox scrutiny.[33]

In the judgment of Orthodox clergy, Presbyterians continued to bear primary responsibility for the bad news coming from Alaska. In effect, their civilizing project and social vision had dispossessed First Peoples who could only expect to be thought of as part of society if they could claim the rights of citizenship based on individual demonstration of having internalized the characteristics of American Protestant society. Protestants in the United States had dared to believe that despite various denominational loyalties, a shared commitment to the basic contours of both church history and the history of doctrine in the exceptional American context would inoculate them against the bitter battles over Christology and scriptural inerrancy that had broken out in European Protestant circles.

The translation from German and the widespread use of Karl Rudolf Hagenbach's "genial" works that had skirted those controversial questions persisted after the scholar's death in 1875, but proved in the end, illusory.[34] The tensions created in the unresolved question of the right of individual conscience versus duties owed to a confessional statement of belief

33. Assaad Elias Kattan, "The Ways of Polemic Literature: Vatican I in *al-Hadiyya*," *Ostkirchliche Studien* 62, no. 1 (2013): 136–142, at 137, 142.

34. Zachary Purvis, "Transatlantic Textbooks: Karl Hagenbach, Shared Interests, and German Academic Theology in Nineteenth-Century America," *Church History* 83, no. 3 (September, 2014): 650–683, at 682.

erupted among Presbyterians in the heresy trial of Charles Augustus Briggs in 1891. At first glance the crisis appeared to be one where "claims for institutional authority . . . stood against claims for individual intellectual liberty. . . ." In fact, however, Briggs' trial also brought to light questions about due process and the protection of individual rights of conscience. At trial, Briggs complained that claims that he was teaching heresy had not been properly submitted to the opinion of the various presbyteries of his denomination. That failure revealed that "arguments about jurisdiction and procedure were more than legal stratagems; they reflected Briggs's commitment to what he considered the correct way to promote theological progress."[35] By the end of the nineteenth century, other liberal Protestant leaders avoided the dogmatic questions in favor of renewed efforts at social reform. Their movement, which came to be labelled the Social Gospel, had produced celebrated ministers such as Washington Gladden, George Herron, and Walter Rauschenbusch. In their interpretation of Christianity they insisted that "Jesus taught a social ethic, not an individualistic one." But no less so than the more aggressive Presbyterians like Jackson, the Social Gospel leaders were just as convinced "of the need to convert, assimilate, and 'Americanize' the newly arrived foreign born." Their condescending attitudes toward non-Christian religions extended to their disdain for Roman Catholics and, when they noticed them at all, the Eastern Orthodox. What they expected from both First Peoples and ethnic arrivals was simple: deference.[36] Historians of the political tradition of

35. Harvey Hill, "History and Heresy: Religious Authority and the Trial of Charles Augustus Briggs," *U.S. Catholic Historian* 20, no. 3 (Summer, 2002): 1–21, here at 15, 19. Jackson was among those who supported the prosecution of Briggs. For an argument that missionary experience of American Protestants abroad beginning in the 1890s broadened attitudes about religious and racial minorities in the United States see David A. Hollinger, *Protestants Abroad: How Missionaries Tried to Change the World but Changed America* (Princeton: Princeton University Press, 2017). For the late nineteenth-century Swiss Reformed battle over conscience versus confessional authority, see Sarah Scholl, "Freedom in the Congregation? Culture Wars, Individual Rights, and National Churches in Switzerland (1848–1907)," *Church History* 89, no. 2 (June, 2020): 333–349.

36. William G. McLoughlin, *Revivals, Awakenings, and Reform: An Essay on Religion and Social Change in America, 1607–1977* (Chicago: University of Chicago Press, 1978), 162, 178.

"progressives" in the United States have pointed to these reformers' distaste for legislation emanating from those deemed uninformed or insufficiently sophisticated. Instead, they came to rely on more elite judicial and executive ways of circumventing recalcitrant local and state officials to advance their agendas of social and political reform.[37]

By the time the Orthodox hierarchy began to emerge in the lower forty-eight states of the late nineteenth century, Russian Orthodox leaders both clerical and lay in North America had begun to take note of the importance of legal and civil rights and liberties and the need to be vigilant in protecting them from violation by those beyond the boundaries of Orthodox Christianity. But with regard to the problem of property law, especially as it pertained to religious bodies, American civil church law had already established precedents by which local, state, and federal legal authority "creates, guards, and enforces the civil, contract, and property rights" of religious groups.[38] Orthodox controversies initially contributed little or nothing to the manner in which American law dealt with corporations, church constitutions, implied trusts, schisms within churches, or questions of tax exemptions. With regard to the rights of an individual member of the clergy, however, the 1917 casebook compiled by Carl Zollmann did take note of a conflict between an Illinois Greek Orthodox congregation and its priest. When a clergyman who had not been dismissed or defrocked was prevented from entering the church to perform his duties, the court ruled, he had the right to pursue via civil law an action against the parish for breach of contract.[39] Struggles over property and contract,

---

37. For two differing perspectives, see Christopher Lasch, *The True and Only Heaven: Progress and its Critics* (New York: Norton, 1991) and Gabriel Kolko, *The Triumph of Conservatism: A Reinterpretation of American History* (New York: Quadrangle Books, 1967); on progressive tactics, Adam R. Shapiro, *Trying Biology: The Scopes Trial, Textbooks, and the Antievolution Movement in American Schools* (Chicago: University of Chicago Press, 2013).

38. Carl Zollmann, *American Civil Church Law* (New York: Columbia University, 1917; New York: AMS Press, Inc., 1969), 3. Citations refer to the AMS Press edition.

39. *Ziankas* v. *Hellenic Orthodox Church*, 170 Ill. App. 334, cited in Zollmann, *American Civil Church Law*, 347. It is not clear that Orthodox immigrants were familiar with the early North American Catholic struggles with trusteeism and the laws surrounding charitable trusts. For the literature and some of the issues that

increasingly revealed that a culture of deference to religious and civil authority showed little sign of deepening as the new century dawned. Instead, claims to the rights of contract, property, and the kind of ecclesial society where the laity would take a more aggressive and assertive role than had ever been possible in traditional Orthodox lands were understood and used by lay leaders. The Orthodox lay arrivals quickly recognized the importance of the laws of property and contract protected by an American constitutional tradition that unintentionally would alter the social ethos of twentieth-century Orthodox communities in North America.

As the various ethnic and linguistic strains of Orthodox had begun the process of raising funds at the local level to finance and build the first churches in the United States, a *de facto*, but not quite *de jure* version of Protestant governance emerged in the absence of a fully developed hierarchy and clergy. That development was paralleled by the unanswered question of who rightfully claimed authority over the "diaspora" of Orthodox groups in the United States. Orthodox life began to evolve along Protestant, not Catholic lines of governance. With the death of the original territorial parish corporation, and the original form of a sole corporation that had vested the holder with the right of holding the property of the parish, the Catholic Church's recognition as "an ecclesiastical body . . . [that] had a juristic personality and legal status" emerged as part of the U.S. treaty with Spain at the conclusion of the Spanish-American War. But no such standing yet existed for the American Orthodox.[40]

Within a matter of a few decades both Orthodox clerics and converts from among the First Peoples of Alaska demonstrated how quickly they would respond to a perceived assault on both collective and individual civil, religious, and property rights. Because of the unplanned nature of immigration to the United States by a variety of ethnic Orthodox believers, and in the face of a small clerical and hierarchical presence in North America, the Orthodox Christian churches evolved in a manner that guaranteed debates over property and contract rights understood by the laity that had founded and financed the local parishes of their tradition in this foreign land. The social ethos assumptions that lay behind those conflicts came

---

arose between the late eighteenth-century and the 1840s, see Roeber, "The Long Road to *Vidal*," 414–441.

40. Zollmann, *American Civil Church Law*, 38–110, at 47.

from the Protestant culture into which the Orthodox had arrived. Hierarchs and clerics pointed to a body of canonical measures that defended hierarchical and clerical privileges and honor, the inheritance of a vastly different ecclesiastical tradition from either Western Catholic or Protestant Christianity. The context for the working out of these tensions had begun in nineteenth-century Alaska, but by the ethnically more diverse early twentieth century spread to the lower forty-eight states, where debates over freedom of expression and conscience exploded because of the Bolshevik Revolution that provoked a global crisis among the Orthodox. The mix of hostility and suspicion in the aftermath of the revolution targeted the fragmented Orthodox despite evidence that both in the United States and in Russia itself, admiration of the American tradition of civil, religious and property rights found expression in public and private writings. The visions of society the Orthodox had begun to develop by the early twentieth century had grown out of the context created by the cultural Protestantism but now the increasingly individualistic, secular, and pluralist society of the country the Orthodox—sometimes with mixed feelings—called home.

3

PLURALISM AND THE RIGHTS OF FREEDOM OF SPEECH AND EXPRESSION

To answer Witte's and Alexander's query about how the Orthodox understand the "meaning of freedom of speech and expression," it seems wisest to cast the response in terms of the context of American pluralism. This is so because the Orthodox, like any other American religious tradition, co-exist in a relationship to state authority where at times it appears that the intersection of freedom and pluralism can both promote and at times obstruct the way in which the Orthodox understand their own liberties and those of others. In fact, a second interaction has proven to be just as fraught, and that is the one within the Orthodox Church itself. As the historical evidence demonstrates, conflicts among Orthodox bishops themselves over the role of one "primate" versus the synodical consensus of all bishops in matters of church governance cannot easily be separated from the claims of American Orthodox lower clergy and laity that they also have a right to have a voice in such matters. For the bishops, such claims awakened nightmare memories of a long series of disputes over the control of church property; the way in which ecclesiastical or spiritual courts are conducted; and how procedural rights are understood and applied. Thus, the Orthodox engagement with their rights and those of "others" remained intimately connected to debates over rights within the Orthodox Church. Because those connections remained both complex and current, this latter engagement, though linked to questions of freedom and expression in American society as a whole, receives its own separate treatment after the current chapter in two stages and two interrelated chapters—one involving the right of an American Orthodox Church to be entirely self-governed, and the other that analyzes the reaction against that rights claim.

We begin with a series of observations about pluralism itself. Then, to comprehend how the Orthodox regard the current state of their relationship to state authority since the twentieth century rights revolution, we must also understand the history of the "external" pluralism conflicts beginning in the late nineteenth-century. Because of the speed with which conflicts over rights of religious expression and opinion continue to find their way into the courts, any conclusions we can draw must, perforce, remain somewhat tentative.

I. Pluralism

Scholars of varying disciplines who have written about pluralism in terms of the importance of the right to freedom of religious expression and opinion have addressed the possibility of permanent tension existing between conflicting identities and commitments held by different individuals and communities—some of whom hold overtly secular, others explicitly religious convictions. The Orthodox in North America only began in the late 1960s to assess the advantages as well as the challenges posed by a country committed to freedom of speech, opinion, and expression. Given both the predominance of Protestantism in American life and the frigid relationship between the Orthodox and the Roman Catholic Church, only with the calling of the Second Vatican Council did the Orthodox begin to assess the novel affirmation within Catholicism of the American commitments to the right to religious liberty and freedom of expression.

The American Jesuit John Courtney Murray's insistence that a pluralistic nation-state and society marked by religious freedom posed no threat to Roman Catholic teachings met with alarm and condemnation when he first began writing. The Roman Catholic condemnation of pluralism as an unfortunate necessity in non-confessional Roman Catholic monarchies and states remained intact well into the twentieth century. Some conservative Catholic commentators lamented Leo XIII's apparent endorsement of both natural law and natural rights in his encyclical *Rerum Novarum* as an ill-advised move toward accommodating secular notions of natural rights, including the sacredness of private property. But with the issuing of Vatican II's *Dignitatis Humanae*, whose primary authorship could be traced to Murray, Catholic teaching appeared to acknowledge the positive contribution of states and societies where pluralism, marked by freedom of religious choice and expression, were the norm. Those who have studied the American Jesuit's thought conclude that Murray was primarily interested in emphasizing the advantages of the Church's pragmatic approach to the realities of pluralism: freedom of religious choice and expression. He was not interested in attempting to construct a systematic evaluation of how those realities could be squared with a natural law position favored by Thomists in the Roman Church.[1] By 1978 at least John Meyendorff among American Orthodox commentators appeared to endorse at least some aspects of Murray's arguments.[2]

Not only non-Orthodox Christians, but Jewish commentators, such as Lenn Goodman, encouraged frank and open discussion of real differences in public fora—the only way Goodman believed Americans could avoid the accelerating tendency of both individuals and groups to retreat into isolation and anxiety about the "other." John Inazu's call for "confident pluralism" echoed some of Goodman's plea, with Inazu grounding his calls for such confidence in the ability of both individuals and groups to be clear about their own identities, values, and commitments before they could expect to engage with those with whom they foresee, or experience, difference. In both cases, the writers' concerns focused not so much on the threat of state intrusion upon rights but rather upon conflict with other citizens

1. For two differing assessments of Murray's work and its impact, see Timothy W. Burns, "John Courtney Murray, Religious Liberty, and Modernity: Part I: Inalienable Natural Rights," and "Part 2: Modern Constitutional Democracy," both in *Logos: A Journal of Catholic Thought and Culture* 17, nos. 2 and 3 (Spring and Summer, 2014): 13–38; 49–65; and Michael Novak, "Public Arguments: Murray After 26 Years," *Crisis Magazine* (May 1, 1993), https://www.crisismagazine.com /1993/public-arguments-murray-after-26-years> (accessed December 11, 2020). For the broader context and an argument that a cautious groundwork for Murray was laid by French Catholic theologians by the mid-twentieth century, see Leonard Francis Taylor, *Catholic Cosmopolitanism and Human Rights* (Cambridge: Cambridge University Press, 2020), 23–65.

2. John Meyendorff, *Living Tradition: Orthodox Witness in the Contemporary World* (Crestwood, NY: St. Vladimir's Seminary Press, 1978), 143, while admitting the passing of Christian monarchies and states, nonetheless worried about whether the embrace of pluralism could result in the Church succumbing to agendas set by others in such a society.

voicing their convictions in free and open expression while living in a shared social and political community.[3]

The distance travelled by the Orthodox in embracing a freedom of opinion and expression that included due regard for a commonly shared identity with "others" became clear in the early decades of the twenty-first century. But events also illustrated how an American Orthodox commitment to freedom of opinion and expression was not shared with Orthodox believers and regimes abroad. Many Orthodox (and other American Christians) for example, reacted with dismay to the U.S. Supreme Court's June 2015 decision that ruled same-sex marriage to be a protected legal right under the Constitution[4]. The Assembly of Canonical Orthodox Bishops of the United States of America rejected the Court's declaration of the legal right of same-sex relationships as "marriage" as incompatible with the Church's received teaching on marriage, gender, and sexuality.[5] Concerned foreign observers of U.S. social, racial, and economic tensions shared with the American Orthodox bishops a shocked reaction two years later to the white supremacist rally in Charlottesville, Virginia that purported to be a defense of values deemed to be threatened by immigrants, people of color in general, and LGBT persons, none of whom would be included in this extreme defense of traditional values. The Assembly of Canonical Orthodox Bishops of the United States of America condemned as unacceptable any purported defense of values that based itself on the fiction of "race", "ethnicity," or any other form of "identity" that excluded fellow humans from full recognition as God's children created in his image and likeness. The bishops raised no doubts about the rights of American citizens to assemble, to voice their opinions, and to attempt to persuade others of their values and visions of what American society should look like. But the bishops insisted upon a deeper recognition of a common

---

3. Lenn E. Goodman, *Religious Pluralism and Values in the Public Sphere* (New York: Cambridge University Press, 2014); John D. Inazu, *Confident Pluralism: Surviving and Thriving through Deep Difference* (Chicago: University of Chicago Press, 2016).

4. *Obergefell v. Hodges*, 576_(2015)

5. "Response of Assembly of Bishops to *Obergefell v. Hodges*," July 2, 2015, https://assemblyofbishops.org/news/2015/response-of-assembly-of-bishops-to-obergefell-v.-hodges

humanity even as they avoided invoking the word "rights" in their call for a defense of "core human values."[6]

That freedom of religious expression could not be claimed as a universally endorsed right by the Orthodox worldwide also now became clear. In May 2017, American Orthodox participants had joined Catholic and Protestants in Washington, D.C. for the World Summit in Defense of Persecuted Christians. Sponsored by the Billy Graham Evangelistic Association, the summit had emerged from meetings between the evangelical preacher Franklin Graham and the Russian Orthodox Metropolitan Hilarion Alfeyev. Originally scheduled to be held in Russia with the support of President Vladimir Putin, the meeting was moved to the United States after the election of Donald Trump, at the suggestion of the Russians, in part due to new restrictions imposed by the Russian government (with the support of the Russian Orthodox Church) on Protestant proselytizing in Russia.[7]

Yet these events take on their proper meaning and significance only if we reach back into nineteenth-century conflicts and concerns. For example, between the mid-1960s and the 1980s, Greeks, Russians, and other historically Orthodox Americans turned away from what had long been their historic allegiance to the Democratic Party. Increasingly they became supporters of the Nixon-Agnew defense of the so-called silent majority. In part this shift can be traced to the perceived determination of the Republican Party to continue an unqualified opposition to the menace of Communism. But the Orthodox shift also occurred because of rough agreement

6. "Response to Racist Violence in Charlottesville, Virginia," https://assembly ofbishops.org/news/2017/res[pmse-to-racist-violence-charlottesville-va August 18, 2017.

7. For one analysis of the meeting and its background from the Assyrian International News Agency, see Tom Strode, "Christian Persecution Focus of Global Summit," Baptist Press, May 12, 2017, http://www.bpnews.net/48862 /christian-persecution-focus-of-global-summit, accessed August 20, 2018. For a Russian assessment of the growing relationship between Western voices anxious about "traditional values" and the conservative elements within the Moscow Patriarchate, see Andrey Shishkov, "Two Ecumenisms: Conservative Christian Alliances as a New Form of Ecumenical Cooperation," transl. April L. French, *State, Religion and Church* 4, no. 2 (2017), 58–87. I am grateful to Alfons Brüning for bringing the essay to my attention.

with evangelicals and Catholics in opposing abortion, same-sex marriage, and federal government attempts to regulate local school district policies for transgender students. An additional impetus for the Orthodox positions on such values issues came from the conversion of former evangelicals and Episcopalians in the 1970s and 1980s—with some romanticizing Mother Russia or some other supposedly traditional Orthodox culture and becoming increasingly alienated from what they perceived to be a secular United States. These Orthodox became almost completely countercultural in their definition of Orthodoxy.[8]

Russia—in actual political reality rather than the romanticized image embraced by American converts to Orthodoxy—was nonetheless not singular in its claim to be a defender of traditional values while denying freedom of expression, opinion, and religious association to non-Orthodox. Recent survey results from the Pew Center's Global Restrictions collections revealed that "governments interfered in at least a few instances in over 75 percent of Orthodox Christian majority countries."[9] Often enough, as one scholar has demonstrated, a romanticized historical narrative of a supposed "symphonia" or deep cooperation between Orthodox state authority and the Church has been "adjusted" to suit the objectives of state rulers

---

8. For a general survey of the Orthodox in the United States, see John H. Erickson, *Orthodox Christian in America: A Short History* (New York: Oxford University Press, 2008); for the convert responses see for the former evangelicals, Peter E. Gillquist, *Becoming Orthodox: A Journey to the Ancient Christian Faith* (Ben Lomond, CA: Conciliar Press, 1989), and by the former Roman Catholic Rod Dreher, *The Benedict Option: A Strategy for Christians in a Post-Christian Nation* (New York: Sentinel, 2017); for conversion stories based on selected interviews in a variety of American Orthodox parishes, Amy Slagle, *The Eastern Church in the Spiritual Marketplace: American Conversions to Orthodox Christianity* (Dekalb: Northern Illinois University Press, 2011). On the "middle of the road" tendencies of most American Orthodox, that he labels as practitioners of "Traditional orthopraxy" see Anton C. Vrame, "Four Types of 'Orthopraxy' among Orthodox Christians in America," in *Thinking through Faith: New Perspectives from Orthodox Christian Scholars,* ed. Aristotle Papanikolaou and Elizabeth H. Prodromou (Crestwood, NY: St. Vladimir's Seminary Press, 2008), 279–308.

9. Roger Finke and Dane R. Mataic, "Recent Findings on Religious Freedoms: A Global Assessment and American Update," in *Human v. Religious Rights? German and U.S. Exchanges and their Global Implications*, ed. A.G. Roeber (Göttingen: Vandenhoeck & Ruprecht, 2020), 127–152, at 133.

and hierarchs, neither of whom actually wish the other to be in control of the respective spheres of life. They nonetheless find each other useful when trying to control non-Orthodox rights claims to freedom of religious belief and expression.[10]

These conflicts throw into relief the observations of non-Orthodox ethicists who have contributed to the debates over pluralism by pointing out the conundrum that "to advocate pluralism, we must paradoxically maintain a kind of approval of moral judgments of which we disapprove . . . it is not merely a question of recognizing that in different situations different judgments will be appropriate; for in that case there is no disagreement."[11] The challenge became much more acute as Orthodox Christians confronted changes in public law that had already led non-Orthodox ethicists to observe that "to advocate moral pluralism is to say that something which should in principle not be done, should continue to be done all the same. And to advocate it plausibly is harder than may at first appear . . . [because] a plea for variety of moral practice very easily turns into an undermining of existing practice. Apart from culturally embedded practices, moral plurality quickly becomes self-contradictory . . . to assert the right of plural moral judgment requires a careful account of the systemic social differences that make that right intelligible. So explanation of difference is the essence of a policy of mutual forbearance."[12]

The Orthodox theologian Emmanuel Clapsis was one of the first to address the challenge of Orthodox Christians living in a world characterized by pluralism. His assessment began with the judgment that citizens in such societies place a special, primary value on personal freedom. He concluded that "Christians should be committed to the fundamental ideas of democracy . . ." while retaining the right to be sympathetic critics of the failings of individual societies and states. What is necessary on the part of all participants he argued, is a sense of "shared political values."[13] Since Orthodox

10. Mikhail Antonov, "Church-State Symphonia: Its Historical Development and its Application by the Russian Orthodox Church," *Journal of Law and Religion* 35, no. 3 (December, 2020): 474–493.

11. Oliver O'Donovan, *Church in Crisis: The Gay Controversy and the Anglican Communion* (Eugene, OR: Cascade Books, 2008), 50.

12. O'Donovan, *Church in Crisis*, 50, 52.

13. Emmanuel Clapsis, "An Orthodox Encounter with Liberal Democracy," in, *Christianity, Democracy, and the Shadow of Constantine*, ed. George E.

Christians have lived for centuries under regimes that respected neither "personal freedom" nor the "fundamental ideas of democracy", those living in countries like the United States inherited attitudes and institutionalized aspects of the Orthodox way of life that challenged free expressions of opinion especially when those values manifested themselves as criticism of traditional views of authority, privilege, and power.

The Greek Orthodox theologian Stanley Harakas identified the Archbishop of the Greek Orthodox Archdiocese as a critical figure in the Orthodox struggle to take part fully in the social and political debates that had intensified in the wake of the rights revolution. Nothing, in Harakas' opinion was more important than Archbishop Iakovos' endorsement of the Civil Rights movement. Relying on Ernst Troeltsch's 1911 monumental and seminal *Social Teachings of the Christian Churches*, Harakas argued that Orthodox Christianity had little difficulty identifying with the mystical tradition that was predominantly focused on the personal dimension of religious experience. Neither was it hard to understand, he continued, especially where the Orthodox were a persecuted, or a barely-tolerated minority, the kind of sectarianism that emphasized corporate and group identity and deep suspicion of the "other." But Harakas thought the third of Troeltsch's typology that the German sociologist himself located in the Orthodox as well as Roman Catholic, Reformed, and Lutheran confessional churches remained underdeveloped in actual Orthodox experience. What Troeltsch called the "church type" focused on identifying itself while nonetheless acknowledging the value of "the social, political, economic, and cultural dimensions of life," even with what was "not church."[14] The challenge of facing up to pluralism, Harakas concluded, where the Orthodox right to freedom of expression is but one voice among many, had been hampered by the history of a church that enjoyed for much of its past the protection of its rights and privileges by Orthodox emperors, kings, and

---

Demacopoulos and Aristotle Papanikolaou (New York: Fordham University Press, 2017), 111–126, at 112, 122, 123. See also Emmanuel Clapsis, ed., *The Orthodox Churches in a Pluralistic World: An Ecumenical Conversation* (Geneva: World Council of Churches, 2004).

14. Stanley Harakas, "Orthodox Christianity in American Public Life: The Challenges and Opportunities of Religious Pluralism in the Twenty-First Century," *Greek Orthodox Theological Review* 56, nos. 1–4 (Spring-Winter 2011): 377–397, at 383.

princes. The collapse of that model, and the impossibility of recreating it, Harakas argued, confronted the Orthodox with the truth that "there is little experience in recent Orthodox history, thought, or practice that helps the Orthodox Church deal with pluralism." While lauding the belated Orthodox engagement with rights claims that emphasized the dignity of each human, an engagement that flowed from its own identity of being the Church, Harakas observed that the American Orthodox Church, because of "its scattered and small numbers . . . will be continually involved in shifting, temporary, and varied strategic and tactical associations directed toward specific social and moral goals [requiring] a certain moral and social agility . . ."[15]

The parts of the world recognized as the homelands of the Orthodox shared with the medieval and early modern West an awareness of "weak legal pluralism." In such a world, there might exist "different jurisdictions for specific territories or social groups, which nonetheless remain more or less under the hierarchical supervision of a larger state or empire."[16] Unlike their Western counterparts, however, Orthodox theologians and canonical experts had historically remained cautious when confronting claims for rights that might pit the local family unit, the parish, even a diocese or metropolis against the recognized right to deference exercised by a sovereign, or in the case of the Church itself, the decrees and canons of the universal councils and the hierarchs. At first glance, then, the fundamental question the Orthodox continued to struggle with when faced with an intensifying pluralism: Would the Orthodox have to understand themselves as what Lebanese philosopher and diplomat Charles Malik, called a "permanent minority," in a non-Orthodox world even while embracing the legal and constitutional advantages of living in an ethos marked by the explosion of social media? There, the freedom to express opinions on public platforms and personal blogs has revealed how fragile shared political and social values have become. Even a consensus about what constitutes knowledge appears to be lacking. The Orthodox will have to be clear among

---

15. Harakas, "Orthodox Christianity in American Public Life," 388, 392.

16. Richard J. Ross and Philip J. Stern, "Reconstructing Early Modern Notions of Legal Pluralism," in *Legal Pluralism and Empires, 1500–1850*, ed. Lauren Benton and Richard J. Ross (New York: New York University Press, 2013), 109–141, at 109.

themselves as well as in their engagements with non-Orthodox about what they endorse in the ongoing process of determining the reliability of evidence and most probable truth statements achieved through rigorous open exchanges of opinion. Under such circumstances, the challenges facing the likely permanent minority Orthodox both with regard to the internal governance of the Church and the engagement with a pluralist and fragmented society have intensified exponentially since the beginnings of the rights revolution.[17]

II. Remote Origins of the Orthodox Response to Pluralism and the "Other"

Because of the catastrophe of the Bolshevik Revolution, Russian Orthodox engagement with the rights to freedom of expression and speech that had briefly flourished in the late nineteenth century came to a halt. Declarations regarding the rights of Christians—defined as a majority with regard to Russia itself—had been accompanied in Tsarist Russia by the conviction that law itself is coercive, and was not regarded as having a positive role, certainly not one on a par with religion and morality.[18] For Russians who fled the Revolution in the second decade of the twentieth century, however, the right to freedom of conscience, speech, and expression found eloquent defenders. In 1926 Nikolai Berdyaev published an essay that attacked what he identified as "Russian clericalist tendencies and a clerical ideology . . . a geriatric sclerosis, completely incompatible with creativity and freedom." The burning question the Orthodox had to face, he concluded "is whether Orthodoxy does or does not recognize freedom of

---

17. See for various cases on social media and First Amendment issues, David L. Hudson, Jr., "Social Media," *The First Amendment Encyclopedia*, 2017. https://mtsu.edu/first-amendment/article/1561/social-media (accessed December 16, 2020). On the critical question of "social epistemology," Jonathan Rauch, "The Constitution of Knowledge," *National Affairs* 37 (Fall, 2018), at https://national affairs.com/publications/detail/the-constitution-of-knowledge (accessed November 10, 2020). On Malik, see Chapter Eight.

18. See the analysis by Mikhail Zherebyatyev, "The Russian Orthodox Church's Interpretation of European Legal Values (1990–2011)," in *Eastern Orthodox Encounters of Identity and Otherness: Values, Self-Reflection, Dialogue*, ed. Andrii Krawchuk and Thomas Bremer (New York: Palgrave MacMillan, 2014), 207–17.

conscience as the preeminent basis of spiritual life." Unlike Protestant individualism, however, Berdyaev argued, genuine Orthodox freedom of conscience functions even at the level of an ecumenical council whose authenticity "is discerned and affirmed by the free conscience of the people of the Church." Bishops maintain the unity of the Orthodox Church, he asserted, but "lordship over the entire creative life of the individual and of the collective does not belong to him." Instead, the "churching of life" depended upon the "placing of greater responsibility upon all the people of the Church" where freedom of choice and expression "does not have an official, formal, juridical stamp of 'churchliness.'"[19]

The understanding of rights and obligations tied to the authority of a (preferably Christian) ruler came naturally to Russians given both the East Roman and the Tsarist history upon which they built their own self-understandings. The engagement with notions of rights that applied to groups of persons—rights dependent upon shared language and culture—among the Orthodox in North America did not spring from exclusively American conditions or definitions. Over the course of the nineteenth century, the Orthodox Church in Russia had been forced to confront the implications of the Russian Imperial government's own move from toleration to actual religious freedom for the many non-Orthodox subjects of the Tsar. The move toward a codification of rights began at the level of regarding such laws as a way of firming up the relationship of specific communities to the Emperor. In the process, however, the confirmation of those rights at least cautiously entertained the possibility that individual entitlement was understood as a right. Nonetheless, "if we understand citizenship to comprise a set of uniform, individual, and equal rights," then no one in Imperial Russia was a citizen.[20]

Berdyaev's frustrations over the interrupted engagement among the Russian Orthodox with the question of freedom of conscience and expression

19. Nikolai Berdyaev, "Church Discord and Freedom of Conscience," transl, Alvian N. Smirensky, *The Wheel* 21/22 (Spring/Summer, 2020): 6–18, at 7, 8, 16, 17.

20. Paul W. Werth, *The Tsar's Foreign Faiths: Toleration and the Fate of Religious Freedom in Imperial Russia* (Oxford: Oxford University Press, 2014), 4, 6, 73, 258 and especially 257–266, at 265: "The prominent place of the Orthodox Church in post-Soviet Russia suggests that the tensions described in this book have not been entirely resolved even today."

emanated from the promising, but unfulfilled work of the Moscow Council of 1917–18. Governed by the Russian Holy Synod since the time of Peter the Great, the Russian Church took immediate advantage of the first phase of the Revolution of 1917 to call a National Council. Among its many objectives a critical one emerged in the words of Metropolitan Antonii Vadkovskii of St. Petersburg, who demanded that the local parish be recognized as a "legal person" with the "right to own property."[21]

When it gathered in Moscow in 1917, the Russian sobor approved various documents that elaborated a vision of "synodality" that recognized the rights of the entire Church to be consulted before authoritative statements were pronounced by a newly restored Patriarch. The latter was identified as the First Hierarch of the Church of Russia in the document "The Definition on the Rights and Duties of the Most Holy Patriarch of Moscow and All Russia."[22] For both those favoring the restoration of the Patriarchate with his moral and legal rights and those who favored a greater emphasis on the conciliarity of the Russian Church "the most important theological argument was that of *conciliarity*, of *sobornost'*. This concept was central in all the arguments for or against the restoration of the patriarchate."[23] Given its long connections to the throne, the members of the sobor could not conceive of a Church that had been stripped of the right to own property, nor were they interested in entertaining a separation of the Church from an Orthodox Russian state authority, a standing they refused to give to the Bolshevik regime. The final session of the sobor accepted a heavily revised document "The Position of Women in the Life of the Church" that sidestepped the question that had been raised about the restoration of women to the diaconate, but did grant new rights for women to serve as psalmists and readers in local parishes, including the right to serve as the elected officer of the Parish Assembly, as the church warden or *starosta,* in cooperation with the priest-rector. In a forlorn attempt to defend the Church now stripped of its collective juridical personality and hence incapable of owning property under an increasingly hostile

21. Nicholas Ferencz, *American Orthodoxy and Parish Congregationalism* (Piscataway, NJ: Gorgias Press, 2006), 48.

22. Hyacinthe Destivelle, O.P., *The Moscow Council (1917–1918): The Creation of the Conciliar Institutions of the Russian Orthodox Church* (Notre Dame, IN: University of Notre Dame Press, 2015), 71–123, at 85–6.

23. Destivelle, *Moscow,* 79.

regime, the sobor bestowed juridical personality on the parish church itself as well as on the parish community at large. By insisting on the rights of each juridical person, the faithful at the local level would hopefully have been given "the right to defend their churches before the civil authorities."[24]

By the early twentieth century, Russian theologians, led primarily by Vladimir Soloviev and his student Sergius Bulgakov, had abandoned the historical Russian attempts to invoke the memory of the East Roman Empire and the supposed symphonia between Emperor and the Orthodox Church in assessing the privileges, honors, and rights of each. Bulgakov in particular singled out the American experiment in the separation of Church and State and its emphasis upon the sacredness of individual human dignity. Criticism of Tsarist control of the Church that began with the abolition of the Moscow Patriarchate under Peter I had escalated to such a degree that by the time of the Revolution of 1917, some estimates suggest that "as many as 90 per cent of the church's top officials welcomed the revolution when it came."[25]

In actual fact, the deep roots of disagreements about the freedom of expression and the respective rights of bishops, clergy, and people in Imperial Russia—and those of the non-Orthodox "others"—had been planted at least a century earlier. Scholars rightly caution against assuming that the Orthodox Church had, since the reign of Peter the Great, become nothing more than a department of the Imperial state. Still, by the time of Nicholas I's codification of Russia's laws, "the laity as such factored little into what these laws construed as the local ecclesial establishment." The reaction against the reform initiatives of Tsar Alexander II by his successor guaranteed the rejection of any notion of the "rights" of the laity to be involved in church affairs much less their rights to express opinions about matters of state. At the same time, in their struggle to serve their parishioners

24. Destivelle, *Moscow*, 105, 102.

25. For the details, see Aristotle Papanikolaou, *The Mystical as Political: Democracy and Non-Radical Orthodoxy* (Notre Dame, IN: University of Notre Dame Press, 2012), 28–43, at 32. For additional reflections on the manner in which Russian theologians struggled to come to grips with their relationship to the West, see Vera Shevzov, "The Burdens of Tradition: Orthodox Constructions of the West in Russia (Late 19th-Early 20th CC.)," in *Orthodox Constructions of the West*, ed. George E. Demacopoulos and Aristotle Papanikolaou (New York: Fordham University Press, 2013), 83–101.

many among the local clergy became convinced that they were "more burdened than honored by being the bishop's representative in the local parish," and "called for independence from hierarchy in parish affairs." These tensions had already found expression in the divergent theological works of both Makarii Bulgakov (1816–1882) and Aleksei Khomiakov (1804–1860) before the crisis that brought down the Romanov rule of Russia. And the disagreements would carry over into the Russian diaspora in Western Europe and North America, as well, guaranteeing a fractured response to the questions of the rights of freedom of expression and precisely who had a right to be involved in making decisions that affected local parish life and its relationship to a pluralistic society.[26]

An inherited tendency to think of rights as appertaining to lawfully designated bodies or offices in both church and state—and exclusively in both cases articulated by elites, not ordinary subjects—was not unique to Russia. This manner of thinking would also receive additional impetus because of the reports of Ottoman assaults on Armenian Orthodox Christians beginning in the 1890s, and more infamously, during World War I. Concern for the free and open expression of religious rights—particularly the defense of the collective rights of persecuted Christians—intensified among the Orthodox scattered in the variety of ethnic and linguistic "diasporas" of the United States as a result.[27] Disputes over "rights as authority" and religious rights of supposedly protected groups forced the Orthodox to examine how to engage the practical consequences of the freedom of religious belief and expression with their more familiar understanding of rights and privileges connected to an office in the institutional Church.

The rise in the immigration of Greek-speaking Orthodox to North America from 1890 to 1920 revealed a need among Greek speakers to

26. Vera Shevzov, *Russian Orthodoxy on the Eve of Revolution* (Oxford and New York: Oxford University Press, 2004), 16–53, at 17, 26–29; 43, 52.

27. For the impact on American public opinion of the Armenian genocide, see Peter Balakian, *The Burning Tigris: The Armenian Genocide and America's Response* (New York: Harper Perennial, 2004), 3–10, 70–72, 166–173. See also, for the argument that British authorities purposefully repressed evidence that the Armenian genocide was an attack on religion, Michelle Tusan, "'Crimes against Humanity': Human Rights, the British Empire, and the Origins of the Response to the Armenian Genocide," *American Historical Review* 119, no. 1 (February, 2014): 47–77.

identify themselves with the freedoms and rights of America, and not various communities or geographic locations that remained hostile to a constitutionally grounded, representative democratic state. Anti-Greek riots had occurred in the United States prior to World War I—most notoriously in 1909 in Omaha, Nebraska, but in other parts of the country as well. The rebirth of the Ku Klux Klan at Stone Mountain, Georgia in November 1915 gave additional impetus to anti-immigrant, anti-Catholic, anti-Jewish, and anti-African American sentiments that had already manifested themselves in late-nineteenth century American life. Within six years, the Klan had spread across the country boasting at least 100,000 members and preaching the need for a defense of white, Protestant "one-hundred-per-cent" Americanism. Although violence against African Americans and threats made against ethnic groups marked the Klan's rise to dominance in many states, "the major theme, however, was the rich vein of anti-Catholicism, which the Klan was to mine avidly during the 1920s, and it was this more than anything else which made the Klan." Nonetheless, "to the Negro, Jew, Oriental, Roman Catholic, and alien, were added dope, bootlegging, graft, night clubs and road houses, violation of the Sabbath, unfair business dealings, sex, marital 'goings-on,' and scandalous behavior as the proper concern of the one-hundred-per-cent American."[28]

Greek Americans fell afoul of the Klan in part because of their socio-economic status as small shopkeepers who were feared by Klansmen recruited from Protestant men "clustered in the three categories of lower white-collar employees; petty proprietors, managers and officials, and skilled tradesmen."[29] In their attacks on Greek Orthodox Americans, the Klan did not focus on the potential socio-economic threat represented by immigrant labor and ownership. Rather, the Klan's obsession with the threat posed by Catholicism drew the Orthodox into the same supposed web of conspiracy against Americanism. The Catholics could be accused of hostility to republican institutions and support of papal monarchism. The Orthodox fell under suspicion "from the republican conviction that tyranny bred rebellion. Klan writers thus blamed the Russian Orthodox Church

28. David M. Chalmers, *Hooded Americanisms: The First Century of the Ku Klux Klan 1865–1965* (New York: Doubleday & Company, 1965), 33.

29. Nancy Maclean, *Behind the Mask of Chivalry: The Making of the Second Ku Klux Klan* (New York: Oxford University Press, 1994), 52–74, at 54.

(equivalent in their minds, to the Roman Catholic Church) for the Russian revolution . . ."[30] By extension, Greek Orthodox, who had known only repression and tyranny under the Ottomans, were just as unlikely to be capable of understanding American values and political virtues.

By 1921, Greek Americans in Atlanta recognized that the rise of the Klan demanded a response to counter its growth. They also saw how, in the post-World War I cultural climate, popular literature and forms of propaganda used freedom of expression to a devastating impact on Orthodox communities. The use of media demonstrated the potential of spreading the Klan's message even among Americans who were not inclined to join the organization. "When we move away from a singular focus on the paying membership of the Klan organization, and the vagaries of the rise and fall of that membership, we better appreciate the cultural clout of the Klan movement." Klan members "produced newspapers, created books and films, staged plays, recorded jazz music, built a radio station with national reach, even fielded baseball teams against Jewish and Catholic opponents. They did so largely divorced from—and often in contention with—the organization's leadership, an organic expression of a lived ideology."[31] How to defend Orthodox rights to freedom of speech and expression in the face of this hostility galvanized Greek Americans, but the impetus did not come from the Orthodox clergy.

The Order of American Hellenic Educational Progressive Association was formally organized on July 26, 1922 in Atlanta, Georgia, within the heart of the Invisible Empire of the Klan. The reality of Greek American life—as opposed to the caricature of a cohesive, united, formerly oppressed and potentially un-American Greek presence—stood behind the formation of AHEPA as much as did concerns generated by Klan propaganda. What the organization's own founders recognized as a Greek propensity for individualism and disunity had to be overcome if Greek speakers were to respond to anti-Greek propaganda and efforts at intimidation. In the deep divisions of pro- and anti-royalist factions within Greece and the Greek American community. the founders recognized the geographic and linguistic differences that had long separated Greeks in various parts of the

30. MacLean, *Behind the Mask of Chivalry*, 95–97, at 96.
31. Felix Harcourt, *Ku Klux Kulture: American and the Klan in the 1920s* (Chicago: The University of Chicago Press, 2017), 182.

Old World. Pre-World War I attempts to create a Pan Hellenic Union had collapsed, and even after half a century of AHEPA's existence, its membership counted for "only about 2 ½ % of the entire population of Americans and Canadians of Greek descent. . . ."[32]

The language of AHEPA's charter illustrated how intent its founders were to "inculcate loyalty and patriotism to and for the country in which we live . . . allegiance to its flag; support to its Constitution; obedience to its laws and reverence for its history and traditions." But beyond a general patriotism, the charter also insisted on its intent "to instruct its members, by precepts and examples, in the tenets and fundamental principles of government, and in the recognition and respect of the inalienable rights of mankind."[33] The choice of words that echoed Jefferson's rhetoric in the Declaration of Independence signaled the determination of Greeks in America to link the American revolutionary defense of the rights of mankind to the traditions of Athenian democracy, which was made to stand in for Greeks as a whole. Both Greek and Slavic-speaking immigrants found the atmosphere of post-World War I America increasingly perilous. The "turbulent years following the First World War, when the volatile contingency of racial meanings and the fluidity of cultural and political immigrant affiliations . . . turned to militant strategies of conformity and racist policies of exclusion." Especially for immigrants who were associated with the working-class union movement, the threat of being branded as "un-American" escalated in the decade following the end of the war. A "deployment of Americanism as an ideology to extinguish diversity and neutralize working-class activism demarcated the boundaries of whiteness in relation to Americanness, understood as uncompromising cultural and political conformity to the middle-class values of 100 percent Americanism."[34]

32. George J. Leber, *The History of the Order of AHEPA* (Washington, D.C.: The Order of AHEPA, 1972), vii. On the divided Greek community before World War I, and the "individualism" issue, 160–61, 174–75, 184–85.

33. Leber, *History of the Order of AHEPA*, 147.

34. Yiorgos Anagnostou, *Contours of White Ethnicity: Popular Ethnography and the making of Usable Pasts in Greek America* (Athens, OH: Ohio University Press, 2009), 29–61, at 50–51. For further details on the Greek-American struggles during these years, Alexander Kitroeff, *The Greek Orthodox Church in America: A Modern History* (Ithaca: Cornell University Press, 2020), 39–57.

That trend can be attributed to the impact of constitutional novelties such as the passage of the Eighteenth Amendment that ushered in the experiment in alcohol prohibition and simultaneously appeared to be an assault on the social habits of ethnic and religious minorities. For Orthodox immigrant parishes, no less so than for Roman Catholics and observant Jewish communities, being targeted by Protestant reformers and bearing the impact of unsavory propaganda spread by the Ku Klux Klan led to the inevitable conclusion that this was an example of "native-born Protestants against everybody else . . . [as] American Jews had opposed the Eighteenth Amendment with the near unanimity and absolute vehemence that seized American Catholics." The sentiments of a Philadelphia Jewish Rabbi could have stood for the opinions of Orthodox Christians of the 1920s as well: "'Prohibition is an Anglo-Saxon-Protestant issue that we . . . ought to keep out of.'"[35]

The U.S. Supreme Court and the courts in general played no role in defending the civil rights of those being targeted by the Klan and the members of Congress who successfully imposed a restrictive immigration policy by 1924 designed to block the arrival of the ethnic and religious minorities who were the objects of Klan activities. After allowing for some restriction of civil liberties during World War I, the Court came to exhibit during the 1920s a limited sympathy for a "libertarian" philosophy embodied in Justice Oliver Wendell Holmes who "in a series of opinions . . . asserted that all political ideas and opinions should be given the broadest possible scope for expression, and should be restricted only if they created an immediate danger of unlawful action or material injury."[36] By the 1920s, the "nationalization of the Bill of Rights" unfolded with a slow but steady inclination of the Court to incorporate "the First Amendment in the due process clause of the Fourteenth Amendment. . . ." (*Stromberg v. California* 283 U.S. 359 (1931).[37] Nevertheless, Holmes himself, having paved the way for the abandonment of natural rights claims as the basis for the government's police powers, grew uneasy at the notion of an unlimited ex-

---

35. Daniel Okrent, *Last Call: The Rise and Fall of Prohibition* (New York, London: Scribner, 2010), 148, 186, 192.

36. Alfred H. Kelly, Winfred A. Harbison, and Herman Belz, *The American Constitution Its Origins and Development*, 6th ed. (New York: W.W. Norton & Company, Inc., 1983), 525–549, at 530.

37. Kelly, Harbison, Belz, *American Constitution*, 531, 533.

pansion of rights discovered by the Supreme Court. "Instead, Holmes argued that the Court should limit itself to protecting those few rights recognized by societal consensus as fundamental."[38] Despite his reputation among those admirers who saw him as the pioneer of "legal realism," Holmes remained reluctant to overturn precedent, and, while spurning "moral" notions of "right" rather than strictly legal ones, remained intent throughout his career until his death in 1921 on determining the "limits of the law."[39]

The cases that helped to shift the Court's interpretation of rights to free speech issues and not the rights of individuals to religious liberty of conscience became clear by the time of the *Burstyn v. Wilson* 343 U.S. 495 (1952) decision. There, the Court held that neither individual nor group religious sensibilities justified a state's attempt to give special protection to religion even when a group faced "contempt, mockery, or ridicule." Because of Justice Douglas' striking opinion issued in the same year (*Zorach v. Clausen* 343 U.S. 306 1952 at 313) that "we are a religious people," the Orthodox who were aware of the decision may have wondered where the boundaries now lay between freedom of expression and assaults on "a religious people" even if the United States as a sovereign power was not understood to be a "Christian nation."[40]

By 1952, Russian Orthodox believers in the United States were bitterly disappointed when the Supreme Court affirmed, in a case of ejectment, the right of the now-Bolshevik regime in Moscow to ownership of the venerable St. Nicholas Cathedral in New York City.[41] The justices rejected the prior decision of New York courts that had pointed out that the U.S. had not recognized the legitimacy of the Bolshevik regime in Russia and that therefore a transfer of possession and use of the Cathedral to autonomous Russian Orthodox in the United States who claimed to have established themselves by 1925 was wholly appropriate. Those Russian Americans had rejected the legitimacy of a Russian Patriarch

---

38. Bernstein, "A History of 'Substantive' Due Process," 2.

39. White, *Law in American History* 3: 11–90, at 25–26.

40. Kelly, Harbison, Belz, *American Constitution*, 545, 655.

41. *Kedroff v. St. Nicholas Cathedral* 344 U.S. 94 (1952). The following relies upon the analysis of the case provided by Richard W. Garnett, "'Things That Are Not Caesar's': The Story of Kedroff v. St. Nicholas Cathedral," in *First Amendment Stories,* ed. Richard W. Garnett and Andrew Koppelman (New York: Thomson Reuters/ Foundation Press, 2012), 171–191.

thought to be incapable of freedom of expression, manipulated by a hostile Soviet regime. Justice Jackson recognized the potency of that position taken by the Orthodox Russians and the New York court in *Kedroff v. St. Nicholas Cathedral*, but rejected their argument, stating that by allowing the bishop appointed by Moscow to take possession: "New York law must yield to the authority of a foreign and unfriendly state masquerading as a spiritual institution."[42] The *Kedroff* case, so the Court stated in its majority opinion, boiled down to the danger posed to liberty at large when the authority of an individual state or the Federal government presumed to interfere in "the free exercise of an ecclesiastical right, the Church's choice of its hierarchy."[43] Within a generation of the Court's 1952 decisions, however, the Orthodox would have to confront increasingly difficult questions about whether they could rest content with the direction of both "judicial decisions and public conversations about religious freedom [that] tend to focus on matters of individuals' rights, beliefs, consciences, and practices. The distinctive place, role, and freedoms of groups, associations, and institutions are often overlooked. . . . [A] legal regime that is designed to protect only this reduced notion of religious freedom will, *Kedroff* suggests, leave vulnerable and unprotected important aspects of that freedom."[44] The decision in *Kedroff*, by relying on the 1871 *Watson v. Jones* decision that recognized internal church court decisions as final, "failed to realize that the application of *Watson v. Jones* might itself be viewed as violating the constitutional prohibitions against establishment of or denial of free exercise of religion. This inconsistency within the *Kedroff* opinion has thrown the law surrounding church property disputes into uncertainty."[45]

42. *Kedroff v. St. Nicholas Cathedral* 344 U.S. at 131.

43. *Kedroff v. St. Nicholas Cathedral* 344 U.S. at 119.

44. Garnett, "'Things That Are Not Caesar's'," 184. On the changing nature of the laws surrounding the issue of the right of association, see below.

45. Daniel E. Curtis, "Judicial Intervention in Church Property Disputes—Some Constitutional Considerations," *Yale Law Journal* 74 (1964–1965): 1113–1139, at 1132–3. https://digitalcommons.law.yale.edu/fss_papers/1594. On the related question of whether "neutral principles" have resolved the tension between the free exercise and establishment clauses of the Constitution, see Chapter Five.

III. Pluralism and the Debates over Civil Rights

As the Orthodox struggled to reconcile inherited notions of rights and duties consistent with their own tradition, far more radical challenges began to alter how legal experts regarded questions of objective law and whether one could even talk of a human "nature." By the 1950s, the behavioral movement that John Watson had pioneered beginning in 1913 had become the "behavioral sciences" that "comprised the specifically identifiable behavioral aspects of biology, psychology, sociology, economics, political science, anthropology, and law. Eschewing all possible value assumptions, exponents emphasized the working out of new methods for understanding and predicting behavior, particularly quantification, mathematical symbolization, and model building."[46] By 1954, the landmark *Brown v. Board of Education* in its famous Footnote 11 incorporated both sociological and psychological data in order to buttress its decision on "modern authority" to declare that equal protection of the laws "guaranteed by the Fourteenth Amendment" had to be extended to African American students. The debate over whether the courts of the United States should properly be involved in social policy questions was not only hotly debated at the time, but now reverberated with increasingly divisive results in cases involving both civil and religious rights that the Orthodox had to navigate as they came into their own as a recognized religious group in a gradually more pluralistic post-World War II America.[47]

Scholars who have analyzed the expansion of rights claims in the United States since the 1950s invariably repair to the *Brown* decision as the "contagious example of the civil rights movement on other outside groups" that

46. Merle Curti, *Human Nature in American Thought: A History* (Madison: The University of Wisconsin Press, 1980), 372–406, at 373, 403.

47. On the Brown decision, and criticisms of the process of reasoning as well as the objective of social reform, see variously Learned Hand, *The Bill of Rights* (Cambridge, MA: Harvard University Press, 1958), 73–4; Alexander M. Bickel, *The Supreme Court and the Idea of Progress* (New Haven, CT: Yale University Press, 1978); J. Skelly Wright, "Professor Bickel, the Scholarly Tradition, and the Supreme Court," *Harvard Law Review* 84, no. 4 (Feb., 1971): 769–805; Richard Kluger, *Simple Justice: The History of Brown v. Board of Education and Black America's Struggle for Equality*, revised and expanded edition (New York: Alfred A. Knopf, 2008).

spread a "new rights language" throughout American society.[48] Indeed, "the sheer volume of rights invention and rights disputes in the fifty years after Brown has no historic parallel."[49] At one level, there is no escaping the conclusion that "rights claims invite sharp distinctions between the rights-invaded self and other . . . popular claims of rights" that have had an increasingly difficult time "talking directly and sustainedly about common possessions, common interest, and entangled and interdependent destinies." As a result, the consciousness of rights "not only transfers personal wounds into the realm of justice; it simultaneously translates private experience into general claims and potentially universalizing language. This is the solidaristic dynamic in rights movements."[50]

As Stanley Harakas pointed out in his analysis of pluralism, the person who called his Orthodox flock to identify their own "rights-invaded self" with others was the former Ottoman Empire subject Demetrios Koukouzis (1911–2005), who became the Greek American Archbishop Iakovos. Beginning his priestly ministry in the 1940s, Iakovos would eventually (until his forced retirement in 1996) hold the title of Archbishop of North and South America. He would also take the first, bold and controversial step of confronting the rights revolution and bringing the Orthodox into that conversation. In the case of both Iakovos and the exiled Russian Orthodox theologian, Alexander Schmemann, the Orthodox found voices that exemplified for that generation the "confident pluralism" characterized by the civic virtues of *"tolerance, humility* and *patience"* that appeared to hold the promise of reconciling an ancient church's traditions with the realities of a pluralistic society.[51]

Among the longest sagas exemplifying tolerance, humility, and patience, the struggles of both the First Peoples of the Americas and of African Americans for equal civil and social rights continued to unfold as uncompleted journeys. Historians of the African American struggle have long recognized the critical role the Black Churches played in spearheading the twentieth-century contours of the civil rights movement. The founding leaders of the

48. Daniel T. Rodgers, "Rights Consciousness in American History," in *The Nature of Rights at the American Founding and Beyond*, ed. Barry Alan Shain (Charlottesville: University of Virginia Press, 2007), 258–279, at 273.

49. Rodgers, "Rights Consciousness," 275–76.

50. Rodgers, "Rights Consciousness," 276.

51. Inazu, *Confident Pluralism*, 85.

National Association for the Advancement of Colored People had included Protestant White clergy and laity as well. But an Orthodox engagement with these pivotal aspects of the rights revolution in twentieth-century America only emerged after World War II under the leadership of Iakovos, and in the face of considerable opposition. The Archbishop's participation in the famous Selma March did not reflect a primary concern about economic justice for African Americans. It is also unclear whether Iakovos shared Martin Luther King's own late conviction that the struggle for civil rights was, in the end, also a battle for human rights.[52]

Rather, Iakovos' determination to confront the issue of civil rights stemmed as he himself said, from "formative memories of Greek suffering on his native Adriatic islands, under harsh occupation by the Ottoman Turks."[53] Memories of discrimination and the denial of rights of religious expression in the United States, however, did not mean that Iakovos' endorsement of the civil rights movement resonated in the Greek Orthodox community at large—or among any other Orthodox jurisdiction. From Greek immigrant memories of the mixed reception they had received in a United States characterized by a Protestant and predominantly northern European cultural and social ethos came a decidedly divisive reaction regarding the pursuit of civil rights by marginalized minority groups. Greek Orthodox desire to be thought equal participants in the political and social milieu of the United States struggled at the same time with a fierce determination to preserve both the Greek language and, on the part of more conservative Greeks, the local Orthodox parish as guardians of Greek identity, one that had been forged in the nineteenth-century independence movement.[54]

52. For King's grappling with human rights (which King understood primarily as an issue of economic rights) see Thomas F. Jackson, *From Civil Rights to Human Rights: Martin Luther King, Jr., and the Struggle for Economic Justice* (Philadelphia: University of Pennsylvania Press, 2007), who in his analysis of the Selma protests and march never mentions the Orthodox Archbishop's presence and participation, 219–225.

53. Taylor Branch, *At Canaan's Edge: America in the King Years 1965–68* (New York: Simon & Schuster, 2006), 106.

54. For a survey of this tension within Greek Orthodox communities between separate identity and integration, Peter C. Moskos and Charles C. Moskos, *Greek Americans: Struggle and Success,* 3rd ed. (Cambridge, MA: Harvard University Press, 1995).

Iakovos' appearance in Selma and at the memorial service held for the murdered Unitarian minister James Reeb emanated from what he identified as the obligation of the Orthodox Church "to fight, when it felt it must, for the rights of mankind. . . ."[55] Iakovos' willingness to invoke the "rights of mankind" came as close as any Orthodox theologian did at that time to endorsing the United Nations' document on universal human rights. Far more than Iakovos (or the Orthodox, or European Americans as a whole) would recognize for many years, racialist prejudice against African Americans had deepened, not ameliorated, in the last decades of the nineteenth century. Despite the profound change in constitutional law inaugurated by the "Reconstruction Amendments,"[56] the imposition of Jim Crow laws in the southern United States became manifest in repeated outbreaks of lynchings and race riots, and such laws hardened the contours of what an eminent African American historian labelled the racial geography in the United States from the 1870s to the 1930s: "The Old Order Changeth Not."[57]

In seeking to explain whatever ails minority communities in the United States, analysts are more certain than ever that lack of access to education, good nutrition, and health care account for the pathologies of these groups.[58] In applying the doctrine of "strict neutrality," as one scholar has

55. Albert Jordy Raboteau, "In the World, not of the World, for the Sake of the World: Orthodoxy and American Culture," *Orthodoxy in America Lecture Series* (New York: Fordham University Office of Development and Human Relations, 2007), 3, https://publicorthodoxy.org/wp-content/uploads/2017/01/raboteau2006.pdf. See also, Kitroeff, *Greek Orthodox Church*, 124–127.

56. Eric Foner, *The Second Founding: How the Civil War and Reconstruction Remade the Constitution* (New York: Norton, 2019).

57. John Hope Franklin, *Racial Equality in America* (Chicago: University of Chicago Press, 1976), Chapter Two, 37–74 for the "Old Order" quotation, originally the title of one of the lectures collected in this volume; C. Vann Woodward, *The Strange Career of Jim Crow: A Commemorative Edition,* with afterword by William S. McFeely (New York: Oxford University Press, 1955; Oxford: Oxford University Press, 2001), citations from the 2001 edition; Michael Perman, *Struggle for Mastery: Disenfranchisement in the South, 1888–1908* (Chapel Hill: University of North Carolina Press, 2001); and most recently, Henry Louis Gates, Jr., *Stony the Road: Reconstruction, White Supremacy, and the Rise of Jim Crow* (New York: Penguin Press, 2019).

58. Nina Zablonsky, *Living Color: The Biological and Social Meaning of Skin Color* (Berkeley: University of California Press, 2012); and Robert Wald Sussman,

insisted, courts and citizens cannot ask for "racial neutrality" that rests on a fiction of "symmetry," i.e., that "all considerations of race are symmetrical and equally suspect"—a claim that ignores the historical reality of "this nation's inclusion/exclusion asymmetry in matters of race, choosing an abstractional, ahistorical, and acontextual formalism" over demonstrable historical fact.[59]

The violent reaction of many ethnic Roman Catholics to the initial attempts at integrated housing and schools in the 1960s reflected how central the understanding of rights tied to a specific language and national culture had become in American communities. It would be an unfair exaggeration to suggest that ethnic Roman Catholics made no effort to transcend the problem of ethnic and racial tensions or that they ignored the civil rights claims of African Americans. But the tendency to identify with the traditions of a specific linguistic-national past revealed that the Orthodox on this particular issue shared much more in common with their Roman Catholic counterparts than many were inclined to concede. And, where Roman Catholics eventually developed the notion of a "national parish" that tried at least on a temporary basis to address the demands made by non-English speaking Catholics, another model that emerged by the early twenty-first century was the "shared parish," where English-speaking and Spanish-speaking Catholics share the same physical plant and are members of the same parish, but still maintain separate worship services in their respective languages. While this model could be said to preserve a sense of the collective rights of a specific ethnic-linguistic group, it overlooks the question of how the freedom of expression in religion might be defended, or violated given

---

The Myth of Race: The Troubling Persistence of an Unscientific Idea (Cambridge, MA: Harvard University Press, 2014). Still invaluable as an introduction to the complex issues of race and slavery from ancient to modern times is Michael McGifferet, ed., "Constructing Race: Differentiating Peoples in the Early Modern World," special issue, *The William and Mary Quarterly* 3rd Ser., 54, no. 1 (January 1997).

59. Ronald Turner, "On Neutral and Preferred Principles of Constitutional Law," *University of Pittsburgh Law Review* 74 (Spring 2013): 433–489, at 486, 487. doi:10.5195/lawreview.2013.261. On the mortality rates among young black males, Elliott Currie, *A Peculiar Indifference: The Neglected Toll of Violence on Black America* (New York: Metropolitan Books, 2020).

the preponderance of attention bestowed upon the collective identity of a dominant ethnic-linguistic group.[60]

The hesitancy to be identified with civil protests of the 1960s or any behavior that might be considered dangerous to the Greek commitment to honor stemmed in part from the effort the majority of Greek Orthodox had invested in distancing themselves from a more radical past. Immigrant Greek participation in the IWW, the Community Party-USA, and the Socialist Labor Party had been a visible, controversial, and now unwelcome memory of Greek American life since the 1940s.[61] The post-World War II civil war in Greece served even further to marginalize the more radical strains in the Greek American experience, especially after the policies of the Truman Administration made it clear that anti-communism would be a litmus test of whether Greeks in the United States were genuine Americans. How fragile the freedom of opinion and expression still remained in Greece itself emerged with startling clarity in 1967 when the rise of a military dictatorship in Greece "sparked a protest movement that was a somewhat anemic reprise of the radical/liberal alliance of World War II." Moreover, the growing success of the Greek Orthodox Church itself, coupled with the fact that by the 1960s "about three in four Greek Americans [were] native born" meant that this ethnic group had "moved, in the main, into middle-class vocations and into the suburbs." Whatever memories of marginalization might have kindled a sense of shared grievance with African

60. For the history of Catholic resistance to integration in Chicago, Arnold R. Hirsch, *Making the Second Ghetto: Race and Housing in Chicago, 1940–1960* (Cambridge: Cambridge University Press, 1983), 68–99; but see also Timothy B. Neary, *Crossing Parish Boundaries: Race, Sports, and Catholic Youth in Chicago, 1914–1954* (Chicago: University of Chicago Press, 2016); Brett C. Hoover, *The Shared Parish: Latinos, Anglos, and the Future of U.S. Catholicism* (New York: New York University Press, 2014); and for an exhaustive study of the changing nature of Catholic parishes with data on the persistence of specific ethnic-linguistic celebrations in mixed parishes, Mark M. Gray, Mary L. Goutier, and Melissa A. Cidade, *The Changing Face of U.S. Catholic Parishes: Emerging Models of Pastoral Leadership Project* (Washington, D.C.: National Association for Lay Ministries, 2011).

61. Dan Georgakas, "Greek American Radicalism: The Twentieth Century," in *Reading Greek America: Studies in the Experience of Greeks in the United States,* ed. Spyros D. Orfanos (New York: Pella Publishing Company, 2002), 63–84, at 63.

Americans proved to have very little purchase within the Greek Orthodox Archdiocese Iakovos headed.[62]

The disputes about the rights of the Orthodox that required navigation in unfamiliar and at times threatening waters also laid bare deep disagreements within the Orthodox Church itself. Those disagreements continue to swirl about the rights claims and privileges of Orthodox bishops, clergy, and laity. So intense and divisive have those disagreements remained that they continue to undermine the capacity of the Orthodox to present a united front to a pluralistic society. In no small part, the persistence of those disagreements has also compromised Orthodox Christian capacities to evangelize North American society, and to retain the loyalty of its own faithful, especially the young. The question of internal Church structure and governance, and the image the Orthodox hope to convey to others about their claim to be "the" Christian church has pushed to the foreground the demand for an understanding of what "rights" mean within the Orthodox Church. Moreover, those discussions have proven to have international implications that extend far beyond the demographically small North American Orthodox Church, and illustrate how stubbornly "historically Orthodox" parts of Orthodox Christianity have resisted a growing American Orthodox claim to have the right to be a self-governed, self-determined Church. Those disagreements have laid bare not only disputations about the process by which an Orthodox community has achieved sufficient maturity to be self-governing, but also who among the historic Orthodox Patriarchates exercises the right to recognize and to grant the legitimate claim of such communities to be universally recognized as a fully independent, self-determining Orthodox Church. By the last third of the twentieth century, those disagreements took on concrete, and divisive significance that remain unresolved more than half a century later.

62. Georgakas, "Greek American Radicalism," 82; Charles C. Moskos, Jr., "The Greek Orthodox Church in America," in *Reading Greek America*, pp. 85–97, at 85. Considerable irony surrounded the lauding by AHEPA of Vice President Spiro Agnew (a member of the Protestant Episcopal Church) only a short time before his disgrace and resignation from office.

CHAPTER

4

RIGHTS OF AND FOR A SELF-GOVERNED AMERICAN ORTHODOX CHURCH

The right to freedom of expression and religious liberty Orthodox Christians claimed as their own in a pluralistic society could not be limited to concerns about infringements of those rights from outside their Church. The struggle over rights of and for an American Orthodox Church broke out in earnest by the 1920s among the post-Bolshevik Revolution remnants of the original Russian Mission to North America. The Greek Orthodox, while at the time not direct participants in that struggle, nevertheless held no monopoly on internal struggles to claim the rights of full citizens while maintaining a quasi-separate cultural identity within American society. However, little sympathy was shown for the denial of civil rights and freedom of expression suffered by non-Orthodox.

Eastern European Slavic-speaking Orthodox who had arrived in large numbers in the late nineteenth and early twentieth century encountered outright hostility, including prejudice against their religious faith and their ethnic customs. Most strikingly, by the time one of their newspapers (*Svoboda*) began reflecting on the poor treatment working people received at the hands of American business leaders and the police, that treatment was compared to the abuse suffered by African Americans. Yet the comments on the appearance in 1895 of a biography of the abolitionist John Brown claimed that the oppression suffered by Ukrainians was worse than that inflicted upon African Americans. The editors did concede however, that the brutality, including the lynching of African Americans severely undercut the American claim to be the land of "liberty" and of civil rights. At the same time, the assertion of the superiority of Slavs over African-Americans received endorsement in the claim that in the United States "whites ruled over blacks, the superior race over the inferior," whereas in the places of Slavic emigration, "among us, our own ruled over our own. . . ."[1]

Slavic speakers who arrived as immigrants in the United States had in many cases been Greek Catholics, most from the Sub-Carpathian regions of Central Europe. Between 1900 and 1930, however, "the conversion of tens of thousands of Carpatho-Rusyns to Orthodox Christianity" had injected not simply disputes over freedom of expression, but more commonly, arguments over property rights into these Orthodox communities.[2] Even before events in Russia overwhelmed the American Russian Diocese, when a large number of these former Eastern Rite Ruthenian Catholics who had immigrated to the United States decided to become Orthodox, their leader Alexis Toth, in joining the Russian Diocese of Alaska and North America, had begun the slow and delicate process of putting church properties into the hands of bishops. As was the case with all strains of Eastern Orthodox in America, "from their beginning these parishes were owned by the congregations, not any diocese."[3] Lay resistance to hierarchical claims of rights over their property reflected not just a lay determination to guard their identities and freedoms, which they considered to be just as much theirs as those enjoyed by their Protestant neighbors. It also revealed how much they craved the approval, or at the least, tolerance, from those "others."

Escalating anxieties over religious rights and freedom of expression also came naturally to the Arab American Orthodox Palestinian arrivals in the United States, who by the 1930s had become enmeshed in the spiraling conflict between Arab Muslims and the Jewish population of Palestine. They faced the excruciating question of whether they should be participants in the pan-Arabic revolt of 1936–39 intent on defending Arab rights,

---

1. Joel Brady, "Transnational Conversions: Greek Catholic Migrants and Russky Orthodox Conversion Movements in Austria-Hungary, Russia, and the Americas (1890–1914)" (unpublished PhD diss., University of Pittsburgh, 2012), 56–90, at 72, 74 quotation from the newspaper *Svoboda* (Shamokin, Olyphant, Pa., n.d.)

2. For a summary of these events, see D. Oliver Herbel, *Turning to Tradition: Converts and the Making of an American Orthodox Church* (Oxford: Oxford University Press, 2014), 1–60, at 28.

3. Nicholas Ferencz, *American Orthodoxy and Parish Congregationalism* (Piscataway, NJ: Gorgias Press, 2006), 121.

or whether they were instead representatives of an Arab Christian national identity, with the rights and privileges peculiar to them alone. The long history of Arab Christians surviving as a minority subject to periodic persecutions had not changed the fact, in the opinion of one scholar, that "to the Syrians, religion, morality and racial status are different aspects of one and the same thing."[4]

Orthodox Christians who faced expulsion or persecution for their faith, whether in Soviet Russia, Eastern Europe, or the Middle East, found refuge along with non-Christian refugees in Article 14 of the 1948 Universal Declaration of Human Rights that declared "everyone has the right to seek and to enjoy in other countries asylum from persecution." That article received additional support at the 1951 "Convention Relating to the Status of Refugees." In the American context, one might have expected these affirmations to have been invoked in the testimony of the Orthodox Archbishop of Shanghai and San Francisco, John Maximovich.

Fleeing Soviet Russian persecution, a group of White Russians had left via China until the communist victory over the Chinese Nationalists forced another exodus, this time to the island of Tubabao in Guiuan, Eastern Samar. The Philippine President Elpidio Quirino had not envisioned a permanent settlement but nonetheless allowed the Russians to remain for several years while they pursued their hope to emigrate farther, to the United States. Archbishop John, speaking through Nicholas Alexander of Holy Trinity Orthodox Seminary in Jordanville, New York who accompanied him to Washington, testified on behalf of the Russians before the U.S. Senate's Judiciary Committee's Subcommittee on Amendments to the Displaced Persons Act of 1948. Securing the support of California Senator William Knowland, who had visited the camp in 1949, the Archbishop would eventually rejoice when the 1948 Act as amended in 1950 allowed immigration to the United States in 1951.[5]

---

4. Noah Haiduc-Dale, *Arab Christians in British Mandate Palestine: Communalism and Nationalism, 1917–1948* (Edinburgh: Edinburgh University Press, 2013), 1–17; 152–162; Philip K. Hitti, *The Syrians in America* (New York: George H. Doran Company, 1924), 122.

5. For details, see "The Story of the White Russian Refugees in Tubabao Island, Guiuan Eastern Samar Philippines, 1949–1953," accessed 30 March 2019, https://www.visiteasternsamar.com/2018/11/the-story-of-white-russian-refugees -in.html. See on the general issue of refugees and rights, Carl J. Bon Tempo,

This episode illustrated an Orthodox use of American commitments to religious freedom and human liberty (the words invoked by Alexander). Yet while affirming exiled Russian loyalty to the United States and giving praise for that nation's resolute anti-Communism, the Archbishop did not invoke a claim to the right of asylum. Just prior to hearing his testimony, the same Subcommittee heard from those pleading the case of displaced Arab Palestinians from their homes in the new state of Israel. But even in that instance, the argument for accepting such refugees pointed to the duties of "Christian nations" and their philanthropy and only once mentioned the "rights of the native inhabitants of that area."[6] These instances illustrated that the exercise of the right to asylum—a right that had to be sought because of the threat to freedom of expression and conscience in their original homelands—depended not on the United States' endorsement of the United Nations' Universal Declaration, but on the revision of its own domestic legislation regarding displaced persons. It was on that basis that the Orthodox—along with others who did not share their religious convictions—successfully pleaded their case for refugee status, pointing to the importance of freedom of religious expression.

The post-World War II displacements of persons from historically Orthodox lands contributed to the need of the Orthodox to ask how they would now live as one community of belief among many with fellow citizens who profess no religious belief, and to "changing their relationships with the 'old countries' in general, and the 'mother churches' of those countries in particular."[7] As the Russian Orthodox émigré example suggests, potential conflicts

---

Americans at the Gate: The United States and Refugees during the Cold War (Princeton: Princeton University Press, 2008); Peter Gattrell, *The Making of the Modern Refugee* (Oxford: Oxford University Press, 2013); Elizabeth Borgwardt, *A New Deal for the World: America's Vision for Human Rights* (Cambridge, MA: Harvard University Press, 2005).

6. Subcommittee on Amendments to the Displaced Persons Act, Displaced Persons, HRG-1949-SJS-0016 (1950). https://congressional.proquest.com/congressional/docview/t29.d30.hrg-1949-sjs-0016. For the testimony on displaced Arabic Palestinians, see 346–378 at 354; for the testimony of Alexander and Archbishop John, 383–391 at 385.

7. Elizabeth Prodromou, "Christianity and Democracy: The Ambivalent Orthodox," *Journal of Democracy* 15, no. 2 (2004): 62–75, at 67; Prodromou, "Orthodox Christianity and Pluralism: Moving Beyond Ambivalence?" in *The*

between "church and state," that might boil down to "religious rights" and the need to defend them against state intrusion provided a starting point. Some Orthodox could express limited sympathy for the expression of freedom of religion and expression on the part of non-Orthodox, a denial that had been their own fate in their countries of origin.[8]

The gradual internalization by the Orthodox of the values that surround the commitment to freedom of religious opinion and expression had attracted the attention of Orthodox hierarchs by the 1980s. Some among the bishops confronted the need for a common Orthodox witness in the face of growing moral pluralism that manifested itself as much in a fragmented Church riven by ethnic and linguistic loyalties as in American society at large. Metropolitan Philip Saliba of the Antiochian Orthodox Christian Archdiocese of North America insisted that the Orthodox had to find a way "to blend . . . old and new cultures into some kind of an integrated reality . . . the mission of the Church is not to be subservient to any kind of nationalism. . . . After eighteen years in the episcopate, I have been convinced that Orthodox unity in America must begin on the grassroots level." Failure to confront the reality of pluralism's challenge both within and beyond the Church's boundaries, he concluded, could have but one outcome: "our Church on this continent will remain an insignificant dot on the margin of history."[9] The Antiochian hierarch's retrospec-

Orthodox Churches in a Pluralistic World: An Ecumenical Conversation, ed. Emmanuel Clapsis (Geneva: WCC Publications/Brookline, MA: Holy Cross Orthodox Press, 2004), 22–46; Emmanuel Clapsis, "Human Rights and the Orthodox Church in a Global World," in Alexei Bodrov and Stephen M. Garrett, eds., *Theology and the Political: Theo-Political Reflections on Contemporary Politics in Ecumenical Conversation* (Leiden: Brill, 2020) 51–69.

8. See for example, J. Christopher Soper, Kevin R. den Dulk, and Stephen V. Monsma, eds., *The Challenge of Pluralism: Church and State in Six Democracies*, 3rd ed. (New York: Rowman and Littlefield, 2017). For further reflections on this dimension of pluralism, see Aristotle Papanikolaou and George Demacopoulos, eds., *Christianity, Democracy, and the Shadow of Constantine* (New York: Fordham University Press, 2017).

9. Metropolitan Philip Saliba, "Orthodoxy in America: Success and Failure," homily delivered in St. George Cathedral, Worcester, Massachusetts, Sunday of Orthodoxy, 1984; available at "The Historic 1984 Sunday of Orthodoxy Sermon of Metropolitan Philip," *Antiochian Orthodox Christian Archdiocese of North*

tive analysis of the fragmented state of the Orthodox stemmed from his recognition of the riven social, political and moral climate of American society, where, he queried, "why is it that every time there is a moral issue to be discussed, a Protestant, a Roman Catholic, and [a] Jew are invited for such discussions? How can we explain our Orthodox absence despite the authenticity of our theology and moral teachings?"[10]

Just as a few Orthodox had taken the first tentative steps toward confronting the emerging civil rights movement, the claims for civil rights for minorities had been grounded in religious convictions. Although it remained the case that the voices calling for an expansion of rights between 1962 and as late as 1975 had been framed by "an emphasis on racial discrimination and religious intolerance" the growing instances of linking law and rights shifted away from invoking religious grounds for doing so. As this change occurred it became obvious that "religion and law would never have a straightforward relationship . . . built on different foundations of meaning and . . . different social imaginaries."[11] Neither, as events proved, would the internal debates about governance, property, and procedural safeguards in ecclesiastical courts prove any less fraught.

III. The Orthodox Church in North America and the Limits of Freedom of Expression

Bitter internal disputes over the rights of individual hierarchs versus groups of bishops intensified by the late 1960s, as did the related question of how much freedom of religion and expression was to be permitted within the Orthodox Church itself. Those disputes led back to the intense relationship between religion and law, not only in suits brought against bishops, but also in cases where the charters and constitutions of the Orthodox jurisdictions in North America revealed how dependent those structures were

---

America, February 8, 2016, http://ww1.antiochian.org/node/17372; and in Peter E. Gillquist, *Metropolitan Philip: His Life and His Times* (Nashville, TN: Thomas Nelson Publishers, 1991), 278–284, at 285.

　　10. Saliba, "Orthodoxy in America—Success and Failure," in Gillquist, *Metropolitan Philip*, 284.

　　11. Steven L. B. Jensen, *The Making of International Human Rights: The 1960s, Decolonization and the Reconstruction of Global Values* (New York: Cambridge University Press, 2016), 138–173, at 176, 172.

on governance from abroad. Decisions taken often without consultation with American Orthodox groups alarmed some Orthodox in North America who had grown used to the expectation that free and open expression of opinion and debate about the manner in which the Church governed itself had to characterize Orthodoxy in a pluralist society.

American courts had in the nineteenth century refused to become entangled in the internal disputes arising from contested claims of congregational or hierarchical rights when these were deemed to fall within the jurisdiction of ecclesiastical discipline. "Discipline" is understood to be "founded on divine authority and exercised through church judicial authority," and regarded as "moral or spiritual and not temporal or secular."[12] Courts or tribunals that the Orthodox have constructed to enforce discipline are, like Catholic tribunals, "also ordered hierarchically and there are rules on their establishment, composition (which may include laity) and original and appellate jurisdiction. . . ."[13] Most commonly, Orthodox Christians brought before an ecclesiastical court or tribunal have been clergy, although in the case of the Greek Orthodox Archdiocese, Orthodox laity seeking to be divorced and remarried also must appear before such courts. The degree to which standards of what would be understood in Anglo-American terms as "due process" have been applied to guarantee the protection of the rights of the accused varies considerably. In sharp contrast to Roman Catholic specificity in detailing what offenses and what procedural protections accompany an imposition of discipline, both Orthodox and Anglican traditions are "notable for the lack of juridical precision in the definitional elements of . . . ecclesiastical offences . . . and unlike the Catholic church, juridical instruments do not provide for explicit defences."[14]

The three largest Eastern Orthodox jurisdictions have all operated under a charter or some form of constitution. Each contained language regarding governance that specifies the rights of a Metropolitan Archbishop and bishops of the Church and also addresses the question of ecclesiastical discipline as well. But the history of those charters/constitutions reveals the

12. Norman Doe, *Christian Law: Contemporary Principles* (Cambridge: Cambridge University Press, 2013), 154–187, at 155, 257.

13. Doe, *Christian Law*, 166.

14. Doe, *Christian Law*, 179, 180.

troublesome nature of a key unsettled question: Who should be regarded as the "first" among bishops in North America, and in what relationship would such a person claiming the rights and privileges of first bishop stand with regard to his fellow bishops? Disputes began between the bishops of the Russian mission and arriving Greek speakers in the early twentieth century, and subsequently, between the 1970s and 2009 engulfed the Syrian Orthodox, who by 1969 were known as "The Antiochian Orthodox Christian Archdiocese of North America."

The early twentieth-century disputes cast into relief the conviction among the Orthodox (lay as well as clerical) that when one spoke of rights in such disputes, one was actually discussing power, privilege, and authority. The disputes over the right of jurisdiction did not invoke the term *dikaion*—righteous or just—but instead the Greek term *presbeion*—prerogative or privilege—that had become familiar since the time of the first councils that had established the privileges and rights of honor among the great episcopal sees of the ancient churches. Or at least, this was the sense in which the emerging clergy understood what was being defended. The laity who had built and owned the local parishes understood the dispute to be one between traditional privilege and their own conviction that they were defending both their collective and individual rights in American civil and church law, which for them also was a moral right given the huge investment of time, money, and labor by themselves and their ancestors in acquiring and defending church properties. Nor did they hesitate to give public expression to those convictions in the form of lawsuits brought against bishops.

The year 1907–08 cast a long shadow over the subsequent history of the Orthodox in North America and intensified debates over rights and privileges of competing hierarchs with devastating effects upon the life of the Church as a whole. Despite the herculean labors of bishops Tikhon Bellavin and Raphael Hawaweeny, the attempt to pull together the various linguistic and ethnic strands of the Orthodox under the umbrella protection of the Russian Diocese ended in failure. The March 5, 1907 meeting at St. John the Baptist Church in Mayfield, Pennsylvania had been called by Tikhon to address the need to establish the Russian Diocese as an incorporated body. He had hoped that this would place oversight of all Church matters (including the volatile issue of property ownership) in the hands of the bishops but guarantee the rights of the various linguistic and ethnic groups to maintain their own liturgical traditions. But as one scholar has concluded: "The Sobor was a paradigm of American Orthodoxy: opportunity missed rather than realized."[15] Nicholas Ferencz's analysis of the 1907 meeting focuses upon the critical failure to deal via American law with the crucial issue of the incorporation of the Russian Diocese, the lack of hierarchical trusteeship of all Church properties, and the unwillingness of the various linguistic and ethnic strands of Orthodoxy—especially lay trustee leaders—to acknowledge the need for an American diocese that would have been self-governing even though still connected to the Holy Synod of the Russian Orthodox Church.

In the aftermath of the Russian Revolution and the subsequent splintering of even the modest pan-Orthodox cooperation in the United States, hierarchs facing multiple challenges came to rely on the language of defending their rights and privileges. As the Russian Mission disintegrated into factionalism following the inability of the newly restored Moscow Patriarchate to direct, financially support, or advise its American Diocese, the *Russian-American Orthodox Messenger* reported on the struggle to claim and defend conflicting hierarchical rights. The bilingual paper that had begun publication in New York City in 1896 noted disputes over the "right of jurisdiction" and the "usurpation of rights" and complaints of the denial of rights that flew back and forth among Bishop Anthony of Alaska, Metropolitan Antonii Khrapovitskii, and Metropolitan Platon Rozhdestvensky.[16]

But in contrast to the earlier essays published in both Russian and English that had addressed the question of American legal and constitutional protection of rights, the *Messenger* turned increasingly to internal ecclesial matters. Its editor, at least, had been an enthusiastic supporter of the early stages of the Russian Revolution that promised to sever the connection between the Church and the Russian state. No surviving essays or

15. Ferencz, American Orthodoxy, 187–197, at 196.

16. See the letters reprinted in the issues for July 6, 1922, July 19, 1922, January 1, 1924, April 2, 1924; for a concise summary of the struggles, see John H. Erickson, "Eastern Orthodox Christianity in America," *The Cambridge History of Religion in America, Vol II: 1790 to 1945*, ed. Stephen J. Stein (Cambridge: Cambridge University Press, 2012), 324–343, at 334–335. For an alternative reading of these events from the perspective of the Russian Church Outside Russia, see Fr. Neketas S. Palassis, *A History of the Russian Church Abroad and The Events Leading to the American Metropolia's Autocephaly* (Brookline, MA: Holy Transfiguration Monastery, 1972), 4–49.

private letters allow us to say to what extent this point of view was shared by the faithful within the Russian Mission in North America. The 1917 issues of the *Messenger* totaled 496 pages, an offering that shrank to only 128 for the 1918 issues as the newspaper collapsed from a weekly, "to biweekly to monthly to quarterly to ceasing publication altogether."[17] By January of 1918 the editors reminded readers that the right of religious liberty had been planted by the "blessing of God" and the Orthodox "possess the rights and protections of the laws and constitution of a constitutional country. Who would have believed that Russian Orthodox people here in America . . . could be safer and more tranquil than in the longsuffering and tragic Motherland . . ."[18] After ceasing publication from 1919 to 1921 and again from 1931to 1935, the paper reappeared as the *Vestnik*, a Russian-language-only publication that offered no more commentary on the Orthodox and their engagement with American rights to freedom of religion and expression.

By the 1970s, the majority descendants of the old Russian mission would finally emerge as the Orthodox Church in America (OCA) claiming the standing of "autocephaly." Despite the truth of the conclusion that "we know comparatively little about the term 'autocephalous' and the reality behind it during the ancient and early medieval periods" we can risk adopting the summary statement that with regard to the North American debates, an "autocephalous" church "possesses . . . the right to resolve all internal problems on its own authority, independently of all other churches, and . . . the right to appoint its own bishops, among them the head of the church, without any obligatory expression of dependence on another church."[19]

The claim of what eventually emerged as the Orthodox Church in America to be autocephalous remains controversial and is not universally recognized a half-century after the Russian Orthodox Church in April 1970

17. John A. Jillions, "The *Amerikansii Pravoslavnyi Vestnik (The Russian Orthodox American Messenger)* 1917–18: In the Aftermath of Revolutions in Russia," *St. Vladimir's Theological Quarterly* 61, no. 2 (2017): 195–229, at 216.

18. *Messenger*, January 1918:2 (cited in Jillions, *Amerikanskii Pravoslavnyi*, 218).

19. John H. Erickson, "Autocephaly in Orthodox Canonical Literature to the Thirteenth Century," *Saint Vladimir's Theological Quarterly* 15:1/2 (1971), 28–41 at 28–29.

granted a *tomos*, or formal letter, granting complete self-governance to the "Russian Orthodox Greek Catholic Church in North America", the "Metropolia."

Orthodox canonists have pointed out that the word autocephaly does not occur in the corpus of the canons, those pastoral instructions emanating from councils and synods that aid in the administration of Orthodox churches. Although the word itself occurs in the canonical literature, it is generally descriptive and does not occur as part of a prescriptive method or mandate as to how autocephaly comes about. For those questions, scholars are compelled to look to other kinds of sources.[20] In the North American context, the conflicting claims about what autocephaly is, and how the right to it is obtained, came to be reduced to two: the Ecumenical Patriarchate of Constantinople (Istanbul) relies on a reading of Canon 28 of the Council of Chalcedon of 451 to support its position that peoples and territories not already under the supervision of any of the then-patriarchates (Rome, Constantinople, Alexandria, Antioch, Jerusalem) may enter the Orthodox Church as autocephalous only with the consent and blessing of the Ecumenical Patriarch. The Russian Orthodox Patriarchate argued to the contrary that autocephaly has been granted and recognized by other Patriarchs regardless of whether Constantinople's approval had been obtained. Citing priority of arrival in North America, the Russian Orthodox Church claimed the right to bestow self-governance of its former mission.

Neither claim has proved to be convincing, and stalemate on this question persists half a century after the granting of the 1970 Tomos, not just among the Orthodox in America but globally. The origins of the self-governance principle was neither an American nor a Western development in the evolution of struggles over political and religious authority and freedom of expression. Rather, the decisions taken in Russia during the Moscow Council of 1917–18 laid that groundwork. As we have already noted, the initial focus of that Council remained on the life of the church at the parish and diocesan level, and, for the first time in Russian Church history, envisioned the role of lay and clergy delegates who were not chosen by bishops. They now exercised more than a merely consultative presence. Fiercely opposed by the most conservative and pro-monarchist

20. Alexander Rentel, "Autocephaly with a Canonical Perspective," (lecture, St. Tikhon's Seminary, 29 October, 2019). https://www.stots.edu/news_191105_2.

elements in the hierarchy who denounced any lay role in the governance of the local or the national church, this singular accomplishment of the council came first. Only subsequently did a second focus on the office of the patriarch emerge as an equally heated topic of debate. As the last of the three sessions of the council had been interrupted by Bolshevik intervention, it had become clear that the council saw itself as a "constituent assembly" that had established the local council as the supreme power in the Church. The principle of "conciliarity" among all the bishops emerged from these debates to such a degree that over the long twentieth-century history of the Russian Church "these three elements of the 1917–1918 Council—the patriarchate, the conciliar institution (with the participation of lay people in the local council), and the parish statute" gave a distinct profile to the Russian Patriarchate, but only abroad, neither in the Soviet Union, nor in today's Russia.[21]

Such a profile was hard to reconcile with the ancient history of councils and the claims to quasi-monarchical governance of bishops who had been called together for councils by emperors. The Russian Patriarchate was not so much restored as re-captured a version of pre-Constantinian episcopacy in a different form and function from that of the ancient patriarchates of the Orthodox Church that had emerged by the time of the Council of Chalcedon in 451. The Bolshevik disbanding of the Council and the subsequent imposition of a totalitarian state apparatus interrupted the realization of what such a Church would look like. But among a group of exiled Russians, first in Europe, and subsequently, in North America, a version of such an Orthodox Church did emerge.

Until its abrupt and unexplained abolition by the Ecumenical Patriarchate in December 2019, the Russian Exarchate in Europe and its theological Institute of St. Sergius in Paris had enjoyed the protection of the Ecumenical Patriarch. That refuge began after the exiled Metropolitan Eulogy "then the spiritual head of the Russian Orthodox in France, sought the canonical protection of Ecumenical Patriarch Photius II. In 1931,

---

21. Hyacinthe Destivelle, O.P., *The Moscow Council (1917–1918)*, 73–123; 166. For the diversity of opinions and practices in pre-revolutionary Russian Orthodoxy, see Vera Shevzov, "Letting the People into Church: Reflections on Orthodoxy and Community in Late Imperial Russia," in *Orthodox Russia: Belief and Practice under the Tsars*, ed. Valerie A. Kivelson and Robert H. Greene (University Park: The Pennsylvania State University Press, 2003), 59–77.

Constantinople received Metropolitan Eulogy and his parishes . . . it embraced and lived out the most important reforms of the Moscow Council of 1917–18, including the adoption of the Gregorian calendar and (in the Council's recreation of the Patriarchate) the embrace of an Orthodoxy that could exist with the powers of church and state separated."[22]

Despite the emergence of the OCA by 1970 subsequent events revealed that the ability of the Orthodox in North America to express themselves freely and to govern themselves suffered severe setbacks. That pattern emerged as the result of intrigues carried out in authoritarian political contexts that began, but did not end, with the Cold War. A decades-long campaign initiated by Soviet Russia in the 1940s against the role of the Ecumenical Patriarch in Istanbul lay at the heart of the refusal on the part of most Orthodox Patriarchs to recognize the Russian Church's grant of autocephaly. Suspicion among Russian Orthodox exiles in Europe and North America surrounding the freedom of expression allowed to the newly restored Russian Patriarchate appears to have been justified, as evidenced by the partial opening of the KGB archives in Russia. The Moscow Patriarchate reestablished in 1918 was thoroughly infiltrated by the Soviet secret service. That reduction of the patriarchate to a department of the Soviet state included the person of Metropolitan Nikodim—code name Svyatoslav—who served as the main discussion partner with whom the then-Metropolia in North America dealt in its quest for autocephaly. The Tomos granted by Moscow in 1970 contains an internal contradiction regarding territorial integrity that was seized upon by its opponents as the main reason for the non-recognition. That non-recognition was clear in the case of the Greek Orthodox—but more complicated and nuanced among the Syrian and Lebanese Arabic-speaking Orthodox that had in 1970 not yet achieved their own internal unity to become today's Antiochian Orthodox Christian Archdiocese of North America.[23]

22. Katherine Kelaidis, "The Russian Exarchate: A Eulogy," *The Wheel* 20 (Winter, 2020): 6–9 at 7. Following the Russian invasion of Ukraine in February, 2022 the parish in Amsterdam voted to leave the Russian jurisdiction and asked for protection from the Ecumenical Patriarch in Istanbul. For details, see below, Conclusion.

23. Nikodim remains a controversial figure; for an argument that he was somewhat independent of the Khrushchev regime but never deviated from Soviet foreign policy statements and positions, see Dimitry Pospielovsky, *The Russian*

Analysts of Soviet Russia in the 1960s point to two important developments that provide some context. The first was the cultivation of a modified official nationalism that attempted to curb excessive nationalist movements among the many republics and ethnicities of the Soviet Empire. But the objective was clear—while a limited nationalist identity might be tolerated, in the end, this was supposed to be secondary to feelings of Soviet patriotism and thus only a very limited version of ethnic nationalism was tolerated among Ukrainians, Carpatho-Russians, Poles, and the Baltic Soviet states. Second, the Brezhnev years in Russia were captives of the three major foreign crises of the Czech revolt of 1968, Vietnam 1965–75, and Afghanistan 1979–89. The Brezhnev doctrine justified Soviet intervention anywhere it saw a threat to Soviet security. But coupled with this was the desire to avoid an actual nuclear confrontation with the West and hence the era of détente resulted in the SALT treaty of 1972.[24]

Despite the reputation of the Khrushchev years as a thaw in Soviet relations with the West, the opposite was true with regard to the Church. The anti-religious campaign from 1958 to 1964 resulted in the closure of half of Russia's churches, disproportionately in Ukraine; reduction of clergy and seminaries and the arrest and internment of both clergy and lay believers. Of the 63 monasteries and sketes that existed in 1958, only 18 survived by 1966.[25]

Church under the Soviet Regime 1917–1982, 2 vols. (Crestwood, NY: St. Vladimir Seminary Press, 1984), II: 296–298 and 359–63.

24. Kivelson and Suny, *Russia's Empires*, 333–34; 343.

25. Scott M. Kenworthy, *The Heart of Russia: Trinity-Sergius, Monasticism, and Society after 1825* (Washington. D.C.: Oxford University Press for Woodrow Wilson Center Press, 2010), 373, 374; Joan Delaney Grossman, "Khrushchev's Anti-Religious Policy and the Campaign of 1954," *Soviet Studies* 24, no. 3 (January, 1973): 374–86; Donald A. Lowrie and William C. Fletcher, "Khrushchev's Religious Policy, 1959–1964," in *Aspects of Religion in the Soviet Union, 1917–67*, ed. Richard H. Marshall, Jr. (Chicago: University of Chicago Press, 1971), 132–37; John Anderson, *Religion, State and Politics in the Soviet Union and Successor States* (Cambridge: Cambridge University Press, 1994).; John Paul Hinka, *Religion and Nationality in Western Ukraine: The Greek Catholic Church and the Ruthenian National Movement in Galicia, 1867–1900* (Montreal: McGill-Queen's University Press, 1998); Nicholas E. Denysenko, *The Orthodox Church in Ukraine: A Century of Separation* (DeKalb: Northern Illinois University Press, 2018).

Even with the fall of Khrushchev, the Brezhnev regime did not improve conditions; no new churches or monasteries were permitted. On a broader front, dissent was crushed in 1966–68, with special attention paid to Ukrainian intellectuals accused of writing subversion in the Ukrainian language and "undermining 'the eternal friendship' between the Russian and Ukrainian peoples."[26] In 1967 the followers of the Russian Christian universalist Nikolai Berdyaev were put on trial, many of whose followers were Orthodox Christians. This background makes the rationale behind the willingness of the Moscow Patriarchate to consider granting the Metropolia autocephaly all the more peculiar. But the roots of that decision lay within a larger and older strategy in which the Metropolia was a minor player. The Soviet regime under Josef Stalin had already by 1944 formulated a strategy to move the center of global Orthodoxy from Istanbul to Moscow, a plan that provides some understanding of Greek Orthodox alarm at the prospect of an autocephalous North American Orthodox entity created by Soviet fiat and subsequent determination to bring the North American Orthodox more directly under the control of the Ecumenical Patriarch.

Even before World War II ended in Europe, Stalin had entertained a proposal to hold an ecumenical Christian congress in Moscow with the dual purpose of uniting all non-Catholic Christians against the Vatican and making Moscow the new global center of all Eastern Orthodox Christianity. The election of Patriarch Alexii in February 1945 put in place a man who would attempt to call under his own authority a pan-Orthodox council that envisioned claiming the role of Ecumenical Patriarch for Moscow. Ignoring the role the Bolshevik Revolution had played in frustrating a pan-Orthodox Synod called by Constantinople in 1923, Alexii and his allies made a sufficiently convincing proposal that the Soviet government by 1946 endorsed a pre-council conference to be held in Moscow in 1947. If all went as Moscow hoped, an actual Ecumenical Council would take place the following year honoring a celebration of the 500th anniversary of Moscow's self-proclaimed autocephaly of 1448. By ensuring Soviet domination of all but the patriarchates of Constantinople, Alexandria, and Jerusalem, little seemed to

---

26. Michael Khodarkovsky, *Russia's 20th Century: A Journey in 100 Histories* (London: Bloomsbury Academic, 2019), 154.

stand in the way of a plan to advance Soviet foreign policy via the Moscow Patriarchate.[27]

Soviet Russian determination to exercise political control over a church in the arch-enemy territory of the United States had been clear since the 1940s. The Greek Orthodox alarm over the term "autocephaly" as it emerged by 1970 focused on the impossibility of a "partial autocephaly." The final language of the 1970 Tomos of Encephaly meant self-determination for the OCA but not authority over the other Orthodox diaspora jurisdictions in North America, not even those of Russian and Central European Slavic traditions. As Patriarch Alexii in his letter to Ecumenical Patriarch Athenagoras claimed, the remaining "sister Churches, having their own branches in America" would continue to govern their own affairs. Given the Kremlin's campaign to isolate Constantinople that had begun in the early 1940s, Alexei's claims reassured no one. The resulting standing of the OCA resembled more an "autonomous" than a fully "autocephalous" Church.

An autonomous Orthodox church can submit candidates for its chief or governing bishop but the final choice remains with a patriarchate that is not obliged to accept the local church's choice. This "autonomous" option had been raised and rejected by the Metropolia decades earlier. Political restrictions imposed by Moscow as a prerequisite for Russian reconciliation with the Metropolia arose between 1945 and 1947. Negotiations had taken place revealing that if the Metropolia wanted to be recognized by Moscow, the North Americans would have to accept the calling of a council chaired by the Moscow Patriarch's representative. Second, autonomy reserved to Moscow the right to accept or reject candidates for the episcopacy. Third—and the real issue—an American council would have to adopt an official position not to engage in any "political activity" against the

---

27. This summarizes Chapter Nine of Daniela Kalkandjieva, *The Russian Orthodox Church, 1917–1948: From Decline to Resurrection* (Oxford: Routledge, 2015), 307–344; see 319 on agreement of the pro-Russian Antiochian Patriarch Alexandros III for the Russian proposal; 320–21 on the refusal of Constantinople, Alexandria, Jerusalem, the Church of Greece and Cyprus, and the eventual denial by the Russians of the plan to establish Moscow as the "Third Rome", 331. On the frustrated 1923 Pan-Orthodox Congress, see Patrick Viscuso, *A Quest for Reform of the Orthodox Church: The 1923 Pan-Orthodox Congress, An Analysis and Translation of Its Acts and Decisions* (Berkeley, CA: InterOrthodox Press, 2006), and specifically on the "diaspora" of various Orthodox in North America, lv–lviii.

Soviet regime. The definition of "political activity" remained the sole pre-rogative of the Moscow Patriarchate and the whims of Josef Stalin. No one in the Metropolia—nor in the Ecumenical Patriarchate—harbored any illusions about what this would have meant given the close relationship and subservience of Patriarch Alexii I to Joseph Stalin revealed in the fawning terms the Patriarch used in eulogizing Stalin upon the latter's death.[28]

The most convincing explanation for the Kremlin's approval of auto-cephaly for the Metropolia can be found in the Soviet conviction that the Vatican, the United States, and the Ecumenical Patriarchate represented the most dangerous *troika* threatening the domestic and international interests of the Soviet Empire. The timing of the Soviet objective of exercising some influence over American Orthodox affairs had its roots in the Greek Orthodox presence in the United States and their complicated relationship to the original Russian Mission. The Metropolia's own original canonical claim to be self-governing—made in 1924 to avoid Soviet control—had been rejected by Moscow just two years after the Greek Orthodox Archdiocese had been created to care for Greek Orthodox or those of "Greek ancestry." The Metropolia's relations with the White Russian pro-monarchist Russian Church Outside Russia had also dissolved in the 1920s, resumed fitfully in the 1930s, but again had been broken by the 1950s. A 1965 proposal to create an American Orthodox synod with the Greek Archbishop as its primate was vetoed by the Russian Patriarchate. It was that rejection that explains the reaction of the Ecumenical Patriarch Athenagoras in 1966—a year later—to the Metropolia's request to become an Exarchate of the Ecumenical Patriarchate along the lines of the Western European Archdiocese in Paris.

Athenagoras' insistence that only the Russian Church could address the Metropolia's status bewildered the Americans. Most of the Metropolia's members had never been "Russians" but "Rusyn", i.e. Carpatho-Russians, Ukrainians, Galicians; post-1945 immigrants to the US produced no significant growth in the Metropolia. Small increases in the parishes directly under the Patriarch of Moscow came a distant second compared to those

---

28. John A. Jillions, "The Tomos of Autocephaly: Forty-six Years Later," *Orthodox Church in America*, April 7, 2016. https://oca.org/news/headline-news/the-tomos-of-autocephaly-forty-six-years-later; Pospielovsky, *The Russian Church under the Soviet Regime* 2: 296–98

who opted for the Russian Church Outside Russia, the White Russian Tsarist exile church that had never recognized the legitimacy of the Moscow Patriarchate after the death of Patriarch Tikhon Bellavin. By the late 1960s approximately 15 to 20 per cent of the Metropolia membership consisted of converts from Protestant, Roman Catholic, or other religious backgrounds. The 10 foreign-born Metropolitans of the Metropolia vetoed a 1967 proposal to change the name of the Metropolia from the "Russian Orthodox Greek Catholic Church of North America" only to find that the majority of straw votes cast by delegates to the All American Sobor favored the change.[29]

The conventional histories of the events between 1967 and 1970 claim that the growth of Soviet interest in détente encouraged the move toward autocephaly.[30] Yet the Moscow Patriarchate retained control of St. Nicholas Cathedral in New York City that had only by the 1950s been declared by the U.S. Supreme Court to be the property of the Soviet-dominated Russian Patriarchate. This control was now expanded to include any parish that wanted to remain under the Patriarchate of Moscow. If the vision and intent of the Russian Orthodox Church had been to create an autocephalous Church that would unite all Russian and Slavic-tradition Orthodox in promoting the emergence of a united American Orthodox Church, the Patriarchal parishes should have been ordered to join the OCA. Greek Orthodox canonists both in the United States and in most of the ancient patriarchates recognized this and reiterated a long-standing argument that a "partial" autocephaly cannot exist for a given geographic or political entity. The autocephaly of a Metropolia composed of non-Russians would not impede the objective of maintaining a Russian Patriarchal base of operations in New York City.[31]

The retention of Russian authority over parishes in the United States built upon a long-standing disagreement over the rights of Orthodox

29. John H. Erickson, *Orthodox Christians in America* (New York: Oxford University Press, 2008), 95–6; Mark Stokoe and Leonid Kishkovsky, *Orthodox Christians in North America 1794–1994* (n.p.: Orthodox Christian Publications Center, 1995), 96–7.

30. For example, Stokoe and Kishkovsky, *Orthodox Christians*, 99–100.

31. For the Greek arguments, see the essays collected and published as *Russian Autocephaly and Orthodoxy in America: An Appraisal with Decisions and Formal Opinions* (New York: Orthodox Observer Press, 1972).

bishops in North America. Apologists among Greek speakers wanting to demonstrate priority of arrival claimed a presence at New Smyrna (Florida) in 1768 despite historians' conclusions that those Greek speakers were predominantly Greek Catholic emigrants from Menorca, Corsica and not from Orthodox communities. Neither those claims nor those of the Russians about who arrived in North America first carries any particular weight or significance in assessing the complicated question of just what autocephaly is, and the "right" to grant and receive it. Nor does it matter if New Orleans is claimed as the oldest site of an Orthodox presence in the United States by 1864 (the linguistic identity of the members of that Orthodox group remains unknown); nor whether the transfer of the 1794 Russian mission from Russian imperial Alaska to San Francisco adds any clarity to the Russian claim of the right to grant autocephaly. Bishop Tikhon Bellavin was by 1907 already a lame duck bishop since he had received the call to return to Russia to become first, Archbishop of Jaroslavl, then Archbishop of Vilnius, and finally, Patriarch of Moscow. His eventual successor Platon Rozhdestvensky received in 1908 a suggestion from his own clergy that the Greek Orthodox in North America needed to be invited to be more active participants in the organization of Orthodox life in America. But Platon responded that in his opinion the Greeks were characterized by "self sufficiency . . . in questions of religion and faith," noting that in his initial four months in America no Greek contacted him or any other Russian bishop.[32]

Some scholars have argued that the Ecumenical Patriarch did acknowledge the presence of the Russian hierarchy in North America and refrained from sending a bishop until 1918. For ten years responsibility for America had lain in the hands of the Church of Greece. Athens in 1918 decided "to appoint a resident bishop" the pro-republican supporter Meletios Metaxakis "accompanied by two leading Greek bishops, Alexandros Demoglou and Chrysostomos Papadopoulos, as well as Amilkas Alivizatos, an eminent lay theologian."[33] During the controversies generated by the granting of the 1970 Tomos, Patriarch Alexii II of Moscow claimed that the 1908 Tomos from Constantinople placing the Greeks in North America under the authority of

---

32. Erickson, *Orthodox Christians in America*, 53–54.

33. Alexander Kitroeff, *Greek Orthodox Church in America* (Ithaca: Cornell University Press, 2020), 31–38 at 33.

the Church of Greece occurred while his predecessors in the Holy Synod had been in contact with Patriarch Joakim III of Constantinople regarding the appointment of a Greek bishop for America.[34] Nothing came of this contact (if in fact, it occurred) and no Greek bishop appeared on American shores for ten more years. The 1908 Greek Tomos remains significant since it advances the argument that the Ecumenical Patriarchate possesses the exclusive right and obligation to determine canonical order over all "Orthodox communities outside the canonical geographical boundaries of the Holy Churches of God."[35] But the Tomos of 1908 explained that this was a purely administrative decision "to unite the Greek communities of Europe, America, and elsewhere, to the Most Holy Autocephalous Church of Greece. . . ." Upon his arrival in the United States, Metaxakis claimed that only then was he "informed of the presence of a Russian Bishop on American soil without the permission of the Ecumenical Patriarchate." Metaxakis, after his arrival in 1918, and Platon, after his return to North America in 1921 each expected the other to acknowledge his right to be considered the primate, or first among bishops, illustrating the competing claims about episcopal rights, privileges, and preeminence over different linguistic communities—claims that have persisted to the present day. One significant difference emerged a short time later: at his enthronement as Ecumenical Patriarch in 1922 the opportunity to unite two million Orthodox of varying linguistic backgrounds into "an American Orthodox Church," was apparently no longer Metaxakis' objective. With the creation of the Greek Orthodox Archdiocese of North and South America under the direct supervision of the Ecumenical Patriarchate,

34. Panagiotes N. Trempelas, *The Autocephaly of the Metropolia in America*, transl. and ed. George S. Bebis, Robert G. Stephanopoulos, and N.M. Vaporis (Brookline, MA: Holy Cross Theological School Press, 1974), 25. For the claim in the March 17, 1970 letter of Patriarch Alexii to Patriarch Athenagoras regarding Patriarch Joachim III's "negotiations with the Russian Holy Synod concerning the appointment of a Greek Bishop to America," see the collection of correspondence published in the *Saint Vladimir's Theological Quarterly* 15:1/2 (1971), 60. I have been unable to find confirmation of this claim after contacting both Greek and Russian scholars who have access to respective archival materials. Patriarch Athenegoras did not respond to this claim in his correspondence with Alexii or his successor Patriarch Pimen.

35. For the quotations and more elaboration here and in the next paragraph, see Ferencz, *American Orthodoxy and Parish Congregationalism*, 134–38.

the 1922 charter revealed that the Archdiocese's purpose was to "nurture the religious and moral life of American citizens of the Orthodox faith who are either themselves Greek or of Greek ancestry."[36]

By the 1930s the tensions between royalists and republicans in Greece and abroad had diminished somewhat. The pacification of the political struggles within Greek-American communities subsided in part because of the influence of Aristocles Sperou, born in Epirus in 1886, who took the monastic name Athenagoras and by the 1930s arrived as the new archbishop of the Greek Archdiocese.[37] Athenagoras enjoyed the advantage of being associated neither with the pro-royalists in Greece nor with the liberal republican followers of Eleftherios Venizelos. Athenagoras' task of uniting the Greek speakers of his Archdiocese prevented neither his pursuit of ecumenical relations nor his guarded support of English language translations of the Greek Orthodox Church's liturgical texts. But even before his election as Ecumenical Patriarch, Athenagoras had made clear during World War II that no one should doubt "where the archdiocese stood in relation to the right-wing, pro-monarchist exiles versus the left-wing pro-republican partisans . . . while no friend of the left, Athenagoras did not let the Greek political conflict interfere with church life directly."[38]

Between 1942 and 1944 American military intelligence officials became concerned about the possibility of communist insurgencies throughout the Balkans that might bring the entire post-war region under Soviet influence as Axis control of the region collapsed. The alliance with Soviet Russia against the Axis did not allay anxiety among American military leaders about the fate of that region of Europe. Informal contacts with Orthodox bishops including the Albanian Fan Noli, the Serbian bishop Dionisije Milivojevich and Athenagoras competed against increasing attempts by the Soviet regime to secure, whether by threats or financial support, the subordination of the Balkan Orthodox.[39] Despite Stalin's hesitation to

36. Cited in Erickson, *Orthodox Christians in America,* 68.

37. Ferencz, *American Orthodoxy,* 143–47; Kitroeff, *Greek Orthodox Church,* 58–94.

38. Kitroeff, *Greek Orthodox Church,* 81.

39. For the Soviet attempts, see Kalkandjieva, *The Russian Orthodox Church,* 307–44; For the OSS and (later) CIA contacts with Athenagoras and the other Orthodox bishops, see U.S Central Intelligence Agency, *The Study of Foreign Political Developments in the United States.* CIA-RDP89–01258R000100010004-2,

support the communists in Greece for fear of alienating the western allies, the renewed Greek Civil War of 1946–49 confirmed Athenagoras' deepest worries and had repercussions in the United States. The settlement of refugees fleeing from the war re-intensified the determination of many to identify the Church with Greek national, cultural, and linguistic interests and to be less concerned about relations with Orthodox Christians of other national or linguistic traditions. Even before the end of World War II, Athenagoras had become alarmed at the possibility of Soviet influence in Greece itself, well-aware of the Communist Party allegiances and sentiments within Greece. His sentiments were recognized in Moscow and convinced the Kremlin that Athenagoras was little more than a puppet-operative of the United States.

Athenagoras' election as Ecumenical Patriarch in 1948 intensified Soviet Russia's anxieties because the Ecumenical Patriarch Maximos had been forced to resign. Although the details of the resignation remain unclear, "one of Maximos's biographers suggests he was forced to step down amid considerable Byzantine intrigue and controversy created by the political polarization between the West and the Soviet Union . . . Maximos had close relations with Russian Orthodoxy, and consequently he was suspected of being 'soft' toward the Soviet Union." Athenagoras, because of his American citizenship and his anti-communist convictions secured the public support of the Turkish government in Ankara.[40] But his elevation alarmed Moscow even more for now Athenagoras enjoyed a global status and a physical presence in NATO-allied Turkey. What remains unclear are Athenagoras' reactions by the early 1960s to the Metropolia's initial outreach to Moscow. The subsequent publication of the correspondence between the Ecumenical Patriarchate and Moscow shows that the former was aware of the efforts at

---

Washington, D.C.: CIA, 1944, https://www.cia.gov/readingroom/docs/CIA-RDP89-01258R000100010004-2.pdf (accessed May 10, 2019); on the Greek Civil War, C.M. Woodhouse, *The Struggle for Greece 1941–1949*, with an introduction by Richard Clogg (London: Hurst & Co., 1976; Chicago: Ivan R. Dee, 2002). Citations refer to the Ivan R. Dee edition.

40. Kitroeff, *Greek Orthodox Church*, 92, 93. On Maximos' earlier acceptability to Turks, Greeks, and Russians, but then the perception that he was insufficiently committed to defending the Ecumenical Patriarchate, see Alexis Alexandris, *The Greek Minority of Istanbul and Greek-Turkish Relations, 1918–1974* (Athens: Center for Asia Minor Studies, 1992), 237–246.

reconciliation between the Metropolia and Moscow in 1961, the formalization of negotiations in 1963, and then the abrupt cessation of progress. Soviet archives reveal that since 1945—before Athenagoras became Ecumenical Patriarch—the Soviets had begun a concerted campaign to isolate and deny the Patriarch of Constantinople's role as "first among equals."

At the Rhodes Orthodox conference of 1961 called by Athenagoras, the assembled hierarchs agreed that unanimity among themselves had to be preserved in any dealings with non-Orthodox Christians. That demand came from Moscow. It was triggered by the decision of the Vatican to invite Orthodox observers to attend the Second Vatican Council in Rome. The Vatican first approached Constantinople, recognizing that see's historic and canonical role as primate among the Orthodox churches. Moscow sent signals that it would not approve observation by the Orthodox in Rome. While the Vatican met with the Patriarchs of Alexandria, Jerusalem, Cyprus, Greece, and Antioch, Moscow's Metropolitan Nikodim informed the Romanians, Bulgarians and Polish Orthodox that Moscow would not approve sending observers.[41] Then, in a maneuver that revealed the real objective of embarrassing Constantinople, Moscow informed the Vatican that it would send its own representatives. Outflanked by Moscow, Athenagoras convened another meeting at Rhodes in 1964 where the principle of unanimity was revoked. Each Orthodox Patriarchate was declared free to deal with Rome as it saw fit.[42]

Athenagoras' and Pope Paul VI's 1965 lifting of the mutual 1054 excommunications of Rome and Constantinople further alarmed the Kremlin. In that same year the Paris Exarchate of exiled Russians that had been established in 1930 under the protection of the Ecumenical Patriarchate now surfaced again as a topic of controversy that involved the American Metropolia. Moscow's ambitions to make its influence felt even beyond the occupied nations of eastern Europe included pressure put onto the Exarchate to return to the Moscow Patriarchate. The Paris group refused. Under pressure from Moscow, Patriarch Athenagoras notified the Paris

41. That Nikodim was working with the KGB (as"Svyatoslav"), Christopher Andrew and Vasili Mitrokhin, *The Sword and the Shield: The Mitrokhim Archive and the Secret History of the KGB* (New York: Basic Books, 1999), 487.

42. Radu Bordeianu, "Orthodox Observers at the Second Vatican Council and Intra-Orthodox Dynamics," *Theological Studies* 79, no. 1 (2018): 86–106; 79, 95.

Exarchate that it must return to Moscow. Instead, the Parisian exiles pro-claimed themselves an independent archdiocese; in 1971 the Ecumenical Patriarchate accepted it back again as an Exarchate.[43]

How Soviet influence could have been exercised on an Orthodox bishop resident in a NATO-allied country (Turkey) remains unclear. Athenago-ras had declined in May 1966 to entertain the proposal from the Metropolia that it become an exarchate on the Paris model. He then encouraged the Metropolia to approach Moscow to resolve their canonical standing. A year later in June, he "instructed the Greek Orthodox archdiocese in the USA to suspend eucharistic communion with the Metropolia. One assumes that this step was taken in response to pressure from the Moscow Patriarchate."[44] At the same time, Athenagoras hoped that he could still bring the Metro-polia under his protection by creating an exarchate similar to the one that had been granted to Paris in 1930. A surviving letter from John Meyendorff to Nikodim in September 1968 may have been the spur to Moscow to pur-sue autocephaly more aggressively to prevent Athenagoras from realizing his exarchate plans.[45]

Because of the speed with which Moscow moved to grant autocephaly to the Metropolia, Athenagoras professed shock as news emerged by 1969 that the granting of a tomos from Moscow was imminent. Athenagoras' successor in America, Archbishop Iakovos, reacted negatively to the an-nouncement of the OCA's autocephaly. Despite the wording of the 1970 Tomos of Autocephaly that this was the Orthodox Church *in*—not *of* America, Iakovos pointed out the canonical danger in his May 1970 letter to Theodosius, the Patriarch of Antioch, that the OCA "will seek the grad-ual coercion of others, or the actual subjection to them of all Orthodox churches in America when they believe [this to be] possible"[46] Iakovos was

43. Serge Keleher, "Orthodox Rivalry in the Twentieth Century: Moscow versus Constantinople," *Religion, State & Society* 25, no. 2 (1997): 125–137, 132.

44. Keleher, "Orthodox Rivalry," 133.

45. The letter is cited in Andrey Kostryukov, "Granting of Autocephaly to Orthodox Church in America in the Light of the Documents of Church Archives," *St. Tikhons University Review* 70, no. 3 (June 2016): 93–103, at 101n37, https://www.researchgate.net/publication/304583171. I thank Scott Kenworthy for bringing this to my attention.

46. Cited by Jillions, "The Tomos of Autocephaly: Forty-Six Years Later;" for this and the correspondence and other documents among the patriarchs and other

aware that far from reconciling all Russian and Eastern European Slavic Christian arrivals in North America under an autocephalous OCA, the tomos instead guaranteed continued patriarchal presence, the hostility of the exiles who had created a Russian Church Outside Russia, and the presence of an OCA whose claims to autocephaly the Kremlin knew would be rejected by Constantinople.[47]

Between 1970 and 1996, tensions escalated between Constantinople and Moscow to such an extent that by 1996 Moscow had "ceased commemorating the ecumenical patriarch of Constantinople in the diptychs." The more aggressive members of the Moscow Patriarchate "are suggesting that the time has come for Moscow finally to gain the quasi-universal primacy of the Orthodox world . . . and that the 'Third Rome' (Moscow) should replace 'New Rome' (Constantinople)."[48] The claim of Moscow to be the "Third Rome"—though never officially adopted or accepted by either the Holy Synod nor the subsequently restored Patriarchate of Moscow—nonetheless found its way into the disputes over the rights of local parishes to align themselves more closely with Moscow—or distance themselves from it—within a few years' of the former Metropolia's disputed claim to be an autocephalous church.

The venerable parish of St. Basil, founded in 1904 was incorporated in 1924 in Simpson, Pennsylvania. The Pennsylvania Court of Common Pleas of Lackawanna County issued an equity decree in 1927 that vested the church property "solely in the name of the corporate congregation." Only in 1956 did this parish recognize a bishop, deciding to affiliate itself with the Metropolia. The Patriarchal Church of Moscow attempted to block this

---

parties, see the special issue of *St. Vladimir's Theological Quarterly*: Alexander Schmemann, ed., "Autocephaly in the Orthodox Church in America," special issue, *St. Vladimir' Theological Quarterly* 15, nos.1–2 (1971). Many of the materials have been collected in Ionut-Alexandru Tudorie, ed., *The Time Has Come: Debates over the OCA Autocephaly Reflected in St. Vladimir's Quarterly* (Yonkers, NY: St. Vladimir's Seminary Press, 2020).

47. Kostryukov argues (unconvincingly) that ridding the Moscow Patriarchate of insolvent parishes played a role in the decision since it had first considered abolishing its American exarchate in 1958 but kept parishes without providing financial support. Had this been a major consideration, the Patriarchal parishes should have been ordered to join the OCA.

48. Serge Keleher, "Orthodox Rivalry," 135.

decision but lost the case. But by 1982, as the now-named OCA voted to adopt the Western or Gregorian calendar, St. Basil, in accord with a majority vote of its members, chose to leave the OCA and affiliate itself with the Russian Church Outside Russia (ROCOR). Attempts by the OCA to block this decision—arguing that the "property of St. Basil's was held by the congregation in trust for the church" (meaning the OCA) failed to convince the courts. "Right to possession" had always rested with the congregation and because no doctrinal issue was involved here, the courts relied on a precedent already set in a dispute between the *Presbytery of Beaver-Butler of the United Presbyterian Church in the United States v. Middlesex Presbyterian Church* 507 Pa. 255 (1985). That decision laid down the principle that when property disputes were at stake, Pennsylvania's courts had to rely upon "the same principles of law as would be applied to non-religious associations. This so-called 'neutral principles' approach represents the most current view of the U.S. Supreme Court as well as to what arguments courts may entertain in light of the First Amendment when they are asked to settle property disputes between members of a religious association. See *Jones v. Wolf,* 443 U.S. 595 (1979)."[49]

The same appeal to the rights of the congregation against those asserted by hierarchs and the church body they represented allowed St. John the Baptist Russian Orthodox Church in Mayfield, Pennsylvania, founded in 1907, to leave the OCA for ROCOR in 1982. The OCA attempted to block the decision and lost on the same grounds. The St. John's parish letter of 1951 that had acknowledged the spiritual authority of the then-Metropolitan Leonty Turkevich nevertheless retained "all property in the corporate name," a position reiterated in parish bylaws in 1962. The conflict between the rights of an American hierarchy and those claimed by American parishes over property relied on principles of American law and the long-cherished defense of property rights.[50]

49. For the cases here and in the next note, see United Judicial System of Pa: https://www.pacourts.us>courts>commonwealth-court. Commonwealth Court of Pennsylvania No. 78 T.D. 1985 1986. PA. 43194; 513 A. 2d 541, 99 Pa. Commw. 264 *Joseph Mikilak Et Al. v. Orthodox Church of America Et Al.* (07/29/86), 273.

50. Commonwealth Court of Pennsylvania No. 1702 C.D. 1986 1988 PA. 40961; 538 A.2d 632, 114 Pa. Commw. 176 *Orthodox Church America Et Al.v Thomas Pavuk Et AL* (03/01/88), 23, 35.

Few members of the OCA as it emerged between 1970 and the 1990s would have anticipated that it would not be clashes over property rights of parishes that would roil the waters within their jurisdiction. Rather, even as the OCA faced non-recognition by many Orthodox patriarchates, the question arose as to whether one bishop, or a consensus of all the bishops claiming the right to be consulted and give their opinions on disputed matters, defined the understanding of authority in the Orthodox Church in America. The eruption of financial scandal and accusations of malfeasance against the Chancellor and the bishops of this jurisdiction came to a head by 1996. In the turmoil that ensued, an unlikely candidate for the role of Metropolitan Primate of the OCA emerged in the person of the young convert James Paffhausen, who took, at the time of his monastic tonsure in 1994, the name Jonah. Over the course of the next decade, Father Jonah helped establish a monastery that eventually found its home in Manton, California. In recognition of his labors in founding mission parishes and his role as abbot of the Manton monastery, he was sent to the OCA's Diocese of the South where in November 2008 he became the auxiliary Bishop of Fort Worth.

The new bishop enjoyed no time in his diocese before being elected eleven days later to the office of Metropolitan Primate at the OCA's All-American Council held in Pittsburgh, Pennsylvania. Most observers have concluded that the new Metropolitan was chosen because he was not implicated in the financial scandal.[51] He was also a fresh and inspiring voice, and his elevation garnered support not only from many clergy and laity, but also from the Holy Synod of Bishops. The hierarchs believed that Bishop Jonah could help the OCA put behind it the recent troubled times and enter a new and hopeful phase in its history. What emerged instead in his short tenure as Metropolitan (2008–2012), however, was the issues of rights, privileges, honor, and power. In his remarks to the All-American Council before his election as Metropolitan, Bishop Jonah had faulted the bishops for authoritarian behavior that showed no awareness of the values of accountability to the whole Church. By 2012, however, in his address

51. The narrative below relies upon my conversations with the Very Reverend John Jillions, who served as Chancellor during Metropolitan Jonah's tenure; the recollections of the canonist and present Chancellor, the Very Reverend Alexander Rentel; and the sources in the following note. . (Conversations and e-mail exchanges with the author, April 2–10 April 2019.)

to the All-American Council held in Seattle, the Metropolitan admitted that he himself had fallen into the very authoritarian behavior he had criticized at the time of his election. This admission stood at the center of the OCA's statement that he had made a "questionable, unilateral decision" that violated the obligation of the Metropolitan to proceed only in consultation with the other bishops of the Church.[52]

The initial enthusiasm that had surrounded Metropolitan Jonah's election began to change to anxiety by 2011. Administrative concerns morphed into a canonical crisis. The young metropolitan showed little appetite for the boring details of administration, was very often absent from the OCA's headquarters; demonstrated an inclination toward regarding the OCA as part of the Russian diaspora and cultural world and showed an inability to follow through on stated policies to such a degree that the other bishops of the Holy Synod began to lose confidence in his ability to lead. His Chancellor asked for and received a blessing to contact each member of the Synod individually and as a result heard of their anxieties about the decline of their fraternal relationship with Metropolitan Jonah. They declared themselves alarmed that he was acting unilaterally, without consulting his brother bishops, or would act in direct contradiction of decisions they had taken together as a Synod. By 2012 the level of concern had deepened to such a degree that some insisted that the metropolitan seek professional counselling. At first he agreed, as he had told the All American Council in November 2011, recognizing that there had been a serious break in relations with the other bishops. But when he later refused to do this, it became clear both to Metropolitan Jonah and to the Holy Synod that his only other option was to resign his office, which he volunteered to do.

52. Archival sources surrounding this controversy remain inaccessible to researchers. We have summarized what can be gleaned from the public statements available at: Orthodox Church of America, "His Grace Bishop Jonah Addresses Questions and Concerns," November 11, 2008, https://oca.org/holy-synod /statements/metropolitan-jonah/jonah-15aac-qna; the Holy Synod of the Orthodox Church in America, "Statement from the Holy Synod Regarding the Resignation of Metropolitan Jonah," July 16, 2012, https://web.archive.org/web/20130312214247 /http://oca.org/PDF/NEWS/2012/2012-0716-holy-synod-statement.pdf; and the recollections of the OCA canonist and chancellor the Very Reverend Alexander Rentel and the former Chancellor, the Very Reverend John Jillions (personal communication to the author, March–April, 2019).

The OCA crisis over the rights of bishops would now also engulf the Greek Orthodox Archdiocese and subsequently, the Antiochian Orthodox Christian Archdiocese. In all three instances, the question of the rights, privileges, and obligations of a synod of bishops versus those of a singular figure of episcopal authority once again focused the attention of the Orthodox on this troublesome issue. The OCA disputes cannot accurately be reduced to a supposed conflict between American standards of procedure and rights versus those of an ancient canonical tradition. Yet some did point out that increasingly Metropolitan Jonah had turned for mentorship to the Moscow Patriarch's Metropolitan Hilarion Alfeyev. In the latter's foreword to the monograph that detailed the work of the 1917–18 Council, Hilarion cautiously endorsed its goals by admitting that "it is the task of the Russian Church to continue the reflections begun by the Council of Moscow. . . ." In actual practice, the monarchical rule of a patriarch—the option favored by the patriarchists at that council—remained the model Hilarion himself appears to favor, one that characterizes the Moscow Patriarchate in the twenty-first century.[53]

Following the resignation of Metropolitan Jonah on July 6, 2012 and the election of Metropolitan Tikhon (Mollard) on November 13, 2012, the Holy Synod of the OCA at its meeting in Detroit three years later in October 2015 set up "general procedural standards" for spiritual courts following the Atlanta Georgia All American Council's approval to move to more permanent general rules for canonical procedure. Article XV clearly stipulates that all members of the OCA are entitled to "canonical process" and have "legitimate rights" according to the "norm of law" (although presumably meaning the canons of the Church, not provisions of due process

53. Hilarion Alfeyev, "Forward to the French Edition," in Destivelle, *The Moscow Council*, xi; on the "patriarchists", 76–93. Alfeyev's preference for a monarchic role for each autocephalous Patriarch emerges in his interpretation of the history of the governance structures of the Church. See Hilarion Alfeyev, *Orthodox Christianity Volume I: The History and Canonical Structure of the Orthodox Church* (Yonkers, NY: St. Vladimir's Seminary Press, 2011) 325–44. For an alternative reading that does not address the tension between synodality and Patriarchal *presbeia*, see Lewis Patsavos, "The Primacy of the See of Constantinople in Theory and Practice," *Panorthodox Synod*, September 13, 2018, https://panorthodoxcemes.blogspot.com/2018/09/the-primacy-of-see-of-constantinople-in.html (accessed May 30, 2019).

taken from Anglo-American civil law). A provision for ecclesiastical courts already existed in earlier OCA statutes, but the aim of the revisions under Article XV focused on the right of all to due canonical process in ecclesiastical courts. The revisions also allowed the bishops to develop detailed church court procedures outside the less flexible framework of an All American Council. Not everyone agreed with this revision since some believed that the protection of rights should be provided for not in the form of diocesan discretion over procedures, but uniformly in the statute itself, whose revision would have required the action of an All American Council.[54] The resignation of Metropolitan Jonah appeared, at first glance, to reaffirm the Orthodox Church in America's determination to govern itself based on the principles laid down (but never fully implemented) at the 1917–18 Moscow Council. Jonah's resignation represented a victory of sorts for those in the OCA who were determined that this Orthodox Church be thought of and governed not as part of some larger Russian world but as the American realization of the interrupted Moscow Council's model for church governance based on the principle of sobornost. Yet events would prove almost immediately that opposition to the rights of the American Orthodox to govern themselves would continue both within the ranks of the OCA, and more ominously, within the two other major "jurisdictions" among the Eastern Orthodox in North America, the Greek Archdiocese of North America, and the Antiochian Orthodox Christian Archdiocese. Both jurisdictions shared a Byzantine-era heritage of liturgical worship styles, sometimes tense relationships between Greek and Arab speakers, but most importantly, a move toward self-determination in the 1990s that suffered sharp reversal by the second decade of the twenty-first century.

54. For the Statute and the Resolution, see Orthodox Church in America, "The Statute of the Orthodox Church in America: Article XV, Ecclesiastical Courts," https://www.oca.org/statute/article-xv (accessed July 25, 2016); "Resolution of the Holy Synod on Canonical Procedures for Church Courts," October 21, 2015, https://oca.org/holy-synod/statements/holy-synod/resolution-of-the-holy-synod -of-the-orthodox-church-in-america.

5

"GREEK" NORTH AMERICAN ORTHODOX RIGHTS

The addition of the word "Greek" to Orthodox Church continues to confuse non-Orthodox—and with good reason. On one hand, the term Greek Orthodox can correctly designate Orthodox Christians whose everyday speech or citizenship in the republic of Greece accurately reflects who they are. But as alert readers by now will also have recognized, the term has a broader meaning as well. It signals those Orthodox whose worship rituals, music, and customs find their roots in the many peoples, cultures, and languages of the Eastern Roman Empire. Thus, not only Greek speakers, but those who spoke and read Syriac, then Arabic, may also be understood to be Greek Orthodox. Even Armenians, Georgians, and Copts share (on a more limited basis) an indebtedness to the Greek Old and New Testaments and the writings in the Greek language of many early church fathers. It is this second, broader understanding of Greek Orthodox that concerns us here.

The resignation of Metropolitan Jonah of the Orthodox Church in America occurred only 13 years after a similar resignation had occurred within the Greek Archdiocese of North America. On August 19, 1999, Greek Orthodox Archbishop of America Spyridon Papageorgiou ended what one historian described as "a traumatic event in the life of Orthodox America. Unquestionably, it will go down in the collective memory as the most dramatic dispute in the Greek Archdiocese since the 1920s." The controversy caught the attention of non-Orthodox journalists and exemplified the first, extensive use of social media, blogs, and websites—the growing new form for freedom of opinion and expression—that further alarmed the most tradition-minded among hierarchs both in America and abroad.[1] But the events of the late 1990s had their roots in a growing estrangement between the Ecumenical Patriarchate and Archbishop Iakovos that had begun in the 1970s. Between 1997 and 1999 a clash between a claim of faculty rights at Hellenic College/ Holy Cross Greek Orthodox School of Theology and the demand of Archbishop Spyridon and his supporters for obedience from the administration and faculty of the institution had led to the Archbishop's dismissal of four of the seventeen members of the faculty. The controversy caught the attention of non-Orthodox publications, notably the *Chronicle of Higher Education*.[2] Both the Archbishop and his opponents had recourse to civil courts in the course of the dispute, the Attorney General of Massachusetts being approached by those who pointed out that in firing the faculty the Archbishop bypassed the bylaws of the institution and did not consult the Board of Visitors. In turn, as attacks mounted (predominantly from the newly formed groups *Voithia* and Greek Orthodox American Leaders (GOAL)), Archbishop Spyridon in turn used the Federal courts in an attempt to block GOAL's use of the Archdiocesan mailing list to continue its campaign against him. For his part, the Archbishop believed he was operating within his rights, privileges, and duties as Archbishop; his opponents just as firmly believed he showed no understanding of American constitutional and legal procedures crafted to ensure the protection of faculty in freely expressing opinion and raising controversial questions in the course of their duties as qualified teachers in an Orthodox institution of higher learning.

1. What follows here depends on my attempt to reconcile the account provided in Alexander Kitroeff, *Greek Orthodox Church in America: A Modern History* (Ithaca: Cornell University Press), 2020, 115–227 and personal conversations and e-mails with the Reverend Anton Vrame and Professor Andrew Walsh as well as with Walsh's articles "Unexpected Consequences: The Revolt Against Archbishop Spyridon in the Greek Orthodox Archdiocese of America, 1996–1999," in *One Calling in Christ: The Laity in the Orthodox Church*, ed. Anton Vrame (Berkeley, CA: InterOrthodox Press, 2005), 57–74; Walsh, "Those Revolting Greeks," *Religion in the News* 2, no. 3 (September 1, 1999), http://www2.trincoll.edu/csrpl /RINVol2No3/Revolting%20Greeks.htm.

2. Kit Lively, "Faculty Firings Throw a Greek Orthodox College Into Turmoil," *Chronicle of Higher Education*, July 18, 1997; Beth McMurtrie, "Hellenic College Reinstates 4 Professors in Wake of Archbishop's Resignation," *Chronicle of Higher Education*, September 10, 1999.

In the end, the alienation of the other Greek Orthodox bishops who believed that Spyridon was violating their episcopal rights proved fatal to his tenure as Archbishop. But the bishops did not take the lead in opposing the removal of Iakovos and the tightening of control over the Archdiocese by the Patriarch of Constantinople. Instead, both lay and clergy speakers at the Archdiocesan Council meeting in October articulated their concerns. The speakers included Yorka Linakis, a former member of the New York State Supreme Court, the attorney John Angelis of Kentucky, and the priest Thomas Paris, who all warned the visiting patriarchal delegation of how unaware Constantinople appeared to be about the realities of Orthodox life in North America. As the Greek American historian Kitroeff concluded, "Father Paris's tone and words were unprecedented in high-level meetings of the archdiocese and showed how wide the rift had grown between many leading members of the Greek Orthodox Church in America and the Patriarchate of Constantinople."[3] Warned by accrediting agencies regarding the dismissal of an administrator and trustee by the Archbishop, Spyridon ordered an amendment to the bylaws that guaranteed that he, "by virtue of his archiepiscopal office, is the highest, canonical, ecclesiastical and spiritual authority of the Institution." But it was not faculty or lay protest, but the opposition of the other bishops that made the difference because the Archdiocesan Charter of 1977 had stipulated that when the Archbishop did act as the "highest canonical, ecclesiastical, and spiritual authority" of the school, he did so only with the advice and consent of the entire episcopal assembly.[4]

The Archbishop did not lack supporters among the clergy and laity. That support, however, varied in terms of geographic region with (for example) strong backing emerging in Florida where Spyridon was well known and had family members. By contrast, his opponents were especially prominent in the Chicago area, a fact that was taken up in detail by writers reporting the controversy for readers of the *Chicago Tribune*.[5] The former acting

3. Kitroeff, *Greek Orthodox Church*, 228–236, at 235–6.

4. See Stephen P. Angelides, "Seminary Scheme gives Spyridon autocratic authority," *Voithia*, March 27, 1999, http://www.archbishopspyridon.gr/spyridon_1999/voith_angelides_27mar99.html.

5. Steve Kloehn, "Feud Forces Out America's Greek Orthodox Leader," *Chicago Tribune*, August 20, 1999, https://www.chicagotribune.com/news/ct-xpm-1999-08-20-9908200104-story.html.

director of finance for the Greek Archdiocese, George Chelpon, made clear in his deposition to the Supreme Court of the State of New York that contrary to accusations of financial mismanagement, the Archbishop had improved procedures that guaranteed more accountability and transparency in the handling of archdiocesan finances.[6]

Behind this uproar loomed the fate of Spyridon's predecessor, the much-beloved Archbishop Iakovos who had been forced in 1996 to resign as Archbishop by the Ecumenical Patriarch Bartholomew. Spyridon's mandate—to attempt to govern an archdiocese deeply resentful of that forced retirement—led some to conclude that his tenure was fated from the outset. In his own reflections on the controversy, the Archbishop continued to articulate his worries. His choice of terms revealed how much the original Protestant "social ethos" into which Orthodox Christians had entered in the nineteenth century still haunted the nightmares of Orthodox hierarchs. Spyridon was convinced that the Archdiocese had become infected by American values he identified with Protestantism and that what was at stake was the privilege, right, and responsibility of the Ecumenical Patriarch over the Greek Archdiocese. The Archbishop's conclusion proved to be prophetic since Patriarch Bartholomew decided to revoke the 1977 charter and in the 2003 version advanced the claim of the Ecumenical Patriarch that he alone was the sole interpreter of the Greek Archdiocese's charter. The claim made by the Ecumenical Patriarchate in 2003 reflected a growing unease among other Orthodox hierarchs in traditional Orthodox lands with what they regarded as the over-indulgence on the part of American bishops of lay and clergy insistence upon participation in decisions of how the Orthodox should best be governed in North America through open and free expressions of opinion and assessment. The fear of the Ecumenical Patriarchate that it was losing control over the Greek Archdiocese in North America remains the best explanation of what happened to the Greek Archdiocese between the emergence of the Orthodox Church in America and the subsequent controversies over the charter/constitution of the Greek Archdiocese.

Article 6 of the 2003 "Charter of the Greek Orthodox Archdiocese of America" addresses the "Responsibilities and Rights of the Archbishop."

6. Greek Orthodox Stewards of America, "Affidavit of George Chelpon filed in Court by Archdiocese in Suit Brought by Simos C. Dimas," June 10, 1999, http://www.archbishopspyridon.gr/spyridon_1999/gosa_chelpon_10jun99.html.

Article 7 does the same for the Metropolitans. In Article 9 regarding Spiritual Courts the "operating procedures" pay no attention to secular law but only to those "Regulations hereafter promulgated by the Eparchial Synod and approved by the Ecumenical Patriarchate." Clergy under Article 16 can be transferred because such decisions remain "the exclusive right and privilege" of the hierarchs.[7] But even the right of Greek Americans to submit names to the Ecumenical Patriarchate for consideration in the selection of a new Metropolitan proved to be elusive. In 2017 the Holy Eparchial Synod of the GOA would decide to send the Patriarchate the name of Bishop Sevastianos of Zela as the new Metropolitan of Chicago. At the last minute, however, the Ecumenical Patriarch cancelled the election and in the ensuing controversy between the GOA and the Patriarchate revealed once again the Patriarch's insistence that he alone possesses the right to interpret the Archdiocese's charter as he sees fit.[8]

By 2010, the Holy Eparchial Synod of the GOA reported that it had "finalized the text on Regulations for Spiritual Courts." By 2014 those regulations were published and under Article 3 the "Responsibilities and Rights of the Archbishop" received primary attention. In Part Four, under "Dispute Resolution Procedures" readers were directed to an Addendum B where "Spiritual Court Proceedings" began with the statement that "Nothing herein shall limit or prohibit a Hierarch or the Eparchial Synod, in his/its sole discretion, from convening a Spiritual Court(s), for any reason, in accordance with the Holy Canons and Traditions of the Church and the provisions of the Charter. Nothing in these Dispute Resolution Procedures shall be deemed to affect, in any way, the jurisdiction or actions of a Spiritual

7. For the charters and regulations of the Greek Archdiocese see: Greek Orthodox Archdiocese of America, "Official Charter of the Archdiocese," January 18, 2003. https://www.goarch.org/documents/charter. For protests against the charter and the perception that it insufficiently protected the right of the archdiocese to have its election of a future metropolitan affirmed by Constantinople, see Sophia A. Niarchos, "Patriarchate-Granted Charter and New Regulations Among Issues at Clergy-Laity Congress," *Greek News*, July 26, 2004. https://www.greeknewsonline.com/patriarchate-granted-charter-and-new-regulations-among-issues-at-clergy-laity/ (accessed May 10, 2018).

8. Theodoros Kalmoukos, "Election of Metropolitan of Chicago Canceled," *Orthodox Christian Laity*, July 13, 2017. https://ocl.org/election-metropolitan-chicago-canceled/.

Court." Priests whose service "is interrupted for any reason" and who are not reassigned were deemed to "have the right to request that the matter be heard by the Synodal Committee on Clergy Affairs." But the Rules of Procedure stipulated that "Formal rules of secular courts shall not apply" in dispute resolutions. Only the Eparchial Synod, a hierarch, or the chancellor possesses the right to initiate a review or appeal of a dispute. Moreover, "no formal rules of evidence shall apply to these Dispute Resolution Procedures."[9]

The Arabic-speaking American Eastern Orthodox Christians had over time become aligned both with the autocephaly objective of the new Orthodox Church in America and with the vision of Metropolitan Iakovos for a Greek Archdiocesan charter that he had hoped "would make the Greek Orthodox Church more attractive to the faithful by providing more local decision making and allowing the church to seek to attract all those of Eastern Orthodox faith in the Americas."[10] Whatever the hopes that had been raised by the 1977 charter were dashed in the 1990s. In that reversal, the Antiochian Orthodox Christian Archdiocese played an unexpected, if major role.

The old relationship between the Metropolia and Arabic-speaking Americans had improved dramatically by the 1950s after the disastrous collapse of the episcopacy of Aftimios Ofiesh in the 1930s, the man who had been chosen as successor to Bishop Raphael Hawaweeny of Brooklyn. Hawaweeny had been brought to the United States as a priest under the Russian Holy Synod to minister to Arabic-speaking parishes that were part of the Russian mission. Arabic-speaking parishes under the Russian-approved bishop Ofiesh remained briefly with the Russians, then effectively became self-governing. With Ofiesh's decision in 1933 to marry and leave the Church, the Russian Metropolia issued a canonical release to the remaining pro-Russian parishes to the jurisdiction of the Patriarch of Antioch directed to Bishop Emmanuel Abo-Hatab, one of two bishops Ofiesh had ordained in 1927—Sophronios Bashara for a diocese of Los Angeles and Abo-Hatab for the diocese of Montreal.[11]

9. "https://www.goarch.org.documents/Regulations"https://www.goarch.org .documents/Regulations. See Addendum B-4 Dispute Resolutions Procedures, Spiritual Court Proceedings.

10. Kitroeff, *Greek Orthodox Church*, 184.

11. This and the following paragraph summarize Constantine Nasr, *Antony Bashir: Metropolitan & Missionary* (Yonkers, NY: St. Vladimir's Seminary Press,

Those Arabic-speaking parishes who were determined to operate directly under the Patriarchate of Antioch were able to achieve their objective when Patriarch Gregory Haddad chose Archimandrite Victor Abou-Assaley to be the leader of the Antiochian Orthodox Church in North America. The conditions within the Patriarchate of Antioch itself at the time were nearly as chaotic as those in North America. Patriarch Gregory died in December 1928 and two rival patriarchs were elected, Metropolitan Arsenius (Haddad) of Latakia, and Metropolitan Alexander (Tahan).[12] Internal rivalries and disagreements within the Synod in Damascus would characterize the next 40 years of that patriarchate's history, directly affecting the Arabic Orthodox communities in North America. A young priest named Antony Bashir was called by Archbishop Victor to work with him, but Victor died in 1934 after only a year as Metropolitan. Bashir succeeded Victor as vicar of the Syrian Orthodox Archdiocese. With Metropolitan Theodosius representing the (now recognized) Patriarch of Antioch Alexander III, an election took place in 1935 that resulted in Antony Bashir becoming Victor's successor. Father Samuel David had been promised the post of auxiliary to Antony but then the patriarchate reversed itself and blocked his ordination. David then sought and obtained ordination by three Russian bishops, Adam Phillipovsky of Philadelphia, Arseny Chuhovits of Detroit, and Leonty Turkevich of Chicago—without the blessing of their own Metropolitan Theophilus or that of the Patriarch of Antioch. The same day David was ordained, in New York Bashir was ordained archbishop of the Archdiocese of New York and all North America by the patriarchal representative Metropolitan Theodosius and Archbishop Vitaly of the Russian Orthodox Church. The Russians in America repudiated the ordination of David and insisted that the question of legitimate ordination belonged to the Patriarch of Antioch. The exiled Russian Synod of Bishops in Serbia at Sremsky Karlovtsy claimed the authority over Russian clergy outside Russia. With the support of Alexander of Antioch and of Bashir, it nullified the ordination and excommunicated David. Rehabilitated in 1939, David was

---

2012), 13–18; 37–92. See also Sean J. La Bat, "The Holy Catholic and Apostolic Church in North America, 1927–1934, A Case Study in North American Missions," (M.Div. thesis, St. Vladimir's Orthodox Theological Seminary, 1995).

12. On Patriarch Alexander's career, see "Patriarch Alexander III (Tahan)," *Canadian Orthodox History Project*, February 27, 2021, https://orthodoxcanada .ca/Patriarch_Alexander_III_(Tahan).

given the title of archbishop and Antony that of metropolitan. Political factionalism within the Synod of Damascus continued to produce decisions favoring Bashir at some points, and David at others. The brief period of peace in the late 1950s shattered at the death of Samuel David and continued division intensified between Bashir and the newly consecrated bishop for Toledo, Michael Shaheen. This split among the Arabic speakers and the resulting confusion created about a dozen parishes who formed the Archdiocese of Toledo under Shaheen while Bashir presided as the Metropolitan of New York. Shaheen served as Archbishop of Toledo for 13 years until a reconciliation with New York was effected by Antony Bashir's successor, Metropolitan Philip Saliba, who accepted Shaheen as auxiliary archbishop in 1975—five years after the OCA's reception of the 1970 Tomos of Autocephaly from Moscow.

The response of the Arabic-Orthodox to the OCA's tomos reflected the influence exercised by Antony Bashir on Orthodox life in the United States. Bashir in 1955 began sending seminarians to St. Vladimir's Orthodox Theological Seminary and an Antiochian convert priest Paul Schneirla began teaching Old Testament at that institution that owed its profile to a faculty drawn from the Paris Institute of St. Sergius. In his recollections of Bashir, Alexander Schmemann, who labored for the Metropolia with Moscow, noted Bashir's support for a non-ethnic school that would promote the emergence of an American Orthodox Church. In its multilinguistic and cultural composition and governance structure, this Church would be unique among the Orthodox worldwide. It was Bashir whom Schmemann credited with the organization of the Standing Conference of Orthodox Bishops. Schmemann's recollection of Bashir emphasized that St. Vladimir's was supposed to function as "the nucleus of an American orthodox reality." And for Bashir, "St. Vladimir's was not a Russian Seminary. He never used the term 'Russian Seminary' when referring to St Vladimir's; he was always clear about it."[13]

The Antiochian Patriarchate and its American Archdiocese reacted to the 1970 Tomos with two very different, but related responses. Metropolitan Philip Saliba had come to the United States as a deacon at the invitation of Archbishop Samuel David, not Antony Bashir. But Saliba, supporter of the use of English in liturgical services, was a poor candidate for the

13. Nasr, *Antony Bashir*, 99, 129.

parishes that formed the Toledo Archdiocese. Sent by Bishop David to the Greek Archdiocese's Holy Cross Greek Orthodox School of Theology in Boston, Saliba and his fellow Toledo Antiochian Emile Hanna were at first instructed in English. At the end of their first year they were dismayed to learn that English-language instruction was to be discontinued. All classes would be conducted in Greek. All of Antony Bashir's students left Boston. Saliba and Hanna wanted to follow them to St. Vladimir's Seminary but Samuel David informed his two seminarians that they could return to Boston, repatriate themselves to Lebanon and Syria, or forego seminary training and be ordained parish priests immediately. Rejecting all three options, Saliba found work, earned his undergraduate degree in history at Wayne State University, and only in 1959 was ordained a priest by Metropolitan Antony Bashir before having completed all of the necessary degree requirements for a master's of divinity degree. Bashir then fulfilled Saliba's wishes and sent him to St Vladimir's, where he began his relationship with the renowned theologians Alexander Schmemann, John Meyendorff, and Thomas Hopko all of whom had taught, or been shaped by the European Exarchate's St. Sergius Institute in Paris.[14]

From the time of his student days at St Vladimir's Saliba supported the seminary, not only by continuing to send students as Bashir had done, but also by giving additional money. From Paul Meyendorff's reading of his father John Meyendorff's papers, it is clear that Philip knew of the Metropolia's negotiations with Moscow, as did Archbishop Iakovos of the Greek Archdiocese. Both served as the vice chair and chair respectively of the Standing Conference of Orthodox Bishops and both had been briefed about what was taking place.[15] The announcement of the granting of the tomos occurred on April 10, 1970. It took more than a year for the Patriarchate of Antioch to issue a letter of non-recognition—in contrast to the Patriarch of Alexandria's refusal in December 1970, the Patriarch of Jerusalem's decree of non-recognition in March 1971 that echoed the more extensive denunciation of the autonomous Church of Greece. Not until

14. Metropolitan Philip's recollections in an interview included in Nasr, *Antony Bashir*, 157–60.

15. Paul Meyendorff, "Fr. John Meyendorff and the Autocephaly of the OCA," *St. Vladimir's Theological Quarterly* 54, nos. 3–4 (2010): 441–448, https://churchmotherofgod.org/salvation-history/new-life-church-history/6308-fr-john-meyendorff-and-the-autocephaly-of-the-oca.html.

July 1971 did Antioch issue a short and irenic statement. The reason for the delay was the unexpected death of the Antiochian Patriarch Theodosius in September 1970. Metropolitan Philip had already signaled at the General Assembly of the 24th Annual Convention of his archdiocese in Miami in 1969 that he opposed an ethnic identity for his archdiocese. He insisted on dropping the word "Syrian" from the title of the archdiocese and called for the founding of an autocephalous Orthodox Church at the earliest opportunity. The aging and ill Patriarch Theodosius VI was aware of Metropolitan Philip's intentions. Theodosius had deferred to the wishes of the American participants in the Special General Assembly that had met in March 1966 in New York and voted for Saliba to succeed Bashir as metropolitan.[16]

Archimandrite Ellis Khouri was sent to the patriarchate to head the American archdiocesan representatives at the meeting of the Holy Synod. Khouri met with Patriarch Theodosius, the two consulted, and Theodosius convened the synod at the Monastery of the Prophet Elias. Despite a determined campaign on the part of five bishops within the Synod of Damascus to reject the legality of the American Special Assembly and any role played by the laity in the selection of bishops, Theodosius not only prevailed over them at that meeting but in his last four years of life appointed a new group of metropolitans to break the political machinations that had disturbed the meetings of the Synod since the 1930s. By the summer of 1970, however, the patriarch was quite ill. As the Holy Synod met in September of 1970—five months after the granting of the Tomos by Moscow and four months after his receipt of the alarmed letter from Archbishop Iakovos about the OCA—Theodosius died. The new patriarch, Elias IV of Aleppo, joined the Patriarchs of Alexandria and Jerusalem in refusing recognition of the

16. For the rejections of the OCA's autocephaly, Panagiotis Trempelas, *The Autocephaly of the Metropolia in America* (Brookline, MA: Holy Cross School of Theology Press, 1974), 45–67. On the divisions within the Synod of Damascus and Theodosios' critical role in affirming the American Special General Assembly and support for Philip, see Antony Gabriel, "A Retrospective: One Hundred Years of Antiochian Orthodoxy in North America," in *The First One Hundred Years: A Centennial Anthology Celebrating Antiochian Orthodoxy in North America*, foreword by the Most Reverend Metropolitan Philip, ed. George S. Corey, et al. (Englewood, NJ: Antakya Press, 1995), 243–291; at 269–275.

OCA's autocephaly. In part, this decision reflected the difference in the educational backgrounds, experiences, and world views of the two men.

Theodosius had been born in the region of Mt. Lebanon and then lived in Beirut where he attended the École des Trois Docteurs before doing further study in Damascus. Joining the teaching faculty at the Balamand Monastery in Lebanon, he was sent to northern Iraq, learned Turkish, then returned to be then sent to Constantinople where he became fluent in Greek. This exposure to the influence of the French in Lebanon, and to the variety of contexts in which Orthodox Christianity survived in the Middle East made the cosmopolitan and pro-Western Theodosius aware of the challenge the United States posed as a land of immigrants and multiple cultures and histories.

Metropolitan Elias by contrast, had been born in Lebanon and his entire education took place in the Middle East with the single and important exception of time spent at the Ecumenical Patriarchate's theological school on the island of Halki near Istanbul in 1939. Elias referred to the members of his patriarchate as Arab Christians and by 1974 became a participant in the Organization of Islamic Cooperation. He became known as the "Patriarch of the Arabs," an identity given him by King Faisal of Saudi Arabia. His short reign of only nine years was preoccupied with the deteriorating political conditions in the Middle East and in building the Balamand Theological School of St John of Damascus. He also inherited the continuing North American split between Toledo and New York. It would take another five years before that schism was resolved and it was that success that brought Elias to the United States for a visit in 1977 just two years before his sudden death. Elias intended to solidify and perpetuate a unified Arab diaspora in North America that had not existed since the death of Raphael Hawaweeny in 1915. The OCA's autocephaly threatened to undermine that goal given the long-standing tensions between the pro-Antioch and pro-Russian Arab parishes. In his letter announcing to Moscow that he would not officially recognize the OCA, Elias noted that he had been visited by "a bishop" and Alexander Schmemann. It appeared to him logical that an American church would eventually emerge because the Arab Christians born in the United States had "forgotten the language of their fathers." The patriarchate agreed that "only the autocephalous Churches in consultation and agreement can proclaim an 'Autocephalous Church in America' and on the basis of this stand we regulate our ecclesiastical relations."[17] Elias' perspective remained that of someone who still understood the North American Archdiocese in linguistic-ethnic terms, even while lamenting the vanishing of Arabic from the reality of everyday life there. A curious note appeared in the February 11, 1972 issue of the *Religious News Service* purporting to be from someone who claimed that Elias' letter did not represent the position of his own synod.[18]

No written documentation survives in the Antiochian Archdiocesan archives of how Metropolitan Philip Saliba reacted or responded to the issuing of the OCA's Tomos of Autocephaly. No letters, cables, or minutes of meetings reveal how he viewed the eventual non-recognition of the OCA's autocephaly when that was issued by the new Patriarch Elias in July, 1971. Yet Saliba did not order the patriarchal decision to be read in the parishes of the archdiocese nor was notice taken of the decision in the pages of the official organ of the archdiocese, *The Word Magazine*.[19] But in his "Charge" to the 26th Annual Convention of his Archdiocese held in Boston a month later in August of 1971, Philip revealed his position. Reviewing the less-than-exemplary conduct of the Synod of the Patriarchate, Saliba promised continued support. Nonetheless, he concluded, "I feel that we have reached a moment of truth where we must seriously examine the possibility of a united and independent Orthodox Church in North America." To a round of applause, Saliba insisted that the American Orthodox must

> refuse to be a part in an absurd, historical dispute between Moscow and Constantinople. I believe that, due to the uniqueness of the Orthodox situation in this hemisphere, neither Moscow nor Constantinople alone can resolve our problem. . . . two main obstacles stand like a plague in the way of Orthodox unity in America—ethnic chauvinism and historical romanticism . . . if for any reason our efforts

17. *Russian Autocephaly and Orthodoxy in America*, 74.

18. *Religious News Service* has not preserved archival records from the 1970s. https://wikipedia.org/wiki/Elias_IV_of_Antioch. See the note to Patriarch Elias' letter in Trempelas, *Autocephaly of the Metropolia*, 47.

19. I am grateful to The Right Reverend Bishop John Abdalah for confirming my conclusions from the archival copies of *The Word* magazine for 1970–72.

should fail, we must be prepared to shape our own destiny in North America by joining hands with the progressive Orthodox forces who have decided to go forward and liberate themselves from the tyranny of history [Prolonged Applause].[20]

Elias' successor, Patriarch Ignatius Hazim, encouraged the more cosmopolitan and pro-Western perspective on Orthodoxy in the modern world and support for a unified and self-governing American Orthodox Church that had characterized Theodosius' patriarchate. Educated in Beirut, Hazim had been a student of the Lebanese philosopher and diplomat Charles Malik, who had begun studies in Germany before finishing his doctorate at Harvard.[21] Hazim's education continued at the St. Sergius Institute from 1949 to 1953, where he was a student of Professors Schmemann and Meyendorff. His concern for the deteriorated quality of Orthodox knowledge and practice among the young in the Middle East brought him and his contemporary George Khodr together in founding the Orthodox Youth Movement in the 1940s that produced the eminent monastic Elias Morcos, whose monastic brotherhood of St George in Deir el-Harf at Mt. Lebanon played a crucial role in the revitalization of monastic life in Lebanon. It was Ignatius' visit to the United States in 1985 that moved forward the acceptance of the Protestant Evangelical Orthodox Church into the Antiochian Archdiocese.

Antiochian priests who were seminarians in the early 1970s recall Metropolitan Philip observing that American Orthodox unity had to wait until the Antiochians got their own house in order—meaning the end of the schism between Toledo and New York.[22] The reaction of Philip to the OCA's Tomos in 1970 reflected the fragile Arabic-American parish life

20. "Minutes of the General Assembly of the XXVI Annual Convention of the Antiochian Orthodox Christian Archdiocese of New York and All North America," "The Metropolitan's Charge," reprinted in *The Word* 39, no. 9 (November, 1971): 3–8, at 6–7; 7–8.

21. A.G. Roeber, "Orthodox Christians, Human Rights and the Dignity of the Person: Reflections on Charles Malik (1906–1987)," *Journal of Eastern Christian Studies* 70, nos. 3–4 (2018): 285–306; https://orthodoxwiki.org/Ignatius_IV_(Hazim)_of_Antioch.

22. The recollection of then-seminarian the Very Reverend George Alberts (private communication with the author, October 2, 2019).

at that time, as well as the deeply pro- and anti-Western attitudes that still pitted different members of the Holy Synod in Damascus against one another about the Archdiocese in North America.

The internal struggles in and between Greek and Russian Orthodox in North America intensified by the 1990s because of the role played by the Antiochian Orthodox. The Russian Orthodox Church, while still recognizing the autocephaly of the Orthodox Church in America, even after the collapse of the Soviet Union, presented no model for respecting freedom of expression or religious freedoms of non-Orthodox, and made no effort to close its patriarchal parishes. Instead, it reestablished relations with the Russian Church Outside Russia, a jurisdiction that justifies its presence in North America as one dedicated to maintaining a Russian identity abroad, with no interest in promoting an autocephalous Orthodox Church of North America.[23]

The question of episcopal rights and those of accused clergy—that then also raised the question of the rights of bishops to control church property—surfaced in the Antiochian Archdiocese that grew rapidly under the leadership of Metropolitan Philip. His decision to receive the Evangelical Protestant Orthodox in 1986 set the stage for the difficulties that followed. Critics of Metropolitan Philip argued that had a strict application of the canonical procedure for receiving and ordaining clergy been followed (on an individual basis and not at one liturgy on one day) the later conflagration at the parish in Ben Lomond, California might have been avoided. Although the newly received Evangelical Orthodox were allowed for a time to continue practices that were not in accord with normal Orthodox liturgical practice, the eventual clash between Metropolitan Philip and the Ben Lomond priest John Weldon Hardenbrook centered on three related, but separate questions: What is the authority of the bishop over liturgical practice, the discipline of both clergy and laity, and the property of the parish church? If a schism occurs in a parish, which faction is the true Church still in communion with the canonical Archdiocese? Did the facts presented

23. On Russia's retreat since 2009 from endorsing religious rights for non-Orthodox, see Kristina Stoeckl, *The Russian Orthodox Church and Human Rights*; Finke and Mataic, "Recent Findings on Religious Freedoms." See also my introduction in the same volume, A.G. Roeber, "Introduction," in *Human v. Religious Rights? German and U.S. Exchanges and their Global Implications*, ed. A.G. Roeber (Göttingen: Vandenhoeck & Ruprecht, 2020), 7–21.

in a spiritual court reveal that the canons, ecclesiastical law and practices had been violated, and if so, what were the appropriate remedies?

Hardenbrook's pleas before a spiritual court held on May 26, 1998 (after he had been laicized) included claims that he had been singled out for discipline because of his decision to place himself under the spiritual guidance of the controversial abbot Ephraim of St. Anthony's Monastery in Arizona. Disturbed by the influence a Greek-speaking monastic community might exercise upon his own archdiocese, Metropolitan Philip had issued a directive on May 9, 1997 stipulating that spiritual fathers or confessors that were not members of the archdiocese were forbidden to Antiochian clergy and faithful. But Hardenbrook's claim about the importance of this issue played no role in the proceedings of the spiritual court, and the resultant civil suit brought by Hardenbrook and those who followed him. His refusal to accept the authority of the Archdiocese manifested itself in language that referred to the convened archdiocesan spiritual court as a "kangaroo court" or "Military Court Martial." In a letter to the metropolitan in January of 1997 he had informed Philip that none of the clergy in his parish should be laicized or moved until Hardenbrook had continued his personal consultations with each one, ending his letter with the claim "I am sure this is standard procedure."[24]

The concern for correct procedure of spiritual courts and the discipline of clergy had been on Metropolitan Philip's mind before the conversion of the Evangelical Orthodox in 1986. At his request, the Very Reverend John Badeen (who had earned degrees in law, political science, and business administration, and served as Chancellor and Chief Justice of the Ecclesiastical Court in the late 1970s) composed a document entitled "The Archdiocesan Spiritual Court."

Badeen completed his work shortly after Metropolitan Philip had successfully unified Toledo and New York into a unified archdiocese. Badeen's draft identified the Court as "the tribunal of first instance." All

24. Aspects of the controversy can be followed in D. Oliver Herbel, *Turning to Tradition: Converts and the Making of an American Orthodox Church* (New York: Oxford University Press, 2013),130–145. For Hardenbrook's account before the spiritual court, see Fr. John Weldon Hardenbrook, "Fr. John Weldon Hardenbrook's Defense," *Ben Lomond Tragedy: Opposing the blacking out of history*, May 26, 1998, https://benlomond.wordpress.com/1998/05/26/fr-john-weldon-hardenbrooks-defense/ (accessed 10 October 2019).

matters were "assigned . . . for hearing and adjudication by the Metropolitan Primate" who also appoints the three voting members. In treat-
ing "General Rules of Procedure" the document requires the appointed
Archdiocesan Advocate to identify the "alleged action/s of the accused"
and then cite "the applicable canons of the Holy Church, or rules and
practices of the Antiochian See, or rules, practices, edicts, etc. of the
Archdiocese. . . ." A person accused had thirty days from "receipt of the
complaint to file an answer thereto, in writing." Any person accused
"shall be entitled to choose an advocate from the clergy list of the Archdiocese, and to private counsel if he so chooses." The term "rights" occurred
seldom except in the section dealing with "Pre-Hearing Discovery" where
proceedings are to move forward "with due regard to the rights of the
parties." Ultimately, "the Court may impose such procedural sanctions
upon the parties to this action, as are necessary to serve the ends of justice." The sanctions dealt with failure to comply or respond to the court's
request for submission of evidence. In the hearing itself, "each party
shall have the right to examine the witnesses presented by the other or
called on the initiative of the Court." Ultimately, "the Metropolitan Primate may, in exercise of his authority, reject any part or all of the findings of the Court. He may affirm, reduce, or suspend the prescribed
penalties." The right of appeal to the Court of Appeals of the Greek
Orthodox Patriarchate of Antioch and All the East was guaranteed "in
accordance with the canonical procedures of the said Court." The application of penalties to anyone found guilty were to be based on the canons
of the ecumenical councils, local councils, "and the Holy Fathers. Their
application . . . is subject to approval of the Metropolitan Primate, who
must use pastoral discretion, which belongs exclusively to his office, in
applying penalties." An amendment to the document stipulated that the
purpose of the procedures was to safeguard "the rights of the parties,
and yet serving justice, which is the paramount motive."[25] The terms

25. Typescript copy in author's possession. Its identification and origin I owe
to information supplied by His Grace, the Right Reverend Bishop Basil of the
Diocese of Wichita (ACOANA). (Correspondence with author, March 30, 2019).
The current version of issues regarding "discipline and Spiritual Courts" differs
from this earlier version and the word "right" is seldom used; e.g., the accused
will have "the opportunity to answer the charges against him" and the "accused
clergyman is entitled to ask another clergyman of the Archdiocese or a counselor

"pastoral discretion", and "serving justice" sum up the meaning of the term *oikonomia*.[26]

The procedural safeguards developed by Badeen were strengthened even further by the late 1990s because of the work done by Charles Ajalat, the attorney who served as the counsellor to the Spiritual Court. He had set in place an even more rigorous set of procedures to guarantee the rights of the accused as well as those of the archdiocese. The refusal of Hardenbrook to sign and return a model constitution that stipulated that parish property belonged to the archdiocese—and the attempt to argue that the parish retained control on the basis of an "implied trust"—was rejected by the California state courts.[27] The basis for that rejection lay in the manner in which American constitutional and case law had evolved since the seminal 1871 Supreme Court decision *Watson v. Jones* that held that Federal courts could not get involved in internal questions of church doctrine. If an American congregation belonged to a hierarchical denomination, American courts had to defer to hierarchical determinations regarding disputed property issues. In the case of the *Serbian Eastern Orthodox Diocese v. Milivojevich* (1976), *Watson* had been extended to apply to state courts who could exercise no jurisdiction over decisions of hierarchical churches regarding the rights of bishops, or related matters touching on property

---

to aid him in his hearing with the jury." See Fr. Joseph J. Allen et al., eds., *Clergy Guide of The Self Ruled Antiochian Orthodox Christian Archdiocese of North America*, 3rd ed. ([Englewood, NJ: Antiochian Orthodox Christian Archdiocese of North America, 2011), 47–50, at 48, 49 paragraphs f and n.

26. For an overview of the term and its relationship to equity, see the literature and discussion in Roeber, *Mixed Marriages*, 52–66. I am indebted to the Vicar General of the Archdiocese, the Very Reverend Thomas Zain, who has observed that spiritual courts have since been called and conducted on a much more informal basis than those developed in the 1998 proceedings. (Correspondence with author, March 30, 2019, April 2, 2019).

27. Transcript of "Before The Spiritual Court Of the Antiochian Orthodox Christian Archdiocese of North America In Re The Matter of John Weldon Hardenbrook, et al." Tuesday, May 26, 1998 contain the results of the revised procedure and the guarantee of the chair of the Spiritual Court that the rights of everyone involved in the dispute were going to be rigorously protected. (Copy in the author's possession; Ajalat's role in strengthening the procedural rules cited here noted with his permission).

disputes, even if those hierarchical decisions emanated from courts located outside the boundaries of the United States. Two years later in *Jones v. Wolf,* however, the long-standing insistence that courts observe a "compulsory deference" to the internal decisions of a hierarchical body appeared to be altered somewhat since that decision stipulated that any ecclesial disputes were to be judged by the same standards of "neutral principles of the law" that apply in cases involving non-religious entities.

The concept of "neutral principles of law" had originated from Judge Learned Hand's 1958 Holmes Lecture at Harvard on judicial review and Herbert Wechsler's disagreement. Wechsler had claimed that "neutral principles" could be found in the Constitution's own language, and not in any supposed motives of legislators.[28] The court in *Jones* had used this claim to inform lower courts that they could now consider the actual decisions of courts rendered by hierarchs as well as relevant secular case law that touched on property matters. Whatever else the Supreme Court intended in its decision in *Jones,* the cumulative effect of both *Jones* and *Serbian Eastern Orthodox Diocese* suggested that it might be possible to challenge the interpretation of hierarchical decisions arrived at by whatever constitutes the "final authority." This significant shift in American constitutional law pertaining to churches may well have given Hardenbrook and his attorneys confidence that if they argued on the basis of "neutral principles" (which they did) they would win.[29] In this instance, however, it was the archdiocese that prevailed in the courts.

While Hardenbrook bridled at the Metropolitan Archbishop's insistence on obedience to the ecclesiastical law of the Church, some of the recently converted evangelical Protestants (and some lifelong Orthodox) criticized

28. For a review of cases and opinions on this concept, see Turner, "On Neutral and Preferred Principles of Constitutional Law," *University of Pittsburgh Law Rev*iew 74 (2012): 433–489.

29. The cited cases can be followed at "Significant Supreme Court Rulings," *Pew Research Center: Religion & Public Life,* March 31, 2011: https://www.pewforum .org/2011/03/31/churches-in-court8 (accessed March 31, 2011). . For Hardenbrook's appeal and the California court rejection of his appeal, dismissing both the invocation of implied trust theory and reliance on *Jones v. Wolf* (1979 443 U.S.), see *Metropolitan Philip v. Steiger,* 82 Cal. App. 4th 923 (2000) at https://law.justia .com/cases/california/court-of-appeal/4th/82/923.html (accessed 05 August 2019).

the Metropolitan for being too lax in his discipline of the clergy. Those demands erupted over the remarriage of the widowed priest Joseph Allen. The decision of the Metropolitan to allow Allen to remain a priest after having entered a second marriage brought to the fore the question of whether an individual bishop—because of his authority over his own diocese or metropolis—possessed the right to depart from the normal canonical prohibitions against second marriages of deacons and priests. That question had been raised at the 1923 Pan-Orthodox Congress held in Constantinople but remained unresolved because of the different positions taken by various bishops who attended. Some had argued that only a general synod of an autocephalous church could address this issue; others opposed even that possibility. By acting alone, Metropolitan Philip appeared to his critics to have moved beyond what conservative canonists would have pointed to—the general prohibition—but to the refusal to countenance even a synodal reassessment of the prohibition, insisting that only an ecumenical council could address the problem.[30] To his supporters, the metropolitan demonstrated that he was not interested in being an authoritarian figure but was instead intent on showing compassion to a widowed priest.[31]

Distressing though the Ben Lomond case may have been to Metropolitan Philip, even before it was resolved, a much deeper disappointment shook the Antiochian Archdiocese. In 1994, after repeated earlier urgings from the Orthodox Church in America, and now with the support of the Greek Archbishop Metropolitan Iakovos, but at the instigation of a lay leader in the Antiochian Archdiocese, the bishops of the Standing Conference of Orthodox Bishops in America met in an unprecedented "Episcopal Assembly." Hosted by Metropolitan Philip in October 1994 at the Antiochian Village in Ligonier, Pennsylvania, the meeting began with Archbishop Iakovos, who, as the chairman of the SCOBA and in recognition of the stated aims of the assembly, hoped that the Ecumenical Patriarch would accept proposals for an end to the various "jurisdictions" of

---

30. For details, see Roeber, *Mixed Marriage*, 171–72, 191 and at length, Patrick Viscuso, *A Quest for Reform of the Orthodox Church: The 1923 Pan-Orthodox Congress An Analysis and Translation of Its Acts and Decisions* (Berkeley, CA: Inter-Orthodox Press, 2006).

31. Herbel, *Turning to Tradition*, 130–145 and Joseph Allen, *Widowed Priest: A Crisis in Ministry* (Minneapolis, MN: Life & Light Publishing, 1994).

the Orthodox thus helping pave the way for the creation of a united Orthodox Church of North America.[32]

Since the subsequently ill-fated Spyridon had some months before the Ligonier meeting indicated that both he and the Ecumenical Patriarch supported an end to ethnically defined Orthodox jurisdictions in the diaspora, the bishops who met at Ligonier must have assumed that they had the implicit blessing of Patriarch Bartholomew to achieve just that end. Attempting to allay fears on the part of the mother churches that an autocephalous North American Orthodox Church would neglect them, Charles Ajalat, in his response to Alexander Rondos' paper, argued that in the court of international secular opinion, the opposite would be the case—the Orthodox in North America would be taken even more seriously because of their involvement in international charitable and ecumenical work—but that the indispensable prerequisite for the future of the Church was a sense of ownership shared by all members of the Church, laity and clergy alike.[33]

In its report to the Assembly, the International Orthodox Christian Charities, a trans-jurisdictional effort comprised of laity and clergy, pointed to its effort to leave day-to-day operations "to the professional staffs, and Executive Directors/Chief Executive Officers. This combines the best in western organization with the Orthodox understanding, as St. Ignatius said, that 'where the bishop is, there is the Church.'"[34] When the various bishops addressed the question of how to resolve the "Problem of the Orthodox Diaspora," (the title under which their remarks were summarized

32. On the calling and consequences of the Ligonier meeting, see George Bedrin and Philip Tamoush, eds., *A New Era Begins: Proceedings of the Conference of Orthodox Bishops in Ligonier, Pennsylvania* (Torrance, CA: Orthodox Theological Press, 1996); Thomas Fitzgerald, *The Orthodox Church*, 108–110; George C. Michalopoulos and Herb Ham, *The American Orthodox Church: A History of Its Beginnings* (Salisbury, MA: Regina Orthodox Press, 2003), 180–184.

33. Charles Richard Ajalat, "IOCC and the Broader Context: Are There Lessons to be Learned?" in *A New Era Begins: Proceedings of the 1994 Conference of Orthodox Bishops in Ligonier, Pennsylvania*, ed. George Bedrin and Philip Tamoush (Torrance, CA: Oakwood Publications, 1996), 73–87.

34. Bedrin and Philip Tamoush, eds., *A New Era Begins*, 62–86, at 77. Spyridon's interpretation of his role can be followed in his authorized biography, Justine Frangouli-Argyris, *The Lonely Path of Integrity: Archbishop Spyridon of America, 1996–1999* (Athens: Exandas Publishers, 2002).

in the published proceedings of the meeting) the solution proposed by the Patriarchate of Alexandria endorsed the position of Constantinople, that "the whole diaspora of the world is within the jurisdiction of the Ecumenical Patriarchate. . . ."[35] The positions put forward by "Antioch, Moscow and Romania strongly oppose the Alexandrian theory on the authority of Constantinople. . . ." Nonetheless, while opposing Constantinople's universal claims, the other three Churches argued that the "normalization" of diaspora conditions could and should be resolved prior to the calling of a Pan-Orthodox Council, and this normalization should be done by the Ecumenical Patriarch who has "an important function: that of initiating new procedures." Constantinople should relinquish the appeal to Canon 28 of Chalcedon; its Greek Archdiocese should be returned at least as an intermediate step to the autocephalous Church of Greece, and as a result, "the position of honour of the Ecumenical See, *primus inter pares*, would be grounded in the witness of the right and pure faith, and not be expressed by capturing areas or by the submission of other parts of the Church."[36]

Perhaps the argument put forward at Ligonier that the Orthodox in North America should not be labelled or understood as a "diaspora" but a mature church alarmed the respective mother churches abroad. Nor was everyone in North America ready to endorse such a move. Metropolitan Vsevolod Maidansky, the head of the small eparchy of Ukrainians under Constantinople's authority, refused to sign the documents endorsed by the other bishops. Fearful that both the OCA and possibly the Antiochians were being used by Russia to delegitimize Constantinople, Maidansky led his small group the following year, in 1995, into union with the Ukrainian Orthodox Church-USA that also entered into communion with the Ecumenical Patriarchate. Some have speculated that Maidansky was responsible for alarming Constantinople about a supposed plot by Archbishop Iakovos to declare himself the primate of an autocephalous North American Church. His close personal friend and contemporary Metropolitan Nicholas of the Carpatho-Rusyn diocese was equally unhappy with the Ligonier proposals. But the Ecumenical Patriarch had already been informed of the plan for Ligonier after a meeting of the Inter-Orthodox Preparatory Commission that had met in Geneva to discuss the "Orthodox Diaspora."

---

35. Bedrin and Tamoush, eds., *A New Era Begins*, 124, 127.
36. Bedrin and Tamoush, eds., *A New Era Begins*, 137, 138.

That commission had endorsed the creation of an Episcopal Assembly for each diaspora region around the world. The Ecumenical Patriarchate's rejection of the statements that came from Ligonier may well have reflected his conviction that the North American meeting would short-circuit the plans already laid for creating Episcopal Assemblies. Constantinople's rejection of Ligonier removed the Greek Orthodox Archdiocese (the largest of all the North American jurisdictions) from any further movements toward resolving the question of self-government. It also showed how reluctant many Orthodox were to endorse a free, open expression of opinion and speech in matters pertaining to the internal life of the Church.[37]

The Antiochian Archdiocese had weathered the Ben Lomond storm of the 1980s and had appeared, until the ill-fated Ligonier meeting, to be moving forward toward Metropolitan Philip's objective of aiding the emergence of a self-governing and unified Orthodox Church of North America. Instead, it suffered the rebuke of the historic patriarchates and itself became embroiled in a dispute over the right of self-determination and what some regarded as an irregular change in the governance of the archdiocese that echoed the turmoil in the OCA and the Greek Orthodox Archdiocese.

Following the successful unification of the Toledo and New York Archdioceses in 1975, Archbishop Michael Shaheen had served as Auxiliary-Archbishop to Metropolitan Philip Saliba until the former's death in October 1992. From 1992 until 2003 Metropolitan Philip was the sole bishop and member of the Holy Synod of Damascus although he had already secured the assistance of auxiliary bishops: Bishop Antoun (1983); Bishop Basil (1992); Bishop Demetri (1995, retired 2003); Bishop Joseph (1991; to the U.S. 1995). The Patriarchate of Antioch had itself adopted in 1972 "The Primary Canons (Constitution) of the Roum Orthodox Patriarchate of Antioch" as its fundamental law. Developments in North America over the next 35 years unfolded in the shadow of—some argued—against—the bylaws of that constitution.

37. For the context behind Metropolitan Vsevolod's position, see Nicholas E. Denysenko, *The Orthodox Church in Ukraine*, 122–33. See also Kitroeff, *Greek Orthodox Church*, 222–227. I have been informed that neither Metropolitan Nicholas nor Metropolitan Vsevelod put into writing or agreed to interviews explaining their opposition to the Ligonier meeting. I am grateful for communications from Denysenko, the Very Reverend Nik Ferencz, the Very Reverend Gabriel Rochelle, and Professor Gayle Woloschak.

The Holy Synod of Damascus created by a formal resolution in 2003 what some in America understood to be genuine dioceses in the North American Archdiocese and as a consequence, the establishment of a local synod over which the metropolitan archbishop would preside with the diocesan bishops as members of the Synod. The resolution raised the then-auxiliaries Antoun, Basil, and Joseph to the dignity of diocesan bishops. In 2004 the archdiocese met in a general assembly at Pittsburgh, Pennsylvania and formulated a new constitution which Metropolitan Philip asserted was authoritative for the archdiocese. The new constitution based its legal authority on Article 2, Section 15 of the Religious Corporation Laws of the State of New York. Its ecclesiastical authority came from the Holy Synod in Damascus of which the metropolitan archbishop in North America is a member. The archdiocese was defined as the local synod. Later that year, the Holy Synod in Damascus issued a revised version of this document and in a letter to Metropolitan Philip in 2006 Patriarch Ignatius maintained that this was the authoritative document that governed the archdiocese. In 2004, three additional bishops had been ordained as diocesan bishops in Damascus (Bishop Mark, Bishop Thomas, and Bishop Alexander). All were enthroned in their respective dioceses between 2004 and 2005.[38]

The Pittsburgh constitution created an archdiocese that was "autonomous"—i.e., it now had an actual synod with diocesan bishops and under this constitution could elect its own diocesan bishops while submitting to Damascus names for future metropolitans for confirmation or rejection. The name of the archdiocese preferred by Patriarch Ignatius and agreed to by Metropolitan Philip was the "Self-Ruled" rather than the "Autonomous" Antiochian Christian Archdiocese of North America. The archdiocese functioned under this constitution and name from 2004 and in theory does so to the present day—except that on February 24, 2009 substantial changes were imposed from Damascus on the governance of

38. The information contained in this and the next paragraphs are taken from the Searchable Archives of the Orthodox Christian Laity site from January 2005 to September 27, 2011 at https://web.archive.org/web20151009151707/http://archive.ocl.orgBROKEN LINK (accessed December 10, 2019); and the documents under "Chancellors Letters 5.17.09"; "Ajalat Retires 8.6.09," http://www.ocanews.org/newsBROKEN LINK (accessed December 10, 2019); and "Special Meeting of the Archdiocesan Synod is Held," http://ww1.antiochian.org/node/19183 (accessed December 10, 2019).

the supposed dioceses. Moreover, the description of the archdiocese as "self-ruled" disappeared from its official letterhead despite the resolution of 2003 that had granted irrevocable self-rule.

On February 24, 2009 the Holy Synod in Damascus issued a declaration stating that it had "normalized the status of Bishops across the entire See of Antioch." By virtue of this declaration, the diocesan bishops of North America were reduced to the status of auxiliaries. On April 24, 2009, at a meeting at the Chancery in Englewood, New Jersey, a "Resolution Affirming Obedience to the Decision of the Holy Synod of Antioch of February 24, 2009 which Normalized the Status of Bishops Across The Entire See of Antioch" was signed by Metropolitan Philip. Bishops Antoun, Joseph, and Thomas signed as auxiliary bishops. Bishop Basil did not sign the document, nor did Bishop Mark, nor Bishop Alexander who wrote "This decision is already in effect and does not need my signature."

Protests erupted as the Holy Synod's decision became known, with the St. Raphael Clergy Brotherhood of Wichita, Kansas writing to the metropolitan asking for clarification as to what the decision meant and why it was taken. Members of the board of trustees requested the legal opinion of the chancellors, attorneys Robert A. Koory and Charles R. Ajalat, who responded with a letter and opinion addressed to Metropolitan Philip and the "Members of the Local Synod and Members of the Board of Trustees," dated May 13, 2009. The chancellors prefaced their opinion by noting that they had reviewed the patriarchate's own constitution and bylaws and the resolution of the Holy Synod "irrevocably granting our Archdiocese Self-Rule, as well as our Archdiocese Constitution." In their opinion both the February 24 and April 24 resolutions were "invalid," "inapplicable," "inconsistent," and "ill-advised." The chancellors observed that the resolutions contradicted the resolution of the Holy Synod that had granted irrevocable self-rule, as well as the constitution of the archdiocese and what they called "the irrevocable creation of three diocesan bishops by the self-rule Resolution itself, the election and consecration of three bishops under the Constitution as diocesan bishops for North America and the enthronement of these various bishops [in] their respective dioceses."

The opinion then noted the absence of a quorum at the Holy Synod sessions in Damascus (only nine members in attendance) that violated the patriarchal constitutional requirement that a call to meet had to be issued by the patriarch or on the basis of a written request by three members of the synod. Moreover, only an amendment of the patriarchal constitution could make a structural change such as demoting diocesan bishops to the rank of auxiliaries, not an amendment of bylaws that only touches on procedural issues. Even if the decision made some sense elsewhere in the patriarchate, the chancellors argued it was inapplicable to North America. The synod could not have intended by a mere resolution to void its own previous resolutions without stating so directly. Nothing in the self-rule resolution specified that the archdiocese was subject to the Holy Synod in matters relating to the internal governance of the archdiocese. The archdiocesan constitution stipulated that the abolition of the local synod would have to come in the form of an amendment "duly passed by a General Assembly of the Archdiocese".

Since the canons governing the Patriarchate of Antioch place all auxiliary bishops under the authority of the patriarch, the 2009 decision did not alter entirely the self-rule of the North American Archdiocese since the auxiliaries serve not directly under the patriarch but under the authority of the metropolitan archbishop. A further confusion, however, appeared in the way the office of a "diocesan bishop" who is the final authority in his diocese was understood. A "diocesan bishop" is an alien notion and foreign to the way the ancient patriarchates understand episcopacy. Only a metropolitan is a self-standing bishop, while auxiliaries hold the title of a vanished see city and do not operate except as an immediate aid to the metropolitan to whose office they are likely to succeed eventually. The result of the 2009 decision taken in Damascus was to create American Antiochian auxiliaries who are neither auxiliaries in the historically understood sense, nor are they truly diocesan bishops, nor are there genuine Antiochian dioceses in North America.

The decision of the Holy Synod that changed diocesan bishops back to the standing of auxiliaries—but without titles to long-vanished episcopal sees as is the normal practice in naming a bishop "auxiliary"—could not be reconciled easily with the long-standing and openly declared objective of Metropolitan Philip for not just an autonomous, but an autocephalous American Orthodox church. That he was not wholly at ease with members of his own local synod, however, and that it was he who initiated the process to reduce the diocesans to auxiliary status became evident two years later. Responding to pressure from priests in the Diocese of Toledo, he ordered the auxiliary bishop Mark to take up new duties as the auxiliary bishop of the Diocese of Eagle River (Alaska) and the Northwest. Bishop Mark refused the assignment and left the archdiocese in January 2011 for the Orthodox Church in America. On December 11, 2011 three new auxiliary bishops were ordained at the Patriarchal Monastery of Our Lady of Balamand, Lebanon (Bishops John, Anthony, and Nicholas). At that same ordination liturgy, Patriarch Ignatius elevated Bishop Joseph to the rank of archbishop, a move that appeared to signal the Patriarch's choice for a successor to Metropolitan Philip. Upon the death of Metropolitan Philip in 2014, Archbishop Joseph was approved by the Holy Synod after his name and two others had been submitted by the archdiocese.

These disputes illustrate two critical questions: first, how much of the Anglo-American concern for due process in the protection of legal rights could the Orthodox absorb and affirm regarding the free exercise of opinion and expression—especially when questions arose pertaining to self-determination, to property, to civil liberties in a pluralist society? Second, the challenge of living in a pluralist society pushed to the fore the question of whether the canonical tradition based on Roman law has promoted a synodical, fraternal frame of governance by synods of bishops who meet with lay, presbyteral, and diaconal advisors—or did that canonical history favor the magisterial and autocratic governance by a monarchical primate from the patriarchal down to the diocesan level? How much pluralism can exist within the bounds of a global Orthodoxy that continues to struggle with the rights of individual bishops, bishops as a group, and their relationship to their presbyters, deacons, monastics, and laity? The danger of an escalating retreat from dialogue and honest engagement with the realities of a society increasingly aware of "differences" intensified as the Orthodox also faced these internal questions. As one Orthodox bio-ethicist who has responded to episcopal requests for counsel has observed, historically, "it is . . . [a bishop's] responsibility to consider that all views of his flock are appropriately handled and that he can be a proper advocate of even the smallest of voices in the Assembly. This model is one that the Church has used for millennia and is still the norm in predominantly Orthodox countries . . . but I am no longer convinced that it can work well in this complex and diverse world. Can a hierarch really be expected to be an expert in subject matters ranging from birth and beginning of life to dietary restrictions to social justice to complex theology . . . [to] understand the complexity of issues to be considered in examining scientific, political, social, and ethical views of an issue?"[39]

39. Gayle E. Woloschak, *Faith, Science, Mystery*, ed. Bishop Maxim Vasiljevic (Alhambra, CA: Sebastian Press, 2018), 76.

These questions have been recognized for some time, but the disagreements among the Orthodox regarding how to answer them have proven to be intractable. In no small part, the reason for the delay in resolving these tensions can be traced to the alarm with which the Orthodox have confronted the refashioning of expanding rights claims surrounding sex, gender, and marriage. No cluster of rights claims can at present compare in volatility and in theological significance with these issues: the Orthodox understanding of what it means to be male and female, and how and whether the Orthodox can assess the shifting claims made for sex, gender, and marriage. Those claims have also intensified internal debates about the rights and responsibilities of the male holder of the episcopacy as the icon of the fatherhood of God and how women and sexual minorities in the Orthodox Church can articulate their concerns in an ecclesiastical culture that has not always endorsed freedom of opinion and expression internally as successfully as it has affirmed those values in the pluralist society in which it has taken root and flourished. What is still missing in the Orthodox Church in North America and indeed globally, is a settled principle of freedom of expression and opinion that recognizes both the realities of increasing pluralism as well as the critical importance of primacy and conciliarity among bishops, clergy, and laity.

6

THE ORTHODOX, SEX, AND MARRIAGE
BEFORE THE RIGHTS REVOLUTION

In May 1974 the Orthodox-Roman Catholic Theological Consultation issued an "agreed statement" on the issue of abortion and the "right to life." Since this was a statement only, the members of the Consultation could not go into any detail about where and how they grounded their conviction that "the 'right to life' implies a right to a decent life and to full human development, not merely to a marginal existence." The Consultation specified that their understanding of the right to life included "the unborn, the mentally retarded, the aging, and the underprivileged. . . ." Thus, based upon a "common Christian tradition" they claimed a "right of the unborn to life."[1] This statement reflects the teaching that there is a moral right to life, and for the Orthodox, one grounded not in the wishes or policies of human authorities, but one that is built into the "image and likeness" revelation of who God is, and who humans are created to become. Even now with *Roe v. Wade* having been overturned by the U.S. Supreme Court, if the Orthodox intend to demonstrate that Orthodoxy is a way of life encompassing body, soul, and spirit, they will have to continue to resist what the Roman Catholic ethicist Charles Camosy has described as the "secularization of medicine and medical ethics." The Orthodox will

---

1. "An Agreed Statement on Respect for Life," The North American Orthodox-Catholic Theological Consultation, May 24, 1974, Washington, D.C. https://www.usccb.org/committees/ecumenical-interreligious-affairs/agreed-statement-respect-life.

have to remain committed to facing "the complex arguments to be had about abortion in the case of sexual violence or when the mother's health is in danger (and I think such arguments do have merit)" but in a manner that nonetheless will "not discard the fundamental human equality of the prenatal child. Prenatal children must not be erased from the abortion debate, nor should their mothers."[2]

I. Setting the Context for the Debates over Marriage

No issue focused on rights has defined the frontlines of the culture wars in the twenty-first century United States as has the conflict between religious defense of the moral right to life of the unborn and the legal rights of women to self-determination in matters of reproductive decisions. That conflict in turn has now raised the question about whether the state is bound to accommodate religion when religious teachings conflict with legal rights to self-determination, or whether religious rights are trumped by the appeal to rights invoked by women, or by sexual or ethnic minorities, based on individual freedom, equality, and the state's obligation to protect all persons from "dignitary harm."[3] Agreement on what constitutes human dignity and who gets to decide what this means continues to elude those debating the nature of rights. Moreover, those who disdain a religious grounding for moral claims of human dignity are no further along now than they were some forty years ago when Arthur Allen Leff argued that "there cannot be any normative system ultimately based on anything except human will."[4] More than 40 years after the United States Supreme

2. Charles C. Camosy, *Losing Our Dignity: How Secularized Medicine Is Undermining Fundamental Human Equality* (Hyde Park, NY: New City Press, 2021), 111.

3. Robert Post, "The Politics of Religion Democracy and The Conscience Wars," in *The Conscience Wars: Rethinking the Balance between Religion, Identity, and Equality*, ed. Susanna Mancini and Michel Rosenfeld (Cambridge: Cambridge University Press, 2018), 473–484, 481.

4. Arthur Allen Leff, "Unspeakable Ethics, Unnatural Law," *Duke Law Journal* 6 (1979): 1229–1249, at 1229–30. For a more recent analysis, Samuel W. Calhoun, "Grounding Normative Assertions: Arthur Leff's Still Irrefutable, But Incomplete, 'Sez Who?' Critique" *Journal of Law and Religion* 20, no. 1 (2004–2005): 31–96.

Court decision *Roe v. Wade* 410 U.S. 113 (1973)and now even in the wake of the reversal of that decision in *Dobbs v. Jackson Women's Health Organization* profound disagreements persist on the question of the moral rights of the fetus and the legal rights of a woman. But in the meantime, the full impact of the rights revolution has expanded to include a focus on same-sex marriage and issues raised by transgender persons that pit commitments to civil rights equality against religious rights in ways that mirror but go far beyond the ongoing conflicts surrounding abortion. Some have now claimed that dignitary rights and those of self-determination should be understood as part of human rights. In the most recent iteration, those claiming to defend traditional values, especially in historically Orthodox countries such as Russia, have advanced "society-protective arguments, which shift the focus in the abortion debate away from the woman and the fetus to society as a whole."[5]

Those on the political and cultural left have, however, advanced arguments that appear to be very little different from those of their opponents. Douglas NeJaime and Reva B. Siegel have claimed that "[c]onscientious refusals to assist with morally controversial acts create a harmful social meaning" to such an extent that "if granting a religious accommodation would harm those protected by the antidiscrimination law or undermine societal values and goals the statute promotes, then unencumbered enforcement of the statute is the least restrictive means of achieving the government's compelling ends."[6] As Douglas Laycock points out, this argument appears to take away the constitutionally guaranteed right to free speech on the part of conscientious objectors on the specious invocation of the government's "compelling interest" in "stamping out 'social meanings.'"[7] In expanding

---

5. Susanna Mancini and Kristina Stoeckl, "Transatlantic Conversations: The Emergence of Society-Protective Antiabortion Arguments in the United States, Europe, and Russia," in Mancini and Rosenfeld, eds., *The Conscience Wars*, 220–257, at 222.

6. The essay appeared first in Douglas NeJaime and Reva B. Siegel, "Conscience Wars: Complicity-Based Conscience Claims in Religion and Politics," *Yale Law Journal*, 124, no. 7 (May, 2015): 2516–2591; the citation here is from the critique offered by Douglas Laycock, "Religious Liberty for Politically Active Minority Groups: A Response to NeJaime and Siegel," in *Religious Liberty*, 5 vols, (Grand Rapids, MI: W.B. Eerdmans, 2010–2018), 4: 814–832, at 816.

7. Laycock, "Religious Liberty," 817.

their argument to a global context, NeJaime and Siegel claim that the only "genuinely pluralist exemption regime" they can envisage is one dedicated to protecting "dignitary harm" by "limiting accommodation in ways that respect the convictions of the believer *and* one's fellow citizens. . . ."[8]

The complex story of constitutional history and jurisprudence plays a part in any discussion of rights claims in the U.S. context. When legal and constitutional historians address the issue of "substantive" due process, for example, they focus on the claim that there are "implicit" or "unenumerated" rights that in the late nineteenth century the Supreme Court held to have protected corporations from government regulation. But over the course of the first half of the twentieth century, the Court increasingly deferred to legislative restrictions on "ordinary commercial transactions." More importantly, the Court by the 1960s rejected state statutes that had interfered with the ability of

> married couples to receive information about, and to employ, contraceptives for the purposes of birth control. In that case, *Griswold v. Connecticut*, the majority opinion announced that the Court had been invited to revive 'substantive' understandings of 'liberty' in the Due Process Clause, but had 'decline[d] that invitation' because it '[did] not sit as a super-legislature to determine the wisdom, need, and propriety of laws that touch . . . social conditions.' So instead of reading 'liberty' in the Fourteenth Amendment substantively, to create a right in married couples to use contraceptives in the practice of birth control, the Court majority located the right in 'privacy,' a 'penumbral' constitutional right emanating from various specific guarantees in the Bill of Rights and the Ninth Amendment.

Yet only eight years later, the Court located a woman's legal right to procure abortion again in "personal liberty" rights found in the Fourteenth Amendment.[9] Along with non-Orthodox fellow citizens, Orthodox Christians in the United States remain opposed to unrestricted abortion

---

8. NeJaime and Siegel, "Conscience Wars in Transnational Perspective: Religious Liberty, Third-Party Harm, and Pluralism," in Mancini and Rosenfeld, eds., *The Conscience Wars*, 187–219, at 218, 219.

9. G. Edward White, *Law in American History Volume III:1930-2000.* Oxford University Press (2019): 510–599, at 511.

on demand as a legal right, reject it as a moral right, but are somewhat divided on their agreement or opposition to the shifts in the rationale for defending liberties and rights, and where to ground such claims—i.e., in privacy, liberty, equality, or a defense of a common social good?

To assess these claims we need to review the history of the women's rights movement in the United States and the pre-rights revolution understandings of marriage among the Orthodox. Only then can we begin to comprehend the reactions that set in beginning in the 1970s on the part of those concerned about perceived dangers to traditional values. But as the court cases and commentary already noted indicate, those debates have enmeshed a larger discussion of sex, gender, identity, and conscience that manifested itself in the *Obergefell v. Hodges* decision to affirm the legal right of same-sex marriage, a decision based in part on endorsement of a substantive due process argument by the majority of the Supreme Court justices. So complex have these debates become that we must examine the rise of feminism and especially gender feminism in a subsequent chapter, even though some of those issues cannot convincingly be assessed apart from the longer history of the Orthodox and their understanding of marriage between one man and one woman.

We begin with the history of the Orthodox in America and their early experiences with questions of marriage and understanding of gender, male and female. Within the ranks of the Orthodox in the United States many have concluded that the battle for the defense of traditional marriage and values has now been lost on a social and political level. As a result, the question of a possible recovery of an expanded role for women within the Orthodox Church in ministry—especially the diaconate for women—has fallen under the shadow of the perceived threats to marriage and the roles of men and women in the Church. Consequently, the Orthodox Church finds itself embroiled in even more intense debates over whether the rise of gender feminism and new theories of sexuality now threaten the Church internally in its theological anthropology, and not merely in the public sphere where conflicting rights claims continue to escalate. These debates about sex and gender require the separate and extended treatment that follows this historical review of the Orthodox views of men, women, and marriage for they have also revealed the most serious theological exchanges among Orthodox Christians in the United States that swirl around an inherited iconographic understanding of the male bishop as the father of his community, guaranteeing a unity with the servanthood of deacons and the

Holy Spirit's wisdom, counsel, and apostolic witness of the presbyters. Where, in that iconography, do women belong? And what can the Orthodox say about questions of transgender persons? Those questions come into focus only when we have first examined the pre-"rights revolution" Orthodox engagement with marriage and the long-accepted understanding of what it means to be male and female.

Orthodox belief that humans are created male and female stands in opposition to claims that identity can be reduced to a gender question determined by social and cultural conditioning. But even if that belief is a given, what implications does it hold regarding the dignitary rights, and the responsibilities of men and women in the Orthodox Church and in the pluralist society in which they, single, married, heterosexual, homosexual, or transgender, live and struggle toward the goal of union with God? Overall hang the rapidly changing assessments by legal scholars, legislators, and policymakers of whether and how religiously based convictions on such critical issues as marriage, gender, and sexuality can or cannot any longer be "accommodated" in the United States. A significant number of legal and constitutional commentators now reflect the conviction of some Americans that such accommodation is inherently incompatible with the defense of legal and civil rights. Indeed, some scholars have pointed out that the decision to insist on same-sex unions as marriage placed those unions on the same level of equal dignity with what had traditionally been regarded as marriage. By insisting on parity of definition, the state sends "a message effectively implying that traditional religious beliefs on the subject are officially disfavored or rejected." Nor can such a decision be regarded as "expressive" only, for in areas such as public school curricula where attitudes toward gender and sexuality are shaped "the state has not only sent a message implying that . . . [traditional] religious beliefs are to that extent wrong . . . [but also] that these religious teachings are backward and hurtful." Whether the (apparently) triumphant secular point of view will be willing to accommodate traditional marriage dissenters brings us full circle back to the assertion we made at the beginning of this book, that the Orthodox have embraced some, but not all, types of rights claims in their experience of being a minority church in a diverse society comprised of religious and non-religious citizens.[10]

10. Steven D. Smith, "Die and Let Live? The Asymmetry of Accommodation," *Southern California Law Review* 88, no. 3 (March 2015): 703–725, at 708, 709.

Concerns over the apparent incompatibility of the claims made by some in the rights revolution and traditional Orthodox, Catholic, and Protestant convictions regarding marriage, gender, and sexuality are not confined to conservative commentators. After a long career devoted to ensuring that in the United States it was "safe to be gay," Andrew Koppelman has made public his worry that the emerging secular consensus may not be "one that's safe for religious dissenters."[11] The most aggressive of secular scholars reject accommodation of any religious institution that reflects heteronormativity and opposes non-binary teachings about men and women in supposedly patriarchal structures. What Koppelman worries about (informed by the history of antisemitism in Europe) is the "stigma of moral pollution . . . associated with religion itself. Conservative Christians have good reason to fear becoming a despised outlier caste. . . ."[12]

II. From Women's Rights to Gender Studies

Scholars who have specialized in the areas of women's studies and gender studies point out that a major shift occurred in scholarly circles by the 1980s. Earlier, research regarding men and women had proceeded under the assumption that the understandings of "male" and "female" despite cultural differences in expression, had a global core meaning that did not change all that significantly over time. Thus, studies of "the family" and subsequently of "women" typified anthropological, sociological, political, and historical research. By the 1980s, however, "gender" increasingly replaced "women" as the topic of interest, and because of this shift, the Orthodox now face a much steeper challenge in reconciling their received tradition regarding what it means to be human with the assumptions that now predominate in many Western university and American law school faculties.[13]

11. Andrew Koppelman, "Gay Rights, Religious Accommodations, and the Purposes of Antidiscrimination Law," *Southern California Law Review* 88, no. 3 (March 2015): 619–659, at 621.

12. Koppelman, "Gay Rights," 657.

13. For a summary of the literature and issues, see the four entries under "Gender" in Joan Shelley Rubin and Scott E. Casper, eds., *The Oxford Encyclopedia of American Cultural and Intellectual History* 2 vols. (New York: Oxford University Press, 2013), 1:443–464.

The first use of the term "rights of women" in the American context surfaced in the broader debates over women and the "rights of man" that had
drawn upon both ancient philosophy and "inspiration in the mechanical
innovations then being applied to industrial production, and in the discover-
ies of medical physiologists about the human body itself." Combining these
sources with a developed tradition of natural law and natural rights, Mary
Wollstonecraft by the 1790s combined a traditional invocation of a "knowledge of human nature" with her irritated dismissal of Jean-Jacques Rousseau's "nonsense," in supposing that "If women are by nature inferior to
men, their virtues must be the same in quality, if not in degree, or virtue is a
relative idea; consequently, their conduct should be founded on the same
principles, and have the same aim."[14] It was this essay in the American context that first "raised the question, both directly and indirectly, of women's
political participation." The publication struck a nerve and three years later
more copies of it were found in American libraries than Thomas Paine's
Rights of Man. But the arguments that Wollstonecraft employed were quite
conservative, relying as they did upon an already developed understanding
of natural rights, and at no point suggesting that any intrinsic conflict existed between revealed religion and the assertion of women's civil or political
rights.[15] When in 1798 Charles Brockden Brown published an essay on "The
Rights of Woman" in his *Weekly Magazine*, an uneasy disconnect was laid
bare, namely, between a revolution fought with an appeal to natural rights
and the fact that the new republic nonetheless "denied equal rights to all
black people and to nearly one-half of the white population: women."[16] The
traditional connection between rights and duties, one that Wollstonecraft
and nearly every other writer still took for granted, had no chance to be

14. Susan Groag Bell and Karen M. Offen, eds., *Women, the Family, and
Freedom: The Debate in Documents*, 2 vols (Stanford: Stanford University Press,
1983), I: introduction, 14; Mary Wollstonecraft, *A Vindication of the Rights of Women
with Strictures on Political and Moral Subjects*, first American edition (Boston:
Peter Edes for Thomas and Andrews, 1792), 58.

15. Rosemarie Zagarri, "American Women's Rights before Seneca Falls," in
Women, Gender and Enlightenment, ed. Sarah Knott and Barbara Taylor
(Houndsmills, UK: Palgrave MacMillan, 2005), 667–691, at 667 and 670.

16. Rosemarie Zagarri, *Revolutionary Backlash: Women and Politics in the Early
American Republic* (Philadelphia: University of Pennsylvania Press, 2007), 11.

tested beyond the brief flirtation in New Jersey that first bestowed, then by 1807 took away, women's voting rights.[17]

In order to move more American males to consider positively the notion of women's political rights as a critical part of citizenship, however, even more volatile questions emerged in the course of debate. Among them, issues surrounding sexuality, domestic violence, divorce, and control over the size of families revealed that the notion of women's rights might move forward officially on the lines of civil rights and legal protection of citizenship and voting. In actuality, such rights claims pointed to deeper questions about what it meant to be male, female, and exactly how one possessed legal and civil rights in the American social and political context. The increasing significance placed upon the possibility of rational choice exercised by the individual helps to explain the loosening of divorce laws, but sheds light as well even into the realm of what it meant to be a child. As a result, definitions of what it meant to do justice in American law in controverted cases regarding the standing of men, women, and children focused on "reaching and passing an age of reason and defined childhood as characterized most significantly by an almost complete inability to exercise judgment. In doing so, it elevated reason beyond all other human attributes. It put perhaps too much weight on this sudden transformation, on the difference between and child and an adult." But the implications here were to be long-lasting since this "new emphasis is still fundamental to our law and to our ideas about human development."[18]

By the time the recently consecrated Bishop Innocent Veniaminov began construction in 1844 of St. Michael's Orthodox Cathedral in Sitka, Alaska, the struggle for women's political rights had already begun in the

17. Zagarri, *Revolutionary Backlash*, 30–37. Unmarried propertied women in Lower Canada, by contrast, exercised the franchise until 1834; 37.

18. For a survey of the changes in American divorce and family issues, see Roeber, *Hopes for Better Spouses*, 277–82; on the changing definitions of childhood, Holly Brewer, *By Birth or Consent: Children, Law, and the Anglo-American Revolution in Authority* (Chapel Hill: University of North Carolina Press, 2005), 351. For a more skeptical reading of the reforms of divorce law and the argument that "gendered hierarchies defy radical transformation, despite otherwise significant cultural and economic change," Kirsten Sword, *Wives not Slaves: Patriarchy and Modernity in the Age of Revolutions* (Chicago and London: University of Chicago Press, 2021), 4, and on the divorce laws, 243–284.

United States. Historians of women's rights in the United States point to the 1848 Seneca Falls convention as an important benchmark in the appearance of such questions as a significant part of American political discourse. Yet it would be the confrontation of the United States with the practice of polygamy in the Church of Jesus Christ of Latter-Day Saints that emerged at almost the same time that made the debates over women's rights even more volatile. This latter controversy in a more visible, national forum of debate tied the rights of women to the ideal of monogamous marriage. Critics of Mormon polygamy (that included women in the forefront of the campaign to advance the political rights of women) sought to deny constitutional protection to polygamous marriage, branding the practice as uncivilized, and un-Christian.

The early history of the struggle for the political and civil rights of women in the United States located that narrative in a struggle for equal education, the reform of property and divorce laws, and the suffrage movement that emerged in tandem with the debates over the civil rights of African Americans in pre-Civil War America. None of those issues attracted the attention of Orthodox commentators with the exception of the issue of slavery, as the condemnation of the American Confederate States by the Ecumenical Patriarch made clear. In the aftermath of the American Civil War, the question of women's political and civil rights resumed, and for some time, continued to argue on the basis that antebellum reformers had done so, arguments that in retrospect remained socially conservative.[19]

19. On the re-telling of women's history in order to advance the rights claims, Teresa Anne Murphy, *Citizenship and the Origins of Women's History in the United States* (Philadelphia: University of Pennsylvania Press, 2013); on the challenges to acceptable female behavior, Sarah Knott, "Female Liberty? Sentimental Gallantry, Republican Womanhood, and Rights Feminism in the Age of Revolutions," *William and Mary Quarterly* 71, no. 3 (July, 2014): 425–456; on women and family size, Susan E. Klepp, *Revolutionary Conceptions: Women, Fertility, & Family Limitation in America, 1760–1820* (Chapel Hill: University of North Carolina Press, 2009); on the question of household governance, and of marital consent and its relationship to political choice, or the lack thereof, Norma Basch, *Framing American Divorce: From the Revolutionary Generation to the Victorians* (Berkeley: University of California Press, 1999), 19–67; Carol Shammas, *A History of Household Government in America* (Charlottesville: University of Virginia Press, 2002).

By the end of the nineteenth century, reformers coupled those efforts to labor and public health reform movements. At the state level, by the early 1900s suffrage existed in some parts of the country, but in the opinion of one of the earliest historians of women's rights, between 1896 and 1910 the entire suffrage issue appeared to be suffering from "unrelieved 'doldrums.'"[20] Eleanor Flexner, heavily influenced by the political and social issues of the 1930s, devoted little attention to the issue of women's rights and the support or criticism of those rights emanating from religious leaders and organizations. When she did turn to the question of who opposed the federal amendment to the Constitution that gave women the vote, Flexner identified the opposition in the American South as the manifestation of fear of African American enfranchisement; the hostility of brewers (predominantly German Americans) in the Midwest; and business and industrial leaders in the Northeast. But religious opposition came especially from Roman Catholic leaders such as James Cardinal Gibbons, who sent an address to the national Anti-Suffrage Convention that met in Washington, D.C. in 1916. Not surprisingly, Flexner offered no observations about the small Orthodox Christian groups in the United States at the time, or their reaction to the suffrage question.[21]

More recent feminist scholarship has shown that the New Woman movement at the turn of the twentieth century had not, as some scholars once maintained been the "almost exclusively . . . white middle-class affair" of an elite. Ethnic women's writers included Lakota, Chinese-American, Mexican-American, and German-American authors who wrote essays that maintained a traditional posture toward the importance of marriage and family, while at the same time managing to "critically discuss ethnicity and gender issues of the time." Their short stories may have been the earliest examples of "strong and critical feminist countervoices to patriarchal and nativist America at the beginning of the twentieth century."[22]

20. Eleanor Flexner and Ellen Fitzpatrick, *Century of Struggle: The Women's Rights Movement in the United States*, enl. ed. (1959; repr., Cambridge, MA: Bellknap Press of Harvard University Press, 1996), p. 255. Citations are from the 1996 edition.

21. Flexner and Fitzpatrick, *Century of Struggle*, 289–99; on Gibbons, 290.

22. Carmen Birkle, "Multiculturalism and the New Woman in Early Twentieth-Century America," in *Feminist Forerunners: New Womanism and Feminism in the*

An even more radical form of early feminism that has come to be identified as "eugenic feminism" rose and fell between the 1890s and the end of World War II. Never convincing a significant number of women or men, the leading figures in that movement are best understood as part of the progressive and elite spokespersons whose advocates were overwhelmingly white and privileged. Never comfortable with the more mainstream eugenicist movement, the advocates for birth control and selective breeding reflected concerns about overpopulation driven by the sexual appetites of the under-educated immigrant, First People, and African American members of society. When the attention of Americans focused again on the question of birth control in the 1960s, advocates for making contraception available had to struggle against the legacy of this older, and only partially repudiated, version of feminism that eugenicists themselves had labelled inconsistent with a strictly eugenicist program. Compulsory sterilization wrongly assumed to have been used first by Nazi Germany had in fact been endorsed in both Great Britain and the United States as parts of an ideology of sexual and social reform.[23]

Roe v. Wade gradually came to be understood among most Americans as a decision that held implications beyond the question of abortion. The Court's decision laid bare a fundamental distinction between those who argued for a relaxation of the prohibition on abortion on the basis of a claim to a constitutional right to privacy and hence a legal right to abortion. Others argued that what was at stake was the legal right of choice. Even though these rights claims stemmed from very different understandings of rights, the capacity of Americans to appeal to the decision "allowed movements to gesture to both ideas and to elide the differences between the two . . . when it was convenient to do so."[24] Even more alarming for

---

Early Twentieth Century, ed. Ann Heilmann (London: Pandora, 2003), 58–75, at 58, 75.

23. Mary Ziegler, "Eugenic Feminism: Mental Hygiene, The Women's Movement and the Campaign for Eugenic Legal Reform, 1900–1935," *Harvard Journal of Law & Gender* 31 (2008): 211–235; Christina Cogdell, *Eugenic Design: Streamlining America in the 1930s* (Philadelphia: University of Pennsylvania Press, 2004); Wendy Cline, *Building a Better Race: Gender, Sexuality and Eugenics from the Turn of the Century to the Baby Boom* (Berkeley: University of California Press, 2005).

24. Mary Ziegler, *Beyond Abortion: Roe v. Wade and the Battle for Privacy* (Cambridge, MA: Harvard University Press, 2018), 3.

those opposed to the equation of legal marriage rights with civil rights were conclusions that compared the history of the *Brown v. Board of Education* decision to the Supreme Court's decision in *United States v. Windsor* (2013) that invalidated part of the Defense of Marriage Act passed by Congress in 1996. That act had upheld the received understanding of marriage as a union between a man and a woman. Setting aside criticisms of a dubious invocation of substantive due process to arrive at the decision based on a reading of the Fifth Amendment to the Constitution, both critics and supporters could agree with Michael Klarman's conclusions, that in neither the case regarding racial equality nor that invalidating DOMA would such a decision have stood any chance in constitutional law except for "dramatic changes in the social and political contexts" of the nation coupled with the composition of the Supreme Court itself. Constitutional and legal doctrine, Klarman observed, meant little to the justices, and apparently just as little to the younger generation whose attitudes and beliefs lie behind the shift in favor of gay marriage that occurred between 1996 and 2013.[25]

Expansion of rights talk in the United States, when it did occur, emanated from a variety of domestic issues ranging from a growing concern for the rights of the disabled, the right of the destitute to have legal representation when being tried, and in matters of human sexual behavior, when gay and lesbian activists decided to build on the Civil Rights legislation of the 1960s as the way to expand the rights of freedom of choice by consenting adults in matters of human sexuality. That decision utilized the "rights of privacy" arguments that had decriminalized sexual activity among consenting adults in the *Griswold v. Connecticut* decision of 1965.[26] That Supreme Court case, coupled with the outbreak of the first AIDS epidemic, galvanized reactions (especially among evangelical Protestants) that had, by the

25. Michael J. Klarman, "*Windsor* and *Brown*: Marriage Equality and Racial Equality," *Harvard Law Review* 127, no. 1 (November, 2013): 127–160, at 129, 138, 155. https://harvardlawreview.org/2013/11/windsor-and-brown-marriage -equality-and-racial-equality/.

26. Anthony Lewis, *Gideon's Trumpet: How One Man, a Poor Prisoner, Took His Case to the Supreme Court and Changed the Law of the United States* (New York: Vintage Books, 1964); *Dusky v. United States* 362 US 402 (1960) mandated a competency hearing before any trial in which the accused must understand the charges and be able to aid legal counsel or act as his or her own attorney; Ziegler, *Beyond Abortion*, 65–73.

1980s, overtaken other kinds of considerations of rights and values, whether rights of asylum, dissent, and even the right to religious freedom—except when that last-named "freedom" or "right" became juxtaposed to expanding rights of LGBT persons.[27]

Historians still debate where to locate the origins of the reactions against the changing attitudes about marriage, human sexuality, and gender. The dean of American evangelical historians, Mark A. Noll, in 1994 identified what he deemed to be a major weakness of his own tradition. In surveying the history of American evangelical Protestantism, Noll focused on what he found to be an overall "distaste for complexity" that functioned sufficiently in the nineteenth and first half of the twentieth century before the growth of the American federal government, urbanization, and the post-World War II erosion of the general ethos of an unofficial Protestantism in the United Sates. Where most evangelicals had historically been politically quiescent, or only at times engaged in active attempts to make American officially Protestant, Noll argues that the very success of the general Protestant ethos led to a kind of pandering to American mainstream culture that was shocked by the events of the 1960s. In rapid succession, U.S. Supreme Court decisions forbade compulsory prayer in schools, as well as Bible reading, the latter acceptable only if this was clearly understood as an investigation of literature, and absent any doctrinal or confessional content.[28]

John Fea, a self-identified historian and member of the "white conservative evangelicals" of a younger generation expressed what he regarded as a long-standing tradition of fear and anxiety among his fellow believers. Even in a more comfortably Protestant age the tradition has often felt its values

27. Seth Dowland, "'Family Values' and the Formation of a Christian Right Agenda," *Church History* 78, no. 3 (September 2009): 606–631.

28. Mark A. Noll, *The Scandal of the Evangelical Mind* (Grand Rapids, MI: William B. Eerdmans, 1994), 12–15. For the engagement of American Reformed Christians with the notion of the "two kingdoms," a Protestant ecclesial realm and a social and political realm informed by the former that seldom attracted the endorsement of evangelicals or Lutherans, see A.G. Roeber, "Das Problem der Zwei-Reiche-Lehre in den USA," in, *Angewandtes Luthertum? Die Zwei-Reiche-Lehre als theologische Konstruktion in den politischen Kontexten des 20. Jhts.* ed. Hans Otte and J. Kampmann (Gütersloh: Gütersloher Verlagshaus, 2017), 348–364, and the abbreviated version above, Chapter One.

to be under attack. Fea located the remote origins of the current anxiety to find a champion to defend traditional values against so-called progressive enemies to older concerns about compulsory racial integration of schools. The integration controversies in combination with the court decisions from 1947 to 1963 appeared to marginalize evangelical values from those of an increasingly multi-racial and multi-cultural society. But Fea also argued that while evangelical reaction to the issues of public school prayer and integration began to galvanize evangelical defense of what they called "values", these skirmishes were paltry compared to the deep anxiety and anger that emerged by the late 1970s over issues of feminism, gay and lesbian activism, and belatedly, abortion.[29]

The former evangelical historian Randall Balmer is also convinced that the origins of evangelical defense of values can be found in the hostility to racial integration that began in the 1960s. But even Balmer admits that in the 1970s as "evangelicals began to venture outside of their subculture," it was the teaching of evolution, and hence the critical question of what it means to be human, male and female, that intensified evangelical hostility to institutionally ensconced values deemed to be hostile to their own. Unlike Noll's lament that evangelicals did not invest sufficiently in the struggle to reconcile faith and rational inquiry, Balmer believes that "institutions are remarkably poor vessels for the perpetuation of faith. . . ." a conclusion that overlooks the fact that especially at the level of local schools, institutions form habits of both faith and learning in a nation's youth, precisely the concern about values that has so exercised America's defenders of traditional values.[30]

The emergence of language that was specific in demanding a defense of traditional values began in 1980 with the Presbyterian Lou Sheldon's founding of the Traditional Values Coalition. From the outset, however, "traditional" and "family" were understood to be interchangeable modifiers of

---

29. John Fea, "Evangelical Fear Elected Trump," *The Atlantic*, June 24, 2018. https://www.theatlantic.com/ideas/archive/2018/06/a-history-of-evangelical-fear /563558 (accessed July 10, 2018). For an insightful survey of the complicated relationship between religion and race in America, see Mark A. Noll, *God and Race in American Politics* (Princeton, NJ: Princeton University Press, 2008).

30. Randall Balmer, *Thy Kingdom Come: How the Religious Right Distorts the Faith and Threatens America: An Evangelical's Lament* (New York: Basic Books, 2006), 109–42, at 116, 142.

the values being advocated and defended. For many followers of Sheldon's arguments, abortion (an issue that initially did not attract much attention or concern among evangelicals)—that was also now defined as a woman's "right to choose" (as enshrined in *Roe v. Wade*)—and the advancement of homosexual rights and values marched hand in hand. Ironically, the long-standing claim for American exceptionalism that argued that the United States still boasted a church-going population unlike the developed societies of Europe began to shift almost at the same time the traditional values coalitions emerged. A generation later, the number of unaffiliated Americans or disappointed evangelicals—the "nones and dones"—has grown steadily. A majority of Americans do not think of themselves as atheists because of these trends, but instead are still inclined toward some kind of "spirituality."[31] Other scholars would point to the rise by 1979 of the Southern Baptist leader Jerry Falwell's Moral Majority as a confirmation of the regional nature of a number of the movements associated with the New Christian Right.[32]

The defenders of traditional values could find support in large sectors of American society because Americans have not favored a legal ban on all abortions, nor more recently a legal ban on same-sex marriage. They have repeatedly shown that they do not approve of abortion on demand and are not eager to promote same-sex marriage. Instead they appear to wish to be as tolerant of those who do not think like them while still upholding some aspects of what they would call "traditional" values, meaning values surrounding sexual ethics and an ideal, if seldom realized, stable family life. Traditional values only rarely come to be invoked with regard to policies such as immigration, asylum, or social welfare although even in the public sphere many Americans, while traditionally skeptical about government ability to respond to their needs, do not favor a radical dismantling of the mix of social welfare and private enterprise they have inherited since the 1930s. For that reason, political scientist Shep Melnick has argued that "a proposition about American politics . . . [remains] just as helpful today as it

31. "America's Changing Religious Landscape," Pew Research Center: Religion & Public Life, May 12, 2015, www.pewforum.org/2015/05/12/americas -changing-religious-landscape.

32. Daniel K. Williams, "Jerry Falwell's Sunbelt Politics: The Regional Origins of the Moral Majority," *Journal of Policy History* 22, no. 2 (April, 2010): 125–47.

was in 1967. Americans . . . are 'ideologically conservative' but 'operation-ally liberal.' . . . most American voters favor a wide array of government pro-grams to promote full employment, increase economic security, improve public health, reduce crime, protect the environment, improve education, reduce discrimination, and promote equality of opportunity. But they are also distrustful of government in general, and centralized, bureaucratic gov-ernment in particular."[33] Americans on the whole believe values decisions to be private and individual—and they remain less inclined to follow instruc-tion or admonitions about values handed down by religious authorities. The clerical sex scandals in the Catholic Church coupled with parallel scandals among Protestant evangelicals have further eroded the credibility of reli-gious leaders as legitimate articulators of traditional values.[34]

The shift away from arguments drawn from a claim to the right of pri-vacy to an insistence on the rights of women based on the claim to equal protection under the Constitution, and the failure of the Equal Rights Amendment to the Constitution, illustrate the interpretive debates over the rights of women and, subsequently, sexual minorities. For some, this shift represented a significant departure from past tactics; for others, the equa-tion of the struggle for the rights of women with that of human rights could be traced all the way back to the founding era of the republic.[35] A trenchant analysis of the evangelical right argues that abortion debates followed by the same-sex marriage debates emerged as defining moments that transformed

33. R. Shep Melnick, *Transformation of Title IX: Regulating Gender Equality in Education* (Washington, D.C.: Brookings Institution Press, 2018), 259, citing Lloyd A. Free and Hadley Cantril, *The Political Beliefs of Americans: A Study of Public Opinion* (Camden, NJ: Rutgers University Press, 1967).

34. Laurie Goodstein and Sharon Otterman, "He Preyed on Men Who Wanted to Be Priests. Then He Became a Cardinal," *New York Times*, July 16, 2018, https://www.nytimes.com/2018/07/16/us/cardinal-mccarrick-abuse-priest.html; Goodstein, "How the Willow Creek Church Scandal Has Stunned the Evangelical World," *New York Times*, August 9, 2018, https://www.nytimes.com/2018/08/09/us/evangelicals-willow-creek-scandal.html; Jay Scott Newman, "The End of the Imperial Episcopate," *First Things*, August 20, 2018, https://www.firstthings.com/web-exclusives/2018/08/the-end-of-the-imperial-episcopate.

35. Linda Kerber, "U.S. Women's History as the History of Human Rights," *Travail, genre et sociétés* 28, no. 2 (2012): 25–44. https://doi.org/10.3917/tgs.028.0025 (accessed June 20, 2019).

older evangelical Christian arguments into what are now known as "rights politics." Evangelicals as a consequence now emphasize their marginalized and threatened status as a minority and hence, are much more sympathetic than their ancestors were to "increasing appeals on the right to rights and pluralism." At the same time, "political liberals have embraced a new kind of community morality regarding equal treatment for sexual orientation, punishing dissent," a position conservative evangelicals see as a majoritarian communitarianism that "demands conformity."[36]

In the opinion of many scholars, the reaction to the second wave of feminism accounted for the rise of the men's movement, which in the evangelical Christian form also informed those evangelicals who would convert to the Orthodox faith during the 1980s. Among these men's movement groups, the Promise Keepers appeared to some to provide for evangelical Protestants a response to the growth of feminist activism and reaffirmed the role of Christian men as the spiritual, and ideally, economic heads of households. Within a relatively short time, however, the Promise Keepers declined from their initially large profile and by the late 1990s had ceased to have much of an impact on the continuing debates over male and female roles in Christian families.[37] Some scholars traced the reactions to feminist criticisms of traditional gender roles to long-term shifts in the nature of the modern workplace, the absence of men from the home, and the subsequent decline of fatherhood itself as a major influence upon the lives of children. Others pointed instead, especially in the American context, to a shift in favor of consumer goods, the decline of educational childhood toys that had once encouraged children to dream of becoming adults and the confusion over what typified masculine role models. That change came to be reflected in the image of men portrayed in the media, suggesting an actual regression into "immaturity" among American men.[38]

36. Andrew R. Lewis, *The Rights Turn in Conservative Christian Politics: How Abortion Transformed the Culture Wars* (Cambridge: Cambridge University Press, 2017), 162, 163.

37. For a succinct history of the movement, see John Bastkowski, *The Promise Keepers: Servants, Soldiers, and Godly Men* (New Brunswick, NJ: Rutgers University Press, 2004).

38. Alexander Mitscherlich, *Society Without Father: a Contribution to Social Psychology* (New York: Harper Perennial, 1992); Gary Cross, *Kid's Stuff: Toys and the Changing World of American Childhood* (Cambridge, MA: Harvard University

Among American Protestant women, a seminal effort to promote "equal partner marriage" appeared in 1974. Letha Dawson Scarponi and Nancy A. Hardesty's *All We're Meant to Be: Biblical Feminism for Today* became a classic text within the second wave of American feminists. Despite its popularity—running into three editions by the 1990s—the work of these evangelical feminists had, at least in the opinion of one scholar, become effectively marginalized by the early twenty-first century. Analyzing the reactions to the Scarponi/Hardesty book, Sally K. Gallagher concluded that any diminution of male authority within marriage inevitably cast doubts on Biblical authority itself. Even within the camp of evangelical Protestant women, a split occurred by 1986 as some became more committed to gender feminism and others remained focused on a moderate defense of both equal partner marriage and what they perceived as the received teaching on the authority of men in both church and society.[39]

Underlying all these cultural shifts, however, lay the collapse of the economic structures that had defined roles for capital, labor, and government for most of the twentieth century. The ruin of the working class household contributed in ways that still reverberate more than half a century later to the realignment of ethnic immigrant families from an identity of full participation within the old Democratic Party's New Deal appeal to ethnic and working-class Americans to a sense of themselves as an increasingly fragile and embattled minority attempting to defend their faith's traditional understanding of family and the roles of both men and women.[40] It was into this Protestant, and belatedly, Catholic engagement with questions of marriage, sex, and eventually, gender that the Orthodox came as late participants.

Press, 1999); Cross, *Men to Boys: The Making of Modern Immaturity* (New York: Columbia University Press, 2010).

39. The third edition of the Scarponi/Hardesty volume was published by William B. Eerdmans Publishing Company in 1992. For Gallagher's analysis, see "The Marginalization of Evangelical Feminism," *Sociology of Religion* 65:3 (Autumn, 2004), 215–237, at 223–27 on the Scarponi/Hardesty book and the eventual split within evangelical feminist circles.

40. Jefferson Cowie, *'Stayin' Alive': The 1970s and the Last Days of the Working Class* (New York: The New Press, 2010).

III. The Orthodox, Marriage, and Sex

Most Orthodox (whether Eastern or Oriental) will only accept commentary or adjustment on questions of sex and marriage to already existing definitions and understandings that do not directly contradict or compromise what emerged as part of the Orthodox witness to the understanding of the meaning of male and female since ancient times. When historians ask about Orthodox memory regarding gender, they do recognize that during the centuries of the East Roman Imperial Church's dominance, "gender was a problem to be solved . . . the valency of gender in Byzantium was ambiguous." One can find examples of varying degrees of ambiguity regarding the standing of eunuchs who appear as angels in some iconography, or of women posing as male monastics in circles close to Constantinople that might well not have been shared by other centers, rural and urban, in the far-flung Eastern Roman Empire.[41] This was so because Christianity at one and the same time continued to reflect the male-centered values of Mediterranean cultures; it accepted a transcendence of temporal necessities that typified male and female identity suggested by Jesus' own affirmation that in the Kingdom after his Second Coming, sexual activity will not play any role comparable to life on earth. Nonetheless the Church also admitted that this revelation could also appear to be "at odds with the Christian affirmation of the body which was given doctrinal expression in the incarnation and the resurrection of the body." Thus "gender was the irritating grain of sand in the oyster that kept bringing this tension to painful consciousness." More than five hundred years after the disappearance of the Eastern Roman Empire, the commitment to the sacrality and givenness of human sexual expression in marriage and the awareness of the irrelevance of sexual expression in the coming kingdom still persists and, remains the irritating grain of sand. The Orthodox, no less than the Roman Catholic Church, reject the separation of sex from gender, i.e., the "ideology of gender" while affirming the importance of research "which tries . . . to achieve a deeper understanding of the ways in which sexual

---

41. Judith Herrin, *Byzantium: The Surprising Life of a Medieval Empire* (Princeton, NJ: Princeton University Press, 2009), 160–169; McGuckin, *The Path of Christianity: The First Thousand Years* (Downer's Grove, IL: IVP Press, 2017), 1104–14.

difference between men and women is lived out in a variety of cultures."[42] A resolution of the question of the moral right to life and the legal or dignitary rights of women and those of same-sex orientation remains part of this commitment both to universal human dignity and the understanding of theological anthropology that insists on the significance of male and female identities.[43]

The abuse of First People women by Russian fur trading company employees gives us the first indicator of North American Orthodox confrontation with issues of sex, gender, and moral rights and the demand for protection of those rights by those in civil authority. Monastic and clerical condemnation of these abuses provoked violent responses, including death threats against the Russian clergy who insisted that indigenous women be respected because they were fellow humans, without regard to whether they had become baptized Orthodox Christians. A report by the Hieromonk Makarrii to the Holy Synod in 1797 reported how the Russian traders "forcibly take women and children as concubines"—in the case of Maxim Kribdin, including a young girl already baptized, into a condition of sexual slavery.[44]

By the early nineteenth century, the Hieromonk Gideon who had been sent from Russia to report on the conditions of both the Orthodox

---

42. Damien Casey, "The Spiritual Valency of Gender in Byzantine Society," in *Questions of Gender in Byzantine Society*, ed. Bronwen Neil and Lynda Garland (Farnham, UK: Ashgate Publishing, 2013), 167–181, at 181. For a non-Orthodox critique of claims that "sex" is merely a socially constructed and culturally relative term, see Helen Joyce, *Trans: When Ideology Meets Reality* (New York: Oneworld, 2022).

43. Congregation for Catholic Education, *Male and Female He Created Them: For a Path of Dialogue on the Issue of Gender in Education* (Vatican City: Congregation for Catholic Education, 2019), para. 6; accessed June 7, 2019, https://zenit.org/articles/new-vatican-document-provides-schools-with-guidance -on-gender-issues/.

44. Letter of Makarrii to the Holy Synod, December 20, 1797, reprinted in Michael Oleksa, ed., *Alaskan Missionary Spirituality* (New York: Paulist Press, 1987), 287–290, at 288. On the fur company itself and its controversial leader Alexander Baranov, see Kenneth N. Owens and Alexander Yu. Petrov, *Empire Maker: Aleksander Baranov and Russian Colonial Expansion into Alaska and Northern California* (Seattle: University of Washington Press, 2017).

mission and the First Peoples revealed the ongoing problem presented by the abuse of First Peoples women. In a letter to Alexander Andreevich Baranov, the manager of the Russian American Company (incorporated and holding the monopoly privilege over the fur trade since 1798), Gideon blamed the institution for providing a cover for the attitude of Russians whose "depraved minds" led them to abandon "family life altogether . . . therefore the poor Americans are, to the shame of the Russians, sacrificed to their immorality."[45] The first encounters of arriving Russians with various tribal groups in the Alaskan area revealed that no marriage ceremony as such existed among these peoples. The closest ritual the Russians could recognize as vaguely similar to marriage was the Sugpiaq practice of having the prospective groom arrange for "a special steam bath for his bride as part of the procedure."[46]

Because of the diversity of marital customs, missionaries received instructions from the bishops who finally emerged in the persons of Innocent (John Veniaminov, 1797–1879) and his successors to overlook irregularities in indigenous marriage customs. In his 1853 communication to Hieromonk Theophan, Veniaminov noted that polygamy was a fact of life among the First Peoples and the practice was not to be dealt with harshly nor could the "forbidden degrees of relationship" prohibitions always be reconciled with "the scantiness of local populations." Furthermore, missionaries were forbidden to make in-depth inquiries into marriages entered into before baptism, nor were such unions to be regarded as a bar to receiving the Eucharist.[47]

Nonetheless, by the 1860s, egregious irregularities continued to occur, and a newer generation of Church authorities was no longer willing to overlook them. The sub-deacon Constantine Lukin arrived in the area of the Kushokwin-Yukon mission. Himself a creole whose mother had been a Kodiak Alutiiq, Constantine had for more than a decade been living with a Yup'ik woman already married to another man. The newly arrived bishop from Russia, Peter Ekaterinovsky (1820–1889), restored the woman to her

---

45. See the letter of Gideon to Baranov from 26 May, 1807 in Lydia Black, *The Round the World Voyage of Hieromonk Gideon* (Kingston, ON: Limestone Press, 1989), 107.

46. Michael Oleksa, *Orthodox Alaska: A Theology of Mission* (Crestwood, New York: St. Vladimir's Seminary Press, 1992), 99.

47. Oleksa, *Alaskan Missionary Spirituality*, 238–251, at 245, 246.

lawful husband and had Lukin dismissed from his service as a lay assistant to the creole Orthodox clergy.[48] The Russian Orthodox discipline of Lukin, however, should not be interpreted only as a form of Russian imperial or colonialist dominance over a creole convert. Starting in the previous century, the Russian Church had moved to put an end within the Empire to its medieval tolerance of common law marriages that had subsequently been blessed by a Church short on parish-level clergy. The extension of a more canonically rigorous discipline of marriage from Russia itself to more recently acquired areas under its influence provides the best context for understanding what occurred a century later in the Kushokwin-Yukon incident.[49]

By 1878, i.e., within a decade of the acquisition of Alaska by the United States, and coinciding with the decision to move the Russian Diocese's headquarters from Alaska to San Francisco, Senator Aaron A. Sargent of California introduced a proposed amendment to the U.S. Constitution to extend to women citizens of the United States the right to vote in federal elections. Rejected by a senate committee in 1887, the amendment would only be adopted in 1920, a particularly inauspicious year for the Orthodox in the United States. In the aftermath of the Bolshevik Revolution in Russia, Patriarch Tikhon Bellavin issued his *ukase* that recognized out of necessity the autonomous standing of the Russian Mission that became known as the Metropolia. Any attention that might have been given to the question of the roles of women—whether of the First Peoples or citizens in the 48 states or in the Church—vanished in the controversies that now surrounded a fragmenting group of Orthodox ethnic churches. No official Orthodox notice was taken of the Amendment itself, nor of the challenges to it that were finally dismissed two years later despite accusations of irregularities put forward by opponents in Maryland, West Virginia, and Tennessee—states where an Orthodox presence was negligible, or non-existent.[50]

At the level of everyday experience, however, the social and political conditions among arriving Orthodox immigrants in the thinly settled areas

---

48. Oleksa, *Orthodox Alaska*, 138–140.

49. For details on the Russian regulation of both common law and mixed marriages, see Roeber, *Mixed Marriages*, 146–56.

50. The Supreme Court affirmed the correctness of the Amendment's procedural move toward ratification in *Leser v. Garnett* 258 U.S. 130 (1922).

of the United States and its territories led to practical adjustments in the roles Orthodox women began to play in both Church and society. In the Intermountain West—the area Sheldon Jackson himself had come from prior to his arrival in Alaska—by comparison with more settled areas of the United States, Greek American women "had more freedom than those in urban centers . . . they drove cars, worked outside the home, could, usually, refuse marriage proposals, and groups of them took vacations together . . . their role in church affairs became active, not merely that of cooking for festivals. The San Francisco, Los Angeles, and Utah Greek churches have had women presidents and women board members have served for many years . . . the Pocatello Greek church . . . dissatisfied with men's handling of church affairs . . . ran a slate of women candidates and succeeded in having all offices filled with women. One man did remain on the board."[51]

Despite differing roles played by immigrant Orthodox women in these isolated incidents, the role of women in Orthodox churches of any jurisdiction did not change dramatically from inherited patterns until after the World War II. From 1917 to 1945 internal developments within the Orthodox Church both in the United States and abroad forced a reassessment of those roles. For the first time Orthodox exposure to other Christians in what became the World Council of Churches began to change the parameters of Orthodox views on the roles of women and marriage. By the time of the post-World War II reorganization of several of the American Orthodox jurisdictions, cautious indications of a willingness to address the roles of Orthodox women in relationship to parish life arose because those women had become participant citizens of the United States, exercising equal voting rights with their spouses. But only in the following generation did the formation of organizations specifically intended to give a voice to women in Orthodox life begin to emerge.

In the late 1940s the Greek theologian and rector of the University of Athens, Evangelos Theodorou began his explorations of the history of women serving as deacons in the ancient Orthodox churches. Although his essays

---

51. Helen Papanikolas, "Greek Immigrant Women in the Intermountain West," in *Reading Greek America: Studies in the Experience of Greeks in the United States,* ed. Spyros D. Orfanos (New York: Pella Publishing Company, 2002), 99–114, at 113, 114.

culminated in the 1949 book *Heroines of Love: Deaconesses through the Ages*, nothing came of his proposal that the Orthodox re-open the question of ordaining women to the diaconate. His later dissertation published in Athens in 1954 also met with silence, in some degree because more pressing concerns regarding the fraught political conditions in Greece and the outbreak of an especially brutal riot against Greeks in Constantinople focused the attention of Greek hierarchs and theologians on those events. But in Theodorou's own words, "the first official response of the Orthodox Church to specifically engage this issue occurred only a full generation later in 1988 when the Ecumenical Patriarchate of Constantinople convened an Inter-Orthodox Theological Consultation on Rhodes where for the first time invited representatives gathered to examine 'The Place of Woman in the Orthodox Church and the Question of the Ordination of Women.'"[52]

Because of the fragmented, ethnic character of Orthodox communities in North America and the continued arrival of immigrants fleeing Eastern Europe in the aftermath of World War II, the Civil War in Greece, and continued unrest in the Middle East, Orthodox women in the U.S. continued to work as housewives, or labored in working-class occupations or in small shops. Like many non-Orthodox women, including Eleanor Roosevelt, when confronted with the proposal for an Equal Rights Amendment to the U.S. Constitution in the 1950s, Orthodox women opposed the Amendment along occupational and class lines. Specific legal rights that had been designed to protect working women found protection in the Hayden Amendment that more radical feminists opposed on the grounds that true equality could not be reconciled with the continued protection of rights restricted to women only.

Orthodox women themselves began raising questions about their standing, and possible roles in the Church with the Zoe movement in Greece in the 1920s. Initially an exclusively male brotherhood movement that began in 1907, the movement's aim at revitalizing lay piety had expanded to include work in missionary efforts as well. By 1938, the reality of women involved in the movement brought about the foundation of an actual sisterhood named Efsevia "after the founder of the Zoe brotherhood and

---

52. Evangelos Theodorou, prologue to *Women Deacons in the Orthodox Church: Called to Holiness and Ministry*, by Kyriaki Karidoyanes FitzGerald (Brookline, MA: Holy Cross Orthodox Press, 1998), xxi–xxviii, at xxiii.

movement, Efseviios Matthopoulos."[53] Eventually utilizing the outlet of the journal *Aktines*, published by the Christian Union of Scientists, and the journal of the Center for the Social Education of the Greek Woman, women authors often writing anonymously, began in the 1950s to argue for women's "rights in education, as well as a clear emphasis on women's rights in the workplace."[54] Drawing a sharp distinction between the secular, often Communist-leaning feminism in Greece, and themselves, the Zoe sisterhoods, until their splintering in 1963, embraced a celibate lifestyle that was nonetheless not monastic, thereby attracting the suspicion of the Greek hierarchs. Despite their relatively conservative form of feminism that still reaffirmed the traditional role of husbands as the head of households, the sisterhood could not survive the reactionary movement within the Zoe brotherhood that repudiated the earlier engagement with changing realities in Greek society. Older Zoe members "disapproved of its young men and women members who socialized and worked together for religious purposes" a judgment propagated especially by the former, and now bitterly disillusioned Greek philosopher Christos Yannaras.[55]

The Zoe sisterhood movement arose in tandem with the post-World War I move on the part of the Greek Orthodox to continue participation in ecumenical ventures, a posture encouraged by the Greek Archbishop in North America, Athenagoras I, who would become the Ecumenical Patriarch in 1950. Stirred in part because of emergency situations created by the horrors of the World War II and the Holocaust, Athenagoras supported the engagement of Orthodox Christians to make common cause with other Christians in the World Council of Churches on issues of concern that did not challenge Orthodox dogmatic teachings. One of the most vocal critics of the Orthodox retreat in the 1960s from engaging seriously the ongoing developments and various strains within feminist understandings of women's rights has traced the origins of the Orthodox women's awareness

53. Spyridoula Athanasopoulou-Kypriou, "Emancipation through Celibacy? The Sisterhoods of the Zoe Movement and their Role in the Development of 'Christian Feminism' in Greece 1938–1960," in *Innovation in the Orthodox Christian Tradition? The Question of Change in Greek Orthodox Thought and Practice,* ed. Trine Stauning Willert and Lina Molokotos-Liederman (Farnham, UK: Ashgate Publishing, 2012), 101–121, at 101.

54. Athansopoulou-Kypriou, "Emancipation," 115.

55. Athansoppoulou-Kypriou, "Emancipation," 110; 102–03.

of rights to Athenagoras' support of Orthodox participation in the World Council of Churches. Leonie Liveris' opinion expressed in an interview with an Australian newspaper, concluded that "'the worlds of Orthodox and feminist theology were mutually exclusive . . . [and] being an Ortho-dox woman meant leaving many things at the door of the Church when you join.'" Her criticism resulted in the primate of the Greek Orthodox Archdiocese of Australia's refusal to endorse Liveris' nomination to serve on the WCC's Commission on Justice, Peace and Creation.[56]

But by the 1960s the Orthodox had been exposed for a generation to wider Christian circles of debate about the role of women in both church and society. And by the 1960s, the criticism of those women who began to ask questions about a more active role in the Church shifted significantly—away from older attitudes that had focused on "women's spiritual and physical weakness, menstrual cycles, incompetence, lack of intelligence, or general inferiority. . . ." Instead, in the wake of the civil rights movement and the first wave of feminism, a new set of questions arose about the very nature of what it meant to be a woman or a man and whether "gender" rather than "sex"—the latter connected to some sense of a biological "essentialism"—now ought to define the conversation. With that shift, questions about sexuality and marriage intensified. Those issues had come into focus outside the United States in the career of the convert Elisabeth Behr-Sigel. A woman of both Jewish and Lutheran religious backgrounds, Behr-Sigel had served a one-year pastorate in the French Reformed Church and later converted to the Orthodox faith.[57]

Yet, just as was the case with the Greek theologian Theodorou, decades would pass before the issues first raised by Behr-Sigel began to be addressed openly. The WCC's 1963 meeting in Montreal had produced firm opposi-tion to the question of women being ordained in the Orthodox Church. And only in 1976—and only because of the urging of the WCC—did the

56. Leonie B. Liveris, *Ancient Taboos and Gender Prejudice: Challenges for Orthodox Women and the Church* (New York: Ashgate, 2005), 178.

57. The following relies upon: Sarah Hinlicky Wilson, "Tradition, Priesthood and Personhood in the Trinitarian Theology of Elisabeth Behr-Sigel," *Pro Ecclesia* 19, no. 2 (Spring, 2010): 129–150, at 130; Sister Margarete Roeber, "Wherefore Man and Woman?," (paper, Holy Assumption Monastery, Calistoga, CA, December 8, 2013) 9–18; 27–32. For a summary of Behr-Sigel's own theological journey, see McGuckin, *The Eastern Orthodox Church*, 263–69.

Consultation of Orthodox Women meet in Romania to begin debating the broad topic of women in the Orthodox Church, and tentatively, what roles they had played in the past, and what future possibilities might be explored.[58]

Despite meetings and conferences between 1976 and the dawn of the new millennium, that the right of women to participate fully in the theological deliberations of the church continued to meet resistance became clear in the spring of 2006. From its inception as a protest church against the Soviet control of the Moscow Patriarchate, the Russian Orthodox Church Outside Russia regarded itself as the only legitimate expression of the Russian Church since the 1917–18 All-Russian Sobor. In preparing for the reconciliation of ROCOR with the Patriarchate of Moscow, an All-Diaspora Council was called in 2006. Despite the claim that they adopted the same rules for participation that had governed the Russian Sobor itself, the assembly of ROCOR included neither monastic nor lay women among its delegates. In "An Open Letter to the Hierarchy of ROCOR" 81 signatories protested this fact, pointing out that "1918 certainly was a different time: women could not vote in the overwhelming majority of countries. . . ." But even in Russia, the women signatories protested, Russian women have, "been included in Councils" further making the "exclusion of women from the All-Diaspora Council in 2006" even more disturbing, revealing "a disconnect between the priorities of our ecclesiastical organization and the actual life and values of the flock." The reality in America—that women "conduct the choirs . . . are members of parish councils . . . head church organizations and . . . teach at the seminary," and as professional women were "lawyers, doctors, scientists, businesswomen and scholars"—needed to be taken seriously. Lest anyone accuse them of being influenced by an alien ideology, the signatories pointed out that "the equality of men and women as God's creation is not a foreign or feminist concept, but a value we as an Orthodox community share, embrace and live by. We have women vote, we do not hide women behind burqas, we encourage women to learn, think and work."[59] The petition laid no claim

---

58. For the WCC reports and the eventual 1976 meeting, see M. Roeber, "Wherefore Man and Woman?," 2–3.

59. "An Open Letter to the Hierarchy of ROCOR," https://www.rocorstudies .org/2021/02/22/an-open-letter-to-the-hierarchy-of-rocor/

to rights of women to participation, but did ground the request in the expanded vision for women's roles in the Church that had emerged in the Russian Council in the previous century.

Despite the petition, no women participated in the council, nor was their request for a commission to examine the standing of women in the church honored. But it was not only the Russian Orthodox in the United States who hesitated to deal with the changing social, economic, and political standing of Orthodox women that had evolved over the course of the previous century. Under the leadership of Archbishop (and later Ecumenical Patriarch) Athenagoras, the Greek Orthodox Archdiocese of North America that had been incorporated in 1921 had convened in 1930 its first biennial Clergy-Laity Congress. A year later Athenagoras founded the Ladies Philoptochos Society to encourage the charitable work of the women members of the Greek parishes. Not until 1982 did the National Sisterhood of Presbyteres come into being, the organization specifically intended to address the concerns and perspectives of priests' and deacons' wives. No specific attention in the form of commissions at the national or diocesan levels addressed prior to the 1980s the changing standing of Greek-American women. Among Arab-American Orthodox, those favoring continued connections to the Russians and those wishing to be under the authority of the Holy Synod of Damascus were finally reunited in the Antiochian Christian Orthodox Archdiocese of North America in 1975. But even before that unification Metropolitan Philip Saliba founded the Antiochian Orthodox Christian Women of North America in 1973. The organization was intended to promote "a spirit of Christian leadership, awareness and commitment as taught in the Holy Orthodox Church," and service and charitable activities and to provide a forum for fellowship among women members of that jurisdiction. In a move that many of the most conservative Orthodox found troubling, Philip also designated March as "Women's Month" and encouraged parishes to invite women in good standing in the parishes to serve as readers, to take the collections, and in some instances, with the local priest's blessing, to offer a reflection or homily on the appointed Scripture read at the Divine Liturgy.

The controversial reception of a Tomos of Autocephaly given by the Russian Orthodox Church to the former Russian Metropolia that renamed itself the Orthodox Church of America in 1970 did not produce any changes in the standing of women or a discussion of the roles of women in this self-consciously American jurisdiction. Nonetheless, and more or less on the same schedule as the other jurisdictions, a generation later by the 1980s a parish in Ohio founded the Holy Trinity Business Women group that specifically recognized the reality of single, working married, divorced, and widowed women whose common identity emerged from their involvement in various workplace environments. The challenges posed by the need to balance increased economic pressure with traditional expectations as women serving various forms of needs within the parish's life accounted for these ad hoc efforts. But no national institution and no pan-Orthodox discussion of the changing role of women in the Church emerged as a result of these efforts within disparate jurisdictions.[60]

The internal debates over the role of women in the American Orthodox context eventually caught up with the pioneering work on women in the diaconate first raised in the 1940s by Evangelos Theodorou. Yet, despite the publication of Presbytera Kyriaki Fitzgerald's monograph on women and the diaconate, American hierarchs and theologians did not engage the issue for almost another generation.[61] Finally, the question of women and the diaconate began in the early decades of the twenty-first century to attract significant attention and corresponding controversy.

For some time, the St. Phoebe Center for the Deaconess had been sponsoring lectures and conferences to assess the historical, canonical, and present day practices of various Orthodox communities on this topic. The decision taken by the Greek Orthodox Patriarch Theodoros of Alexandria in February of 2016 to consecrate several women to what was described as the diaconate galvanized further attention on this issue. So did the decision of the Vatican to investigate whether women could serve as deacons in the Roman Catholic Church. These events elicited a response of thirty-five priests and seven deacons (that subsequently has grown to more than 272 signatories) in the form of "A Public Statement on Orthodox Deaconesses by Concerned Clergy and Laity." The opposition to considering women as deacons emerged primarily from the ranks of the Russian

---

60. For the OCA's 1982 experiment in Ohio see Margarita Berzonsky, "Organizing Business Women to Serve the Church," *Parish Development* 1 (1983), https://oca.org/parish-ministry/parishdevelopment/organizing-business-women-to -serve-the-church.

61. Kyriaki Karidoyanes Fitzgerald, *Women Deacons in the Orthodox Church: Called to Holiness and Ministry* (Brookline, MA: Holy Cross Orthodox Press, 1998).

Orthodox Church Outside Russia and the more conservative parishes of the Orthodox Church in America. Although signatories to the statement did not always include their jurisdiction or patriarchate, of the eighty-four signatories who did identify themselves most can be identified as members of ROCOR, the OCA, and the Russian Patriarchal parishes. Although patronymics are only somewhat useful in identifying the signatories' backgrounds, it is striking how many names came not from the Slavic-speaking Orthodox world, but instead appeared to be those of American Protestant converts. A mere 20 signatories identified with the Greek Orthodox Archdiocese of North America; of the 27 Antiochian signatories, only four names can be identified as Arabic in origin; the balance appears to be American converts.

The disputes over whether "ordination" or "blessing" characterized the historic as well as the present liturgical rite proceeded while the continuous record of women serving as deacons in the monasteries of the Armenian Apostolic Church was ignored (this includes the wearing of diaconal vestments and use of the *rapidia* or fans at the Eucharist and occasional chanting of the gospel). Opponents dismissed the statement of the St. Phoebe Center that the charism of the diaconate in no way implies the possibility of ordaining women as presbyters or bishops. The signatories instead voiced their repeated concern about the danger of women deacons being "forced" on the Church; that they might have "the authority a deacon might exercise over men as well as women" thus questioning the importance of women's submission to men. The signatories also invoked the ominous example of such "innovations" in "heterodox communities." This last concern ironically appeared to be a version of branch theory of Christianity where the issue of women was concerned. Such a position is at odds with the usual claim of the most conservative Orthodox that there is no grace to be found among the heterodox, and hence, presumably nothing much to be learned from their errors, either.[62]

62. For the statement and record of signatories, see "A Public Statement on Orthodox Deaconesses by Concerned Clergy and Laity," January 15, 2018, http://www.aoiusa.org/a-public-statement-on-orthodox-deaconesses; for the Armenian example, Abel Oghlukian, *The Deaconess in the Armenian Church: A Brief Survey* (New Rochelle, NY: St. Nersess Armenian Seminary, 1994); for the St. Phoebe Center statement, "FAQs," St. Phoebe Center for the Deaconess, https://orthodox deaconess.org/mission-vision/faqs/ (accessed October 20, 2017); for the consecration

Although many social, economic, and political issues have fueled the growing concern among the Orthodox on the redefinition of what constitutes marriage, there can be little doubt that the rise of various forms of feminist critiques of marriage and human sexuality in general has played a critical, central role. It is to that history that we must turn now in some detail in order to appreciate how the Orthodox came late in confronting those critiques and how they now ponder what rights, both civil and within the Church itself pertain especially to LGBT persons.

---

by Patriarch Theodoros, see Aurelian Iftimiu, "Theodoros of Alexandria performs first consecration of deaconesses," Basilica.ro, February 22, 2017, https://basilica.ro /en/patriarch-theodoros-of-alexandria-performs-first-consecration-of-deaconesses/; for the Vatican decision, Joshua J. McElwee, "Francis institutes commission to study female deacons, appointing gender-balanced membership," National Catholic Reporter, August 2, 2016, https://www.ncronline.org/news/vatican/francis -institutes-commission-study-female-deacons-appointing-gender-balanced. For the most recent reflections on Orthodox women and the diaconate, see Carrie Frederick Frost, *Church of Our Granddaughters* (Eugene, Oregon: Cascade Books, 2023) and John Chryssavgis, et al., eds., *Deaconesses: A Tradition for Today and Tomorrow* (Brookline, Massachusetts: Holy Cross Orthodox Press, 2023).

7

THE ORTHODOX, GENDER, AND SEXUALITY AND THE RIGHTS REVOLUTION

A s the reaction to Archbishop Iakovos' participation in the civil rights movement demonstrated, by the 1960s the majority of American Orthodox had exhibited little inclination to engage with challenges to traditional, accepted roles of ethnic and racial groups, and even less so, with investigating understandings of what it means to be male, female, and Orthodox. The feminist movement of the 1960s, however, emerging as it did on the heels of the broader civil rights movement that sought economic, political, and social equality for non-White minority groups, challenged the predominantly paternalist culture of Orthodox families, regardless of geographic or linguistic origin. Both Catholic and Protestant Christians in the United States by the 1970s and 1980s also began to confront the question of whether and how it was possible for gay and lesbian persons to remain faithful members of their religious communities. As a result, both Catholic and Protestant authors devoted increasing attention to the issue of human sexuality, marriage, and in the Catholic instance, a "theology of the body" given impetus by Pope John Paul II's own writings. By contrast, almost nothing on the topic appeared from Orthodox theologians until early in the twenty-first century.[1]

---

1. The single most influential treatment remains Thomas Hopko, *Christian Faith and Same Sex Attraction: Eastern Orthodox Reflections* (Ben Lomond, CA: Conciliar Press, 2006). For a summary of the literature on Catholic reflections on human sexuality, marriage, and Pope John Paul's theology, see Anthony Roeber,

The delay on the part of the Orthodox Church in addressing such issues reflected the reality of its division into various jurisdictions increasingly composed of conservative and moderate memberships, with a very small voice of culturally or politically left-leaning participants.[2] Greek-Orthodox writers such as Leah Fygetakis noted in the 1980s that "whether a Greek woman [was] lesbian or heterosexual . . . *philotimo* is so important she has learned at a very young age to make use of lies and deception to cover up any shortcomings or unacceptable behavior . . . Greeks see lying as more socially acceptable than telling the truth if the truth goes outside social norms . . . dishonor comes not so much from breaking the rules as from being caught." Under such social and cultural constraints no discussion of a change in women's roles, no matter how modest, was possible.[3]

As the trajectory of the pursuit of women's rights shifted toward questions of gender and sexuality in the broader society, Orthodox theologians, ethicists, and social scientists had to examine more intently the basis upon which Orthodox teachings about what it meant to be "male" and "female" rested. The deep history of Orthodox reflection on the meaning of human sexuality has produced a wide variety of opinions about the significance of sexual differentiation, what role that difference played at the creation, during human history, and what role it will play in the condition of humanity following the Second Coming of Christ. All remain topics of debate and continue to generate a spectrum of theological opinions.

I. Orthodox Received Teaching and Questions of Gender

It seems wisest to begin with what we might describe as the "received teaching" among the Orthodox regarding God's purpose in creating humans, male and female. The majority of Orthodox theologians have long argued

---

Mixed Marriages: An Orthodox History (Yonkers, NY: St. Vladimir's Seminary Press, 2018), Chapter 4.

2. For a typology of the kinds of Orthodox parishes and communities in the U.S., see Vrame, "Four Types of 'Orthopraxy,'" 279–307.

3. Leah M. Fygetakis, "Greek American Lesbians: Identity Odysseys of Honorable Good Girls," in *Reading Greek America: Studies in the Experience of Greeks in the United States*, ed. Spyros D. Orfanos (New York: Pella Publishing Company, 2002), 291–325, at 305.

that the Genesis account that identifies the creation of humanity in God's likeness included male and female from the very outset (Genesis 1:27–29) The convert apostle Paul, in his letter to the Galatians, recapitulated the Genesis story in Chapter 3 verse 28 of that letter. Although some commentators have attempted to argue that Paul or his amanuensis failed to complete in accurate Greek a series of disjunctions in his list of differences, traditionally, Orthodox scholars would disagree.

Although the apostle wrote that "between Jew or Greek, slave or free," he did not write "male *nor* female" (emphasis added). Instead, while using the Greek *ouk . . . oude* for the distinctions between Jews and Gentiles, slaves and the free, Paul wrote "*kai*" between "*arsen*" and "*thele.*" This intentional reversion to the Genesis coupling of "male *and* female" cannot be seen to carry "exactly the same meaning as 'neither male nor female.'" Instead, the deliberate use of "and" demonstrates that God envisioned and created humanity from before creation itself as identifiably male and female—and these distinctions are permanent—in other words, there neither was, nor will be, an androgynous "human." Although some commentators as well as early fathers including St. Gregory of Nyssa may have been influenced by Philo of Alexandria and Origen in appearing to endorse some version of a "primordial human being" of androgynous form, and a belief in a "dual creation," it was not the Catholic-Orthodox, but the later esoteric communities who had first developed the notion of a "redeemer" of an androgynous *anthropos*. Orthodox interpreters emphasize that the "text stresses sexuality even more than is at first apparent," because God blessed the "be fruitful and multiply" activity of humans immediately (v. 28) and thus, Paul's quotation of Gen 1:27 and then its negation "no male and female" shows that he actually insisted "that baptism in Christ was in no way related to the 'natural-sexual' order of things and thus in no way a 'return'—as in the Anthropos-redeemer myth—to an original status. Baptism was rather the implementation of something utterly new." Not only Galatians, but the "deutero-Pauline epistles to the Colossians and the Ephesians—letters that deal with gnostic tendencies—actually liken the relationship between Christ the redeemer and the church to a marriage (Eph 5: 25–32)."[4] So too, in any future state, the

4. Paul Nadim Tarazi, *Galatians: A Commentary* (Crestwood, NY: St. Vladimir's Seminary Press, 1999), 173–177 at 174, 175, 176. See also Peter C. Bouteneff, *Beginnings: Ancient Christian Readings of the Biblical Creation Narratives* (Grand

distinction of male and female will remain permanent but without the need for specific mutual helpers, nor for procreation. That apparent paradox appears to be related to what Paul elsewhere (1 Cor 6:13) says about the mortal stomach and food—both are created for each other but God will (not "destroy" as in English translations) "liberate from the law," or "render idle and unnecessary" (*Theos kai tauten kai tauta katargesei*) these aspects of the human person.[5]

Orthodox theologians convinced of this received teaching would claim that the true identity of Christians male or female lies in Baptism-Chrismation-Eucharist. The former Pharisee Saul of Tarsus went to great lengths to explain the difference between receiving as a free gift the promise of God versus what could be claimed as a legal right. "If you inherit something as a legal right, it does not come to you as the result of a promise, and it was precisely in the form of a promise that God made his gift to Abraham." Anxious that his point be understood, the convert Paul continued "Let me put this another way: an heir, even if he has actually inherited everything is not different from a slave for as long as he remains a child. He is under the control of guardians and administrators until he reaches the age fixed by his father . . . God has sent the Spirit of his Son into your hearts; the Spirit that cries, 'Abba, Father', and it is this that makes

---

Rapids, MI: Baker Academic, 2008); On Orthodox methodology connecting Old and New Testament texts, Eugene J. Pentiuc, *The Old Testament in Eastern Orthodox Tradition* (New York: Oxford University Press, 2014), 3–61. On Nyssa and differing Orthodox views, Sister Margarete Roeber, "Wherefore Man and Woman? Exploring the Discussion of a Theology of Sex and its Implications for the Ordination of Women to the Priesthood Among Contemporary Orthodox Christian Scholars," (M.A. Thesis, Antiochian House of Studies, Balamand University, 2013). See also Roeber, *Mixed Marriages*, 216–26 and Hans Boersma, *Seeing God: The Beatific Vision in Christian Tradition* (Grand Rapids, MI: William B. Eerdmans Publishing Co., 2018), 425–28.

5. For a Side A reading of Galatians, i.e., endorsing sexual relations between same-sex partners, see the argument of Justin Lee, one of the co-founders of the Queer Christian Fellowship, as opposed to the Side B arguments of Wesley Hill and Ron Belgau: Justin Lee, "The Great Debate: Justin's View," *Geeky Justin*, 2003, http://geekyjustin.com/great-debate/ (accessed April 6, 2021). I am grateful to Dr. Robert Olsen for alerting me to this site. On the two "sides" within the LGBT community, see below.

you a son, you are not a slave any more; and if God has made you son, then he has made you heir."[6]

Orthodox belief and received teaching on the permanent, ontological significance of male and female thus remains irreconcilable with notions of gender as mere socially constructed identifications of personal identity or a self detached from sexual differentiation. The Orthodox cannot alter (without losing their own identity) their acceptance of a teaching that their view of male/female sexuality is rooted in an original intention of God for men and women not only in this life but with regard to their eternal standing as heirs by adoption from before the beginning of creation. But underlying the debates over sexuality and gender, a more serious and related question has also emerged in the wake of gender feminism's emergence, namely, of whether Christians can alter the received teaching of addressing God as "Father, Son, and Holy Spirit." The acceptance of the written, scriptural revelation of the Trinity and the relatedness of both male and female to what humans can claim to know and to narrate about that acceptance remains the critical challenge for those who seek to construct a different narrative from the received teaching regarding both.

In both Protestant and Roman Catholic circles, a first generation of feminist writers such as Elizabeth Johnson, Mary Daly, and Rosemary Ruether advanced radical conclusions that "understanding God as 'Father' . . . serves to reinforce the maleness of God . . . justifies and reinforces patriarchal values and ideals; and . . . both of the above serve to perpetuate an unhealthy understanding of divine transcendence."[7] More recent feminist theologians, however, have attempted to speak of "reforming" rather than carrying out a "revolution" against the received teaching on how Christians are to address God in prayer. Since most of those attempts still remain indebted to Protestant theologians, most Orthodox will not likely find references to Karl Barth or Friedrich Schleiermacher convincing or helpful. Bacon, however, does draw upon the Orthodox theologian Metropolitan John Zizioulas. Despite her admiration for aspects of his work,

---

6. Gal 3.18 and 4.1–3; 6–7. (*Jerusalem Bible* translation). On the complex question of Paul's relationship to "law" in the Second Temple Era see the discussion in Roeber, *Mixed Marriages*, 98–106.

7. Hannah Bacon, *What's Right with the Trinity? Conversations in Feminist Theology* (London and New York: Routledge, 2009), 16, and more broadly, 15–52.

however, Bacon still judged that "Zizioulas' stress on the monarche of God the Father misplaced" and she insists instead that a God "in relationship . . . with the world . . . [i]s not signaled ontologically by the person of God the Father but by the Godhead itself. . . ."[8]

For the Orthodox who remain convinced of the adequacy and correctness of the received teaching, ancient connections linking birth itself, Christian baptism (i.e., adoption by grace into the status of "sons" of God) and marriage (where Christ appears as the Bridegroom of the Church) have been traced back not only to texts but to the iconography of the oldest known-Christian church structure (ca. 250 A. D.) at Dura Europos. The capacity of the ancient Church to use the imagery of marriage to hold both marriage and celibacy together as equally possible forms of growth in likeness toward union with God also set the parameters within which male and female activities, roles, and destinies were pulled forward from the Hebrew scriptures into specifically Christian images and understandings.[9]

In order to ask, however, whether and how the Orthodox in the United States could, or would absorb and apply the understanding of rights claims to ongoing disputes about human sexuality, marriage, and the standing of women in Church and society, we need to return to the specifics of the American controversies that had moved beyond the question of women's roles to that of same-sex and transgender persons and their legal rights in American society and how the Orthodox respond to this extension of rights claims. In that context, we can note other Orthodox voices that have begun to critique the received teaching on the critical issue of what it means to be created male and female—and what to make of human persons whose attractions and sense of self do not match the received teaching's conclusions. It is worth noting that not only Eastern Orthodox, but Oriental Orthodox theologians as well dissent from what one has identified as "a ruinous juridical and legislative nominalism," the outcome of what the sociologist Robert Bellah identified as "expressive individualism." In the Armenian Orthodox Vigen Guroian's analysis, novel notions of what constitutes the dignity of the person appear in the reasoning of some justices of the Supreme Court to rest upon "the belief that self-expression and self-realization of personal desire are

---

8. Bacon, *What's Right with the Trinity*, 72.

9. Michael Peppard, *The World's Oldest Church: Bible, Art, and Ritual at Dura-Europos, Syria* (New Haven, CT: Yale University Press, 2016), 129–140, at 131, 136.

among the very most important values and ends that the law should serve and uphold." Given the reality of the novel interpretation of same-sex partnerships as marriage, Guroian has called for Orthodox clergy to "cease cooperation or collaboration with the government in civilly marrying persons . . . [to] expose the radical discontinuity between the state's definition of marriage and marriage as the church understands it."[10]

Especially with regard to the appropriation by gay and lesbian groups of the civil rights claims pioneered by African-Americans in the 1960s, the move to demand same-sex unions as marriage not only surfaced late, but should not be taken as representative of the LGBT community at large. Orthodox laity and clergy alike have only recently begun to recognize that perhaps the majority of persons in this group of Americans are not interested in marriage but instead would insist on what more than one feminist legal scholar has called for—accommodation by law for "sexual liberty" on the same basis upon which accommodation for religious rights have historically been based that aims at "exemption from the prevailing orthodoxy of marriage."[11]

Setting aside accommodation of sexual liberty claims that the Orthodox cannot affirm, disagreement still persists among Christians who identify as LGBT as to what their sexual orientation or attraction implies with regard to the received teaching that sexual intimacy is reserved for the marriage relationship of one man with one woman. Although no organization can be said to speak for all LGBT Christians in the United States, making a distinction between a hypothetical "Side A" and a "Side B" provides a useful way of sorting out both literature and positions with which Orthodox clergy in particular must struggle in real-life pastoral situations.[12]

10. Vigen Guroian, *The Orthodox Reality: Culture, Theology, and Ethics in the Modern World* (Grand Rapids, Michigan: Baker Academic, 2018), 125–139, here at 126, 127, 131.

11. Mary Anne Case, "Why 'Live-And-Let-Live' Is Not A Viable Solution To The Difficult Problems of Religious Accommodation in the Age of Sexual Civil Rights," 463–492; Melissa Murray, "Accommodating Nonmarriage," 661–702, both in "Religious Accommodation in the Age of Civil Rights Symposium," special issue, *Southern California Law Review* 88, no. 3 (March, 2015), at 664, 685, 695, 701.

12. What follows summarizes the statements at "Side A/Side B Theology Primer," Coming Out for Christians, accessed April 19, 2019, <www.comingout4christians .net/side-a-side-b-primer.html>. For an example of the Side A position see Stephen

Side A claims that a study of Scripture allows the legitimacy of same-sex practice. Much of the argument appears to emerge from a Protestant focus on a Scripture-alone foundation that begins with a re-reading of disputed texts from both the Hebrew Bible and the Christian New Testament buttressed with claims from contemporary authors in the social sciences. Within this group some hold that virginity is expected until entering a "committed relationship;" while others are not convinced that this is necessary. The more conservative of this side is most likely to endorse same-sex marriage and point to the Protestant churches that have approved such unions. The method of argument alone poses significant problems for the Orthodox whose reading, reception, and teaching from the Old Testament has come from its hymnographic and liturgical tradition. For both Catholic and Protestant traditions alike, liturgical practices have tended to use the historical books more and been "predominantly retrospective, looking backward at the events and figures of the past," in contrast to the Orthodox emphasis that "is preeminently prospective, gazing at the eschatological fulfillment."[13]

Side B confesses the position that the Orthodox Church continues to proclaim: that sexual activity is the privilege and duty of the male and female partners who have been blessed by the mystery of marriage. Although some who subscribe to the Side B position may attempt a Christian marriage with a person of the opposite sex, the persistence of same-sex attraction poses a grave challenge for those attempting this resolution of their dilemma.[14] Others, recognizing what appears to be the consensus that same-sex attraction is a given and not a choice, opt for celibacy but recognize the need for emotional intimacy and pursue spiritual friendships to sustain them. Among young members of the Orthodox Churches in the United States, as well as those inquiring about the Church, the perceived lack of sympathy or concern for same-sex youth continues to be a major reason for the departure from, or reluctance to join, the Church. The appalling rate of suicide, either attempted or accomplished, among LGBT

Morris, *'When Brothers Dwell in Unity': Byzantine Christianity and Homosexuality* (Jefferson, NC: McFarland & Company, 2016).

13. Pentiuc, *The Old Testament in Eastern Orthodox Tradition*, 226.

14. See Jonathan Berry with Rob Wood, *Satisfaction Guaranteed: A Future and A Hope for Same-Sex Attracted Christians* (London: Inter-Varsity Press, 2016), 171–182.

youth, to take but one example, requires more than pious expressions of regret on the part of hierarchs and clergy in particular.[15]

Reactions to the presence of LGBT persons within a Christian parish or congregation, Protestant, Catholic, and Orthodox have ranged from violent protests and actual physical attacks, warnings of impending change in what is conventionally labelled traditional marriage, to limited sympathy. When the Protestant Nate Collins organized the first meeting of a group identifying itself as Revoice in St. Louis, Missouri in the summer of 2018, for example, a storm of criticism broke out that he felt compelled to answer. In his response, he made it clear that the group had no intention of demanding a change in the traditional understanding of marriage, but rather was committed to exploring what the meaning of same-sex attraction or sexual identify confusion means for the church if one accepts the position that such attraction, orientation, or identity is given and not chosen.[16]

II. Gender, and Orthodox Critiques of Received Teaching

Among those offering a critique of the Orthodox received teaching, we should note the arguments of scholars such as Bryce Rich and the

15. See the literature and statistics compiled at "Facts about Suicide," *The Trevor Project.* https://www.thetrevorproject.org/resources/article/facts-about -lgbtq-youth-suicide/ (accessed June 29, 2019). In my own 40 years of teaching at various secular colleges and universities in the U.S., this issue and the standing of women in the Church emerged as most-often major questions and concerns posed by students inquiring into the history and teaching of the Orthodox. For an encouraging example of pastoral response to the struggles of those grappling with same-sex questions, see Abbot Tryphon, "Same Sex Attraction: The Homosexual Person in Light of the Orthodox Faith," Ancient Faith, September 7, 2017. https://blogs.ancientfaith.com/morningoffering/2021/same-sex-attraction (accessed February 22, 2021).

16. Nate Collins, *All But Invisible: Exploring Identity Questions at the Intersection of Faith, Gender, and Sexuality* (Grand Rapids. MI: Zondervan, 2017); for the interview responses see Mark Galli, "Revoice's Founder Answers the LGBT Conference's Critics," Christianity Today, July 25, 2018, https://www.christianity today.com/ct/2018/july-web-only/revoices-founder-answers-lgbt-conferences -critics.html.

contributors to the collections of essays *Orthodox Christianity and Gender*; *Women and Religiosity in Orthodox Christianity*; *Tradition and Human Sexuality*. It is also important to note that even the possibility of Orthodox questioning received teaching on matters of sex and gender has provoked criticism and fear that any such discussion portends the erosion of an authentic Orthodox Christianity represented for ultra-conservative Orthodox in the United States by Russia, and proof of an invasive cancer of liberal secularism. Even so, a closer examination of at least one of these very conservative Orthodox communities composed of both converts and persons born into Orthodox families revealed considerable complexity and differing emphases on where the danger to Orthodoxy lies. The West Virginia community composed of both converts and "cradle" Orthodox could not easily be reduced to "the typical narrative we often read or hear" about regions, persons, and communities on the margins of American society. Still, not only in rural Appalachia but in communities scattered predominantly throughout the American South, "far-right Orthodox Christians . . . who . . . felt oppressed and dismissed by those with political power, reacted with fearful dismay at the advancing front of progressivism . . . in what they perceived of as a post-truth era. . . ." [17] If the enemy of traditional Orthodox Christianity could be identified as the liberal democratic pluralistic American society at large and its emphasis on individual rights, the more fearsome danger for members of these communities lies within the Orthodox Church itself if it allows any discussion of the questions of sex and gender that question any aspect of received teaching.

If one takes the time to examine the published results of those wishing to challenge the "received teaching" represented by the authors and titles noted throughout this chapter, it becomes clear that no simple, unified "feminist" or "progressive" set of assumptions and conclusions is shared by all the participants. The introductory essay to the volume *Women and Religiosity in Orthodox Christianity* notes for example that "Feminism—or alignment with feminism as a mobilization connected to challenging sexism—has not emerged as a motivation for women's activism in the

17. Sarah Riccardi-Swartz, *Between Heaven and Russia: Religious Conversion and Political Apostasy in Appalachia* (New York: Fordham University Press, 2022), 184, 182. For an analysis of these tendencies more broadly, see Aram G. Sarkisian, "Orthodox America Has a Lost Cause Problem," https://publicorthodoxy.org/2021/12/03/orthodox-lost-cause/ (accessed April 2, 2022).

Orthodox Church." Kristin Aune concludes that most women in traditional Orthodox lands would not aspire to gender equality in part because
"Orthodox Christianity is a gender essentialist religion—a religion that
sees gender as biologically determined, not a social construct."[18]

The essays contained in the volume *Orthodox Christianity and Gender* focus almost exclusively upon the roles and challenges of women in historically
Orthodox lands, not the United States. Many of the essays complain of the
abuse of complementarity in marriage as an excuse for denying women both
voice and dignity within the Orthodox Church. The editors do, however,
claim that there remains a "theological basis of gender" but Brian Butcher's
attempt to survey a variety of perspectives offers no convincing narrative alternative to those Butcher identifies as "essentialists" and "naïve" Orthodox representatives of received teaching such as the late Father Thomas Hopko and
the exiled Russian theologian Paul Evdokimov. Nor, in the analyses set forth,
do the authors examine the issue of whether "rights" in general, and not only
those pertaining to women, remain fragile because of the long history of authoritarian political regimes and the absence of a tradition of grounding rights
in a constitutional, representative democratic political order.[19]

Among the essays contained in the edited volume *Orthodox Tradition and
Human Sexuality*, Aristotle Papanikolaou devotes a great deal of time and
effort to finding an "hermeneutical key for interpreting Scripture, patristic,
canonical, and liturgical texts" by means of reflecting on the "Incarnation
and the theological anthropology implied by the affirmation of the Incarnation." Yet indebted as his effort is to a reading of the sometimes obscure and
inconclusive speculations of Maximus the Confessor, Papanikolaou is forced
to admit in the end that for Maximus the only excuse for human sexual congress between a man and a woman remains that of procreation. Nor is it
clear that he succeeds in attempting to construct what he calls a "deontologi-
cal approach to sex" other than relying on both Maximus and the equally
vague speculations of Gregory of Nyssa. In this, Papanikolaou gains the

18. Kristin Aune, "Women in Orthodox Christianity: A Foreword," vii–xix,
at xv in Ina Merdjanova, ed. *Women and Religiosity in Orthodox Christianity*
(New York: Fordham University Press, 2021).

19. *Orthodox Christianity and Gender: Dynamics of Tradition, Culture and
Lived Practice.* Ed. Helena Kupari and Elina Vuola (London and New York:
Routledge, 2020), "Introduction", 5; Brian A. Butcher," Gender and Orthodox
Theology: Vistas and Vantage Points," 25–46, at 30, 38.

endorsement of the Emeritus Metropolitan Ambrosius of Helsinki whose introduction cites both Gregory and Maximus to the effect that "sexual differentiation was not God's original intention and certainly it is not part of the reality of resurrection." But no real evidence is given to support such sweeping claims, nor are the disagreements among scholars about how to interpret Nyssa and Maximus acknowledged.[20] It is equally striking that none of these authors chooses to note that the Latin patristic author Augustine of Hippo recognized that progeny or procreation as a good of marriage is the least important, and that it is fidelity that for Augustine allowed one to regard marriage as something sacramental.[21]

Similarly, Bryce E. Rich's contribution to this volume and his more extensive book *Gender Essentialism and Orthodoxy: Beyond Male and Female* explore primarily the twentieth-century exiled Parisian group of Russian Orthodox writers. But he pays little attention to the major difficulty posed by both the Hebrew Bible and the New Testament writings that cannot easily be reconciled with a non-binary claim for the original humans and God's intentions in creating them male and female. In fairness to Rich, his methodology begins with an analysis of patristic reflections on gender in his attempt to contrast "personalism" against what he regards as Russian "essentialism" represented by exiled Russian theologians associated with the St. Sergius Institute in Parish. Yet his Chapter 7 on marriage passes over in silence Christ's own blessing of God's original intention for marriage of one man and one woman, the condemnation of divorce, and the higher standard of marriage demanded by Christ for Christians as opposed to what was permitted in Second Temple Judaism or the gentile religions of the time. He concludes honestly that neither in ancient Israel nor in any Gentile society can one find an affirmation of same-sex relationships but insists that "what is crucial is not complementarity of gender but of persons."[22]

20. Metropolitan (Emeritus) Ambrosius of Helsinki, "Preface"; and Aristotle Papanikolaou, "A Theology of Sex," in eds., Thomas Arentzen, Ashley Purpura, Aristotle Papanikolaou, *Orthodox Tradition and Human Sexuality* (New York: Fordham University Press, 2022), ix-xi; 247–264

21. For some of the relevant literature on Augustine and marriage, see Roeber, *Hopes for Better Spouses*, 2–5.

22. Bryce E. Rich, *Gender Essentialism and Orthodoxy: Beyond Male and Female* (New York: Fordham University Press, 2022), On Hopko and essentialists, 56–91; Chapter Seven on Marriage, 145–63; quotation at 152.

In general, the contributors to the critiques of received teaching tend to approach the problem as a question of hermeneutics but spend relatively little time grappling with the challenge of what, if anything can be rescued from the narrative contained both in the Hebrew Bible and the Christian New Testament as received teaching if questions of what it means to be human, and how humans are to address God, have been misleading, "naïve," and from the questionable perspective of hindsight, inadequate. The critics appear to conclude that "postmodern" denials of the possibility of a trans-historical, trans-cultural narrative about God and humanity offer the only way forward to address the laments, and genuine suffering, of those who find themselves estranged from received teaching.[23]

The sole attempt to address the difficulty of the Scriptures in *Orthodox Tradition* appears in Ektarini Tsalampouni's "Biblical Tradition and Same-Sex Relations: A Difficult Hermeneutical Path." But most of this effort focuses on the scholarship of Protestant and some Catholic biblical experts and claims that Orthodox biblical scholars have remained uninformed by those critical efforts. While one can argue that Orthodox biblical experts have been late in coming to an engagement with critical biblical scholarship, Tsalampouni omits even mentioning the engagement of North American scholars such as Theodore Stylianopoulos, Eugen Pentiuc, George Parsenios, or Michael Legaspi, to name but a few—who do know and use critical biblical methods. More seriously, Tsalampouni provides no examples or approaches that show what an Orthodox engagement might look like. Moreover, the conclusion that the Scriptures remain "a foundational text of the Christian tradition, normative but within its historical and cultural limits" fails to provide a clear understanding of just what this "normativity" consists of. Asking who gets to decide this key question results in a conclusion that will not reassure those who value the received teaching of the bishops aided by their presbyters, deacons, and lay theologians: "not in her institutional form but as the community of members who react to the challenges of their time and interpret accordingly the event of God's salvation through Christ. . . ."[24]

---

23. For example, Butcher's essay in the *Orthodox Christianity and Gender* volume noted above.

24. Tsalampouni, "Biblical Tradition," *Orthodox Tradition*, 79–101, 91.

Nonetheless, one cannot, from a pastoral perspective, help but be sympathetic to Papanikolaou's observation in his essay that the Orthodox Church's demand for lifelong celibacy for LGBT persons imposes a level of asceticism that is not asked of heterosexual Christians. This troubling disparity, however, should lead the Orthodox to ask to what extent and how the received teaching of Orthodox Christianity can accommodate the givenness of same-sex attraction, gender uncertainty, and the attendant struggles of such persons (the Side B viewpoint) in a pastorally consistent manner that is not dependent upon the personal inclinations of a particular bishop or priest. No lay brotherhoods such as those that exist in the Roman Catholic tradition, for example, are part of the Orthodox experience. It might be useful to ask whether the historical experience and wisdom of Orthodoxy's monastic community traditions in dealing with the reality of LGBT persons should be explored more thoroughly to provide at least one option for a lay community of Side B-minded LGBT Christians comparable to Roman Catholic third orders.[25]

Given their small demographic footprint in North America, the Orthodox in the United States have not been major participants or leaders in the debates surrounding these questions of marriage, gender, and sexuality. Voices from the historically Orthodox nation-states and areas of the world for the most part have recorded incidents of intolerance, violence, or marginalization with calls that range from a more pastorally compassionate response to demands for an Orthodox recognition of the legitimacy of sexual activity including marriage of LGBT persons.[26] In the United States, no author has yet emerged among the Orthodox to offer a study that would take up the personal and the pastoral challenges of dealing with the reality of LGBT persons in the Orthodox Church

25. Such an initiative would have to avoid the erroneous opinion of the late John Boswell regarding the "brother-making" or *adelphopoiia* as a quasi-same-sex marriage ritual (John Boswell, *Same-Sex Unions in Pre-Modern Europe* (New York: Vintage Books, 1995)). For the literature on this, see Roeber, *Mixed Marriages*, 9n.2.

26. See Nik Jovcic-Sas "The Tradition of Homophobia: Responses to Same-Sex Relationships in Serbian Orthodoxy from the Nineteenth Century to the Present Day," in *New Approaches in History and Theology to Same-Sex Love and Desire*, ed. Mark D. Chapman and Dominic Janes (Cham, CH: Palgrave Macmillan, 2018), 55–77.

comparable to essays offered by Roman Catholic and Protestant members of that community.[27]

Occasional reflections have appeared by individual American Orthodox Christians, but none has emerged so far that engages Vasileios Thermos' conclusions that admit the givenness of same-sex desire and eschew the Western theological language of homosexual desire (not the homosexual person) as "intrinsically disordered" while nonetheless insisting that marriage between one man and one woman remains normative for the Orthodox. Admitting that same-sex attraction is a given and not a choice still leaves the Orthodox seeking a way to minister to "homosexual and transsexual identity" while recognizing that both "constitute two 'accidents' of human development." Even if the Orthodox do not give gender an ontological status, those who identify with the received teaching of the church would endorse Thermos' conclusion that the identity of male and female enjoys a "status . . . higher than that of the other human attributes . . . a locus from which one is invited to enter the *imitatio Christi* . . . it serves an ontological mission."[28]

Thermos has unfortunately published most of his findings in Greek with the result that those not fluent in that language have not been able to engage his conclusions in detail. From what is available in English, however, one notes especially his analysis of "Adolescent Identity and Religiosity" that young people coming to Orthodoxy from various sectarian groups can also bring "dependent tendencies " to the Church with "an emphasis on 'spirituality,' as psychological experience rather than the practice of love,

27. For examples, Eve Tushnet, *Gay and Catholic: Accepting My Sexuality, Finding Community, Living My Faith* (Notre Dame, IN: Ave Maria Press, 2014); Wesley Hill, *Washed and Waiting: Reflections on Christian Faithfulness and Homosexuality* (Grand Rapids, MI: Zondervan, 2016); Hill, *Spiritual Friendship: Finding Love in the Church as a Celibate Gay Christian* (Ada, MI: Brazos Press, 2015).

28. Vasileios Thermos, "The Orthodox Church, Sexual Orientation, and Gender Identity: From Embarrassment to Calling," *The Wheel* 13/14 (Spring/Summer 2018): 83–90, at 89, 90. Orthodox theologians are not in complete agreement on how to read Maximus the Confessor on the question of the ontological significance of gender despite Thermos' statement. For some of the literature, see Roeber, *Mixed Marriages*, 221n.62. The issue of gender dysphoria cannot be examined as part of the issue of same-sex desire. For some commentary on this issue, see below.

as well as an extreme conservatism and strictness. . . ."[29] More extensively, Thermos has offered an English-language synopsis of his 2016 book (*Attraction and Passion: An Interdisciplinary Approach of Homosexuality.*)[30]

Resolute in his determination not to be thought a partisan of either ultra-traditionalist Orthodox or left-leaning believers, Thermos in the end calls for a deep examination of "wrong stereotypes of the past" while insisting on the received teaching that sexual congress belongs to the marriage of one man and one woman. He acknowledges the special challenge homosexual men (in particular) face in keeping faith with "the important goal . . . to keep loyal to a monogamous relationship. If the person is already loyal to such a relationship, the spiritual feat will be to live in abstinence. And if the person is already fruitful in abstinence, the goal will be virtue and sanctity. And here perhaps surprises are to be seen as to what the Grace of God can accomplish."[31]

American contributors to a conference held in 2015 included one analysis of the controverted question of what "the fathers" had to say about gender; another reflecting on the challenges to pastoral care presented by same-sex marriage; but none assessed an American equivalent to the Russian Natallia Vasilevich's survey of "Sexual Orientation and Gender Identity in the Social Doctrine of the Russian Orthodox Church and Anthropological Challenges."[32] To date, no synod of Orthodox bishops in the United States or elsewhere in the world has given any indication of a willingness to redefine the mystery of marriage. Hence, whatever the nature of these internal debates about the pastoral care of LGBT persons, they remain unlikely to be framed by the language of "rights." Moreover, the degree to which discussion of these issues appears in some cases to demand

29. In Thermos, *Thirst for Love and Truth: Encounters of Orthodox Theology and Psychological Science* (Montreal: Alexander Press, 2010), 69–80, at 78.

30. The English-language synopsis is *Sexual Orientation and Gender Identity Answers and . . . People* (Vasileios Tsangalos, transl. (Athens: EN PLO Editions, 2019).

31. Thermos, *Sexual Orientation*, 38, 39.

32. Valerie Karras, "Patristic Views on the Ontology of Gender," 29–38; Robert Arida, "Response to Myself: A Pastor's Thoughts on Same-Sex Marriage," 119–23; Vasilevich, 66–70, all in *"For I am Wonderfully Made": Texts on Eastern Orthodoxy and LGBT Inclusion*, ed. by Misha Cherniak, Olga Gerassimenko, Michael Brinkschröder (Nieuwegein, DE: Esuberanza Publishing, 2017).

anonymity out of fear of condemnation by hierarchs, clergy, or lay opponents raises the related question of whether the Orthodox endorsement of freedom of conscience, expression, and religious liberty remains difficult to extend to these topics of marriage, gender, and sexuality.[33]

Moreover, it remains difficult to determine what the Orthodox laity in the United States believes and practices with regards to questions of marriage, gender, and sexuality. A recent survey revealed that relatively few among the laity pay much attention to what their bishops write or say, regarding the local priest as the more "authoritative" voice on questions of ethics, morals, and values.[34] Since Orthodox Christianity in the United States remains divided among various jurisdictions with no functional primate or governing body, even if priests are regarded by the laity as their source for understanding Orthodox positions on questions of ethics, values, and rights, priests are not recruited, ordained, and then sent back to their place of origin. Rather, depending on the needs of the particular metropolis or diocese, a priest may serve in one of the many regions of North America and possess little or no connection to the historical and cultural factors that gave shape to the regional manner in which people view ethical questions posed as values or rights.

If Orthodox Christians in the United States take most of their cues about values and rights from the parish priest, it is nonetheless unclear whether those same parish pastors inform themselves about what lay and clerical professionals have offered as aids to reflection on the conflicts between traditional values and claims being advanced by those who regard the traditional as the enemy of LGBT persons. The ethicist priest-scholar John Breck has authored insightful analyses of many questions raised by new developments

33. The contributors to a volume from the "Bridging Voices" research initiative of the Fordham University Orthodox Christians Studies Center remain anonymous. A major lacuna in the collection is the absence of any Side B contributors to Gregory Tucker and Brandon Gallaher, eds., *Orthodox Christianity, Sexual Diversity & Public Policy,* (British Council Bridging Voices Project, 2017–2020). https://www.fordham.edu/download/downloads/id/14882/orthodox_christianity_sexual_diversity_and_public_policy.pdf (accessed April 6, 2021).

34. Alexei D. Krindatch, *The Orthodox Church Today: A National Study of Parishioners and the Realities of Orthodox Parish Life in the USA* (Berkley, CA: Patriarch Athenagoras Orthodox Institute, 2010), 166–67, 177. www.hartford institute.org/research/OrthChurchFullReport.pdf.

in bio-ethics since the debates over values and rights accelerated in the 1980s. By 2002 Breck observed in an essay "Cultural Wars and Orthodox Christianity," that while some Orthodox might endorse positions similar to Roman Catholic ethicists in calling for "'justice' and 'a consistent life ethic'" others fear, for example, that "if the good end of universal health care is bought at the price of a government-imposed, single-payer policy, then the government—under secularist pressure—inevitably would require as well that physicians and other health-care personnel accept the moral perspective of the secular society, a perspective 'free of religious constraints.'"[35] The concern for a government imposition of policies regarding dignitary equality for LGBT persons surfaced when President Barack Obama's use of executive orders and policies via the Department of Education's "Dear Colleague" letters threatened state and local officials with the loss of federal funding if those authorities did not move to protect the rights of transgender students.[36] Whether freedom of expression and opinion are best defended by legislation, or whether the growth of an executive power in the federal government promotes or threatens those rights remain topics of debate—and not only among the Orthodox.[37]

Although no official statements emerged from the hierarchs in response to the Obama administration's directives to schools that they provide access to bathroom facilities to transgender students based on the student's self-identification, such exercises in administrative law emanating from the Department of Education strike many Americans as excessive. Scholars of

35. John Breck, *God with Us: Critical Issues in Christian Life and Faith* (Crestwood, NY: St. Vladimir's Seminary Press, 2003), 234, 235.

36. For an exhaustive analysis of how gender issues have redefined the understanding and application of Title IX forbidding gender discrimination on athletic teams to "gender equality" see Melnick, *Transformation of Title IX*; and especially on the use of the "Dear Colleague" instructional letters from the Department of Education rather than the use of notice-and-comment procedure prior to making policy, 42–53.

37. On this topic see Mark Neely, *Lincoln and the Triumph of the Nation: Constitutional Conflict in the American Civil War* (Chapel Hill: University of North Carolina Press, 2011); Arthur Schlesinger, Jr., *The Imperial Presidency* (New York: Houghton-Mifflin, 1973); Andrew Rudalevige, *The New Imperial Presidency: Renewing Presidential Power after Watergate* (Ann Arbor: University of Michigan Press, 2006).

constitutional and legal history have emerged as critics of administrative law, pointing to executive invasion of legislative and judicial power through its agencies that "make legislative rules dictating what Americans can grow, manufacture, transport, smoke, eat, and drink. . . . . [T]he agencies make binding adjudications—initially demanding information about violations of the rules, and then reaching conclusions about guilt and imposing fines. Only then . . . does the executive exercise its own power—that of coercion—to enforce its legislation and adjudication." Thus, opposition to application of Title IX objectives by administrative, non-elected officials is not peculiar to the Orthodox, or indeed, to Christians in America.[38]

One reaction to the executive orders that have roiled the public school policy has arisen in the growth of homeschooling among the Orthodox in America. No surveys for all American Orthodox jurisdictions exist so far to assess the depth or growth of this phenomenon. Any significant withdrawal of Orthodox children from the influence of public educational institutions subject to Title IX regulations regarding sexuality, gender, and marriage could emerge in the future as an important barometer of Orthodox participation in, or withdrawal from, the regional cultures of the United States and what many perceive to be an attack on traditional and family values carried out in the name of LGBT rights. Lest one conclude that unfounded paranoia lies behind the support for homeschooling among the most conservative Orthodox, one only needs to examine the arguments advanced by some self-styled "progressive" scholars to see that active hostility and not tolerance or "accommodation" characterizes some of those positions. Elizabeth Bartholet's desire to outlaw homeschooling recognizes that statutory approaches will not likely be successful, nor perhaps will be the intervention of the courts. But pressure can be applied in a number of ways in order to guarantee "exposure to varied views and values . . . [and] rights to future autonomous decision-making with regard to employment and lifestyle".[39]

38. The expanding administrative law has its roots in royal prerogative and subverts the democratic-representational republic that was founded in opposition to arbitrary power; see Hamburger, *Administrative Law Unlawful?*, 4; Melnick, *Transformation of Title IX*, 254–60.

39. My queries to the three largest Orthodox jurisdictions produced an identical response: There are no firm statistics for the Greek Orthodox Archdiocese, the Orthodox Church in America, or the Antiochian Christian Archdiocese.

The most important question to ask given the changing arguments advanced by LGBT activists since the advent of the campaign for same-sex rights in the 1970s is whether the Orthodox continue to view sexual attraction and activity as a matter of free choice, or whether sexual orientation is a given. That question had changed among rights activists themselves. Initial arguments were based on the rights of privacy and free choice that then expanded to include arguments similar to civil rights legislation that had forbidden discrimination in matters of employment (Title VII). Nonetheless, even if Orthodox Christians lay aside the ancient/medieval conviction that same-sex activity was chosen, and accept today that same-sex orientation or gender dysphoria is a given, does such a change in understanding do much to help the Orthodox to steer their way through the dilemmas of values versus rights? For example, does acknowledging that same-sex marriage might conceivably deserve standing as a human right for non-Orthodox while maintaining their own received tradition's teaching that such unions cannot be regarded as the mystery of marriage leave Orthodox LGBT persons and their pastors to pursue some other approach to traditional values and rights instead? Can the Orthodox endorse an approval of civil unions between LGBT Side B persons? Is a clear distinction between a civil union entered into by celibate LGBT persons and the mystery of marriage sufficient to be consistent with the whole of Orthodox views of the dignitary rights of all humans? The controversy that erupted around Pope Francis's musings on that possibility suggests that it would be difficult for at least some Orthodox bishops to approve of such an option, although the lack of hierarchical engagement with the distinction between Side A and Side B LGBT positions suggests that the civil union question remains largely unexamined among the Orthodox. But in the United States context, at least one theologian was adamant that the civil rights of same-sex attracted persons, regardless of their behavior had to be respected. To do less is to risk the

---

Impressionistic and anecdotal responses point to endorsement of homeschooling largely from evangelical Protestant converts, and only rarely among the so-called cradle or ethnically Orthodox Christians in the United States. The latter prefer to remain in public schools, or to enroll children in Orthodox, Roman Catholic, or Lutheran Church Missouri Synod parochial schools. The tendency is more marked in the politically and socially conservative regions of the United States. For Bartholet, see her "Homeschooling: Parent Rights Absolutism vs. Child Rights to Education & Protection," *Arizona Law Review* 62, no. 1 (2020): 1–80 at 75.

Church being regarded as engaging in "a denial of such public recognition[and] as an expression of hatred and contempt. . . ."[40]

Recent controversies among the Orthodox in the United States erupted in Spring/Summer 2018 with the appearance of an issue of the journal *The Wheel*.[41] In surveying the reactions to the Supreme Court's own theological anthropology in the wake of the *Obergefell v. Hodges* decision, John Jillions (the former chancellor of the Orthodox Church in America) observed that we lack data and commentary on both the majority and minority opinions of the Supreme Court justices that would enable us to say with any degree of certainty what implications for imparting traditional and family values the 2008 decision may hold for Orthodox places of worship, schools, parish halls, summer camps, and the like. But Jillions also insists that this is only one of two major questions that must also be faced: "What can the Orthodox Church say to LGBT people and their families? And 2) How will the constitutional right to the 'free exercise of religion' be affected?"[42]

With regard to Jillions' first question, other contributors to this issue of *The Wheel* noted the change in Orthodox belief from same-sex attraction as choice to given.[43] Yet does this change show how to reconcile traditional values to broader human rights claims for LGBT persons? Most secular ethicists and those in medical and psychological practice would see no difficulty in deriving moral or ethical teachings from changing evidence

40. For the Roman Catholic controversy, see Colleen Dulle, "Explainer: What Pope Francis actually said about civil unions—and why it matters," *America Magazine*, October 22, 2020. https://www.americamagazine.org/faith/2020/10/22/pope-francis-gay-civil-union-lgtb-context-media-documentary (accessed December 18, 2020). The late Father Thomas Hopko saw no intrinsic theological reason for the Orthodox to oppose civil unions. See Hopko, *Christian Faith and Same Sex Attraction*, 83.

41. "Being Human: Embodiment and Anthropology, Sex, Marriage and Theosis; *Obergefell v. Hodges* and the Orthodox Church," special issue, *The Wheel* 13/14 (Spring/Summer 2018).

42. John A. Jillions, "*Obergefell v. Hodges*: Questions for Orthodox Christians," *The Wheel* 13/14 (Spring/Summer 2018): 117–128, at 118.

43. Brandon Gallaher, "Tangling with Orthodox Tradition in the Modern West: Natural Law, Homosexuality and Living Tradition," *The Wheel* 13/14 (Spring/Summer 2018):50–63, at 58–61.

drawn from contemporary hard science, since the conclusions of scientists themselves continue to be open to challenge and revision, especially with regard to the complicated questions of human biology, neurology, and the evolutionary emergence of *homo sapiens*.[44] That lack of reticence poses serious challenges to believer-scientists who live with the reality that "the scientific community is not friendly toward religion in general." But even more challenging is the parish pastoral situation where ethical decisions on a host of issues demand not just a well-read priest but a "parish team that includes scientists, health care professionals, and others" who are competent to examine such issues "from the ethical, theological, and health-care perspective."[45] Some Orthodox clerics have attempted to master changing scientific evidence on such matters, but generally fail to keep up with the latest scientific literature when approaching the issue (for example) of the given-ness of same-sex attraction. No concrete suggestions have emerged for reconciling such evidence to traditional or family values beyond observing that the Orthodox must "re-think our attitude toward this question."[46]

The nuanced perspective advocated by Thermos (a practicing clinical psychotherapist) is certain not to receive enthusiastic affirmation by those Orthodox attracted to what they take to be traditional authoritative—if not authoritarian—reactions to perceived threats posed by the emerging focus on the positive values given to the Church by same sex-attracted persons and those struggling with psychosexual gender identity questions.

44. See for example the challenges to Charles Darwin's notions of the "tree of life" by the late microbiologist and biophysicist Carl Woese; for a survey of the issues and literature, "Biodiversity: The Three Domains of Life," April 24, 2002, https://www.biology.iupui.edu/biocourses/N100/2k23domain.html; and David Quammen, *The Tangled Tree: A Radical New History of Life* (New York: Simon & Schuster, 2018).

45. Woloschak, *Faith, Science, Mystery*, 32, 41.

46. Lazar Puhalo, *On the Neurobiology of Sin* (Dewdney, B.C.: The Monastery of All Saints of North America, 2016), 118–19. For an additional, non-Orthodox assessment of the "given-ness" of trans-gendered persons' self-perception and the possibility of seeing "their transitioning as a distinctly eschatological act by which the plasticity of the body is employed in the service of healing and wholeness," see Scott Bader-Saye, "The Transgender Body's Grace," *Journal of the Society of Christian Ethics* 39:1 (Spring/Summer, 2019), 79–92 at 92.

Self-identified "progressives" have shown themselves to be just as capable of adopting authoritarian positions that dismiss as homophobic anyone who questions their demands that same-sex or transgender identity and sexual relations be valued exactly and equally as traditional married heterosexual relations have been. The manipulation of Title IX at the hands of the progressively zealous in the U.S. context provides evidence that the attraction to unilateral imposition of values and rights from above is a monopoly of neither the political and cultural right nor the left. The Orthodox determination to avoid being taken captive by partisans of the American culture wars will for some time to come mean that they will have to be satisfied remaining a minority voice not only in the United States but increasingly in traditionally Orthodox societies and nation-states as well.

As if pondering the challenges of increased numbers of mixed marriages and the question of how to minister to same-sex attracted persons were not complex enough, the Orthodox have not yet developed a history of scientific and theological reflection on the even more complex question of transgender issues. Evangelical Protestant such as Mark A. Yarhouse have attempted a reconciliation of authoritative witness in the Bible with the reality of gender dysphoria, "the experience of having a psychological and emotional identity as either male or female, and that your psychological and emotional identity does not correspond to your biological sex . . . [a] perceived incongruity [that] can be the source of deep and ongoing discomfort."[47] Although Yarhouse's summary of his years of research and counselling persons on a broad spectrum of gender variance provides invaluable context, his main concern is to address the response of both the individual Christian and more importantly, the Christian church. Admitting that "scientists do not know what causes gender incongruence," a "rare phenomenon and one in which we have little by way of research to inform the discussion," Yarhouse nonetheless concludes that the Christian community may be best served by adopting a combination of what he refers to as a "disability framework," a "diversity framework," and an "integrity framework." Yarhouse uses these terms to describe those concerned about gender incongruence as evidence of a "fallen world." The disability framework is one that regards such incongruence as evidence of a fallen reality but the person experiencing the incongruence

47. Mark Yarhouse, *Understanding Gender Dysphoria: Navigating Transgender Issues in a Changing Culture* (Downers Grove, IL: IVP Academic, 2015), 19.

as someone suffering from a condition comparable to any medical or psychiatric condition. Diversity frameworks range from the more radical version endorsed by those who would reject sex and gender as categories that hold any meaning to the more moderate forms—all of which are still likely to be viewed warily by many Christians.[48]

If one substitutes for "the bible" the Orthodox "Tradition," and for "sanctification" the concept of "theosis," (with some reservations) it is possible to see how this Protestant evangelical analysis of gender dysphoria might be reconciled to an Orthodox perspective. Yarhouse repeatedly warns that there are no simple, "sound bite" solutions to dealing with gender dysphoria, but that the Church must ask itself "what it will look like to be missional in the years to come" where a truly mission-minded Church will reassure the marginal that they belong, encourage them in their struggle for deepened belief, and focus on the open-ended potential to "become" more in union with God. Yarhouse is brutally honest in reporting that "an estimated 50 percent of people who meet criteria for and receive services for Gender Dysphoria drop out, likely due to frustration with the process or possibly other reasons." But it is not just the individuals who struggle with gender dysphoria who need encouragement to focus on "becoming" rather than assuming that their struggles with gender identity define who they "are." Here, the Orthodox can recognize the kinship of such struggles with their own belief that the whole of life lived in an Orthodox manner should be understood as "becoming" the increasing likeness to God, i.e., recovery of the original image and likeness made possible by God's mercy and love. Too often churches—including the Orthodox—that are focused on integrity of received teaching translate this into a legalistic and accusatory posture that is just as defective as the over-emphasis on tolerance and inclusivity that is dangerously naïve and ignores the evidence that there are some determined to overthrow any normative understanding of gender and sexuality, a position that the Church cannot endorse. "We need good examples of what a church looks like that models and lives out a balance of welcoming and ministry with clear biblical testimony."[49]

A mere five years after Yarhouse's path-breaking study, however, the challenges facing Christian youth in particular have intensified so dramatically

---

48. Yarhouse, *Understanding Gender Dysphoria*, 11, 50–53, 130–31.
49. Yarhouse, *Understanding Gender Dysphoria*, 147, 153, 155, 156.

that Yarhouse has felt compelled to offer a joint analysis with Julia Sadusky that attempts "to distinguish emerging gender identities from gender dysphoria and to provide an update on what has changed in the clinical landscape in the past five years, as well as to offer options for Christians who wish to lean in to this conversation."[50] Both authors admit that we have no reliable evidence that can prove that "gender dysphoria and transgender experiences have existed in some form throughout history and across cultures." Both those who claim that there is nothing new here except for increased awareness and the access to narratives via social media, and those who have labelled the explosion of "gender identity presentations" as a form of "social contagion" may be right. What is most significant in terms of the Church's reaction to this phenomenon, however, seems clear: "the more stringent their community's gender expectations—especially for young women who are told that they must be either stylish and fashionable, or conversely, meek and homely in order to be godly women—the more heightened their sense of displacement may be." Lest parents, guardians and clergy be tempted to despair in the face of such challenges, the authors insist that "the path to sanctification remains the same for us all: prayer, service, and embracing suffering, even as it relates to the unknown territory of gender identity. We are reminded not to be afraid, for our God, who will never leave or forsake us, has called us each by name (Deut. 31:6). In answering his call, we will find him whom our soul has longed for since the day we were born."[51] Thermos, so far, has emerged as the only qualified psychotherapist and Orthodox clergyman who has attempted to examine the complexities of gender identity, and those seeking sexual conversion in the face of sex dysphoria. On the one hand, Thermos remains convinced that while "biological sex is not an ontological feature of humans . . . it cannot be equated to all other features that add to our sense of identity. . . . This something more which characterizes it is its ontological mission, as a 'reconciliation' of the sexes through the ecclesiastical heterosexual marriage. . . . man is called to continue Christ's work Who annihilates divisions, not distinctions."[52]

50. Mark Yarhouose and Julia Sadusky, *Emerging Gender Identities: Understanding the Diverse Experiences of Today's Youth* (Grand Rapids, MI: Brazos Press, 2020), xiii.

51. Mark Yarhouse and Julia Sadusky. *Emerging Gender Identities*, 23, 27, 205.

52. Thermos, *Sexual Orientation*, 59.

II. The Orthodox, Gender, and the Right of Dissent

These questions of marriage, gender, and sexuality can look quite different and intimidating as one moves to the question of how the Orthodox respond to the broader rights claims in American law that surround these topics. As a matter of long-standing historical development, not only the Orthodox but most religious communities in the United States have relied on the "ministerial exception" that served to defend first individuals and increasingly entire religious communities from the purview or interference of the state. The grounds on which courts now decide whether the state has a "compelling interest" in defending the rights of individual citizens within a religious community, however, have shifted in recent years and resulted in a considerable amount of confusion. The discontent with a history of accommodation of religion on the part of some critics (noted in Section I) reveals that it is no longer clear how potential conflicts between the right to religious liberty and civil rights claims will be decided. This is especially the case on many American college campuses, where opposing partisans increasingly cast controversial issues in the language of rights.

The most optimistic assessment of American law with regard to rights based on religious belief emphasized that "for all but about a quarter-century (1963–1990) . . . the [Supreme] Court's Free Exercise decisions have followed a reasonably consistent path. The clause enriches and informs other constitutional liberties, like freedom of speech and association, and protects all faiths from intentionally discriminatory treatment . . . by the government. Except for that quarter-century, the clause has not supported a constitutional right to exemption from the general regulation of conduct that is within the state's power to control."[53]

Other legal-constitutional scholars have argued to the contrary that the debates over gender and sexuality have produced a much more harrowing scenario for religious groups who dissent from the rights claims advanced by the LGBT community. But the first signs of the failure to pursue the merits of what Douglas Laycock calls "accommodation and accountability" began with a tax case. In *Jimmy Swaggart Ministries v.*

---

53. Ira C. Lupu and Robert W. Tuttle, *Secular Government, Religious People* (Grand Rapids, MI: William B. Eerdmans Publishing Company, 2014), 177.

Board of Equalization, the court held "that churches are subject to formally neutral taxes, including sales tax, property tax, and income tax." Legislatures are therefore free to impose such taxation with the sole exception that paying such a tax would "require a believer to violate specific doctrinal tents of his faith." As a result of this kind of reasoning, "all the affirmative, communal, and spiritual aspects of religion are assumed away, placed outside the protection of the Free Exercise Clause . . . [savaging] the rights of churches as social groups or mediating institutions." Handed down two months before the more famous case of *Employment Division, Department of Human Resources of Oregon v. Smith* decision [494 US 872 (1990)], *Swaggart* attracted the attention of constitutional and legal scholars, but not to the degree that *Smith* provoked. In that case, the Court insisted that free exercise claims on the part of religious groups do not trump "any neutral law of general applicability." Beginning as a case that dealt with Native American use of peyote in worship, the case instead revealed a crucial point Michael McConnell identified—that there exists a profound difference between "formal neutrality" versus "substantive neutrality" that we should translate as "liberty" that insists on the "right of religion to be let alone, whether or not other activities and institutions are let alone." Laycock's analysis of the emerging crisis was succinct; "I submit the simple proposition that religious exercise is not free when it is pervasively regulated."[54]

Many state jurisdictions continue to follow a strict scrutiny doctrine of demonstrating a "compelling state interest" in regulating or interfering with religious activity, under which abortion or access to birth control have been argued by opponents. But the *Smith* case in effect declared the State of Oregon free to initiate a criminal prosecution of any worship service. What has prevented states and the Federal government from doing it is "the likelihood of political backlash from Americans who still believe in religious liberty." It is true that *Smith* left open the possibility that religious groups could appeal to a specific state constitution for protection or request a legislative exemption from the "formally neutral" application of the law. But it is political

---

54. The above relies on Laycock's analysis in his chapter "Summary and Synthesis. The Crisis in Religious Liberty," in Laycock, *Religious Liberty Vol 3 Religious Freedom Restoration Acts, Same-Sex Marriage Legislation, and the Culture Wars,* 24–40, here at 29, 30, 31, 32 and at 132.

pressure, not the federal courts, or the Supreme Court, that has prevented the use of what *Smith* created—"the legal framework for persecution."[55] Most scholars have reacted with skepticism at the attempt to speak of "hybrid" rights as a plausible way of reconciling competing rights claims. "Penumbras" and "emanations" that were once used to buttress privacy claims occur less and less in attempts to advance winning arguments to defend a specific religious assembly's right to define and police marriage and issues circulating around sexuality and gender identity.[56]

Some have taken comfort in the 2012 Supreme Court's ruling in *Hosanna-Tabor v. EEOC* that appeared to reaffirm a "special solicitude" for "religious organizations" found in the First Amendment and building upon the passage of the Religious Freedom Restoration Act by Congress in 1994. Not everyone agrees that the 2012 decision actually clarified the precise standing of "expressive associations" in American law.[57] It is true that RFRA restored the pre-*Smith* demand that the state must be able to demonstrate its "compelling interest" argument as the basis for any regulation of religious associations. But whether this is so, especially for minority religious groups involved in litigation over their religious liberty rights, is not so clear. By looking at the involvement of religious minority groups with the American court system, for example, sociologists note that in general, "the overall trend shows sects, cults, and other minority religions holding high rates of involvement in court cases and a low rate of favorable rulings." According to these researchers, "even subtle shifts in religious regulation will affect minority religions . . . even modest changes in the state's regulation of religion will have an immediate impact on the minority

---

55. Laycock, "Summary," 31–33 at 32, 33, 38.

56. W. Cole Durham Jr. and Robert T. Smith, "Religion and the State in the United States at the Turn of the Twenty-first Century," in *Law and Religion in the 21ˢᵗ Century: Relations between States and Religious Communities*, ed. Silvio Ferrari and Rinaldo Cristofori (Burlington, VT: Ashgate, 2010), 79–110, here at 82. I am indebted to Philip Hamburger, John Inazu, and Richard Garnett for discussion of this issue as well to many of the presenters at the Harvard Law School Symposium "Religious Accommodation in the Age of Civil Rights," April 3–5, 2014.

57. *Hosanna-Tabor Evangelical Lutheran Church & Sch. V. EEOC*, 132 S. Ct. 694, 712 (2012). For an example of a skeptical assessment, see John D. Inazu, "The Freedom of the Church (New Revised Standard Version)" *Journal of Contemporary Legal Issues* 21 (2013): 335–367.

religions holding a tension with their surrounding culture. Religious minorities are the first to benefit when religious regulations are lifted, and the first to be stifled when regulations are allowed."[58]

Both Eastern and Oriental Orthodox Christians in the United States face a constantly evolving body of case law and legislative enactments that promise to underscore the necessity of being able to define precisely what is, and is not protected by their conviction of what marriage, human sexuality, gender, and rights claims mean, both strictly within the boundaries of their specific religious community, and beyond to those difficult cases that stand on the borderlands, the margins of assemblies, the "expressive associations" referred to in the decisions. Although many would still take comfort in the classic defense of religious accommodation laid down by Michael McConnell in his famous essay, namely, that "religious liberty is the central value and animating purpose of the Religion Clauses of the First Amendment," the debates over civil rights and religious accommodation have moved far beyond that confident claim. Dissent on the part of Orthodox Christians from attempts to broaden the most recent legal and constitutional rights claims advanced by LGBT activists promises to be among the most contentious of debates.[59]

One scholar's review of the history of McConnell's approach that argued for accommodation that required neither a "strict neutrality" of the government nor absolute "separation" of religion and the state concluded that the consensus behind that approach has collapsed. Rather than hoping for a grand theory about how to handle the rights claims of diffuse groups of Americans, Mark Tushnet has argued that the best courts can do is to attempt "to reach discrete agreements about narrowly defined problems."[60]

For a brief moment in 2019, legislators on both sides of the culture wars appeared ready to propose federal legislation that would promote "Fairness for All." Originating with the Utah Republican representative Chris Stewart,

58. John Wybraniac and Roger Finke, "Religious Regulation and the Courts: The Judiciary's Changing Role in Protecting Minority Religions from Majoritarian Rule," *Journal for the Scientific Study of Religion* 40, no. 3 (September, 2001): 427–444, at 441.

59. Michael W. McConnell, "Accommodation of Religion," *The Supreme Court Review* 1985 (1985): 1–59, at 1.

60. Mark Tushnet, "Accommodation of Religion Thirty Years On," *Harvard Journal of Law and Gender* 38 (2015): 1–33, at 32.

HR 5331-116th Congress (2019–20) asked for new laws that would protect LGBT persons from discrimination while protecting both individual believers and religious institutions from prosecution if they fail to agree with the civil rights claims of their opponents. Before legislators could act, however, the Supreme Court handed down decisions on both state-level restrictions on abortion and on the right of parents to financial benefits when they choose to send their children to accredited religious schools. Michael McConnell's interpretation of the decisions concludes that by observing strict neutrality states are required to provide aid to such religious schools and that such decisions, taken as a whole, are a victory for pluralism and "the right to be different."[61] But what such decisions also suggest is that the courts, rather than Congress or state legislatures, will remain the future adjudicators of what rights consist of and how they are applied.

By the 1960s—described aptly by John Inazu as "the equality era"—the civil rights movement brought significant pressure upon those claiming "freedom of association" to defend racial segregation. Ironically, however, this same era produced the landmark case *Griswold v. Connecticut* and its claim that a constitutional right to privacy existed, albeit nowhere actually explicitly stated in the text of the Constitution. In the course of subsequent cases, however, the right of privacy, even though supposedly producing a "penumbra" of privacy rights remained focused on individuals, not associations. By the time the Christian Legal Society chapter at Hastings College of Law sought recognition as a student organization because its statement of faith (affirming that sexual conduct should be confined to heterosexual marriage) was held to violate the Nondiscrimination Policy

61. On the House Bill 5331 and scholarly support for it, see: Thomas C. Berg, Carl H. Esbeck, Douglas Laycock, and Robin Fretwell, "Letter in Support of Fairness for All," *Alliance for Lasting Liberty*, December 6, 2019, https://fairnessforall.org/letter-in-support-of-fairness-for-all/ (accessed June 6, 2020); for McConnell's analysis of the Supreme Court cases (including *Espinoza v. Montana* on states' obligation to follow strict neutrality and the protection of Little Sisters of the Poor from providing contraceptive coverage in health insurance, see: Michael W. McConnell, "On Religion, the Supreme Court Protects the Right to Be Different," *New York Times*, July 9, 2020, https://www.nytimes.com/2020/07/09/opinion/supreme-court-religion.html. For the cases themselves, see "Opinions from 2020," *Justia US Supreme Court Center*, accessed April 7, 2021, https://supreme.justia.com/cases/federal/us/year/2020.html.

of the school, its appeal to expressive association was denied. That denial was upheld on appeal from the U.S. Court of Appeals for the Ninth Circuit and by the Supreme Court of the United States. As a result, "at the close of the equality era, the right of association bore little resemblance to the right of assembly that had existed for almost two hundred years. . . ."[62]

Case law so far continues to protect as an undisputed right the decision of clergy to bless marriage in accord with the stated theology of their "expressive association" (albeit separated from the right of assembly as Inazu laments). But it remains unclear whether appeals to expressive association in an era where the legal standing of equal citizenship before the law is the societal and legal norm will indefinitely provide that protection. Furthermore, with breathtaking speed, the proponents of same-sex marriage linked their cause to the history of civil rights to such a degree that within a single generation, American public opinion swung away from opposing same sex marriage to endorsing it. Given such trends in how the law reflects the volatile nature of American public opinion, the clear articulation of a received oral and written tradition on gender, sexuality, and marriage as they are understood among the Orthodox has to be certain and accessible to anyone outside the Orthodox Church who seeks to understand the Orthodox position. The hard questions of justice and mercy created by lived experiences are bound to play a role in how courts react to challenges laid down by those who regard the "institutionalization" of religious belief as the central obstacle to the realization of their human rights to live out their gender and sexual identity.

In a society marked by continued legal and constitutional controversy about the accommodation of religion, religiously based understandings of gender and sexuality will require the Orthodox to offer the non-Orthodox positive, and not primarily defensive, witness for their convictions. This is even more the case in those instances that arise as the result of calls for defending the civil rights—increasingly identified with human rights—of sexual minorities. The challenge to Eastern and Oriental Orthodox of participating in American civil life despite their disagreements with novel definitions of marriage and so-called binary understandings of gender will

---

62. The above summarizes Inazu's reconstruction of the case law in *Liberty's Refuge: The Forgotten Freedom of Assembly* (New Haven, CT: Yale University Press, 2012), 118–149, at 118, 124, 146, 149.

not go away. That challenge will involve the Orthodox in a common struggle alongside other religious communities, some non-Christian, but especially with other Christians who understand themselves—as both forms of Orthodoxy and Roman Catholicism do—as eucharistic assemblies.[63]

It is no doubt true that, "not every religious belief can be claimed as central, and not every religious practice can be worth dying for." Right belief and right practice about marriage and the understanding of sex and gender however, will continue to be counted among the distinctive markers and identifiers of an Orthodox Christian Church.[64] The most recent debates over accommodation and the potentially destructive implications of the use of neutral principles tied to the power to tax all suggest that the historic reliance upon either the Free Exercise Clause of the Constitution, or the Establishment Clause as the alternative, do not give a clear picture of how the Orthodox are to understand what rights individuals and religious institutions possess under American law.

Whatever options other Orthodox communities in the world find appropriate, the Orthodox in the United States need to be aware of the advice of the lawyer and scholar Douglas Laycock. In reflecting on the failure of the Roman Catholic bishops in the United States to convince even their own people of their understanding of correct Catholic teaching on issues of marriage, birth control, and human sexuality, Laycock observed that "bishops are of course free to demand that government and secular social service agencies exclude gays and lesbians and unmarried straight couples from adopting children or providing foster care. But that is not an argument for religious liberty; it is an argument for regulating secular life." The temptation to create by imposition a Christian nation—what appears at times to be an attempt at reviving an integralist vision of a seamless cooperation between church and civil authority—continues to lie at the root of some Orthodox Christians' inability to adopt and be content to look first

63. See on this challenge from a non-Christian perspective Abdullahi Ahmed An-Na'im, *What is an American Muslim? Embracing Faith and Citizenship* (New York: Oxford University Press, 2014).

64. John Witte Jr. and Joel A. Nichols, "The Frontiers of Marital Pluralism," in *Marriage and Divorce in a Multi-Cultural Context: Multi-Tiered Marriage and the Boundaries of Civil Law and Religion*, ed. Joel A. Nichols (Cambridge: Cambridge University Press, 2011), 357–378, at 371.

of all to its own internal commitment to dignitary rights for all its baptized and chrismated members.

Disagreements over rights claims surrounding sex and morals present bishops with a choice of endorsing exemption versus repeal of laws they find morally repugnant. This, in short, is "the difference between seeking religious liberty for Catholic institutions and seeking to impose Catholic moral teaching on the nation. The bishops can argue for either or both but conflating the two fatally undermines the argument for religious liberty." Just so, "with regard to same-sex relationships, the obvious compromise is for the churches to leave same-sex couples alone and for the gay-rights movement to leave the churches alone . . . but if the bishops demand that government discriminate against same-sex couples in adoption and in marriage, they should hardly be surprised that the gay-rights movement responds with hostility and that it resists claims to religious liberty."[65] An awareness of how Christian churches in the past have become associated with despotic, reactionary, and repressive regimes, suggests that, for example, an Orthodox choice to continue fighting the sexual revolution that was part of the general rights revolution "may be to permanently turn much of the country against religious liberty—or at least to turn public opinion towards a very narrow, more French-like understanding of religious liberty."[66]

American Orthodox Christians will find little of value to guide them in looking to historically Orthodox lands where the Church either enjoyed privileges as a protected minority under an imperial regime (such as the Ottoman Empire) or where it could count on the active imposition of law on society by Christian rulers, which continues to be the case in present-day Russia. The first order of business for the Orthodox in the United States will continue to be one of coming to grips with their own history of the encounter with various rights languages, properly understood in the American context. The challenges of living in a pluralist society; on cherishing and defending freedom of speech and opinion; on contested questions of marriage, sex, and gender require a thorough knowledge of the liberal democratic-representative heritage of American rights. As one of the

65. Laycock, "The Bishops and Religious Liberty," in Laycock, *Religious Liberty* 4: 728–732; 730, 731.
66. Laycock, "Religious Liberty": 734–784, at 771.

preeminent non-Orthodox legal scholars and authors has summarized current dilemmas, "Christians and other religious believers have marched to the culture wars without ammunition—substituting nostalgia for engagement, acerbity for prophecy, platitudes for principled argument, bumper sticker issues for holistic reformations . . . they must think much more seriously about their roles as 'prophets, priests, and kings' in a secular age."[67]

67. John Witte, Jr., *Church, State, and Family: Reconciling Traditional Teachings and Modern Liberties* (Cambridge: Cambridge University Press, 2019), 377–78.

8

HUMAN RIGHTS CLAIMS AND THE ORTHODOX IN AMERICA

As a reader who has come this far will now recognize, answering Witte's and Alexander's queries about how the Orthodox navigate the "regime of human rights" depends upon whose history of various rights claims one chooses to follow. It is also the case that understandings of the meaning of "human rights" have changed significantly from the 1940s, when the Orthodox did engage with those discussions and definitions. The examples in the preceding chapters show that elastic and increasingly broad claims have come to be made under the rubric of human rights for rights that were historically understood as political, legal, or civil rights. It is also the case that optimistic and pessimistic narratives now characterize how Christian observers understand the history of rights. What do people mean when they invoke the term "human rights"?

Several key questions continue to divide scholars who have attempted to provide clarity from their respective perspectives as theologians, philosophers, historians, social scientists, or legal experts. For some time now, legal scholars and philosophers have been troubled by questions that emanate from disagreements over whether political, legal, and moral rights can or should be subsumed under the "human rights" rubric. In the American context, for example, the language that surrounds the extension of the right to marry has been cast not only in legal terms, but also with appeals to what some have identified as "moral rights talk" that has become identified with "human rights." But as Michael Perry has argued, "not every right internationally recognized as a human right—is a legal right in every country [and] some have insisted . . . that 'moral' rights are not really rights, that the only genuine rights are legal rights, that so-called 'moral' rights are phony . . . rights."[1]

To extend this example, legal scholars and philosophers have argued that barring LGBT persons from marriage might "disadvantage" these individuals but such a policy would not automatically constitute a violation of "the right to moral equality."[2] That violation would occur only if laws enforced by the government result in an abrogation "of the right to religious and moral freedom."[3] In his more recent reflections, Perry has continued to demand that attention be paid to the question of whether it is critical to find a "grounding" or "foundation" for human rights since many secular scholars dismiss this as a hopeless quest, because there is no consensus about whether there is such a thing as "human nature." Beyond this first question, an equally difficult one has arisen because as Perry explains, some insist that an "orthodox" definition of "human rights" exists and these are rights that all humans possess "simply in virtue of their humanity." Some then go on to argue that we should distinguish those rights from the "political" version of human rights. And yet others argue that this "orthodox meaning is mistaken" because even if some rights are legal, and in other cases, rights are moral, what has happened over time is that "for better or worse, the language of rights—especially the language of human rights—is now a common feature of moral discourse throughout the world, and is likely to remain so." But Perry concludes his analysis with his assertion that he finds no secular argument convincing for talking about the morality of human rights except a vague kind of "agapic sensibility—the agapic orientation to the Other." Perry appears willing to affirm the possibility for a non-theist to rely on this "agapic sensibility" and to ignore the challenge of "foundationalism." It is not clear, however, whether Orthodox Christians can be permitted to give up on the "foundational" question. If they insist upon it, however, Perry observes that even among theists, no consensus has emerged about whether human rights understood as moral rights are enforceable, even if Christians affirm that God will hold everyone accountable. Not all theists agree that the church should be

1. Michael J. Perry, *Human Rights in the Constitutional Law of the United States* (New York: Cambridge University Press, 2013), 19–26, at 23.

2. Perry, *Human Rights*, 140.

3. Perry, *Human Rights*, 146.

involved in trying to enforce moral rights. Perry is a staunch defender of the "morality of human rights for democracy," advancing his argument that the "three pillars" of democracy are "the human right to democratic governance, the human right to intellectual freedom, and the human right to moral equality." In his view of the international, global "regime" of human rights, constitutionalism is so crucial that when we speak of "the political morality of human rights . . . we may fairly regard it as an integral part of that morality."[4]

Perry's perspective is especially useful since he is one of the most eminent American legal and constitutional authorities to address the disagreements among scholars from various disciplines about what is meant by "human rights." But he is also important because some of his argument receives endorsement from the American philosopher Nicholas Wolterstorff, who writes from the perspective of the Reformed Christian tradition. Wolterstorff, however, is much more insistent that no secular argument can convincingly "ground" human rights and provide a defense for either legal or moral rights. That defense emerged from the biblical witness of ancient Israel, and subsequently, Christianity. Wolterstorff is also of special interest because his work a decade ago attracted the attention and commentary from one of the few Orthodox scholars in North America who has written about human rights, Aristotle Papanikolaou.[5]

Before turning in more detail to Wolterstorff's assessments of human rights and those of Catholic authors, we should turn our attention to the first-generation human rights discourse that emerged in the 1940s and the Orthodox role that, like Wolterstorff, located the moral and legal expressions of human rights in the Christian tradition and its roots in the Hebrew Bible. For this opening approach to assessing the "regime of human rights" we need to acknowledge Orthodox understandings of what the term

---

4. Michael J. Perry, *A Global Political Morality: Human Rights, Democracy, and Constitutionalism* (Cambridge: Cambridge University Press, 2017), 8; 23; 40–4; 43–87; 9. Perry outlined in his earlier work the question about whether human rights could be grounded in secular thought and what role courts should play given the growing concern over the "judicialization" of human rights. See his *Toward a Theory of Human Rights: Religion, Law, Courts.* (New York: Cambridge University Press, 2007), 20–29; 60–77.

5. For his assessment of Wolterstorff, see Papanikolaou, *The Mystical as Political*, University of Notre Dame Press (2012),115–125.

meant in that first-generation context, with special attention paid to the North American conditions and audiences. After doing so, we must then turn to how theists ground a claim for human rights, especially given the expansion of human rights claims in the second generation. Here, we can recognize that the Orthodox, like their Roman Catholic and Protestant counterparts, exhibit both pessimistic and optimistic responses to the question about whether human rights are compatible with the understanding of what it means to be human, and who God is in relationship with humans. We must also then acknowledge secular defenses for grounding human rights to ask if, and under what conditions, the Orthodox should cooperate in defending human rights in a world where both the secular and the religious promise to continue in sometimes tense co-existence.[6]

I. The Orthodox and the First Generation of Human Rights

President Franklin Roosevelt's 1940 and 1944 State of the Union addresses urged the expansion of rights guaranteed by the U.S. Constitution (freedom of speech and worship) to include freedoms from want and fear (with the rights to health care, education, employment, housing, and fair economic competition). These additional inclusions illuminated what the president expected the hoped-for postwar organization of the United Nations would endorse.[7] How Roosevelt would have reconciled the conflict between

---

6. The identification of the "generations" of human rights is also problematic. Conventionally, everything from the French Revolution to the United Nations Declaration has been labelled "first generation," with the "second generation" encompassing the realization of broad principles by state authorities after World War II to include economic, social, and cultural rights. Some then see a "third generation" that perhaps begins with the 1972 "Stockholm Declaration of the United Nations' Conference on the Human Environment" as the signal for the rise of "solidarity" expressions with non-Western peoples and issues thought to have been largely ignored in the earlier "generations." I argue that the United States and the Orthodox in North America paid little attention to "human rights" before the 1970s and hence, a simpler paradigm of "two generations" is more useful for understanding why the term becomes controversial.

7. On the ethical dilemmas facing those attempting to implement the "four freedoms," see William F. Felice, *The Global New Deal: Economic and Social Human Rights in World Politics* (Lanham, MD: Rowman & Littlefield, 2003).

his own Christian beliefs about rights and those of the non-theist members of the United Nations we cannot know. When Eleanor Roosevelt reflected on the process that eventually led to the United Nations' adoption of the Universal Declaration of Human Rights, she signaled that an Arabic Orthodox Christian understood and appreciated the Western tradition of natural law, natural rights, and human rights. Charles Malik (1906–87), later the Lebanese ambassador to the United Nations and the United States, had studied philosophy in his native country before beginning doctoral work at Harvard. When the Human Rights commission began its work, the Chinese delegate Peng-chun Chang suggested that the Declaration relied too heavily on Western ideas and that "there is more than one kind of ultimate reality." Roosevelt herself concluded that, even though Chang had spoken to John P. Humphrey, the permanent head of the Division of Human Rights in the U.N. Secretariat, it "was really directed at Dr. Malik, from whom it drew a prompt retort as he expounded at some length the philosophy of Thomas Aquinas." In the end, it was not the proposal to study the principles of Confucianism that nearly derailed the Commission's work, nor Malik's encomium to the Angelic Doctor. Rather, it was the Soviet Union's insistence that each article of the Declaration should end with the statement "This shall be enforced by the state."[8]

For the roots of FDR's pragmatic commitment to rights grounded in his own Episcopalian faith see Jonathan Alter, *The Defining Moment: FDR's Hundred Days and the Triumph of Hope* (New York: Simon & Schuster, 2006) and Christine Wicker, *The Simple Faith of Franklin Delano Roosevelt: Religion's Role in the FDR Presidency* (Washington, D.C.: Smithsonian Books, 2017).

8. Eleanor Roosevelt, *On My Own* (New York: Harper & Brothers, 1959), 77–78. See also Allida Black, et al., eds., *The Eleanor Roosevelt Papers: Vol. I The Human Rights Years, 1945–1948* (Detroit: Thomason Gale, 2007), 4 February 1947, 506–07 for Malik's observations on personal liberty and the importance of the human person; and Roosevelt's own reflections in "My Day" for December 10, 1948, 969–72 that despite the absence of an explicit "mention of God" in her opinion "the spirit of the declaration was inspired by Christianity and it never would have been written if there had not been many people behind it who were motivated by the Christian spirit," here at 970. Dutch representatives had argued for and failed to persuade the delegates to adopt a definition about "equal and inalienable rights" "*based on man's divine origin and immortal destiny. . . .*" 971n3. For a survey of the history of the Universal Declaration and Malik's insistence on the importance of the right to change one's religion see Johannes Morsink,

The influence of the Roman Catholic theologian Jacques Maritain in preparing the UNESCO report that preceded the formation of the actual commission has long been acknowledged. So too, is Maritain's influence upon René Cassin, the secular Jewish French Commission member. It was Cassin who suggested that the wording in Article One, on the nature of the human person, should ground the claims for universal brotherhood and equality in "dignity and rights" in the agreed-upon conviction that humans "by nature" possessed "reason and conscience." Malik, however, wanted a stronger statement, and citing the American Declaration of Independence, wished to substitute "by their Creator" for "by nature." Cassin objected for fear that a theist reference would alienate the Russians—who in turn wanted the entire article deleted—because it is too indebted either to "eighteenth-century French philosophy . . . or the Bible."[9]

Malik, who also spent many years in the United States as well as in his native Lebanon during his long career as academic and diplomat, is remembered today for his role in helping to shape the 1948 United Nations Declaration on Universal Human Rights. But outside his native Lebanon, he has not figured in Orthodox debates on human rights that have been shaped by Greek or Russian partisans. Partly, the neglect of Malik's thought stems from misidentification. The Harvard legal historian Mary Ann Glendon, in describing Malik's work on the UN Commission, concluded that he was a Thomist, given his admiration for Aquinas. The decision of two of his brothers to become Catholic priests also played a role in obscuring how Orthodox Christianity provided the soil for the deep roots of Malik's theological anthropology. In the context of Malik's fierce criticism of Soviet statist thinking about defining rights, he did speak about the inviolability of individual freedom of conscience. But Glendon noted that when Eleanor Roosevelt talked of "individual" rights Malik talked about "persons" "to emphasize the social dimension of personhood and to avoid connotations of radical autonomy and self-

---

The Universal Declaration of Human Rights: Origins, Drafting, and Intent (Philadelphia: University of Pennsylvania Press, 1999), 26–7, 342n47.

9. Andrew Woodcock, "Jacques Maritain, Natural Law and the Universal Declaration of Human Rights," *Journal of the History of International Law* 8 (2006): 245–66, at 247; Mary Ann Glendon, *A World Made New: Eleanor Roosevelt and the Universal Declaration of Human Rights* (New York: Random House, 2001), 89.

sufficiency." Malik emerged in the Commission debates as the champion of the vision of humans as by nature endowed with reason and conscience, a claim rejected by the Soviets and by Saudi Arabia's volatile delegate Jamil Baroody, who, like Malik, had been born a Lebanese Christian.[10]

Born in the village of Bterram in the White Mountains of Lebanon, Malik's family were descended from highly educated cosmopolitans who saw to it that the young Malik received a Western education at what was then the American Mission School for Boys. The young Malik's original academic interests did not hint at his later career in politics and philosophy. Only after leaving Lebanon and the American University of Beirut where he had majored in mathematics and physics did he develop the interests for which he later became famous. His brief sojourn in Cairo preceded a decision to pursue a career in philosophy, which was interrupted by the political upheavals of World War II and the subsequent, repeated crises that engulfed his native Lebanon.[11] Malik's own recollections about the formation of his convictions regarding human rights focused on his years serving at the Orthodox Divine Liturgy in Bterram, Al-Koura with his uncle, Father Mikhail Nicolas Malik. He referred to the "four pillars of my faith" as "The Church, the Bible, the tradition, the liturgy. . . ." His view of the world, he insisted, was not based on "rational-philosophical argument" but instead was part of what he lived—and his insistence on the priority of "being" as opposed to "epistemology" in philosophy remained a core conviction throughout his life. No one, he argued, had a "right" to question his faith in the absence of rational proof because all humans operate on the basis of "the degree of awareness of that faith and the ability

10. What follows in the next pages is taken selectively from A. G. Roeber, "Orthodox Christians, Human Rights and the Dignity of the Person: Reflections on Charles Malik (1907–1987)," *Journal of Eastern Christian Studies* 70, nos. 3–4 (2018): 285–306; Mary Ann Glendon, *The Forum and the Tower: How Scholars and politicians Have Imagined the World, From Plato to Eleanor Roosevelt* (Oxford: Oxford University Press, 2011), 199–217; and her earlier work *A World Made New*, 37–170, at 37, 41, 42 109, 147–8.

11. See variously Aksam J. Merched, "People of Bterram: Dr. Charles Malek," last modified April 10, 2012, http://people.bterram.com/CharlesMalekDEAD LINK (accessed April 9, 2021).

to articulate it,"[12] Malik connected the lived experience of his Orthodox faith to his philosophical conviction that "epistemological orientation is the fundamental fallacy of modern times . . . my whole argument is that naturally, originally and by itself, the mind is not oriented towards itself . . . but toward being—that is, ontologically. . . . First and foremost, then, I must come to terms with being—namely, I must be—and then try to express it as simply and faithfully as I can, or, more precisely, let it genuinely express itself through me."[13]

Although Malik began his graduate career in philosophy at Harvard under Alfred North Whitehead, he felt drawn toward the German philosopher Martin Heidegger's work on being and moved to Freiburg-am-Breisgau in 1932. Assaulted on the streets by SA thugs for his supposedly "semitic" appearance, Malik returned to Harvard to complete his Ph.D. in 1937 under Whitehead. Despite his personal loathing for the racialist politics of the Nazis, however, Malik retained a lifelong respect for Heidegger. Apologizing to Heidegger in 1957 for missing a colloquium on Hegel's thought and therefore being unable to be present for the bestowal of an honorary degree, Malik wrote from Lebanon "permit me to take this opportunity to tell you how much your work has meant in my life and thought and to pray that you be given many a year still to pursue the quest of truth and being." Malik arranged a major international conference for the aged philosopher in Rabiya in 1974 to honor the then-85-year old, who was unable to make the journey but sent his greetings and appreciation to his former student.[14]

Malik had managed to begin an academic career in the 1940s both at American universities and at the American University of Beirut, where he pioneered the foundation of that institution's department of philosophy. But his academic life abruptly ended in 1945 when he received the appointment to represent Lebanon to the United States and the newly founded

12. Charles Malik, *The Wonder of Being* (Waco, TX: Word Books, 1974), dedication and p. 12.

13. Malik, *Wonder of Being*, 31, 32–33.

14. Library of Congress Archives Division, *Charles Malik Papers, Correspondence*, Box 20:5 23 Heidegger, Martin, September 1957; November 1974. Charles Malik, *Charles Malik to Martin Heidegger, September 1957; November 1974*, Library of Congress Archives Division, *Charles Malik Papers, Correspondence*, Box 20:5; 23.

United Nations. Malik never completed his own philosophical writings, and we remain uncertain about the degree to which his thinking on the importance of being and the human person can be traced to Heidegger's influence. Most probably, his reading of Heidegger merely reinforced his already existing Orthodox understanding of human personhood. Nonetheless, in remarks made to Richard Scott of the philosophy faculty at the American University about his mentor Whitehead, Malik revealed a good deal as he reminisced about his former "Whiteheadian outlook" which he had long since abandoned because "I see reality not in terms of process and cosmology but in terms of persons, spirit and what is distinctively human. . . . What interests me now, and in fact ever since I concluded my dissertation on Whitehead, and indeed even during the writing of it, is not the cosmological ideas of Whitehead, but fundamental human spiritual attitudes, including, perhaps, why Whitehead as a human being should have allowed himself to slip in the first place into his utterly unhuman interpretation of man, spirit, and culture." No systematic approach of "the universe," Malik continued, could account for "the distinctively human phenomena of existence, such as guilt, sin, temptation, forgiveness, love, friendship, peace of mind, rebellion . . . as we have them in . . . the Psalms, the New Testament. . . ." Whitehead's omission of such key elements of this "existing man" demonstrated that the Harvard philosopher was "more of a technician and aesthete than . . . a person who is on fire to come closest to the deepest human-spiritual achievements of history. I do not believe in any philosophy that obliterates man."[15] God, humans and "the spirit" outweighed all "processes" for Malik and no "speculative scheme" could substitute for the "concrete, living, historical tradition of God, namely, in the church." The same holds true for finding the human because it is "in the concrete, personal living-dying-suffering being of human existence" that Whitehead's "system" fails. In the end, Malik wrote, "I desperately miss God, man, spirit, fellowship, understanding, repentance, forgiveness and love in Whitehead, and these to me are everything."[16]

15. Malik, *Charles Malik to Richard Scott,* 1 May 11, 1971, *Malik Papers,* 115:1.

16. Continuation of letter to Scott (Ibid.), and see 115:2 for Malik's acceptance of a proposal to direct a master's thesis on "Heidegger's conception of man with some reference to its Christian implications."

Despite having resumed his academic career in 1960 at the American University of Beirut and at the Catholic University of America, Malik had become embroiled in the Cold War politics of the Suez Crisis of 1956 that pitted the Lebanese Christian President Camile Chamoun against the Druze leader Kamal Jumblat, who despised Malik in particular for his opposition to Arab Nationalism led by the United Arab Republic's Gamal Abdel Nasser (1918–1970).[17] In 1958, Malik protested the intervention of the UAR in Lebanese affairs to the UN Security Council, a position from which he never wavered. Opposed to Ba'athist secularist versions of Arab nationalism as well as Muslim- or Christian-led varieties, Malik was dismayed when Lebanon descended into outright Civil War in 1975. Malik was invited as the sole non-Maronite to join what became the Lebanese Front that linked him to the Phalangist leader Pierre Gamayel and Lebanon's former President Camille Chamoun.[18] For Malik, as he revealed in a 1982 speech and repeated in another address in 1984, the critical question had to be asked whether by the turn of the millennium, faced with the rise of an increasingly aggressive Arab Muslim ideology, any future would exist for Christians "east of the Mediterranean."[19] A foreign observer in 1980 described Malik as someone of enormous presence and influence even among his enemies. But he also noted that "the younger Arabs are more suspicious of moralistic rhetoric and of any religious approach to life, and they are attracted to philosophies such as Marxism or existentialism, both of which Malik deplores."[20]

How Malik would have assessed the renaissance of interest in Aquinas on the part of a younger generation of Orthodox scholars, whether those interests would have kept his brothers in the Orthodox Church, and how he would have integrated his own interests and perspectives on that topic,

17. Samir Khalaf, *Civil and Uncivil Violence in Lebanon: A History of the Internationalization of Communal Conflict* (New York: Columbia University Press, 2002), 108–120; Wade R. Goria, *Sovereignty and Leadership in Lebanon 1943–1976* (London: Ithaca Press, 1985), 40.

18. Walid Phares, *Lebanese Christian Nationalism: The Rise & Fall of an Ethnic Resistance* (Boulder, CO: Lynne Rienner Publishers, 1995), 119–149.

19. Phares, *Lebanese Christian Nationalism*, 126, 147.

20. David C. Gordon, *Lebanon: The Fragmented Nation* (London: Croom Helm, 1980), 226–28, at 227.

we will never know.[21] What emerges from Malik's writings is his commitment to investigating where the dominant strains of the Western philosophical and theological traditions could be brought into harmony with his own Orthodox faith. He remained consistent in rejecting any form of ethnic nationalism that compromised his understanding of Orthodox Christianity. His ecumenical sympathies for Maronite, Roman Catholic, and some Protestant theology and piety were evident with regard to the proper understanding of the human person.

Malik's "personalist"—as opposed to purely "individualist"—commitments to human rights emanated from his Orthodox liturgical life as a young man as well as his fascination with Martin Heidegger's philosophical focus on the problem of being. Yet, one is struck by how little he appeared to be influenced by personalism—whose main exponents were Jacques Maritain and earlier, Max Scheler—although he was aware of their work.[22] Malik also showed no awareness or dependence upon Russian Orthodox philosophers and theologians of his time. Paul Valliere's investigation of the thought of Vladimir Soloviev, Nikolai Berdyaev, Pavel Florensky, and Sergei Bulgakov,[23] for example, explores what Valliere describes as the common characteristic of each of these thinkers, namely "the Orthodox seeker of dialogue with the world."[24] If Valliere's analysis is correct, Malik might have been enthusiastic about Bulgakov's, Bukharev's, and Soloviev's "expressions of a world-affirming, historically engaged Orthodox faith seeking to sanctify the

21. For examples of this renewed interest, see for example, Christopher Livanos, *Greek Tradition and Latin Influence in the Work of George Scholarios: 'Alone against All of Europe'* (Piscataway, NJ: Gorgias Press, 2006); A. N. Williams, *The Ground of Union: Deification in Aquinas and Palamas* (New York: Oxford University Press, 1999); Marcus Plested, *Orthodox Readings of Aquinas* (Oxford: Oxford University Press, 2012).

22. Malik's surviving papers reveal no correspondence with Maritain, but he was aware of Max Scheler's critique of Kant and the importance of experience as the basis for ethics (*Sittlichkeit*). Malik, *Malik Papers, Correspondence, Boxes 1–75*; see also *Wonder of Being*, 36–41.

23. Paul Valliere, *Modern Russian Theology: Bukharev, Soloview, Bulgakov: Orthodox Theology in a New Key* (Grand Rapids, MI: William B. Eerdmans Publishing Company, 2000).

24. Valliere, *Modern Russian Theology*, 334.

ever-expanding range of human vocations."[25] Each of the Russian thinkers also contributed reflections on the nature of the "person" as well. But no evidence survives to show that Malik was aware of or drew from these fellow Orthodox thinkers.[26] Nor has anyone discovered a Russian awareness of Malik. That same silence surrounds the connection to Heidegger among other Orthodox thinkers. Although Semen Liudvigovich Frank (1877–1950) has been described as "one of Russia's most articulate philosophers" and his 1915 book *The Object of Knowledge* as "a forerunner of sorts to Martin Heidegger's *Being and Time*," Malik appears to have developed his own conclusions about connecting Heidegger's insights to his own Orthodox beliefs in isolation from Frank's work.[27]

Nor was Malik a correspondent or reader of the young Greek Orthodox scholar Christos Yannaras. By the 1960s, Yannaras also explored the connections between Orthodoxy and Heidegger's critique of Western metaphysics, but with different results.[28] Yannaras believed that Heidegger had accurately identified the dead-end of Western philosophy but erred in his affirmation of "the absence of the God of onto-theology." "It is with a sort of genius," Yannaras concluded, "that Heidegger analyzes the notions of estrangement (*Entfremdung*)—that consciousness of nothingness (*Nichts*) from which human existence emerges." It was Heidegger's courage to refuse solace in a rationalization of this estrangement that opened the possibility for a "re-creation" of humans in Christ, Yannaras argued. Yannaras drew on the pseudo-Dionysian tradition of "the unknowability of the God beyond being," to develop his argument that "there exists no other possibility of

25. Valliere, *Modern Russian Theology*, 345. Neither did Malik ever indicate a sympathy for, or interest in, the Sophiology of Bulgakov. See Valliere, "Sophiology as the Dialogue of Orthodoxy with Modern Civilization," in *Russian Religious Thought,* ed. Judith Deutsch Kornblatt and Richard F. Gustafson (Madison: The University of Wisconsin Press, 1996), 176–192.

26. For more specifics on the Russians, see the literature and discussion in Andrew Louth, *Modern Orthodox Thinkers: From the Philokalia to the Present* (Downers Grove, IL: Inter-Varsity Press, 2015), 13–76.

27. Robert Slesinski, "S. L. Frank's Intuition of Pan-Unity," in *Russian Religious Thought,* ed. Kornblatt and Gustafson, 199–212, at 199, 212.

28. The following synopsizes Christos Yannaras, *On the Absence and Unknowability of God.* See also, Louth, *Modern Orthodox Thinkers,* 248–259.

relationship (existential communion) of creatures with the Creator outside the human person."[29] Some critics have concluded that Yannaras became increasingly negative, saying that he wrote bitter "anti-Western" polemics and put an exaggerated emphasis upon the "Greekness" or "Hellenic" mission of Orthodoxy to rescue the West from the "religionization" of Christianity.[30] Others have argued that Yannaras' encounter with Heidegger resulted in an evolution of his thinking, concluding that "Western nihilism could be overcome only through Eastern apophaticism and personalist ontology."[31] Yannaras appears to have identified issues within Orthodoxy that tally with the Malik argument that "Western civilization" cannot be confined to a specific geographic area, much less to linguistic or national identities. As Basilio Petra explains in his summary of Yannaras' claims, some Orthodox churches were guilty of perpetuating "a mythological cosmology and anthropology (the myth of the prelapsarian world) . . . incompatible with the data of modern science, without such a dualism being considered problematic in any way . . . content to offer a space of psychological refuge—a mythical world—corresponding to humanity's desires and instinctual needs, and in some sense, being a project of them. This last point should be noted especially, because not only does Yannaras *not* accuse the West of this, but he states clearly that such mythological cosmology/anthropology has to be rethought on the basis of the findings of modern science (which is a part of Western modernity)."[32]

29. Yannaras, *On the Absence and Unknowability of God*, 7, 90. 86.

30. Pantelis Kalaitzidis, "The Discovery of Greekness and Theological Antiwesternism in the Theological Generation of the '60s," in *Turmoil in Postwar Theology: The Theology of the '60s*, ed. P. Kalaitzidis, Ath. N. Papathansiou and Th. Abatzidis (Athens: Indiktos Publications, 2009), 429–514.

31. Basilio Petra, "Christos Yannaras and the Idea of 'Dysis,'" in *Orthodox Constructions of the West*, ed. George E. Demacopoulos and Aristotle Papanikolaou (New York: Fordham University Press, 2013), 161–180, at 161.

32. Petra, "Christos Yannaras," 177. Yannaras appreciates aspects of the work of Metropolitan John Zizioulas of Pergamon, whose path-breaking work one assumes Malik would have hailed, appeared two years before his death. John D. Zizioulas, *Being as Communion: Studies in Personhood and the Church* (London: Darton, Longman & Todd, 1985). Nonetheless, Zizioulas misinterpreted Yannaras' analysis of Heidegger, a mistake Yannaras has highlighted in recent comments about his reading of the German philosopher. See Christos Yannaras,

Malik would have been sympathetic to Yannaras' affirmation of the centrality of a believing community as the proper context within which to understand any notion of rights. But Malik would not have endorsed any conclusion that reduced Orthodox witness to a bunkered, ghetto-like defense against alternative voices and understandings of rights, all of which Yannaras lumped together as the pernicious influence of "the West." Malik's lifelong fascination with Western art, architecture, literature, and music tied him to what experts on the thought of Heidegger have pointed out remained important to the German philosopher as well. By the end of his career, "Heidegger's interpretation of the poetic word has a theological element in it. He places the theological element of thinking in the poetical work of the poet. Heidegger's philosophy thus has its own theology within the thinking of being."[33] Heidegger's own philosophical anthropology, focused on an actual reverence for observation and experience of everyday life, served as the basis for a kind of phenomenological anthropology. The German philosopher's "attitude of the philosophical life" demanded that "only by being true to these experiences of life can one free oneself from the concepts that have been alienated from life, yet at the same time serve as fetters for it."[34] Those seeking to understand what a Heideggerian anthropology might look like need to attend first of all to the "search for fundamental ontology, the core human characteristics, that dominated Heidegger's philosophy." Since Heidegger was not primarily interested in anthropological questions "he did not prioritize the social. He saw it as one component of being within the total human posture in the world . . . to the extent that we are serious about the attempt to critique the whole idea of social relations as our starting and ending point, an inspection of Heidegger's notion of being-in-the-world may provide an

---

Norman Russell, *Metaphysics as a Personal Adventure: Christos Yannaras in Conversation with Norman Russell* (Yonkers, NY: St. Vladimir's Seminary Press, 2017), 43–48.

33. Ben Vedder, *Heidegger's Philosophy of Religion: From God to the Gods* (Pittsburgh, PA: Duquesne University Press, 2007), 215–78, at 277. The impact of Heidegger's work on reassessments of Greek philosophy itself can be followed in Drew A. Hyland and John Panteleimon Manoussakis, eds., *Heidegger and the Greeks: Interpretive Essays* (Bloomington: Indiana University Press, 2006).

34. Vedder, *Heidegger's Philosophy of Religion*, 31.

image of one kind of social anthropology that might result from such a critique.[35]

Although indebted to Heidegger, Malik criticized some aspects of his mentor's philosophical anthropology because it never confronted "adequately the question of realization and becoming. Nor . . . to draw the necessary personal-practical consequences from the radical limitations of all philosophy. . . ."[36] As a result, the "idolatry of 'the self,'" highlighted the crisis that led Heidegger, and Malik himself to probe "the cry of the naturally wondering soul, the ontologically bewildered mind. No epistemological or verbal cleverness or subterfuge can possibly silence this cry: only death can silence it. This is the cry of the unspoiled child. Not only can we not enter into the kingdom of heaven until we are born again and become like children, but in so far as the kingdom of the world is a sort of vestibule to the kingdom of heaven, we cannot even step into that vestibule without the anguished cry of being. Only as we reestablish our right relationship to being, in wonder and in awe and in 'standing still,' can we begin to see things as they really are."[37]

Malik later addressed how to draw practical and personal consequences from his theological anthropology. In a series of reflections on the contemporary world, he expressed his conviction that "life and being always come first."[38] Malik proclaimed his faith in the value of a broad understanding of the "classical Western values"—"freedom, personality, excellence, rank, objective truth, faith in God, and the primacy of the spirit. . . ."[39] In connecting these philosophical reflections to his Orthodox convictions and the role of the state, Malik insisted that the Church had to demand from every state respect for "the natural principles of justice, truth, the common good, the dignity of man, and that man can never be treated as a means only . . . [these] spring from the nature of things, and ultimately from the mind of God Himself."[40] Rejecting apathy, indifference, or

---

35. James F. Weiner, *Tree Leaf Talk: A Heideggerian Anthropology* (Oxford: Berg, 2001), 5, 81, 82.

36. Malik, *Wonder of Being*, 41.

37. Malik, *Wonder of Being*, 47, 48.

38. Charles Malik, *Christ and Crisis* (Grand Rapids, MI: William B. Eerdmans Publishing Co., 1962), xv.

39. Charles Malik, *Christ and Crisis*, 4.

40. Malik, *Christ and Crisis*, 25.

complacency, Malik insisted that Christians had a "sacred duty to promote justice, give everybody his due, educate the ignorant, tend the sick, recognize the good everywhere . . . and rejoice in the truth wherever we find it. . . ." Humans were trapped in "the most original of all sins: the slothful inertia of being whereby the source and ground of all being is forgotten . . . Trial, temptation, suffering, chastening, death, the Cross, these then appear to be necessary in order to remind us who we are." Christians were obligated to understand, that "what is at stake here is justice, truth, and man . . . order that is not based on natural justice, on the dignity of man, and on the trust of truth to vindicate itself, cannot flow from the mind of Christ, nor can it merit His love."[41] The human, he wrote, "is as *fated* and *doomed* to be free and responsible as to struggle and care." Whether one opted for Heidegger's insight that "man is a struggling-caring being" or the teaching of the Bible that "man is a being estranged from the ground of his being"[42] made no difference for Malik. Humans struggle for peace because every human "*is essentially* a struggling being."[43] And whether at the personal level or in the attempt to bring peace among nations, a sense of justice had to guide all such efforts but in all such matters of the law, "the most decisive element is the living agreement of free agents."[44] Impatient with abstract theories, Malik insisted that "it is the unique decisions that count . . . history is primarily responsibility and decision. . . ."[45] His critique of the very Western civilization that he prized focused on weakness he traced to the West's condition: "divided, infiltrated, softened, unsure of itself, morally weakened, congratulating itself over veritable crumbs, repeating the wonderful slogans of 'man,' 'freedom,' 'truth,' without, however, filling them with full-blooded content, apparently unwilling ascetically to pay the price of rising to the spiritual heights of which it is certainly capable. . . ."[46]

Malik admired the ancient Greek focus on "the exercise of reason and an incredible curiosity to investigate and know everything . . ." and conviction that "knowledge is the realization of the unity of man as man, and

41. Malik, *Christ and Crisis*, 72, 78, 90–91.

42. Charles Malik, *Man in the Struggle for Peace* (New York: Harper and Rowe, 1963), ix.

43. Charles Malik, *Man in the Struggle for Peace*, xiii.

44. Malik, *Man in the Struggle for Peace*, xix.

45. Malik, *Man in the Struggle for Peace*, xxii.

46. Malik, *Man in the Struggle for Peace*, xxix.

therefore of the essence of all men." For Malik, the exercise of reason and conscience defined the "civilized" no matter where they were geographically located.[47] Malik, throughout his life pursued his conviction in the possibilities of what humans could "become" and as a consequence he rejected "the ancient Greek fallacy which asserts that knowledge is virtue. . . ."[48] Dismissing what he described as "subjectivist" interpretations of nature, Malik returned to his focus on Heidegger and the importance of being, of the fully human person "fundamentally oriented towards being . . . marvel[ling] at the infinite mysteries of nature, because after all the human mind itself is a given fact of nature."[49]

Malik expressed his admiration and sympathy for the world of Islam he knew at first-hand, especially "its absolute faith" in the transcendent "Creator of the heavens and the earth and all that is between them"—but Islam, in his judgment, was not part of the Western understanding of civilization.[50] Instead, in speaking of his "entire cumulative tradition," Malik invoked the Christian Scriptures and a list of saints that included "Augustine, Chrysostom, Basil, Ephrem, John of Damascus, Aquinas and Teresa . . . the great Protestant theologians such as Jonathan Edwards and Karl Barth. . . ." He himself, he asserted, was "sufficiently steeped in the Greek orthodox liturgy and tradition, to feel quite confident that my reading of the will of Christ on the subject of the university is not egregiously off the mark. All these people believed in the living will of Christ and sought it and trusted that he would reveal it to them."[51]

Malik identified himself with "the peculiar genius of the West, where variety, individuality, and freedom are ultimate" but nonetheless wondered if the West had lost its way by refusing to ponder the question of "what do you make of man, reason, nature, destiny, and God?"[52] In his private correspondence he also revealed his concern and deep irritation at his own Orthodox Church's failure to articulate why a commitment to human dignity required a forceful defense of Christian theological anthropology in dealing with a

47. Charles Malik, *A Christian Critique of the University* (Downers Grove, IL: InterVarsity Press, 1982), 17, 19.

48. Charles Malik, *A Christian Critique of the University*, 73.

49. Malik, *A Christian Critique of the University*, 34.

50. Malik, *A Christian Critique of the University.*, 55.

51. Malik, *A Christian Critique of the University*, 103–04.

52. Malik, *Man in the Struggle for Peace*, 213, 228.

pluralistic society, whether in the United States or his own native Lebanon. Malik's relationship with many influential Orthodox hierarchs eroded over time because of his conviction that they were too willing to accommodate Muslim threats to Christian rights in Lebanon. An admirer of the tenacity of the Maronite community's insistence on defending Christian rights, Malik attended Maronite services in the United States, praised Maronite defense of "religious and cultural freedom" that had long served as a bridge between the West and "the culture of the Near East," and shared Naef Basile's conviction that "without the Maronites there would be no Lebanon as we know it today." Malik was convinced that the defense of "religious and cultural freedoms" would only survive under the protection of an internationally recognized state.[53] Malik's primary dedication remained that of attempting to promote as much cooperation and reconciliation among the Middle East's Christian populations as he deemed possible. His rejection of pan-Arabism put him at odds with some younger Orthodox Christians. His long-standing friendship with Metropolitan Antony Bashir, the leader of the New York-based Antiochian Orthodox Christian Archdiocese, led Malik, like the Metropolitan, to criticize the founding of the state of Israel as inimical to the rights of the Palestinians. But Malik's views did not extend to sharing the enthusiasm for pan-Arabism expressed by a younger generation of Orthodox leaders (including Bashir's successor in the United States, the later Metropolitan Philip Saliba).[54]

Malik had hinted early in his career at his instinct that rights, to have any meaning, had to be more than vague moral sentiments. He had shared with Harvard professor of philosophy William Ernest Hocking in 1947 his report of the Drafting Committee of the Commission on Human Rights. Hocking endorsed much of what the Draft Declaration would finally

53. Malik, *Charles Malik to Metropolitan Antony Bashir, February 7, 1946,* Malik Papers, 5:7; and Malik, *Charles Malik to Naef Basile, April 18, 1962,* Malik Papers, 5:8. Malik described his fellow religionists in Lebanon to Metropolitan Antony Bashir by concluding "the Orthodox faithful here are good and solid. I cannot say the same of their spiritual leaders." Malik, *Charles Malik to Metropolitan Antony Bashir, February 25, 1963,* Malik Papers, 5:7.

54. For this issue, see Nasr, Constantine. *Antony Bashir: Metropolitan & Missionary.* Yonkers, NY: St. Vladimir's Seminary Press (2012), 205–06; Archbishop Philip Saliba and Dr. Najib E. Saliba, *Broken Promises and White House Meetings* (Englewood, NJ: Antakya Press, 2015), 1–15, 188–198.

contain but asked pointedly whether all humans had equal moral and legal rights and raised the disturbing question about whether "my right is a power to deflect your conduct." Agreeing with Malik that humans had certain rights that derived from their "nature as a being having reason as conscience," Hocking was unhappy with the mixing of "legal" aspects of rights with the human since as he put it, presumably a list of rights was meant to suggest what rights the "human individual in his community" possessed prior to law and since the law sometimes fails to implement such rights, the listing was intended to identify them, even if they failed to obtain legal protection. Hocking added that "I would exempt all legal implementation" from a list of moral rights "such as the right to affection and to the loyalty of friends—but only such rights as ought to be in the constitutions of modern states." Hocking asserted that "each individual has one fundamental right, the right to do his human task, and this means, to play his part in history. This right, which is at the same time a duty, implies the existence of the community. Hence each individual has a right to a continued society as a condition of fulfilling his human task: his 'fundamental duties to society' are a part of his fundamental right."[55]

Malik's devotion to his Orthodox faith, in tandem with his philosophical convictions about the universal quality of the human "anguished cry of being," led him to insist that no group of humans could be excluded or deemed to be unfit holders of rights. Refusing to blame the worsening situation in the Middle East exclusively on Israel or the Arabs, Malik denounced "the dark impulses of the mob, and on what Dag Hammarskjold once called (in confidence to me) 'competitive Arabism.'" Those policymakers who opted for encouraging "authoritarian, non-democratic, even if necessary military, government in the Arab world," should be ashamed of themselves. Their endorsement of "what is called Arab nationalism (whether of the Nassserite or the Baathist or some other stripe)" betrayed Malik's insistence that all peoples were "fit for freedom," and could not be abandoned to some lesser condition that violated their human rights that he continued to link to both duties to "a continued society" and that society's own continued existence.[56]

55. Malik, *William Earnest Hocking to Charles Malik, August 3, 1947,* Malik Papers, 20:12, 1, 3, 4.

56. Malik, *Charles Malik to William Earnest Hocking, January 10, 1955*, Malik Papers, 20:12, and Malik, *Charles Malik to William Earnest Hocking, February 5, 1965*, Malik Papers, 20:13.

Malik at times appeared uncertain about whether he advocated acceptance of the Christian's role as that of a quiet witness who would remain permanently on the margins of society, or alternatively, a more zealous engagement in the struggle to realize a Christian social and political understanding of human rights. For example, to an American audience he could claim that as an Orthodox Christian "to live in a modicum of peace in this world, a Christian . . . must . . . accept the sad lot of belonging to a *permanent* minority . . . Christians at times get themselves overworked about the state of the world. This is not a sign of faith but of the exact opposite."[57] Malik's philosophy and his theology was characterized by bearing the cross of making a commitment to a life characterized by an asceticism that recognized the limitations as well as the obligations of being engaged with others who did not necessarily share his faith and understanding of human rights. He was also focused on "the healthy and joyous contemplation of being. I want to come out of myself into this wide world and seek the truth in history, life, and objective suffering . . . these independent beings outside of men . . . excite my greatest wonder."[58]

Given Malik's unhappiness with Lebanese Orthodox leaders in the face of unjust treatment at the hands of Muslims, coupled with the plight of Palestinian refugees (what he understood to be a lamentable acceptance of *dhimmitude*); his call for acceptance of a Christian destiny to be that of the "permanent minority" appears somewhat odd. As Malik's growing dismay over the failure of the United States and the West in general to attend to its own moral failings increased, he concluded that the status of permanent minority was the likely role Christians were to play in voicing their correct understanding of human rights. Malik's own ensnarement in the Lebanese Civil War suggests how fragile has been the Orthodox capacity to inform or convince non-Orthodox neighbors of an Orthodox understanding of the nature of personhood and the social and political consequences that result from that conviction—the right of Christian communities to co-exist with non-Christian majorities. Malik recognized that the response of Orthodox Christians to the challenge of being both evangelists and patient sufferers depended upon

57. Malik, *Christ and Crisis*, xiv–xv; 4. 25, 65.
58. Malik, *Charles Malik to Wasfi Hijeb, October 2, 1952*, Malik Papers, 20:8.

circumstances they cannot control. The Christians of the Middle East, he recognized, had at their disposal the ancient liturgical tradition that has served the Church when it "is driven into the catacombs, whether physically or socially and spiritually," when it is forced to cease being "evangelical save unto itself . . . it turns then liturgical, preserving the entire deposit of faith behind symbol and song. It dies, so to speak, that the faith may live."[59]

Never sympathetic to those who imagined there to be an Arab Christian identity shared with Arab Muslims, Malik remained rooted in his Orthodoxy, that of an Eastern Christian who stood for a "fundamental acceptance of what is deepest and most authentic about the West."[60] Malik's reception in his own country has remained controversial. Because of his two brothers' conversion to Catholicism and subsequent ordination to the Catholic priesthood, because of Malik's admiration for the philosophical acuity of Aquinas, and due to his involvement in ecumenical affairs, he was not well received by many among the hierarchy and clergy in Lebanon. As a diplomat and as a professor of philosophy, he enjoyed a much more positive reputation, at least until the outbreak of the Lebanese Civil War. But because of his numerous commitments, Malik never managed to publish the major synthetic philosophical work he had drafted even though it was under contract at the time of his death. No critical biography of Malik exists, and with the exception of two volumes of religious essays in Arabic edited by his son and an evangelical pastor in Beirut, little has emerged from within Arabic-speaking Orthodox circles on his human rights perspective.[61] Even in Malik's lifetime, his

59. Charles Malik, "The Near East," in *The Prospects of Christianity throughout the World*, ed. M. Searle Bates and Wilhelm Pauck (New York: Charles Scribner's Sons, 1964), 83–104, at 87.

60. George Sabra, "Two Ways of Being a Christian in the Muslim Context of the Middle East," *Islam & Christian Muslim Relations* 17, no. 1 (2006): 43–53, at 48.

61. For a generally negative view of Malik as an unwitting representative of "orientalism" see the remarks by his cousin-in-law by marriage, Edward Said, in *Out of Place* (New York: Vintage Books, 1999), 264–280. Said apparently never heard or accepted Malik's conclusions about Christianity as a permanent minority, accusing "Uncle Charles" of dreaming of a "Christian Lebanon," perhaps because of Malik's later role as an intellectual leader and the only non-Maronite member of the

insistence upon the human right to change one's religion brought him into conflict with a fellow Lebanese Jamil Baroody, who as Saudi Arabia's representative had rejected the right to change religion and the freedom to marry and "took issue with the statement that all human beings are endowed with reason and conscience. That, he said, was not, and never had been, true."[62]

Exchanges between the Greek and Russian voices about human rights have ignored Malik's work and have devoted little attention to the perspective of Middle Eastern Christians.[63] The predominant themes emanating from various academic disciplines are now decolonization, international

---

Lebanese Front. I am indebted to Professor Dr. Assaad Elias Kattan of the University of Münster for his analysis (and personal memory) of Malik and his reception in Lebanon. Kattan's judgment is further confirmed by the fact that although the later Patriarch of Antioch Ignatius IV (Habib Hazim) studied with Malik in the 1940s at the American University, no correspondence between him and Malik survives in Malik's papers; Malik, Malik Papers, General Correspondence, 1904–1982. Nonetheless, the patriarch visited his former professor as the latter was dying and remained on good terms with him throughout Malik's life. I am indebted to Malik's son Dr. Habib Malik for this information (Dr. Habib Malik, Private correspondence to the author, August 21, 2015.) For a further investigation of Malik's own musings on whether a Christian Arab culture is possible, see Najeeb G. Awad, "Is Christianity from Arabia? Examining Two Contemporary Arabic Proposals on Christianity in the Pre-Islamic Period," in *Orientalische Christen und Europa: Kulturbegegnung zwischen Interferenz, Partizipation und Antizipation*, ed. Martin Tamcke (Wiesbaden: Harrassowitz, 2012), 33–55, at 55.

62. Glendon, *Forum and the Tower*, 154, 148. Malik recognized the Saudi regime's uneasy relationship with the Wahabist Islamic movement that had become since the 1930s increasingly focused on the dangers posed by non-Muslims. Saudi Arabia would become the only Muslim-majority state to abstain from voting on the acceptance of the Universal Declaration of Human Rights.

63. For an example of this tendency, see the essays in Vasilios N. Makrides, Jennifer Wasmuth, Stefan Kube, eds., *Christentum und Menschenrechte in Europa: Perspektiven und Debatten in Ost und West* (Frankfurt am Main: Peter Lang, 2016), and my review of the same in *Theologische Revue* 112, no. 6 (December, 2016), 502–04. For a rare exception to this pattern, see Assad E. Kattan and Fadi A. Georgi, eds., *Thinking Modernity: Towards a Reconfiguration of the Relationship between Orthodox Theology and Modern Culture* (Tripoli, Leb.: St. John of Damascus Institute of Theology University of Balamand, 2010).

law, individual versus collective rights, but there is seldom found an accurate assessment of the initial contributions made by Malik.[64]

Neither an uncritical defender of the Western liberal state nor of the rights of individual persons, Malik insisted on the role played by intermediate institutions in society that stood as a buffer between the state and the person. By intermediate institutions Malik meant "families, syndicates, universities, and churches. It was he who was behind the only right in the Declaration that specifically devolves to a group . . . Article 16 paragraph 3 . . . : The family is the natural and fundamental group unit of society and is entitled to protection by society and the state."[65]

Malik knew that the sufferings of Christians in the Middle East "is not counted to them for righteousness: it is a cosmic waste. That is why they do not 'count' in the total Christian scale; that is why there is no inspired Near Eastern Christian literature read in Helsinki and Paris, in Burma and Buenos Aires. . . . Man can only suffer: it is God alone who can transfigure suffering into glory. Man can only accept the Cross: it is God alone who can raise from the dead. . . ." For Malik, the challenge of the Orthodox view of any discussion of rights remained bound up with his commitment to "letting the Holy Ghost guide, lead, and direct; entering into the glorious company of the saints through contemplation and ardent prayers of intercession; the quiet of eternity; loving and of being unto death—you can pray and yearn for these things; you can reject them when they come your way; but one thing you cannot do: you cannot produce or create them. They are the free and independent gift of the Holy Ghost."[66]

Malik may have been unduly optimistic about the human capacity to overcome the narrow visions represented by ethno-religious nationalism that dashed his own hopes for his native Lebanon by the time of his death. His prescient warnings about the possibility that, in the face of brutalities

64. For a survey of much of the recent literature and the focus on these themes, see Julia Eichenberg's "Sammelrez: Geschichte der Menschenrechts," at h-soz-u -kult@h-net.msu.edu, December 22, 2016, http://hsozkult.geschichte.hu-berlin.de /index.asp?id=20869&view=pdf&pn=rezensionen&type=rezbuecher.

65. Tony E. Nasrallah, "A Lebanese Role in the UN: Charles Malik," in *The Quest for Peace: A Decade of Politics in the Middle East: proceedings of Selected Conferences and papers 2006–2016,* ed. Georges Yahchouchi (Kaslik, Leb.: Holy Spirit University of Kaslik Press, 2016), 93–102, at 100.

66. Malik, "The Near East," in *The Prospects of Christianity*, p. 103.

·spawned by ethno-religious nationalist impulses, no space would be allowed for Christians "East of the Mediterranean" also have proven to be
prophetic utterances. But he was no less a critic of such tendencies within
his own Orthodox Church. Neither a partisan of an exclusively Christian
state, nor a supporter of pious quietism, Malik's vision of human rights
focused on the "Church, the Bible, the tradition, the liturgy" that opened
for him the encounter with human personhood and the dignity and rights
he strove to defend throughout his life as philosopher, diplomat, but primarily, as Orthodox Christian.

II. The Orthodox, Other Theists, and Human Rights since the 1970s

In the subsequent generation of Orthodox that began reflecting upon the
question of human rights, American Orthodox scholars acknowledged the
insights of Yannaras, but bypassed an assessment of Malik's Orthodox contribution to human rights language. The engagement of the Orthodox
with contemporary controversies over rights in America's pluralistic society has produced different responses from the theologians Vigen Guroian
and Aristotle Papanikolaou. Still, except for a recent exchange that illustrated some of the disagreements and tensions among the Orthodox regarding the issue of human rights and their relationship to political theology
articulated by Papanikolaou, the Orthodox have not engaged the question
of human rights in the American context.[67] Guroian has expressed grave
reservations about the entire project of developing a political theology from
Orthodox theological convictions.[68]

67. Philip LeMasters summarized some of the issues in his paper "Guroian
and Papanikolaou: Reflections on Orthodoxy, Western Democracy, and
Postmodernity," presented at the annual meeting of the Orthodox Theological
Society in America, Holy Cross Greek Orthodox School of Theology, Brookline,
MA, October 2014. I am grateful to LeMasters for providing me with a copy of
the paper. For Papanikolaou's argument, Papanikolaou, *The Mystical as Political;*
see LeMasters' review in *St. Vladimir's Theological Quarterly* 58, no. 1 (2014):
235–39, and Guroian's negative review, "Godless Theosis," *First Things,* April,
2014, www.firstthings.com/article/2014/04/godless-theosis.
68. For Guroian's arguments, see his *Ethics after Christendom: Toward an
Ecclesial Christian Ethic* (Grand Rapids, MI: William B. Eerdmans Publishing

Guroian and Papanikolaou share the conviction that the Orthodox will remain a prophetic minority voice within a pluralist American democracy. They differ insofar as Papanikolaou argues for a political space that the Orthodox can positively endorse that would imply—for example—not advocating for laws against premarital sex or same-sex marriage. The Orthodox must vocalize this if they are simultaneously to remain true to their historically grounded proclamation of who God is and what human dignity consists of, and to their obligation of inviting—not coercing—those beyond the bounds of Orthodoxy to share in that vision. For Guroian, this posture implies more than the rejection of same-sex marriage. It demands articulation of why the Orthodox position is of value and why secular rights claims are based on false assumptions about what it means to be human. Papanikolaou argues that the Orthodox belief in the importance of ascetic suffering as the road to union with God implies encountering the radically "other"—including gay, lesbian, and transgendered persons and communities—and affirming the human dignity and human rights of each individual through endorsing the constitutional and legal right to same-sex marriage.

Despite the American Orthodox concern for domestic rights controversies, differences of opinion on what the Orthodox response should be regarding human rights attracted attention in Europe before American Orthodox engagement with human rights. The impact of the Russian Orthodox Church's apparent endorsement of, and then retreat from, human rights played an increasingly important role in fostering disagreements among the Orthodox in the United States. By 2008, when the Russian Orthodox Church published its document *The Russian Orthodox Church's Basic Teaching on Human Dignity, Freedom and Rights,* notions of freedom and dignity and the "threat to the integrity of religious and cultural traditions" characterized its conclusions. By adopting the rhetoric of "liberal" or "Western" rights discourse, however, the Russian Orthodox simultaneously claimed to "represent, as a dominant religious and moral force, the majority" perspective for Russians, and to identify themselves as an embattled "cultural minority, its approach to human rights represent[ing] a typically protective reaction against

---

Co., 1994) and *Rallying the Really Human Things: The Moral Imagination in Politics, Literature, and Everyday Life* (Wilmington, DE: ISS Books, 2005).

liberal tradition, with distinct overtones of an antiwestern, postcolonial reaction to the dominant language of human rights. . . ."[69] By 2010, conferences in Europe had taken up the question of how and to what extent the Orthodox were prepared to endorse human rights. In a 2009 conference in Nijmegen, Netherlands, only two Americans participated and presented their analysis of how respect for human rights did or did not manifest itself in the form of religious tolerance among the Orthodox.[70] A 2010 conference in Erfurt, Germany explored the question of human rights and Christianity in general but only within the European perspective, with no American participants or contributors.[71] Aristotle Papanikolaou's participation in the Emory University Law School's Center for the Study of Law and Religion resulted in the 2012 publication that lamented that "the Orthodox voice in matters of law and politics is severely underdeveloped. . . ."[72] As if to underscore Papanikolaou's complaint, in the same year his book appeared a collection of essays was also published that reflected a major conference held in 2009 at Radboud University Nijmegen in the Netherlands. In that collection, the Roman Catholic scholar Alfons Brüning noted with concern the accelerating denunciations of human rights by the Russian Orthodox Church. Asserting that Western obsession with "freedom" had effectively undermined any serious commitment to "morality," Russian Orthodox Church leaders had signaled the direction in which, a decade later, military incursion upon a neighboring sovereign state would be

69. Alexander Agadjanian, "Liberal Individual and Christian Culture: Russian Orthodox Teaching on Human Rights in Social Theory Perspective," *Religion, State and Society* 38, no. 2 (June, 2010): 97–113, at 103, 104. For an analysis that traces the cautious endorsement, and the retreat from human rights in the Russian Orthodox Church and the international political agenda of the ROC, see Stoeckl, *Russian Orthodox Church and Human Rights*, 91–118.

70. Christopher Marsh and Daniel Payne, "Religiosity, Tolerance and Respect for Human Rights in the Orthodox World," in *Orthodox Christianity and Human Rights*, ed. Alfons Brüning and Evert van der Zweerde (Leuven: Peeters, 2012), 201–214.

71. Vasilios N. Makrides, Jennifer Wasmuth, Stefan Kube, eds., *Christentum und Menschenrechte in Europa;* see my review of the same in *Theologische Revue* 112, no. 6 (December, 2016): 502–03.

72. Papanikolaou, *The Mystical as Political*, ix.

justified as a defensive measure against Western freedom, individualism, and immorality.[73]

A decade before the European conferences took up the theme of the Orthodox and human rights, a sobering assessment had appeared by a non-Orthodox American legal scholar, Winnifred Fallers Sullivan, who pointed out the increasingly acrimonious disputes over religious rights and concluded that "the guarantee of a right to religious freedom is almost perversely insistent on the necessity of transcendence. While the argument can be made that all rights depend on a religious understanding of the person, the right to religious freedom makes that argument a necessary part of law. Only then can the resulting discrimination against those who claim to have no religion be justified. That is the best argument for legal guarantees of religious freedom. But as with other rights against the state, such rights are paradoxically dependent on state endorsement."[74]

The Armenian American Orthodox legal scholar Mark L. Movsesian echoed Sullivan's' conclusions by 2016, but on a much broader scale. He provided a comprehensive survey of those who assume the importance of grounding the notion of human dignity and rights in an objective standard (for the Orthodox, rooted in the *imago Dei* belief) versus "a subjective conception of human dignity, based on the will of the individual, which most secular human rights advocates prefer." Movsesian concluded that "it is unlikely that advocates of subjective understandings will accept an objective approach that would negate policy goals, such as same-sex marriage, that they view as vital to human flourishing. Indeed, my impression, based on experience in the American legal academy, is that these two sides have increasingly little to say to one another."[75] What these rather grim analyses also point to, however, is the question of whether one can speak of "human rights" without given priority to the right to religious freedom of expression, a question that has been raised by European scholars as well.

73. Alfons Brüning, "'Freedom' vs. 'Morality'—On Orthodox Anti-Westernism and Human Rights," in Brüning and Evert van der Zweerde, eds., *Orthodox Christianity and Human Rights* (Leuven, Paris, Walpole, MA: Peeters, 2012), 125–152. On the invasion of Ukraine, see below, Conclusion.

74. Winnifred Fallers Sullivan, *The Impossibility of Religious Freedom* (Princeton: Princeton University Press, 2005), 158.

75. Mark L. Movsesian, "Of Human Dignities," *Notre Dame Law Review* 91, no. 4 (2016): 1517–1551, at 1518, 1549.

The understanding of "rights" and "personhood" sketched by Metropolitan John Zizioulas in his address to lawyers and jurists at the Academy of Athens appears at first glance to offer a way for the Orthodox to engage with second-generation human rights questions and perhaps even to cooperate with non-theistic advocates of human rights. Zizioulas reminds his readers that individual persons are unique. Yet they also exist in "a unity based on the free relations of persons, whose relations not only respect but affirm otherness, i.e., the absolute uniqueness of every person. This community, in which nobody is capable of being determined alone, but in which all are determined by others in a relationship amongst themselves (but in which this determination of others affirms and establishes the otherness of everyone) is invited to establish the law (*dikaion*) of personhood." As a result, "the Church blesses and encourages every legal development in the direction of protecting persons as unique, unrepeatable, and irreplaceable identities. Thus, the Church supports legal regulations that concern the protection of private life, equal rights, and freedom . . . as well as the protection of honor and respect for all. . . ."[76]

But does a universally shared understating of personhood exist in twenty-first century Eastern Orthodox Christianity, and if so, how does this translate into a discussion of rights? Nicholas Prevelakis has argued that until recently Eastern Christians rarely took up the challenge of explaining how notions of personhood have informed "the kind of political arrangements that they thought were consistent with it."[77] None of the notions of personhood explored in Prevelakis' essay address the specifics of how human rights and an Orthodox response to them appear in the context of American legal, constitutional, and ecclesiastical issues. Prevelakis noted Aristotle Papanikolaou's work, concluding that Papanikolaou insisted that the Orthodox can only endorse a "human rights regime" if claims for human rights are grounded theistically, and if notions of the "individual"

76. John Zizioulas, "Law and Personhood in Orthodox Theology," in *The One and the Many: Studies on God, Man, the Church, and the World Today*, by John Zizioulas, ed. Fr Gregory Edwards (Alhambra, CA: Sebastian Press, 2010), 402–413, at 405, 410.

77. Nicholas Prevelakis, "Eastern Christian Conceptions of Personhood and their Political Significance," in *Personhood in the Byzantine Christian Tradition: Early, Medieval, and Modern Perspectives*, ed. Alexis Torrance and Symeon Paschalidis (London: Routledge, 2018), 173–181, at 173.

are modified to accommodate an Orthodox understanding of persons in communion and not "a framework within which humans appear as separated entities who related to each other legally."[78] The disagreements among Orthodox systematic theologians about "personhood" however, suggest that if a prior consensus must emerge here first, a political constitutional, and legal framework that all Orthodox can endorse in talking about human rights lies somewhere in the future.[79]

As we have already seen in the preceding chapters, in the American context the understanding of the dignitary rights of the individual person and, as a consequence, the regime of human rights appears to be unfolding with less room for theists and a concomitant increase in the emphasis on individual legal claims and defenses of rights. While Zizioulas' endorsement of "equal rights and freedom" appears to be consonant with other theistic approaches that might be shared by the Orthodox with both Roman Catholic and Protestant Christians, such an impression is also deceptive. In the case of both non-Orthodox Christian groups, the same divide between optimists and pessimists has emerged in their understandings of the long history of ancient and modern rights languages. Necessarily selective examples of both positions from both traditions provide a context within which to place Orthodox assessments of human rights. Secular human rights claims appear even more distant and alien to Orthodox understandings, although occasional areas of overlap and common ground do appear, and those should be noted.

In a comprehensive review of how both Catholic and Protestant scholars have tried to come to grips with human rights issues, the Reformed law professor John Witte pointed out the skepticism with which both some Catholic and Protestant writers have viewed human rights.[80] Given the long history of Reformed Christianity in North America, it comes as no surprise that Reformed scholars in America such as Witte (and in the European context, the Dutch scholar Hans-Martien ten Napel) have been

---

78. Prevelakis, "Eastern Christian Conceptions," 177–179, here at 178, 179.

79. For a review of the disagreements and suggestions for reconciling some of those perspectives, Torrance, *Human Perfection in Byzantine Theology*, 1–39; 197–215.

80. John Witte, Jr. and Justin J. Latterell, "Christianity and Human Rights: Past Contributions and Future Challenges," *Journal of Law and Religion* 30 (2015): 353–385, 9n33.

the most vocal in assessing the problems and potential of human rights. Moreover, some have argued that for a human rights regime to flourish and to receive Christian approbation, a prior commitment to religious freedom and rights is indispensable. Ten Napel has reviewed the arguments of those who claim that "classical natural rights" had their roots in the philosophy of Plato, Aristotle, and subsequently in the Western theological tradition of Augustine and Aquinas that have little to do with "modern natural rights." In that "classical" form, part of the argument about rights had to do with a claim that we can define "human nature." Once we reach the works of Thomas Hobbes or Hugo Grotius in the seventeenth century however, so the argument goes, no more attention was paid to the social nature of humans or the need to contain the impact of evil by the exercise of virtues. The triumph of individual self-preservation assumed that individual rights are guaranteed only to the extent that a political authority or state guarantees natural rights in a social compact that presupposes individuals voluntarily agreeing to support the particular monarch or governing authority. But if one agrees with this reading of the history of natural law and natural rights, the Orthodox can hardly endorse modern notions of human rights.[81] The Dutch scholar goes on, however, to make the case for what he calls "pluriform democracy" that the American Presbyterian legal scholar John Inazu develops in his calls for "confident pluralism." Ten Napel argues that what he is advocating cannot be thought of as a uniquely American view of democracy but instead was worked out as early as 1917 in the Netherlands under the heading of "principled public pluralism . . . making the Netherlands a confessionally neutral state, asserting as much as possible equal respect and principled distance to all religious and non-religious worldviews."[82]

Even so, by comparison with Roman Catholic social teaching, "neo-Calvinist thought on democracy in general . . . remained relatively under-developed." A staunch defender of the "mediating institutions" and associations such as families, churches, and other voluntary social groups,

---

81. Hans-Martien ten Napel, "A Natural Law Basis for Human Rights?" *Canopy Forum On the Interaction of Law & Religion*, January 6, 2020. https://canopyforum.org/2020/01/06/a-natural-law-basis-for-human-rights (accessed January 22, 2021); and ten Napel, *Constitutionalism, Democracy, and Religious Freedom: To Be Fully Human* (Abingdon-on-Thames: Routledge, 2017).

82. Ten Napel, *Constitutionalism*, 95.

ten Napel sees these as necessary components of the capacity "to be fully human." For him, no division can exist between Christians and other religions or the non-religious as long as "people of no faith . . . accept that it is a precondition for true freedom not to have to divide one's life into different compartments . . . a principle that cannot be given up today" since it is "a precondition for freedom . . . that is a precondition for constitutionalism and democracy."[83] The commitment to this vision of what being fully human implies in terms of political theology, however, ten Napel admits may be difficult for the Orthodox in their traditional homelands. There, they struggle "to accept a status according to which Orthodoxy would be one among many different churches . . . a social pluralist perspective will likely try to reconcile the entitlements that flow from a universal right with circumstances as they have historically developed in a particular country." It may be so that "the right to religious freedom necessarily trumps other human rights at all times . . ." but it is difficult to see how the Orthodox can claim to be defenders of human rights if they do not make this primary commitment. Even so, while warning about an intrusive state's threat to the human right to religious freedom, ten Napel also points out that the rights of a particular religious group to operate according to its own laws is not an unlimited right. Even though freedom of expression developed in a community "is more central to liberal democracy than religious freedom," "social pluralist theory will also always emphasize that becoming fully human is not an individual matter." Believers "of any kind also have to recognize and respect opposite interests especially when these are equally protected by fundamental rights." Unfortunately, he concludes, increasingly "the right to freedom of religion or belief . . . has become increasingly judicialized. In the process . . . the right paradoxically also becomes more circumscribed . . . and lawyers, courts, and even academic specialists get caught up in an ever more complex web of leading and secondary principles and rules. As a result, not only the right to freedom of religion or belief but human rights in general become less accepted by the population."[84]

In addition to the American legal scholar Inazu, ten Napel singled out for approval the American Reformed philosopher Nicholas Wolterstorff for

83. Ten Napel, *Constitutionalism*, 102–03; 117–18.
84. Ten Napel, *Constitutionalism*, 121, 1234; 127, 135.

his insistence upon the "moral engagement" of citizens.[85] As we have already noted in surveying the social ethos of the Reformed Protestant tradition in early North America, the Scottish Common Sense moral philosophers provided a basis for developing what they had hoped would be a humble but genuine "moral engagement" by Reformed Christians in their dealing with questions of politics and society. Nicholas Wolterstorff's arguments stem from his conviction that we can best understand the dignitary rights claims of contemporary human rights language—and their weaknesses—by examining what appears to come close to the claims about "moral sentiments" advanced by those early modern Christian Scottish Common Sense moral philosophers, especially Thomas Reid. Wolterstorff is explicit in denying that a secular grounding of human rights is possible. He also rejects the claim that modern understandings of natural rights and human rights arose because of a departure from ancient or classical human rights thinking. He is of special interest to Orthodox readers because he uses the Septuagint translation of Scripture in critical places, cites patristic authors such as John Chrysostom, and addresses what he perceives to be the problematic aspects of relying upon "image and likeness" as the foundational grounding for human rights claims by Christians.[86]

But can the Orthodox concur with Wolterstorff's understanding of human rights? A decade ago, Aristotle Papanikolaou gave an overall positive but cautious assessment of the Reformed philosopher's arguments. But it is worth our while to ask if Papanikolaou was correct in asserting that Wolterstorff's understandings of rights as "social" were correct and that Wolterstorff's God and the rights due to him are hard to reconcile with Orthodox understandings of divine-human communion.[87]

Wolterstorff begins by making clear that his central concern is that of moral rights which need to be assessed before one can talk about other kinds of rights. He acknowledges that "justice" and "rights" have become "the most contested part of our moral vocabulary."[88] He goes on to argue that in speaking about justice we need to acknowledge that

85. Ten Napel, *Constitutionalism*, 92–94.

86. All references below are to Nicholas Wolterstorff, *Justice: Rights and Wrongs* (Princeton: Princeton University Press, 2008), here at 60–62; 110–13; 342–61.

87. For Papanikolaou's analysis, see his *Mystical as Political*, 116–124.

88. Wolterstorff, *Justice: Rights and Wrongs*, 1.

"justice is ultimately grounded on inherent rights . . . rights are norma-tive social relationships; sociality is built into the essence of rights. A right is a right *with regard* to someone."[89] Rights are the same as duties "in different words."[90] Wolterstorff rejects the claim that justice can be equated with equality.[91] Thomas Jefferson's famous claim about all men being created equal and endowed with unalienable rights Wolterstorff la-bels "a piece of epistemological bluster, that, if it were true, would ren-der my questions irrelevant."[92] Wolterstorff is not interested in what the Roman Catholic philosopher Alasdair MacIntyre does, which amounts to telling a story of "conflicting understandings of which sorts of things are just and which are unjust."

Wolterstorff intends instead to investigate "a conflict over how we should think about justice."[93] In rehearsing the history of the definitions of *jus* and rights, Wolterstorff argues that all those disagreements come down to a debate "over the deep structure of the moral universe: what accounts for what?"[94] The term "natural rights" has been used in two different ways—one meaning "natural as not conferred by human action versus natural as not conferred at all. I will use the term 'natural' only in the former sense. Rights of the latter sort I will continue to call inherent rights. Natural rights come in two sorts: conferred natural rights and inherent natural rights."[95] Unconvinced that Aquinas provided us with an account of what "justice" consists of, Wolterstorff believes that in our contemporary debates some are fearful of mentioning "natural rights" out of concern that most people will conclude that this is the same as "inherent"—and "lurking in the back-ground all along" is the danger that if we have inherent rights, we don't need God.[96] Wolterstorff dismisses those who have asserted that natural rights cannot be squared with Christianity, because if this is so, "then it is a heresy of long lineage and venerable origin."[97] The roots of the correct

89. Wolterstorff, 4.
90. Wolterstorff, 8.
91. Wolterstorff, 15.
92. Wolterstorff, 319n10.
93. Wolterstorff, 21n1.
94. Wolterstorff, 35.
95. Wolterstorff, 38.
96. Wolterstorff, 42–43.
97. Wolterstorff, 60.

understanding of natural inherent rights are to be found in the Hebrew Bible and the Christian New Testament.

When he begins his exposition of natural rights and human rights Wolterstorff argues that natural rights are not socially conferred and there exist inherent natural rights and these are the ones theologians hostile to the idea are opposed to. But it remains the case that "inherent rights and human rights are not the same." We have failed, he argues, "to note the distinction just made, between a right being inherent to a certain status and that status being intrinsic or essential to the human being who has that status. The idea of nature enters the discussion at two points. Sometimes the issue under discussion is whether it is by 'nature' or by conferral that this right is attached to this status; sometimes the issue is whether there is such a thing as human nature and, if so, whether this status belongs to that nature." Moreover, "not only is the idea of a natural right distinct from the idea of a human right; natural rights and human rights do not necessarily coincide."[98]

Orthodox readers will recognize all too easily the examples Wolterstorff uses to illustrate what he calls "impulses deeply ingrained in human beings." He means the instinct to award those of one's own "in-group" "natural rights" that they would possess "even if there had been no human legislation that conferred those rights on them. There is something about Greeks, something about Athenians, something about white people, something about Aryans, something about Serbs, that sets them apart and gives them an inherent dignity that others lack." It is against this impulse, he argues, that the "recognition of natural human rights" arose.[99]

Rejecting the arguments of Immanuel Kant, Ronald Dworkin, and Alan Gewirth for a secular grounding of human rights, Wolterstorff argues that no "dignity-based" approach can succeed because none of the arguments from capacities for human agency can be successfully tied to the worth of the human.[100] But even a theistic grounding for human rights, Wolterstorff goes on, has been controversial because of the long-standing reliance upon the contested meanings of Genesis 1:26–27. Because of those controversies, Wolterstorff steers clear of "the theological controversies" and attempts

98. Wolterstorff, 317.
99. Wolterstorff, 319.
100. Wolterstorff, 323–341.

to examine the text as a philosopher and expands his literary analysis to include Psalm 8 to conclude that "God created humankind with a uniquely exalted status: in the image of God, as a likeness of God, just a bit lower than God. Being created with that exalted status is intimately connected with being given dominion over the animals."[101] Wolterstorff concludes that the "blessing" or "mandate" given to humans is what should catch our attention, rather than making the mistake of those theologians who "have set the blessing or mandate off to the side and speculated and argued about which resemblances to God ought to be included within the *imago Dei*. That proves hopeless."[102] But neither can this approach "ground" natural human rights because the blessing or mandate to have dominion runs up against the capacities problem and the empirical evidence that "a good many human beings do not have the capacities necessary for exercising dominion."[103]

What we need instead, Wolterstorff states, "is some worth-imparting relation of human beings to God that does not in any way involve a reference to human capacities."[104] That relationship Wolterstorff locates in the belief that "being loved by God gives a human being great worth. And if God loves equally and permanently each and every creature who bears the *imago Dei*, then the relational property of being loved by God is what we have been looking for . . . Being loved by God is an example of what I shall call *bestowed* worth."[105] But Wolterstorff still concludes that even if we "more plausibly interpret image of God along nature-resemblance lines," this does not solve our dilemma because there always exist "human beings who are seriously lacking in capacities on account of human nature being malformed in their case. The image of God is not adequate, all by itself, for grounding natural human rights."[106] Wolterstorff asserts that "if God loves, in the mode of attachment, each and every human being equally and permanently, then natural human rights inhere in the worth bestowed on

---

101. Wolterstorff, 345.

102. Wolterstorff, 347.

103. Wolterstorff, 349. In discussing the meaning of "dominion," Wolterstorff is pursuing an entirely different agenda from "dominionists" among Protestant Reformed groups who mean by the term another version of integralism.

104. Wolterstorff, 352.

105. Wolterstorff, 352–353.

106. Wolterstorff, 352.

human beings by that love. Natural human rights are what respect for that worth requires."[107] Wolterstorff admits that if the theist "holds the convictions about God's love that I have delineated" this does not amount to a "foundationalist argument, but an argument nonetheless." But Wolterstorff then states clearly "I believe that there are natural human rights."[108] Does the reality of natural human rights depend, then, in the end, on faith? Wolterstorff appears to conclude that it does, and that conclusion also carries with it wide-ranging social and political implications.

Wolterstorff examines the "applications and implications" of his argument for "social entities," admitting that his approach is "essentially an elaboration of John Locke's analysis of how rights get conferred onto and within voluntary organization."[109] Wolterstorff traces the "ancestry of theistic requirement theories" to Locke, concluding that "Locke's theory of obligations . . . is . . . a divine requirement theory."[110] In his analysis of the "duties of charity" Wolterstorff connects them to the paradigm of the duty to forgive. But he insists that if we read the command of Christ about forgiveness ("seventy-seven times" in Matthew 18:21–35) we must understand this as a "third-party duty," accepting that "Jesus was speaking on behalf of God, it is toward God that his disciples have a duty to forgive those who wrong them, not toward those who wrong them. And it is God who has a right against them, not the malefactors, to their forgiving the malefactors."[111] Wolterstorff insists that we admit that humans are "by nature tribalists." We have forgotten, he argues, how extraordinary it is that the origins of what he calls our "moral subculture" that recognizes "human rights and person rights" did not arise in the medieval centuries nor in the political philosophy debates of the seventeenth century but in "the Hebrew and Christian Scriptures." Wolterstorff is willing to examine what non-theists have argued about, i.e., a shared if vague human sympathy.[112] But in the end he insists that "the affective side of the self cannot, all by itself, expand or even sustain human rights culture."[113] The moral subculture of rights "is as frail as it is

107. Wolterstorff, 360.
108. Wolterstorff, 361.
109. Wolterstorff, 368.
110. Wolterstorff, 377n31.
111. Wolterstorff, 384.
112. Wolterstorff, 386.
113. Wolterstorff, 392–393.

remarkable. If the secularization thesis proves true, we must expect that subculture will have been a brief shining episode in the odyssey of human beings on earth." But he concludes: "I do not believe the thesis."[114]

Is Wolterstorff's analysis of a "regime of human rights" one that the Orthodox can and should endorse? Papanikolaou expressed guarded affirmation but one accompanied by hesitation. Because Wolterstorff is a philosopher, he does not take up Orthodox theology's tradition of deification. He more recently asserts that "between love and justice there is no tension . . . [and] when I claim that between love and justice there is no tension, the love I have in mind is that to which Jesus was referring—call it *agapic love*."[115] Furthermore, Wolterstorff claims that "Jesus' injunction to love one's neighbor as oneself holds for all human beings."[116] Nonetheless, Wolterstorff asserts the moral virtue of exercising forgiveness, as also commanded by Jesus, was impossible for ancient philosophers. Turning to Thomas Reid, Wolterstorff notes that the Scots philosopher appears to have been unique in seeing that the ancients could only understand virtue as "a prudent prosecution of what is good on the whole for one." Still, "one cannot just insert forgiveness into any ethical orientation whatsoever. There are frameworks of thought within which forgiveness can find no home. Forgiveness entered the world along with the recognition of divine and human worth, of being wronged, of rights, of duty, of guilt. It cannot occur where those are not recognized."[117] Wolterstorff nonetheless argues that liberal democracies in particular have nothing to fear from agapic love even if "liberal democracy is often thought of as inherently . . . a defense [against] the menace of those who insist on loving their neighbors."[118]

Nevertheless, in assessing the American constitutional version of liberal democracy, Wolterstorff concludes that citizens should not ask whether "legislation serves their own interests but whether it serves justice for all and the common good."[119] Wolterstorff's reflections merit the close examination by Orthodox theologians and philosophers alike, many of whom

114. Ibid.
115. Nicholas Wolterstorff, *Justice in Love* (Grand Rapids, MI: William B. Eerdmans Publishing Co., 2015), ix.
116. Wolterstorff, *ibid*., xiii.
117. Wolterstorff, 185, 185n10.
118. Wolterstorff, 235.
119. Wolterstorff, 238.

will also wonder why he chose to advance the notion of agapic love but nowhere takes up the distinctions among *eros, philia, storge,* and *agape* that have attracted renewed attention among Orthodox writers, especially those fascinated with the work of Pavel Florensky.[120] On balance, however, Wolterstorff's regime of human rights appears to be one with which the Orthodox can find considerable grounds for affirmation, despite remaining theological differences surrounding the meaning and potential of sanctification, justification, and theosis.

In the wake of the Second Vatican Council, Catholic engagement with human rights issues have largely focused on the implications of liberation theology and the determination of the Vatican to align itself with the burgeoning Catholic populations of sub-Saharan Africa, Latin America, and Southeast Asia. Because of the long-standing antagonisms between the Church of Rome and the Orthodox, Orthodox engagement with Catholic investigations of human rights did not begin to develop before the 1970s. But more recent Catholic assessments of the alignment with liberation theology in some of its claims have also registered concerns and suggested an approach that might also resonate with the Orthodox. In her review of these developments, Ethna Regan concluded that liberation theology misrepresented "the liberal tradition as completely unconcerned with social and economic rights. The specific contribution of liberation theology lies in its emphasis on the need for systemic and structural fulfillment of these rights. . . ." Especially in the work of Jon Sobrino, Regan found the development of a "defense of the rights of the poor and oppressed as a kind of mystagogy into the life of God." Rather than beginning with "the struggle for human rights from a vision of the human person as *imago Dei* and the ethical imperative born of that vision," Sobrino preferred to begin with the "reality of human right violations, seeing in this reality an initiation into the life of God . . . Those who defend the rights of the poor and oppressed bring the mercy and tenderness of God to bear on situations of

120. Pavel Florensky, *The Pillar and Ground of Truth: An Essay in Orthodox Theodicy in Twelve Letters,* transl. Boris Jakim, introduction by Richard F. Gustafson (Princeton, NJ: Princeton University Press, 2004) See also for a critical assessment of Florensky's philosophy, H.J. Moore, "Antinomism in Twentieth-Century Philosophy: The Case of Pavel Florensky," *Studies in East European Thought* 73 (2020): 53–76, https://doi.org/10.1007/s11212-020-09378-y (accessed March 1, 2021).

suffering and are further initiated into the mystery of God through that experience."[121] At least in the emphasis upon real-life experience, as well as the appeal to a mystagogy of human personhood and suffering, some Orthodox would find this approach to the question of rights instructive, even if they would be reluctant to abandon the *imago Dei* as starting—or at least primary and privileged—partner with Sobrino's emphasis on "this reality [as] an initiation into the life of God."

The most persistently confident voice among Roman Catholics endorsing the continued relevance of a universal claim for human rights appeared in the work of Rafael Domingo in his critique of what he describes as the "traditional religious and current liberal approaches" to the issue of religious rights and freedom. By distinguishing between "God, religion, and conscience; rationality and suprarationality; private and public morality; religious exception and the privilege of abstaining; and recognition, toleration, and accommodation" Domingo argues that an open legal system can secure "a new, coherent and constitutional framework for the protection of the rights to religion and freedom of conscience in this age of diversity, interdependence, and secularization."[122]

A number of Catholic scholars remain less optimistic, warning for example, that those who defend a strong doctrine of rights "might inadvertently subvert the give and take, the needed balancing of competing claims that play essential parts in any political processes. Or worse still, they might subvert their own claims by rendering them unworkable."[123] Most famously, the Catholic philosopher Alasdair MacIntyre rejected the claims

---

121. The point of departure for Catholics remains the Second Vatican Council's 1965 *Dignitatis Humanae,* "Of Human Dignity." Ethna Regan, *Theology and the Boundary Discourse of Human Rights* (Washington, D.C.: Georgetown University Press, 2010), 160, 161–2; Jon Sobrino, "Human Rights and Oppressed Peoples: Historical-Theological Reflections," in *Truth and Memory: The Church and Human Rights in El Salvador and Guatemala,* ed. M.A. Hayes and D. Tombs (Herefordshire, UK: Gracewing, 2001), 134–58; Jon Sobrino, *The Principle of Mercy: Taking the Crucified People from the Cross* (Maryknoll, NY: Orbis Books, 1994).

122. Rafael Domingo, *God and the Secular Legal System* (Cambridge: Cambridge University Press, 2016), 166–169, at 169.

123. Jean Porter, *Ministers of the Law: A Natural Law Theory of Legal Authority* (Grand Rapids, MI: William B. Eerdmans Publishing Company, 2010), 320.

for natural rights and human rights as fictions.[124] Yet those sympathetic to MacIntyre's Aristotleian-natural law approach have pointed out that MacIntyre himself has admitted having been too quick in dismissing human rights claims. It may be possible to arrive at a more sympathetic reading from his perspective. What strikes the non-expert reader of that approach, however, is the entirely different set of sources and authorities invoked by those found among Orthodox and non-Orthodox scholars convinced that it is a Neo-Platonic, not an Aristotleian common ground that Christians, Orthodox, Catholic, and perhaps Protestant alike, all share.[125]

Another Catholic writer, Adrian Pabst, affirms the importance of a "synthesis of theology, philosophy and mysticism that puts a greater emphasis on participation and mediation," invoking what he claims is a common Christian Neo-Platonism, the heritage of both East and West that can rescue the "crisis of liberalism in its secular or religious guise." Unlike Wolterstorff, however, Pabst believes (as does Mark Retter) that Thomas Aquinas succeeded in retrieving a "Neo-Platonist Realism" and hence some definition of justice. But Wolterstorff might also query Pabst to elaborate more extensively about how he envisions the realization of "the common good and its manifold, diverse instantiations in different variants of the good life."[126] Pabst enjoys the enthusiastic endorsement of one of the most distinguished members of the "radical Orthodox" Anglo-Catholic movement, John Milbank, who has also expressed his disbelief in the possibility of reconciling modern notions of natural rights with the classical tradition. While Milbank accepts Brian Tierney's interpretation of the medieval debates, he is not convinced that Tierney sees clearly enough the dimming of the priority of the common good and the pernicious advance of the kind of individualism that lies at the heart of modern notions of natural rights.[127] The Orthodox theologian David Bentley Hart

124. Alasdair MacIntyre, *After Virtue: A Study in Moral Theory* (Notre Dame, IN: University of Notre Dame Press, 1984), 69–70.

125. Mark Retter, "The Road Not Taken: On MacIntyre's Human Rights Scepticism," *American Journal of Jurisprudence* 63, no. 2 (December, 2018): 189–219.

126. Adrian Pabst, *Metaphysics: The Creation of Hierarchy* (Grand Rapids, MI: William B. Eerdmans Publishing Co., 2012), 154–54; 201–71; 442–44 at 443.

127. John Milbank, *Theology & Social Theory: Beyond Secular Reason*, 2nd ed. (Maiden, MA: Blackwell Publishing, 2006), xxxiin56.

on the one hand has greeted favorably the willingness on the part of some Orthodox, Catholics, and Protestants to admit that they share a common "Christian Platonist tradition." They should all admit that at some point an over-fascination for God's will is what provoked the "voluntarist model of freedom" that finally created the misunderstanding that liberty consists of "a personal sovereignty transcending even the dictates and constraints of nature." At the same time, Hart appears to insist that whatever the aberrations that occurred in the history of "rights," they are the children of Christian theologians, not "secularists."[128] As is the case when attempting to assess the recent history of Orthodox engagements with different Protestant evaluations of human rights, so too, Orthodox-Catholic assessments reveal a closer affinity with some Catholic writers less inclined to insist upon a neo-Thomist natural law approach to questions of justice, natural, and human, rights.

II. The Orthodox and Secular Human Rights Regimes

Critics of European Christianity's failures to recognize the human dignity, worth, and preciousness of each individual have, in some cases admitted that even the terms of the debate about shortcomings and the search for "secular" alternatives could not have occurred without the key role Christianity played in initiating the challenges themselves.[129] Because of the disagreements that exist about the adequacy or weakness of secular human rights claims that are admitted by secular participants in those debates, some have asked if human rights should be grounded in moral rights claims, or whether, as philosopher Andreas Niederberger has argued, "human rights theories which start more reconstructively with existing human rights and develop normative foundations on this basis" are not more realistic because they "are open for different justifications of human rights and they consider respective human rights within the horizon of factual political and social constellations."[130]

128. David Bentley Hart, "Foreword," in *Encounter between Eastern Orthodoxy and Radical Orthodoxy: Transfiguring the World through the Word*, ed. Adrian Pabst and Christoph Schneider (London: Routledge, 2016), xi–xiii, at xiii.

129. Tom Holland, *Dominion: How the Christian Revolution Remade the World* (New York: Basic Books, 2019).

130. Andreas Niederberger, "Are Human Rights Moral Rights?" in *Human Rights, Human Dignity, and Cosmopolitan Ideals: Essays on Critical Theory and*

Most analysts agree that Americans, with some exceptions, did not talk or write much about human rights until the 1970s as abuses in Africa, Latin America, and Asia broadened the formerly Eurocentric debates about the origins and articulation of human rights. By 1989, as communism disappeared as the enemy of American values, the role of the Global South in defending the legitimacy of human rights discourse when speaking of economic, political, educational, and asylum issues had become more obvious to scholars. It still failed to attract the attention of most Americans. The debates that began to swirl around values and rights in the United States as we have already noted, began as domestic quarrels over issues of civil rights for minorities, then gender, human sexuality, and marriage.[131] Many Orthodox might envision cooperation with non-theistic advocates of human rights on a number of such issues without demanding prior agreement on where to ground the understanding of human rights. Thus beyond purely national quarrels about human rights, some Orthodox Christians might approve the objectives of Amnesty International, Doctors without Borders, The Children's Relief Fund, to name but a few examples of the concern for righting specific wrongs in the world in general. They might even point to Articles 28 and 29 of the United Nations' Declaration on Universal Human Rights as a source and inspiration for engaging with issues that focus on economic and social justice.[132]

Human Rights, ed. Matthias Lutz-Bachmann and Amos Nascimento (Burlington, VT: Ashgate, 2014), 75–92, at 92.

131. On these developments, see Kathryn Sikkink, *Evidence for Hope: Making Human Rights Work in the 21ˢᵗ Century* (Princeton: Princeton University Press, 2017), 22–136; Jan Eckel and Samuel Moyn, eds., *The Breakthrough: Human Rights in the 1970s* (Philadelphia: University of Pennsylvania Press, 2014).

132. For a version of human rights history in the U.S. that omits engagement with how the Christian populations have participated in that story see Paul Gordon Lauren, "A Human Rights Lens on U.S. History: Human Rights at Home and Human Rights Abroad," 7–39; and on the question of U.S. involvement and commitment to social and economic rights, Hope Lewis, "'New' Human Rights? U.S. Ambivalence Toward the International Economic and Social Rights Framework," 100–141, both in Cynthia Soohoo, Catherine Albisa, and Martha F. Davis, eds., *Bringing Human Rights Home: A History of Human Rights in the United States (Abridged Edition)* (Philadelphia: University of Pennsylvania Press, 2009).

Some partisans of a secular version of human rights that requires no grounding or justification in any form of "theism" have argued that Christianity in general, and not merely the Orthodox, have played no real role in the emergence of what today many understand as human rights.[133] Thus, for example, the Orthodox might at first glance applaud the work of the secular philosopher James Griffin who, in surveying the landscape of human rights claims, concluded in an essay reviewers found especially significant: "we can develop a more precise definition of human rights . . . [by working] from the 'bottom-up', starting with our pre-existing understanding of human rights and uncovering what higher level moral principles it must entail." Griffin's determination to focus on "the notion of personhood, and the claims about human dignity which ultimately reference this notion" center on what he himself calls his "central intuitive idea"—namely that of "agency." Even in societies characterized by only basic educational or informational resources, Griffin finds examples of this kind of agency that prohibits others from interfering with "what one sees as a worthwhile life (call this 'liberty')."[134]

Orthodox Christians, however, as well as Reformed Protestants such as Wolterstorff and Catholic theologians would question Griffin about a possible exaggerated role given to free choice and agency since the ultimate act of liberty for the Orthodox is to choose to say "no" to those aspects of human existence that mistakenly focus on life in this world as the ultimate

133. See the essays in Stefan-Ludwig Hoffmann, ed., *Moralpolitik. Geschichte der Menschenrecht im 20. Jahrhundert* (Göttingen: VandenHoeck & Ruprecht, 2010) that argue for discontinuity between the language of the "rights of man" in the American or French Revolutionary sense and contemporary issues. Hoffmann's own introductory essay traces the near-disappearance of the terms "rights" after 1800, but as is the case with the essays in general, ignores the role of religious convictions in shaping the debates over rights. See Hoffmann, "Einführung: Zur Genealogie der Menschenrechte," 7–40. For further examples of this account of human rights origins, see A.G. Roeber, "Introduction," in *Human v. Religious Rights? German and U.S. Exchange and the Global Implications*, ed. A.G. Roeber (Göttingen: Vandenhoeck & Ruprecht, 2020), 7–21.

134. Paul Bloomfield and Bradley J. Strawser, "A Review of James Griffin, *On Human Rights*," *Analysis* 71, no. 1 (January 2011): 195–197, https://doi.org/10.1093/analys/anq093. James Griffin, *On Human Rights* (New York: Oxford University Press, 2008), 33.

reality. The Orthodox cannot endorse Griffin's focus on self-consciousness, agency, and choice, concepts that for him provide the sole and final say in determining what counts as the basis for human rights.[135] Not only does his position exclude the possibility of human dignity for the unborn but it also fails to address the larger mystery of human consciousness and the unconvincing "non-standard alternatives to materialism . . . [since] with respect to traditional attempts to understand the place of conscious experience in the natural world, we really do continue to face a genuine puzzle. The mind-body problem is still a problem."[136] There is more than a little irony in the fact that in some contemporary Orthodox circles, "rights are directly linked to ethical behavior," in ways that can hardly be distinguished from the unwillingness of American Presbyterian missionaries to recognize citizenship rights for the First Peoples of Alaska unless those persons conformed to a certain standard of "civilized" behavior.[137]

Samuel Moyn's attempt to reduce Christian views of human rights to a belated attempt to prop up conservative or reactionary political regimes has been refuted by theist human rights scholars, and his exaggerations about the lack of attention to human rights before the 1970s have also drawn fire

135. See John Tasioulas' critique of both "foundational" and "functionalist" notions of human rights advanced by James Griffin and Ronald Dworkin, that "something's being a human right in morality is neither a necessary nor a sufficient condition for enacting a legal human right with matching content." Tasioulas, "Towards a Philosophy of Human Rights," *Current Legal Problems* 65 (2012): 1–30, at 5.

136. Joseph Levine, *Purple Haze: The Puzzle of Consciousness* (Oxford: Oxford University Press, 2001), 177. See also John Tasioulas, "On the Foundations of Human Rights," in *Philosophical Foundations of Human Rights*, ed. Rowan Cruft, S. Matthew Liao, and Massimo Renzo (Oxford: Oxford University Press, 2015), 45–70.

137. For an exploration of the limits of intentional cognitive choice as a measure of Orthodox "deification," and a critique of the Russian Orthodox Church's 2008 *Basic Teaching on Human Dignity, Freedom and Rights*, see Petre Maican, "Overcoming Exclusion in Eastern Orthodoxy: Human Dignity and Disability from a Christological Perspective," *Studies in Christian Ethics* 34, no. 4 (June, 2019): 1–14, at 2. I thank Professor Maican for providing me with a copy of his article https://doi.org/10.1177/0953946819859512.

from secular critics.[138] The focus of many secular human rights experts on issues surrounding international law, challenges to democratic values, and reactions against the notion of human rights pursued by various regimes reveals how rarely theistic perspectives shape those conversations.[139]

Ongoing concerns about the plight of Soviet Jews had led to the UN Commission on Human Rights focusing during the period 1965–1967 on a "Convention on Elimination of All Forms of Religious Intolerance." The work on eliminating religious intolerance built upon the attacks on racial discrimination that had received international attention in the early years of the decade. By 1967, however, with the outbreak of the Six-Day War, "Jerusalem symbolized war, religious conflict, Zionism, displacement and battles over sovereignty."[140] As a result of the bitter recriminations that pro and anti-Israeli diplomats hurled at each other in the wake of the war, Charles Malik's old antagonist Jamal Baroody of Saudi Arabia challenged the General Assembly to face up to the unpleasant question of whether the UN or any competent international authority was in a position to decide "where the dividing line between a believer and a fanatic lay."[141] These few examples illustrate why the Orthodox, in company with many, if not most, Roman Catholic and Protestant theists, will not find it easy to endorse

138. John Witte, Jr., "The Long History of Human Rights: Assessing an Influential Revisionist Account," review of Samuel Moyn, *Christian Human Rights* (Philadelphia: University of Pennsylvania Press, 2015), in *Books and Culture,* November/December 2016, https://www.booksandculture.com/articles/2016 /marapr/long-history-of-human-rights.html. See also Mark Movsesian, "Religious Rights," review of *Christian Human Rights*, by Samuel Moyn, *First Things* (January 2016) at https://firstthings.com/article/2016/01/religious-rights (accessed March 21, 2018) and Sarita Cargas, "Questioning Samuel Moyn's Revisionist History of Human Rights," *Human Rights Quarterly* 38 (2016): 411–425, available at HeinOnline (accessed 20 June 2019).

139. See Kathryn Sikkink, "'Human Rights, Responsibilities, and Democracy,' Sikkink Comments on Tasioulas and Moyn Papers: 'Symposium on the Future of International Human Rights Law,'" *Vanderbilt Journal of Transnational Law* 52, no. 5 (November 2019): 1315–1330; and the essays in Kasey McCall-Smith, Andrea Birdsall, and Elisenda Casanas Adam, eds., *Human Rights in Times of Transition: Liberal Democracies and Challenges of National Security* (Cheltenham, UK: Edward Elgar Publishing, 2020).

140. Jensen, *Making of International Human Rights,* 165.

141. Jensen, *Making of International Human Rights,* 172.

human rights claims that ignore or fail to exemplify a defense of what Wolterstorff identified as the Judaic and Christian "moral subculture" upon which any genuine claim of realizing human rights must depend. Even secular philosophers who have examined the problem of ethics in the context of international law have concluded that arguing for human rights on the basis either of status or the well-being of the persons affected has proven to be insufficient. Rather, the Balliol College Oxford University philosopher John Tasioulas has argued, what is needed is an agreement about universal moral right.[142] But our survey of theist arguments appears to suggest at one and the same time that Jesus' call to agapic love is not just for Christians, but at the same time, that the "moral subculture" that has made possible at least halting, if not historically consistent behavior in the social, economic, and political realms is the result of a very specific faith in Old and New Testament understanding of God, persons, and rights.

If the Orthodox are to respond to the query regarding how they navigate the "regime of human rights," the history of engagement so far demands a greater consensus within the Eastern Orthodox community itself before an answer can be hazarded. First, given the importance the Orthodox place on the term "personhood" and the attendant theological anthropology, more clarity and consensus about what this term means must be evident both within the Orthodox Church and in its offering an Orthodox understanding to non-Orthodox, theists and non-theists alike. Second, the Eastern Orthodox will have to make clear to potential critics whether they are willing to endorse freedom of expression, especially in matters of religious choice and identity to avoid the historic temptation to use a connection to state authority to compel submission to social, political, and moral teachings the Orthodox confess. Third, the Orthodox have yet to demonstrate that they have left behind them the temptation to tribalism and the inclination to favor their own rights over those of "the other" however defined.

On April 4, 1917 the first Orthodox bishop ordained in North America wrote a letter offering his support to the newly appointed hierarch of the

142. John Tasioulas, "Exiting the Hall of Mirrors: Morality and Law in Human Rights," *King's College London Law School Research Paper No. 2017–19*, February 10, 2017. http://dx.doi.org/10.2139/ssrn.2915307, (accessed February 26, 2021).

Russian Diocese of the Aleutians and North America. In that letter, Raphael Hawaweeny presented with remarkable candor the challenges that more than a century later still face the Orthodox in North America. Describing himself, the auxiliary bishop wrote "I am an Arab by birth, a Greek by primary education, an American by residence, a Russian at heart, and a Slav in soul." Hawaweeny's loyalty was clear—to "God-saved Russia against ardent enemies of Slavism, Orthodoxy and Christianity, i.e., Germans and Turks."[143] The honesty with which the bishop admitted where his heart and soul lay, who threatened the rights of the Orthodox, and that he was only "an American by residence," encapsulates the struggles the Orthodox have been engaged in for more than a century. If a defense of human rights in the North American context is possible for the Orthodox, they will have to demonstrate to the others in their pluralistic, post-secular society that they are more than merely "American by residence" even as they also identify themselves as members of a global Orthodox community of faith that is still struggling to be fully committed to the upholding of universal human rights. The history of Orthodox engagement with questions surrounding the term "human rights" reveals the Orthodox potential for resolving these questions, but that same history forces the conclusion that the Orthodox must be confident among themselves about how to answer such queries—and that the pursuit of that confidence remains a work in progress.

143. Raphael Hawaweeny, "Letter to Evdokim Meschersky [1869–1935]," December 17, 1914, *Orthodox Church in America Archives*, at https://www.oca .org/history-archives/commemorating-saint-raphael-bishop-brooklyn, (accessed April 20, 2021).

CONCLUSION

As this book was nearing completion, two events of global significance revealed urgent need for the Orthodox in North America to reflect on how they understand rights claims, both in the society in which they live and within the Orthodox Church itself. The outbreak of the COVID-19 pandemic revealed not only the unprecedented global speed and deadliness of the disease. It also laid bare anxieties among some Orthodox Christians about whether public health restrictions on church gatherings represented an assault on their religious rights and liberties. In cases that occurred far beyond the borders of the United States, Orthodox bishops confronted demands that they either close the churches altogether in a defense of the right to life of all members of society and the fraternal obligation to all human beings—or that they refuse to acknowledge what public health officials were saying, and keep the churches open at all costs as a sign of the exercise of faith and the right to practice undisturbed their religious liberties.[1] Despite the waning of the actual numbers of organized

1. The Assembly of Bishops' statements on the pandemic starting in March 2020 can be followed up to 2021 at https:www.assemblyofbishops.org/covid19/news/2021/statement-regarding-developments-in-medicine-covid-19-vaccines-and-immunizations (accessed June 30, 2021); for analysis of the issues surrounding Holy Communion and the risks of infection, see the panels of Orthodox scientists and theologians convened by the Orthodox Theological Society in America at The Orthodox Christian Studies Center of Fordham University, "The Coronavirus (COVID-19) and Communion Practice in the Orthodox Church," YouTube video,

Protestant evangelical Christians in North America, the social ethos of the United States including the Orthodox, continues to be influenced by that tradition. Nowhere did the claim that the government health officials were violating religious rights emerge more stridently than among white Protestant evangelicals (and some conservative Roman Catholics), who also refused to accept the evidence regarding the virulence of COVID-19 and proof that vaccinations were effective and should be received as an exercise of responsible compassion for the elderly, the immune-compromised, infants, and children.[2]

The instructions that eventually emanated from the Eastern Orthodox bishops urged the faithful to follow the scientific, medical, and political advice and regulations of authorities in their specific locality. In doing so, the bishops (without actually citing cases) appear to have endorsed the consensus of American legal and constitutional experts on the exercise of the police power of the state with regard to public health issues. In 1905, the Supreme Court, had in the case of *Jacobson v. Massachusetts* established the conclusion that "compulsory vaccination against a contagious disease such as smallpox was an appropriate public health measure." In 1922 a Texas case (*Zucht v. King*) concluded that the police powers of the state extended to city officials and their ordinances as well, in this instance, holding that vaccination of students in all public and private schools was a reasonable exercise of those powers. By 1944, in another Massachusetts case (*Prince v. Commonwealth of Massachusetts*) the court concluded that not even the family and its invocation of liberty of conscience or religion could block health regulations deemed to be in the

---

2:12:32, recording of a webinar hosted by the Orthodox Theological Society in America, August 22, 2020, https://otsamerica.net/the-coronavirus-covid-19-and -communion-practice-in-the-orthodox-church/

2. On the on-going tension between learned and popular rights claims among evangelicals, see Mark A. Noll, *The Scandal of the Evangelical Mind*. Grand Rapids, MI: William B. Eerdmans (1994), and more recently his essay "Reconsidering Christendom," in *The Future of Christian Learning: An Evangelical and Catholic Dialogue*, ed. Thomas Albert Howard (Grand Rapids, MI: Brazos Press, 2008), 23–70. On the vaccination issue, Elizabeth Dias and Ruth Graham, "White Evangelical Resistance Is Obstacle in Vaccination Effort," *New York Times*, April 5, 2021, https://www.nytimes.com/2021/04/05/us/covid-vaccine-evangelicals.html (accessed April 22, 2021).

public interest. What remains a legitimate area of disagreement among constitutional and legal experts, however, is the question of whether agreed-upon law that the federal government does possess legitimate quarantine powers can or should be understood to extend to include vaccination mandates. Even in the case of state or local officials, the exercise of police powers must be able to demonstrate that the officials have a compelling governmental interest that must be narrowly and specifically identified. Yet, faced with sometimes conflicting policies that pitted local against state officials, Orthodox Christians, like their non-Orthodox neighbors, did not always find the episcopal advice to be sufficient.[3]

However divisive and embittering the arguments that stemmed from the outbreak of COVID-19 may have been, the invasion of the sovereign state of Ukraine by Russia in February 2022 shocked North American Orthodox Christians even more. The invasion forced them to focus on uncertainties about human rights claims and to what extent historically Orthodox people and their governments respect and honor such rights, regardless of religious, political, or social standing of all persons. These conflicts represent yet another instance of how an appeal to rights continues to be used in ways that can appear to distance the rights of religion and a secular understanding of human rights from each other. On balance, with regard to the COVID-19 crisis, wiser counsels prevailed among many of the

---

3. G. Edward White, *Law in American History: Volume II From Reconstruction through the 1920s* (New York and Oxford: Oxford University Press, 2016), 405–07; 570n.50; for the smallpox epidemic and debates over vaccinations in the United States during the period 1898–1903, see Michael Willrich, *Pox: An American History* (New York: Penguin Books, 2012); Scott Bomboy, "Constitutional powers and issues during a quarantine situation," https://constitutioncenter.org /blog/constitutional-powers-and-issues-during-a-quarantine-situation (accessed November 17, 2021; "How much authority do state and local officials have during a health emergency, such as the COVID-19 pandemic?" at https://www.americanbar .org/news/abanews/publications/youraba/2020/youraba-may-2020/state-local -authority-during-covid/ (accessed May 15, 2021); and for a critique of various proposed state legislative measures, "Proposed Limits on Public Health Authority: Dangerous for Public Health" *The Network for Public Health Law* (May, 2021) (National Association of County & City Health Officials) at https://www.naccho .org/blog/articles/webinar-proposed-limits-on-public-health-authority-dangerous -for-public-health (accessed April 30, 2021.)

Orthodox theologians and hierarchs who continued to insist that there can be no ultimate conflict between grace and nature, nor between science and the truth of the Christian gospel. The response of the Orthodox to the Russian invasion, on the other hand, promised to realign loyalties and identities not only among the Orthodox in North America, but worldwide, perhaps permanently.

The military invasion of a neighboring sovereign state by Russia would have elicited condemnation as a violation of international law by secular authorities, regardless of their religious beliefs. But the endorsement of the invasion by the Russian Orthodox Patriarch Kyrill catapulted the sense of crisis among the Orthodox over human rights and the rights and responsibilities of Orthodox Patriarchs to unprecedented heights. Those who questioned how the Patriarch could possibly justify the resulting deaths, and what appears to be incontrovertible evidence of war crimes committed by Russian troops against innocent civilians, had not taken notice of the patriarch's previous history before his election. Yet, the Austrian political scientist Kristina Stoeckl had already identified Kyrill's support for the Russian regime's political agenda that included "restrictive human rights policies of the Russian government." Although in a 2000 article Kyrill as Metropolitan of Smolensk and Kaliningrad had appeared to endorse a "critical engagement with liberal values," by 2008, as head of the Department of External Church Relations Metropolitan, Kyrill had shifted his tactics and conclusions to deploy "two major strategies . . . in the traditionalist take on human rights . . . first an attack on the international liberal and secular human rights regime, and second the availing of human rights in defense against outside interference."[4]

In part, that change of tactics and goals came about as the Moscow Patriarchate lost a case in 2007 that had come before the European Court of Human Rights. A parish in Kyiv, Ukraine had decided to leave its connection to the Moscow Patriarchate and join the Ukrainian Orthodox Church of the Kyiv Patriarchate, a church not recognized as canonical by Moscow. Local officials had denied the attempt. But the European Court found the refusal to be a denial of Article 9 of the European Convention on Human Rights. The conclusion the Moscow Patriarch had to draw was

---

4. Kristina Stoeckl, *The Russian Orthodox Church and Human Rights*, London: Routledge (2014), 42, 43, 49.

that "in the world of international human rights standards, canonical jurisdiction is not a valid argument."[5]

These two developments, while not explaining the willingness of Patriarch Kyrill to endorse the invasion of Ukraine, at least shed some light on his conclusion that Ukraine's increasingly pluralist society and its insistence upon a Ukrainian national identity represented a threat to the peculiar way in which "human rights" discourse could be used both aggressively and defensively by the Russian Orthodox Church in tandem with the Russian regime's determination to reassert political control over former territories of the USSR. The attempt to claim that a military invasion into Ukraine was justified because Ukraine and Russia constituted one, united people, met with massive resistance and repudiation, ironically, even from within the hierarchy, clergy, and people of parishes that had historically been part of the Moscow Patriarchate. But to appreciate fully why this development should not have surprised Russia or Patriarch Kyrill, some historical context is required, with some special attention paid to the creation of an official nationalism on the part of Tsarist Russia that had begun to take shape two centuries earlier. It is not accidental, in other words, that analysts of the Russian invasion have noted the role of Christian nationalism in providing a pseudo-theological justification for the Kremlin's actions, and the manner in which the Russian Orthodox Church played a critical role in creating a narrative by which the international relations of the regime could be cast in terms of a religious rescue operation on behalf of supposedly beleaguered Orthodox threatened by the moral and social degeneracy of the West. Orthodox commentators such as Sergei Chapnin and Cyril Hovorun who have had long personal experience with the Patriarchate of Moscow have reenforced the conclusions of Western analysts.[6]

The perceived need to create a Russian national identity preoccupied the reign of Tsar Nicholas I (1825–1855.) In part, the need arose because of the rapid pace of change that threatened to undermine the autocratic nature of

5. Stoeckl, *Russian Orthodox Church*, 38–9.

6. Ishaan Tharoor, "The Christian nationalism behind Putin's War," *The Washington Post*, April 19, 2022, https://www.washingtonpost.com/world/2022/04/19/patriarch-kirill-orthodox-church-russia-ukraine/ (accessed May 26, 2022); George Soroka, "International Relations by Proxy? The Kremlin and the Russian Orthodox Church," *Religions* 13:3 (March, 2022) https://www.mdpi.com/2077-1444/13/3/208/htm (accessed May 26, 2022).

the Romanov dynasty's rule. Nicholas presided over "the emergence of the Russian intelligentsia, a serious discussion of reforms of the peasant bondage system, and an energetic push for state-directed economic and industrial development." Nonetheless, " a sturdy structure of police surveillance was established. Political repression coexisted with economic growth and intellectual ferment, but autocratic power was in no way compromised."[7]

By the 1840s Moscow's intentions toward the Kyivan Rus became clear. Building on prohibitions issued by Peter the Great of publishing theological books that even hinted at the legitimate separate identity of "small Russia"—i.e., Ukraine or Belarus, the regime pointed to the discovery of the Pan-Slavic Brotherhood of Saints Cyril and Methodius in 1847 as an excuse. The Tsar's policy rejected the idea of Pan-Slavism. By the time Alexander II ascended the throne in 1855, additional restrictions against the use of the Ukrainian language were put into place. Russia moved to abolish Ukrainian language Sunday schools by 1862 and promulgated the argument that Ukrainian was not a language separate from Russian. The Russian version of "official nationalism" sought to avoid Western understandings of "the nation" and "to re-suture nation to state, to the monarch and the state religion at the moment when in Western Europe the political community known as nation was becoming separable from the state . . . and was fast gaining an independent potency as the source of legitimacy."[8]

The ecclesiastical history of the Kyivan Rus and the rise of the Duchy of Moscow have continued to be the source of disagreements among historians, theologians, and Orthodox bishops. No one disputes the arrival of Orthodox Christianity in the person of Greek-speaking missionaries and the rise of the most powerful Varangian prince, Riurik, in 862. But the Scandinavian ruler's attempt to bring unity among "the Chuds, the Slavs, the Krivichians, and the Ves" did not constitute a "founding moment . . . and no Rus state—and certainly no Russian state—was created

7. Valerie A Kivelson and Ronald Grigor Suny. *Russia's Empires.* New York: Oxford University Press (2017), 157.

8. Kivelson and Suny, *Russia's Empires*, 160. The full analysis of the nineteenth-century struggles over a national identity in Ukraine forms the basis of Heather Coleman's current work. For an introduction to her analysis, see her essay "History, Faith, and Regional Identity in Nineteenth-Century Kyiv: Father Petro Lebedyntsev as Priest and Scholar," *Harvard Ukrainian Studies* 34:1–4 (2015–16): 343–372.

in that year."[9] Nor did any such unified "Russian" state emerge with the conversion and baptism of Volodomyr of Kyiv in or about the year 988. Only in the 1650s did "the eastern Ukrainian lands . . . [fall] into the imperial orbit of the Orthodox tsar." Ironically, "While Moscow participated in the creation of the independent Cossacks . . . Ukrainian clerics advanced and profoundly influenced the creation of an idea of Russia."[10] Orthodox scholars and hierarchs alike continue to disagree on the exact meaning of the 1686 subordination of the bishops in Ukraine to the Moscow Patriarchate, with some arguing that the Ecumenical Patriarchate of Constantinople only conceded Moscow's administrative oversight role, while insisting that the Metropolitan of Kyiv remained what from the perspective of ecclesial relations he had always been—the supreme Orthodox authority whose legitimacy stemmed from Constantinople's role in the initial conversion of Volodomyr and his subordinates in the tenth century. That it took the efforts of the nineteenth-century Tsar Nicholas I to seize upon the idea of "Russia" and the fashioning of an official nationality demonstrates both how weak the reality of a Russian state remained, and how plausible the insistence of Ukrainians that theirs was a separate language, culture, and history. From the late nineteenth century and lasting into the present, "intellectuals sought to cultivate Ukrainian culture throughout the fabric of society, primarily through language. Ukrainian politicians and parties imagined diverse reconfigurations of Ukraine, from Ukraine as an autonomous republic retaining some kind of relationship with Russia to Ukraine as an independent nation-state."[11]

9. Kivelson and Suny, *Russia's Empires*, 18, 19.

10. Kivelson and Suny, *Russia's Empires*, 73. For more details on the history of Ukraine, Paul Robert Magocsi, *A History of Ukraine: The Land and Its Peoples* 2nd rev. ed., (Toronto: University of Toronto Press, 2010). On the complex question of ecclesiastical governance in Ukraine, see Borys A. Gudziak, *Crisis and Reform: The Kyivan Metropolitinate, the Patriarch of Constantinople, and the Genesis of the Union of Brest* (Cambridge, MA: Harvard University Press, 1998), and for the first attempt of the Orthodox in Ukraine in the early twentieth century to be recognized as an autocephalous church, see Nicholas E. Denysenko, *The Orthodox Church in Ukraine: A Century of Separation*, (DeKalb: Northern Illinois University Press, 2018), 13–57.

11. Denysenko, *The Orthodox Church in Ukraine*, 209.

The international recognition of Ukraine as an independent nation-state in 1991 should have rendered moot any claims on the part of Russia to control or dominate the political or the ecclesiastical life of Ukraine. The seizure of Crimea by Russia in 2014, like its invasion of South Ossetia and Ahkazia in 2008, provoked not only international political condemnation, but in the case of the Georgian incursion, the condemnation of Catholicos-Patriarch of All Georgia Ilia II, who joined the chorus of Orthodox hierarchs condemning the 2022 invasion of Ukraine. For a quarter-century before the invasion, scholars had been investigating the post-Soviet struggle in Ukraine to construct a new national identity that guaranteed a separate national narrative, but one that recognized the religious and cultural bonds between the two nation-states. These experts were not surprised at the continued invocation of the imagined unity that bound Russia, Ukraine, and Belarus together not merely culturally or in terms of religion, but politically. Both Vladimir Putin and Patriarch Kyrill of Moscow had signaled their insistence upon this narrative long before the invasion. In the broader Orthodox world, however, this version of an official national identity found a receptive audience only in the Orthodox Church in Serbia and the Patriarchate of Antioch, who both failed to call the Russian invasion what it was, remaining silent on the role of Moscow's Patriarch in providing justification for the war. On the contrary, the invasion was perceived by hierarchs such as Ilia of Georgia, and Theodoros of Alexandria as the continuation of an already long-established pattern of aggression on the part of both the Moscow regime and the Russian Orthodox Church's Patriarch.[12]

The events in Ukraine inevitably also produced a crisis within the Orthodox communities in North America, forcing an unwelcome decision

12. On the struggle to construct a Ukrainian national identity after the fall of the Soviet Union, Catherine Wanner, *Burden of Dreams: History and Identity in Post-Soviet Ukraine* (University Park, PA: Penn State University Press, 1998); on the continued invocation by Moscow of Russian, Belarussian, and Ukrainian identity, the condemnations of the majority of Orthodox hierarchs and the loyalty of Serbia and Antioch, see Edward Pentin, "Widespread Orthodox Church Backlash Unleashed Against Russia's Aggression in Ukraine," *National Catholic Register,* March 11, 2022; https://www.ncregister.com/news/widespread -orthodox-church-backlash-unleashed-against-russia-s-aggression-in-ukraine (accessed May 26, 2022).

about whether to label the invasion a violation of international law and human rights and to condemn Patriarch Kyrill's support for the war. The first indication that North American Orthodox would not be able to avoid addressing the crisis came with the publication of "A Declaration on the 'Russian World' (Russki Mir) Teaching." Condemning not only the invasion but the use of language that avoided calling the invasion what it was, hundreds of Orthodox scholars worldwide eventually signed the statement that also rejected any implied right of Russia to intervene by secular or ecclesial means to protect or rescue the values of a purported Russian Orthodox world.[13]

Not surprisingly, the Ukrainian Orthodox Church of the USA on February 25, 2022 issued a condemnation of the "silence of Russian government and spiritual leaders who know the truth . . ." of invasion and failure to call the invasion what it was.[14] On March 6, the largest Eastern Orthodox jurisdiction in North America, the Greek Orthodox Archdiocese, led by Metropolitan Elpidophoros, joined the Ecumenical Patriarch Bartholomew in a swift condemnation of the invasion and the role of Patriarch Kyrill. Since the Ecumenical Patriarchate had recognized the autocephaly of the Ukrainian Orthodox Church in 2018, Constantinople predictably condemned the invasion and restated its blessing of the head of the UOC, Metropolitan Epiphanios. Far more significantly, however, the Orthodox Church in America whose own autocephaly granted in 1970 by Moscow remains unrecognized by Constantinople, also condemned the invasion. In doing so, the OCA joined itself to the courageous condemnation issued by the Moscow Patriarchate's own Metropolitan of Kyiv, Onufrij, who had returned from a visit to the United States just prior to the invasion. The choice of language adopted by the OCA reflected the deepening sense of frustration and outrage many Orthodox observers expressed as the war continued. An initial February 24 statement of support for Metropolitan Onufrij called for Vladimir Putin to end "military operations";

13. "A Declaration on the 'Russian World' (Russki Mir) Teaching," March 13, 2022; https://publicorthodoxy.org/2022/03/13/a-declaration-on-the-russian-world -russkii-mir-teaching (accessed March 14, 2022). In the interest of full disclosure, the author was a signatory to the declaration.

14. "Council of the Metropolia Issues a Statement on the Ongoing War in Ukraine," 24/5 February 2022; https://uocofusa.org/news_220304_2 (accessed May 27, 2022).

the statement concluded by demanding a "cessation of hostilities against Ukraine." By March, however, in a letter of support to Onufrij, the OCA denounced the "unjust war" and on May 20, in an Ecumenical Gathering on Peace in Ukraine, Metropolitan Tikhon openly attacked the Russian invasion of Ukraine. Even so, neither the Greek Orthodox nor the OCA chose to denounce Metropolitan Kyrill by name[15]

In keeping with the Patriarchate of Antioch's refusal to condemn the Russian invasion, its Antiochian Christian Orthodox Archdiocese of North America avoided blaming Russia or naming Patriarch Kyrill but instead released a statement on February 25, reissued on March 15, that called on the Orthodox to "resolve our disputes through fair and open discussions." The statement also prayed for the "health and safety of His Beatitude Metropolitan Onufrij, the Ukrainian Orthodox Church and the Ukrainian people in these difficult times."[16]

Even before the catastrophe of the Russian invasion, those who had studied in detail the history of Ukraine's struggle to articulate a national identity warned that the "Ukrainians have proven that they have a particular regional and cultural tradition that distinguishes them from Russians and other Eastern Slavs." Nonetheless, the "problem of nationalist ideology" remains a serious one because "the damage inflicted by the *Russkii mir* ideology of the Moscow Patriarchate has contributed to gross violations of human dignity through violence and displacement. Orthodox leaders are right to be cautious about the emergence of a blatantly nationalist civic religion in Ukraine. . . ." The pluralist society that has emerged in that nation-state, however, may make the emergence of such a nationalist civil religion as difficult to construct in Ukraine as has been the case in Western nation-states. Whether Ukrainian Orthodox in North America can also escape from the perils of a nationalist diaspora identity will also bear watching for those who wish to see the emergence of a unified Orthodox

15. "Archiepiscopal Encyclical on the Invasion of Ukraine," March 6, 2022 (citing the February 27 denunciation of the invasion by the Ecumenical Patriarch) https://www.goarch.org/-/archiepiscopal-encyclical-invasion-ukraine? (accessed May 27, 2022); For the OCA statements of February 24, March 2, and May 20, see the OCA website for the dates cited and especially www.oca.org /news/p165/ (accessed May 23, 2022.)

16. https://antiochian.org/regulararticle/1159 (accessed May 27, 2022).

Church of North America.[17] On May 27, 2022 the Council of the assembled hierarchs of the Ukrainian Orthodox Church of the Moscow Patriarchate(UOC-MP) issued a formal statement claiming their right to self-governance and rejecting Patriarch Kyrill and the Moscow Patriarchate's hitherto acknowledged role as the final authority in Orthodox ecclesiastical matters in Ukraine. Not surprisingly, Kyrill and his fellow bishops in Russia rejected the legitimacy of the actions taken in Kyiv. Whether the decision would lead to a reconciliation of the Moscow Patriarchate bishops and parishes in Ukraine with the autocephalous church under the leadership of Metropolitan Epiphanias and created by the Ecumenical Patriarchate in 2019 (OCU) remained unclear.[18]

The challenge facing the Orthodox in North America that the Ukraine invasion brought to the fore stems from the inapplicability of both East Roman (Byzantine) and ethnic-nationalist models of church governance, adaptation, and the right to self-determination that developed over centuries of experience. Everyone recognizes that no Orthodox global empire exists or is likely to, and hence, no imperial political authority can compel ecclesiastical obedience, or even cooperation among bishops. Consequently, it has proven difficult for the Orthodox to escape from the reality of the modern nation-state and its role in creating the "conditions of autocephaly" that were "organized upon principles of social, ethnic, linguistic, and political difference" without the presence of an "overarching structure to keep them aligned institutionally or sociologically." The result has been the near-captivity of Orthodox churches to some form of ethnic nationalism, especially for those that have come into being since the rise of the nation-state during the nineteenth century and into the present day.[19] The patterns

17. Denysenko, *The Orthodox Church in Ukraine*, 221.

18. For analyses, see Neil MacFarquhar, "Ukrainian Orthodox Church Breaks with Moscow Over War," May 28, 2022, https://www.nytimes.com/2022/05/28/world/europe/ukraine-orthodox-church-moscow.html (accessed May 30, 2022); Jayson Casper, "'Thou Shalt Not Kill', Ukrainian Orthodox Church Ruptures Relations with Russia," May 30, 2022, https://www.christianitytoday.com/news/2022/may/ukrainian-orthodox-church-condemns-war-moscow-kirill-uoc-mp.html (accessed June 1, 2022).

19. George E. Demacopoulos, "Ecclesiastical Jurisdiction, the Nation-State, and the Specter of Byzantium," *The Wheel* 17/18 (Spring/Summer, 2019): 12–17 at 15.

of voluntary and forced migrations, internationalization of commerce and business, and the resulting pluralist, mixed nature of many societies, including that of North America, have only intensified the difficulties the Orthodox face in reconciling actual, day-to-day experience with the canonical and structural legacies of both imperial and ethnic-national models of what it means to be Orthodox and what rights and privileges belong to all the members of such a church.

How the Orthodox value the dignity and purpose of the fully human person as well as forms of knowledge and wisdom acquired from non-religious sources has also emerged as a troubling topic within which any discussion of rights now occurs. If a review of how the Orthodox in the United States have engaged the question of rights demonstrates anything, it is that putting an endorsement of rights into practice remains a challenge both within the Church itself, as well as with regard to insights and teachings posed by the Orthodox to a post-secular world. That world is one in which religious and secular world views will continue to co-exist, sometimes amicably, sometimes in considerable tension with each other. Despite continued temptation to divide the world, and its history, into religious and secular stories, many scholars in different disciplines have rejected the well-known thesis of the European Protestant sociologist Max Weber and those who have followed him in claiming that the "modern" has no room for enchantment. The myth of disenchantment dies hard, however, despite the fact that "in recent years, support for the classical secularization thesis has withered in the face of religious revivals," and modernity has fashioned its own enchantments.[20]

Where Jason Josephson-Storm is fascinated by the impact of physics on the "human sciences," historians have argued for some time that the turn toward what some critics have claimed to be a more secular understanding of rights had its roots in the horror that emanated from unprecedented violence. The revulsion felt by European Christians at the atrocities perpetrated by the Thirty Years' War (1618–48) on the Continent and the English

---

20. Jason A. Josephson-Storm, *The Myth of Disenchantment: Magic, Modernity, and the Birth of the Human Sciences* (Chicago: University of Chicago Press, 2017): 4. For a variety of critiques of the secularization claim from several disciplines, see the essays in Vyacheslav Karpov and Manfred Svensoon, eds., *Secularization, Desecularization, and Toleration: Cross-Disciplinary Challenges to a Modern Myth* (Cham, Switzerland: Palgrave MacMillan, 2020).

Civil Wars (1641–49) cannot be sidestepped in any serious engagement with the language of rights. What historians have labelled the "crisis of the seventeenth century" boiled down to a simple question: could Christianity in either the Catholic or various Protestant vestures be trusted to respect the consciences, the dignity, and the rights of all, and to sustain a social ethos in which all persons had the opportunity to realize their potential because of a moral subculture that defended especially the marginal, the weak, and the "other"? Many who reflected on this question concluded that the answer was "no."[21] The quest for a stable, predictable, and peaceful society produced what began as a hope that just as mathematical certainty was a form of knowledge that could be shared and agreed upon by many, so too in the realm of human affairs something like this might be possible, and that search ranged from political theory and law to philosophy, theology, and literature. But the quest for certainty and stability that in some instances resulted in republican experiments also gave birth to "sequential bouts of large-scale warfare and aggression . . . [to] products not of republican regimes, but rather of different kinds of monarchies." There was not, and is not now, any inevitable and certain triumph of liberal constitutional democracy, in the West or elsewhere in the world.[22] Realizing that metaphysical certainty in matters of religious conviction could neither be imposed nor taken for granted, several European Christian thinkers in many realms of life ranging from theology to philosophy, literature to law and history, concluded that probable certainty was the best even devout Christians could hope for.

Historian of science Steven Shapin has offered an instructive investigation of the problem confronting the early modern Europeans—how something could be known. Even those who were fascinated by empiricism— knowledge observed from direct sense experience—had no way to prove the reliability of observation either from instruments such as the telescope

21. The classic analysis remains Theodore K. Rabb, *The Struggle for Stability in Early Modern Europe* (New York: Oxford University Press, 1976); for an assessment, Philip Benedict, "Religion and Politics in the European Struggle for Stability," in *Early Modern Europe: From Crisis to Stability*, ed. Benedict and Myron P. Gutmann (Newark: University of Delaware Press, 2003), 120–137.

22. Linda Colley, *The Gun, The Ship, and The Pen: Warfare, Constitutions, and the Making of the Modern World* (New York and London: Liveright Publishing Corporation, 2021), 413.

or the microscope. Worse still, even people like Galileo Galilei believed that human powers of observation had decayed steadily since the Fall, or, alternatively, that sources of knowledge had become corrupted and polluted and that the real task of science was to purify and restore the pristine quality of that knowledge—and this quest lay at the heart of Renaissance humanism and the Protestant Reformation—"back to the sources," "*ad fontes.*" Not everyone was willing to be so reverential toward the past. Some, like Johannes Kepler, argued that ancient knowledge was crude and partial, and by the late seventeenth century the revolt against the ancients became part of the intellectual agenda of some but not all of the early scientists. But Galileo, and philosophers such as René Descartes, Thomas Hobbes, and Blaise Pascal all preferred to base knowledge on experience of what occurs in the world of personal, common sense observation. They now had to include knowledge produced "artificially" by means of telescopes and other instruments.[23]

The great alternative, however, was to reject the attempt to give specific experiences or a particular experiment the claim of certainty—and instead, to begin cataloging and collating as much of what natural historical facts seemed to provide in order to put together massive numbers of examples of what occurred in nature with lots of experiments that rendered accessible such phenomena as the weight of air (hence Robert Boyle's famous barometer experiments). The rejection of the past, in other words, remained very focused and narrow—it was the rejection of specifically Aristotelian notions of nature, but not the authority of human testimony from the past as a whole. What constituted a trustworthy report was what much of the fact-finding was all about—to separate credible testimony from tall tales, especially if those stories contradicted the evidence of the eyes.

The historian Barbara Shapiro has shown that what Shapin traces for us in the realm of observation and eyewitness testimony in the natural science arena was also going on simultaneously in the area of the law, theology, literature, and history as well. Shapiro confirms Shapin's contention that there was never a single scientific revolution and reminds us that people we are interested in who were part of this scientific revolution were not scientists at all as we understand the disciplines today. Robert Boyle, or John

---

23. Steven Shapin, *The Scientific Revolution* (Chicago: University of Chicago Press, 1996), 72–3.

Locke crossed boundaries between natural science, history, theology, and law quite often. But what happened in the seventeenth century amounted to a move away from claims of metaphysical certainty—certainty of knowledge about nature, about humans, about causes, in favor of notions of probability—and that probability was grounded in experience. This move constituted a major intellectual shift since in ancient and medieval thought, probability was associated with opinion and rhetoric—not highly regarded except in the area of casuistry—the form of reasoning by which difficult moral choices were made in uncertain conditions—or as Shapiro also notes, in "dialectic, a nondemonstrative form of reasoning used in argumentation that dealt with opinion." But in the seventeenth century, probability began to claim a real sense of authority because it was grounded in experience. In England under the patronage of the Royal Society, experimental programs increased wherein hypothesizing was put to the test of physical and empirical data. Out of this activity then came notions of probable opinion, the basis for new explanations of why phenomena in nature "worked" a certain way. By contrast, Sir Isaac Newton by the 1670s in a famous debate over optics seemed to claim more certainty for his positions because they were based on mathematical and geometrical principles that appeared in his 1687 treatise *The Mathematical Principles of Natural Philosophy*. Still, Newton, Boyle, and other "scientists," whatever their disagreements about hypothesizing, were committed to empirically observable data and a common ground that said that facts and phenomena were "the basis of natural philosophy."[24]

If we turn to other areas of human life, one can see why the appeal of probability and the testing of hypotheses was especially attractive. Even contemporary observers knew that the violence of the Wars of Religion emerged from the multiple versions of "reformation" and from complex mixes of political, economic, and social tensions. And it is deeply misleading to argue, as some have, that out of "reformation" emerged a "secularized" society.[25] Religious dogmatism that had certainly played its part in

24. Barbara Shapiro, *Probability and Certainty in Seventeenth-Century England: A Study of the Relationships between Natural Science, Religion, History, Law, and Literature* (Princeton, NJ: Princeton University Press, 1983), 38, 58.

25. The argument of Brad Gregory, *The Unintended Reformation: How a Religious Revolution Secularized Society* (Cambridge, MA: Harvard University Press, 2012). For an important critique, see Thomas Pfau, "History without

CONCLUSION

the renewed outbreak of political and social catastrophe of the seventeenth century religious wars explains in part the hostility of post-1648 thinkers to claims of dogmatic certainty—in religious as well as in natural philosophical work and in attempts to rescue ancient understandings of human passions and virtues. The unpredictability of relying upon the supposedly superior passion of the quest for glory, and the long-recognized unreliability of human sexual passion as the basis for creating an ordered society, led to the struggle to rehabilitate the passion for gain—denounced by the ancients as the most ignoble of the passions. Perhaps so, European scholars agreed—but the very predictability of the human temptation to the love of money as the root of all evil suggested that by the paradoxical embracing of this passion, the unpredictability of pursuing glory with the attendant social, moral, and political chaos might be avoided.[26]

Mathematics and mathematical demonstration became part and parcel of the empirical bent of English science, far more so than was the case on the Continent, as the argument for a new view of the human passions began to gain adherents as well. This had two consequences: first, the elaborate mathematics of someone like Newton could only be understood by a small group of experts and this meant that opposition to this new way of doing philosophy or science was also correspondingly small. Most of these treatises were still be written and published in Latin, but in England because of the fascination with empiricism and the collection of data and cataloguing it, all kinds of non-expert amateurs could participate in the program. This made science something that gentlemen could engage in and made it socially acceptable to do so.

Second, in questions of religious belief, the natural theologians conventionally talked about three categories of knowledge—mathematical demonstration being the highest, where intellectual assent was compelled by the logic of the proofs; in second place, physical knowledge based on

Hermeneutics: Brad Gregory's Unintended Modernity," *The Immanent Frame: Secularism, Religion and the Public Sphere*, November 6, 2013, https://tif.ssrc.org /2013/11/06/history-without-hermeneutics-brad-gregorys-unintended-modernity/ (accessed April 22, 2021). For a more satisfactory assessment of the sixteenth century events, Carlos N.N. Eire, *Reformations: The Early Modern World, 1450–1650* (New Haven, CT: Yale University Press, 2016).

26. Albert O. Hirschmann, *The Passions and the Interests: Political Arguments for Capitalism Before its Triumph* (Princeton, NJ: Princeton University Press, 1977).

sensory data; and bringing up the rear, moral certainty. What started to happen in the late seventeenth century in English theological circles was the emergence of the conclusion that while physical and mathematical knowledge could yield infallible certainty (actually conditionally certain since only God was absolutely infallible), religious principles belong to the area of moral certainty alone. This was not thought a bad conclusion at least among some theologians because it showed that one could not compel assent to religious truth—that would negate faith or ethical choosing. It was, such theologians argued, only atheists and doubters who demanded "a religion based on mathematical demonstration or the direct evidence of the senses." Most of the late seventeenth century English theologians' concerns centered on proving the existence of God by an appeal to intellect and reason. But one consequence of this kind of approach was its elitism and the fact that as Shapiro noted "God became more distant as he became more benevolent" (i.e., "reasonable").[27]

If we examine the relationship between religion and science in the late seventeenth century at least in England, we can see that the search for a language and a set of issues where reasonable people could discuss without falling into fatal confessional quarrels explains the attraction for people like Newton, or John Wilkins (the founder of a scientific center at Wadham College, Oxford), who became one of the major contributors to the foundation of the Royal Society dedicated to polite discussion and the willing suspension of attempts to arrive at certainty in matters of religious belief. These developments, along with the impact of the Scottish Common Sense philosophy informed in colonials like Benjamin Franklin, the same reticence in claiming certainty in matters of faith.[28]

Shapiro concludes that by 1700 what was thought of as knowledge and how one came by it—or, as Shapin describes it, what was known, how was it known and what were its purposes—had changed dramatically over the past century. Bacon and Descartes both started their searches for a natural philosophy intent on jettisoning the Aristotelian system of the medieval centuries. But they were also determined to demonstrate that a shared consensus of what constitutes knowledge was possible. The search for new methods of demonstrating knowledge really focused on this central problem.

27. Shapiro, *Probability*, 84, 86, 87.
28. Shapin, *Scientific Revolution*, 113.

But gradually the ground shifted in favor of this empirical, probabilistic approach to knowledge. This shift did not take place in science alone but as Shapiro has documented, in many disciplines including philosophy, law, history, and theology, all of whose practitioners were intent upon finding a consensual, reasoned basis or knowledge. Historians have conventionally talked about the revolution in knowledge by saying that the Renaissance was an age when Aristotelian notions of science were in decline while the Enlightenment was one dominated by empiricism and reason. But if we look at the seventeenth century between Renaissance and Enlightenment in the English context what seems to be happening is that there a real preference for empiricism emerged that marked the English experience as somewhat different from what happened on the Continent. The English appear to have settled for notions of probability and mostly gave up on establishing mathematical and metaphysical certainty either for claiming absolute knowledge of religious truth or of scientific phenomena. And revulsion at the violence of the English Civil Wars and the appalling Thirty Years' War undergirded this determination to avoid religiously motivated violence and destruction. Despite the undoubted importance of figures such as John Locke and Thomas Hobbes in the story of British philosophy and political theory, in North America, it would be instead the Scottish Common Sense figures such as Francis Hutcheson, Thomas Reid, and Adam Smith whose thought shaped the theological and philosophical landscape of North America for the better part of a century.

Shapin ends his discussion by claiming that although there is no one, overarching model for a scientific revolution, there does seem to be a kind of legacy. It includes a depersonalization of nature. No one can escape noticing the very elitist aspect to the abstract and difficult subject matter these Europeans were investigating. The late medical historian Roy Porter explored this development in detail. In his work on modern ideas of both body and soul, especially in his book *Flesh in the Age of Reason*, Porter noted that the problem with the emergence of the "rational soul"' championed by people like Locke, or Descartes is that such notions challenged deeply held convictions ordinary people still defended. What happens when you are no longer conscious? If your body—absent consciousness of it and rational thinking about it—isn't really "you," the idea of a soul and of the resurrection of the body has very little meaning. This kind of advanced scientific reasoning held some attraction to an elite but was impossible to reconcile with the Christian belief in the resurrection of the flesh and the hope of an afterlife. The seventeenth century began with all thinkers about science, religion and all aspects of human life tied to Christian doctrines. Most believed that humans are a compound "of mortal earthly clay and an immaterial and immortal soul that was destined to outlive the dissolution of the flesh, until reunion at the last Judgment." The devaluation of the flesh by increasingly rationalistic approaches to science and scientific method among a small elite also meant that the appeal of this kind of science or religion was distinctively limited for most ordinary people who still thought in terms that reflected a traditional "deep personal psychological attachment to the body" as central to personal identity.[29]

Why conclude the investigation of rights and the Orthodox in America with a review of seventeenth-century European pursuits of the problem of how knowledge is possible? And why is that question crucial to any discourse of rights? What does this have to do with how the Orthodox in North America approach questions of a social ethos; whether they value freedom of expression and religious conviction; what they have to say about the struggles over gender, sexuality, and marriage; and finally, the various regimes of human rights in the face of authoritarian regimes that at times appear to be supported by the Orthodox Church itself?

As we have already noted, by the third decade of the twenty-first century, a serious and widespread assault on the assumptions underlying the pursuit of knowledge has arisen to challenge the very language of rights, however defined, but especially those defended in liberal democratic constitutional states and societies. That assault threatens the developed consensus about how knowledge is acquired, shared, verified, and at least at the present, to constitute the most probable account for truth claims. The spread of conspiracy theories that purport to reveal hidden agendas pursued by elites attacking the values, identity, livelihood, and sense of worth held by people oppressed and marginal in one way or the other can be found in both far-right and far-left accusations. What Jonathan Rauch has identified as a form of "epistemic" crisis in twenty-first century society both in North America and abroad makes it imperative for all who would defend the importance of rights to be able to explain the rootedness of rights in the moral subculture of Christianity and Judaism—and how secular probable

29. Roy Porter, *Flesh in the Age of Reason: The Modern Foundations of Body and Soul* (New York: W.W. Norton and Co., 2003), 94, 79, 108, 470, 471.

knowledge and the growth of liberal democracy have operated not as irreconcilable antagonists—but rather to the advantage of Christian believers.
This could be especially the case if the Orthodox in North America emerge
as an example of what Rauch calls a "thoughtful community." Using the
Wikipedia experiment as an example, he points to the founders' insistence
upon being "reality-based." But far from being an "unstructured, anti-
hierarchical utopia" Wikipedia while being "decentralized was not the
same as being unstructured. Just the opposite. Wikipedia had hierarchies
and gatekeepers, rules and norms, due process and accountability." Although surely not intended, this experiment offers a fascinating model
from which an Orthodox Church in a pluralistic society might profitably
learn and adapt for itself.[30] A rootedness of rights in its own moral subculture, as we have argued throughout, is the product of Christianity's own
history, what makes for a living Tradition. But Rauch himself, in arguing
that there must be something like an elite consensus about just how we go
about defending the probable truth of propositions that can be validated
does not resolve the dilemma that the seventeenth-century debates first
revealed—how do various masters of specialized, elite knowledge commu-
nicate their consensus to ordinary people in order to guarantee a social
consensus about what is, at least most probably, "true"?

Another dimension of this troubling question has arisen because of the
explosion of digital knowledge and the mining of technological information for profit. This development threatens rights as well. Shoshana Zuboff
has labelled this phenomenon "surveillance capitalism."[31] She argues that
early modernity, whatever its real failures and brutalities, did provide a way
for the growth of "institutionalized reciprocities." The "access to afford-
able goods and services was bound by democratic measures and methods
of oversight" that since the 1980s has been undermined, allowing those with
short memories to forget that early modernity's "reciprocity with the social order, however imperfect, appears to have been one of its most salient
features."[32] What has arisen as a second kind of modernity she identifies

30. Jonathan Rauch, *The Constitution of Knowledge: A Defense of Truth* (New York: Brookings Institution Press, 2021), 138–149 at 140.

31. Shoshana Zuboff, *The Age of Surveillance Capitalism: The Fight for a Human Future at the New Frontier of Power* (New York: Public Affairs, 2019).

32. Zuboff, *The Age of Surveillance Capitalism*, 31–32.

with the argument of those who claim that "the public corporation as a social institution was reinterpreted as a costly error, and its long-standing reciprocities with customers and employees re-cast as destructive violations of market efficiency." The deregulation of large sectors of major portions of the economy ended up by "replacing the rich existential possibilities of the second modernity with a single glorified template of audacity, competitive cunning, dominance, and wealth."[33] Echoing the warnings of the French economist Thomas Piketty, Zuboff concludes that raw capitalism cannot be reconciled with the concept of social justice and an attendant concern for human rights. More disturbing still, the explosion of digital knowledge has rewarded those clever enough to construct what Zuboff calls a "private knowledge kingdom and its lucrative predictions that evolve toward certainty in order to guarantee market players the outcomes that they seek . . . this is the dark heart of surveillance capitalism: a new type of commerce that reimagines us through the lens of its own distinctive power, mediated by its means of behavioral modification." Those who can control the "instrumentalization" of surveillance capitalism are in a position to "transform us into means to others' market ends."[34] Zuboff is not content to focus solely on the way in which "personal information" is being mined and exploited for gain. More disturbing, she concludes, is the growth of a fatalism, a popular cynicism that abandons "the human expectation of sovereignty over one's own life and authorship of one's own experience. What is at stake is the inward experience from which we form the will to will and the public spaces to act on that will. What is at stake is the dominant principle of social ordering in an information civilization and our rights as individuals and societies to answer the questions *Who knows? Who decides? Who decides who decides?*"[35]

Even more unsettling, the capacity of a private corporation—to cite but one example, that of Clearview AI—to manipulate facial recognition software that would enable both governmental and private surveillance of any person anywhere in real time may prove to be the most significant assault

---

33. Zuboff, *The Age of Surveillance Capitalism*, 40, 41.

34. Zuboff, *The Age of Surveillance Capitalism* 43–44 summarizing Thomas Piketty, *Capital in the Twenty-First Century* (Cambridge, MA: Harvard University Press, 2014), 334–35; and on instrumentalization, 352, 353.

35. Zuboff, *Surveillance Capitalism*, 521.

on the right to privacy humans have ever known. These technological developments cannot be discussed without raising issues of rights. From an Orthodox perspective, it is difficult to see how such invasions can be reconciled with the Orthodox defense of the integrity, dignity, and relationship to God of the individual person. In facing such an unprecedented challenge and potential threat, the Orthodox will need to draw upon their own history of engaging with various kinds of rights language, and to make common cause with non-Orthodox Christians and non-Christians alike. If the challenge is handled badly, it will pose a threat to all First Amendment rights in the American legal and constitutional tradition to be free from government interference in freedom of expression. It will also pose a grave threat to any recognizable understanding of justice. But failure to curb the ability of a private corporation to make available such invasive surveillance to governments can also encourage even more retreat from public engagement and encourage secret use and potential abuse of power unless restrained in the name of a broader social and political good grounded in the "moral subculture" whose origins and importance Wolterstorff has identified.[36]

Orthodox Christians would be hesitant to endorse without qualification Zuboff's vigorous emphasis upon the sovereignty of individual "inward experience." But Orthodox Christians should be able to affirm on the basis of their own tradition her focus upon the importance of social ordering and the insistence upon taking personal responsibility for moral choices and for defending the rights of all members of a society. More than a small group of experts will be required to participate in asking the epistemic questions she and Rauch have identified especially in the face of the dangers posed by Clearview's invasive face-recognition technology. How should the Orthodox respond?

In the 1956, the film *Friendly Persuasion* presented the anguish of a family whose religious convictions as members of the Society of Friends made it impossible for them to take up arms in the American Civil War. When the war devastated a neighboring town and threatened the safety of

---

36. See for an introduction to this issue, Kashmir Hill, "Your Face is Not Your Own / What Happens When Our Faces Are Tracked Everywhere We Go?," *New York Times*, March 18, 2021, https://www.nytimes.com/interactive/2021/03/18/magazine/facial-recognition-clearview-ai.html (accessed April 22, 2021).

the family itself, however, both father and son felt compelled to take up arms in defense. The film ends with a studied ambiguity about whether force of arms, or only friendly persuasion represents the Christian option for defending the rights of the defenseless in the face of a threat from "the other." In assessing the Orthodox encounter with various kinds of rights claims, it may be possible to advance a cautious conclusion about rights that relates to the dilemma of war the Orthodox have faced in their own long history. Will the Orthodox in the North American context decide that the defense not only of the Church, but of the liberal, democratic, and pluralistic society that has provided this Church with a home and opportunity can only be conducted along the lines of friendly persuasion? Or will apologetics, polemics, and self-pity characterize the Orthodox response to the culture wars and the attendant debates about rights and the epistemic crisis all liberal democratic societies now confront?[37]

The Orthodox ethicist Perry Hamalis has identified a neglected tradition of Christian realism and the pursuit of just peacemaking—expounded by scholars ranging from Reinhold Niebuhr and Jean Bethke Elshtain to Christos Yannaras and others. The rejection of any notion of a utopian "kingdom of God on earth" must include as well demurring on extravagant claims for the "establishment of freedom and democracy." It may be that this engagement is possible for the Orthodox only in the robust debates in the kind of society North Americans now live in. For, as Hamalis points out, the "close ties between church and state/empire in multiple historical contexts" do not provide examples of how the pursuit of Christian realism and just peacemaking is possible for the Orthodox.[38]

Reconciling the privileges and honors, the *presbeia* of hierarchs to the developing American concern for procedural due process, protection of property, and the freedom to express opinion without fear of retribution presents the Orthodox with a related case. The endorsement of the version of human rights articulated by scholars such as Perry and Wolterstorff holds serious implications for the inner life of the Orthodox Church. The

37. William Wyler, dir. *Friendly Persuasion* (1956; Los Angeles: Allied Artists Pictures).

38. Perry T. Hamalis, "Just Peacemaking and Christian Realism," in *Orthodox Christian Perspectives on War*, ed. Perry T. Hamalis and Valerie A. Karras (Notre Dame, IN: University of Notre Dame Press, 2018), 335–359, at 349.

Orthodox are heirs of a canonical tradition that has historically located authority, power, and privileges in the person of bishops and too often at the expense of the need to demonstrate consent and participation by the Church at large. Heirs of the Slavic Orthodox emphasis on sobornost and participant citizens in the Anglo-American legacy of suspicions of pre-rogative power's capacity to pose grave threats to rights and liberties, the Orthodox did not undertake the reconciliation of these birthrights until relatively late in the twentieth century. As the history of the Orthodox in North America demonstrates, this postponement emanated from the eth-nic fragmentation of the Orthodox and international pressures that kept the Orthodox in the Americas focused on events in historically Orthodox nation-states and regions of the world. Because of the "moral absence" of hierarchs for many years in the Americas, a kind of "modified congrega-tionalism" ended up separating the clergy from people that resulted in "two separate streams of authority" in which concern for the "worldly" aspects of property, finances, and lay rights competed with the "rights" the *presbeia* of hierarchs. Whether, as Ferencz hoped, a solution to this stand-off exists in the embracing of "conciliarity" in which "all the People of God, ordained and un-ordained, participate in the authority of the church and the exer-cise of that authority as one, whole Body" remains an unanswered ques-tion regarding rights and privileges in American Orthodoxy more than a generation after he offered his insightful analysis.[39]

One Orthodox attorney has predicted the continued involvement of sec-ular courts in the internal conflicts of churches in disputes over rights where churches are not of one mind about where the ultimate legitimate church authority lies. This is especially the case if that authority can be proven to have violated its own constitution, by-laws, and procedures. Sec-ular courts cannot be counted on to defer to hierarchical authorities if the Orthodox themselves are not united—and they are not—on whether the Ecumenical Patriarch, or some other hierarch or synod constitutes this final authority, even if it is carefully circumscribed as an appellate juris-diction only. This state of affairs suggests that the various jurisdictions of the Orthodox in the United States must take steps to discourage secular courts from determining "whether a church authority acted legitimately"

---

39. Ferencz, Nicholas. *American Orthodoxy and Parish Congregationalism* (Piscataway, NJ: Gorgias Press, 2006), 113–146; 203; 209.

because "accommodation" and the historic deference paid by courts to how churches handle internal disputes appears to be increasingly in doubt.[40]

The most recent example of this pattern has emerged in the proposed Equality Act that explicitly excludes religious organizations from calling upon the Religious Freedom Restoration Act to exempt their personnel policies from the regulation of sexual orientation and gender identity. This is the first time the Congress has explicitly denied the right of religious groups to invoke RFRA. If religious schools are redefined as "public accommodations," the liberal secular law professor Douglas Laycock has argued, religious dissent from the endorsement of LGBT equality claims will no longer be possible. Personnel in religious schools or other organizations will not be exempt. In Laycock's opinion, the legislation goes too far and will further exacerbate the existing divisions in the country. The Executive Committee of the Assembly of Canonical Orthodox Bishops agrees with Laycock's analysis, asking that the leaders of the country to "uphold, and not infringe upon, the religious freedom guaranteed by the Bill of Rights, and to continue to extend the protections afforded by the Religious Freedom Restoration Act."[41]

This pattern of shifting explanations of what rights consist of in the American context can be traced back to the era of the Founding Fathers themselves when no one philosophical or political theory of rights received formal approbation. Nor did Americans pay much attention to a systematic study of where notions of the law and rights were to be found until much later in their history. The study of jurisprudence and its history "commonly equated with legal philosophy, and often . . . thought as including the examination of normative theories about what the purposes of law

40. Matthew Namee, "The Dionisije Conundrum and why Deference Doesn't Work," Orthodox History, https://orthodoxhistory.org/2011/06/14/the-dionisije -conundrum-and-why-deference-doesnt-work/ (accessed April 22, 2020).

41. John McCormack, "A Liberal Law Professor Explains Why the Equality Act Would 'Crush' Religious Dissenters," National Review, May 17, 2019, https:// www.nationalreview.com/2019/05/law-professor-explains-why-the-equality-act -would-crush-religious-dissenters (accessed April 12, 2021); "Statement of the Executive Committee on the Proposed Equality Act," Assembly of Canonical Orthodox Bishops of the United States of America, March 26, 2021, https://www .assemblyofbishops.org/news/2021/statement-of-the-executive-committee-on-the -proposed-equality-act (accessed April 10, 2021).

should be . . . does not begin until the 1880s."[42] When conflicts that were cast in rights language finally reached the level of judicial review of both legislative and federal administrative law in the course of the twentieth century, the results proved to be diverse, and at times, contradictory. The rights claims that surround issues of marriage, gender, and sexuality shifted with remarkable speed from the supposed discovery of a right to privacy, to one of equal protection, and most recently to an assertion that in controverted matters such as abortion or gender identity, maximum individual liberty should be defended on the basis that such a defense constitutes a societal benefit. But in this development, a long-standing tradition of "accommodating" religious rights appears to have suffered significant decline, a pattern noted even by those who would describe themselves as liberal progressives with no particular faith commitments. On balance, nonetheless, the Orthodox Christians of North America now have at their disposal access to critical engagements with their own past in wrestling with the question of rights. If they seize the opportunities the North American context provides them, that wrestling over rights, both within their church and with the broader society, has real potential to strengthen the health and the longevity of rights for both.

42. White, *Law in American History* 3:11.

BIBLIOGRAPHY

Adair, Douglass. "'Experience Must Be Our Only Guide': History, Democratic Theory, and the United States Constitution." In *Fame and the Founding Fathers: Essays by Douglass Adair*, edited by Trevor Colbourn, 152–175. New York: Norton/Institute of Early American History and Culture at Williamsburg, Va., 1974.

Adams, John. "Dissertation on the Canon and Feudal Law" (1765). In *The Works of John Adams, Second President of the United States*, edited by Charles Francis Adams, 9 vols., 3:455–57. Boston: Little, Brown, and Company, 1850–56.

Agadjanian, Alexander. "Liberal Individual and Christian Culture: Russian Orthodox Teaching on Human Rights in Social Theory Perspective." *Religion, State and Society* 38, no. 2 (June, 2010): 97–113.

"An Agreed Statement on Respect for Life." The North American Orthodox-Catholic Theological Consultation. May 24, 1974. Washington, D.C. https://www.usccb.org/resources/usccb-org-respect-for-life.pdf.

Ajalat, Charles Richard, "IOCC and the Broader Context: Are There Lessons to be Learned?" 73–87.

Alexandris, Alexis. *The Greek Minority of Istanbul and Greek-Turkish Relations, 1918–1974*. Athens: Center for Asia Minor Studies, 1992.

Alfeyev, Hilarion. *Orthodox Christianity Volume I: The History and Canonical Structure of the Orthodox Church*. Yonkers, NY: St. Vladimir's Seminary Press, 2011.

Allen, Fr. Joseph J., Fr. Edward Hughes, Fr. Joseph Antypas, Fr. Alexander Atty, Fr. George Aquaro, Fr. Antony Gabriel, Fr. Ghattas Hajal, et al., eds. *Clergy Guide of The Self Ruled Antiochian Orthodox Christian Archdiocese of*

North America. 3rd ed. [Englewood, NJ?]: Antiochian Orthodox Christian
    Archdiocese of North America, 2011.
Allen, Joseph. *Widowed Priest: A Crisis in Ministry.* Minneapolis, MN: Life &
    Light Publishing, 1994.
Allen, Pauline and Bronwen Neil. *Crisis Management in Late Antiquity (410–
    590 CE): A Survey of Evidence from Episcopal Letters.* Leiden: Brill, 2013.
Alter, Jonathan. *The Defining Moment: FDR's Hundred Days and the Triumph of
    Hope.* New York: Simon & Schuster, 2006.
Amar, Akhil Reed. "Creation, Reconstruction, and Interpretation of the Bill of
    Rights." 163–180.
Ambrosius, Metropolitan of Helsinki, "Preface," in *Orthodox Tradition and
    Human Sexuality,* edited by Thomas Arentzen, Ashley Purpura, Aristotle
    Papanikolaou. New York: Fordham University Press, 2022.
American Orthodox Institute of the United States of America. "A Public
    Statement on Orthodox Deaconesses by Concerned Clergy and Laity."
    January 15, 2018. http://www.aoiusa.org/a-public-statement-on-orthodox
    -deaconesses.
Anagnostou, Yiorgos. *Contours of White Ethnicity: Popular Ethnography and the
    making of Usable Pasts in Greek America.* Athens, OH: Ohio University
    Press, 2009.
Anderson, John. *Religion, State and Politics in the Soviet Union and Successor
    States.* Cambridge: Cambridge University Press, 1994.
Andrew, Christopher and Vasili Mitrokhin. *The Sword and the Shield: The
    Mitrokhim Archive and the Secret History of the KGB.* New York: Basic Books,
    1999.
Angelides, Stephen P. "Seminary Scheme gives Spyridon autocratic authority."
    Voithia. March 27, 1999. http://www.archbishopspyridon.gr/spyridon_1999
    /voith_angelides_27mar99.html.
An-Na'im, Abdullah Ahmed. *What is an American Muslim? Embracing Faith
    and Citizenship.* New York: Oxford University Press, 2014.
Antonov, Mikhail. "Church-State Symphonia: Its Historical Development
    and its Application by the Russian Orthodox Church." *Journal of Law and
    Religion* 35, no. 3 (December, 2020): 474–493.
Aral, Berdal. "The Idea of Human Rights as Perceived in the Ottoman Empire."
    Human Rights Quarterly 26, no. 2 (May, 2004): 454–482.
"Archiepiscopal Encyclical on the Invasion of Ukraine," March 6, 2022. https://
    static1.squarespace.com/static/5d73ca0bd74a826972a9a9b5/t/622f692e267
    e34283bc5c0f4/1647274286848/2022+Encyclical+on+the+Invasion+of+Uk
    raine+-+March+6+-+EN.pdf
Arida, Robert. "Response to Myself: A Pastor's Thoughts on Same-Sex
    Marriage." 119–23.

Assembly of Canonical Orthodox Bishops of the United States of America. "Response of Assembly of Bishops to *Obergefell v. Hodges*." July 2, 2015. https://www.assemblyofbishops.org/news/2015/response-of-assembly-of -bishops-to-obergefell-v.-hodges.

———. "Response to Racist Violence in Charlottesville, Virginia." June 13, 2016. https://www.goarch.org/-/response-to-racist-violence-in-charlottesville-va.

———. "Statement of the Executive Committee on the Proposed Equality Act." March 26, 2021. https://www.assemblyofbishops.org/news/2021 /statement-of-the-executive-committee-on-the-proposed-equality-act.

Athanasopoulou-Kypriou, Spyridoula. "Emancipation through Celibacy? The Sisterhoods of the Zoe Movement and their Role in the Development of 'Christian Feminism' in Greece 1938–1960." In *Innovation in the Orthodox Christian Tradition? The Question of Change in Greek Orthodox Thought and Practice,* edited by Trine Stauning Willert and Lina Molokotos-Liederman, 101–121. Farnham, UK: Ashgate Publishing, 2012.

Aubert, Annette G. *The German Roots of Nineteenth-Century American Theology*. New York: Oxford University Press, 2013.

Aune, Kristin. "Women in Orthodox Christianity: A Forward." In *Women and Religiosity in Orthodox Christianity*, edited by Ina Merdjanova, vii–xix. New York: Fordham University Press, 2021.

Awad, Najeeb G. "Is Christianity from Arabia? Examining Two Contemporary Arabic Proposals on Christianity in the Pre-Islamic Period." In *Orientalische Christen und Europa: Kulturbegegnung zwischen Interferenz, Partizipation und Antizipation,* edited by Martin Tamcke, 33–55. Wiesbaden: Harrassowitz, 2012.

Bacon, Hannah. *What's Right with the Trinity? Conversations in Feminist Theology*. London and New York: Routledge, 2009.

Bader-Saye, Scott. "The Transgender Body's Grace." *Journal of the Society of Christian Ethics* 39 No. 1 (Spring/Summer, 2019): 79–92.

Baer, Friederike. *The Trial of Frederick Eberle: Language, Patriotism, and Citizenship in Philadelphia's German Community 1790 to 1830*. New York: New York University Press, 2008.

Balakian, Peter. *The Burning Tigris: The Armenian Genocide and America's Response*. New York: Harper Perennial, 2004.

Balmer, Randall. *Thy Kingdom Come: How the Religious Right Distorts the Faith and Threatens America: An Evangelical's Lament*. New York: Basic Books, 2006.

Banner, Stuart. "When Christianity Was Part of the Common Law." *Law and History Review* 15, no. 1 (Spring, 1998): 27–62.

Barkey, Karen. "Aspects of Legal Pluralism in the Ottoman Empire." In *Legal Pluralism and Empires, 1500–1800,* edited by Lauren A. Benton and Richard Jeffrey Ross, 83–107. New York: New York University Press, 2013.

Bartholet, Elizabeth. "Homeschooling: Parent Rights Absolutism vs. Child Rights to Education & Protection." *Arizona Law Review* 62, no. 1 (2020): 1–80.

Basch, Norma. *Framing American Divorce: From the Revolutionary Generation to the Victorians*. Berkeley: University of California Press, 1999.

Basil the Great. *On Social Justice: St. Basil the Great*. Introduction and commentary by C. Paul Schroeder. Crestwood, NY: St. Vladimir's Seminary Press, 2009.

Bastkowski, John. *The Promise Keepers: Servants, Soldiers, and Godly Men*. New Brunswick, NJ: Rutgers University Press, 2004.

Bedrin, George and Philip Tamlush, eds. *A New Era Begins: Proceedings of the 1994 Conference of Orthodox Bishops in Ligonier, Pennsylvania*. Torrance, CA: Oakwood Publications, 1996.

Behr, John, editor and translator. *The Case against Diodore and Theodore: Texts and their Contexts*. Oxford: Oxford University Press, 2011.

"Being Human: Embodiment and Anthropology, Sex, Marriage and Theosis; *Obergefell v. Hodges* and the Orthodox Church." Special issue. *The Wheel* 13/14 (Spring/Summer 2018).

Beisner, Edward. *Twelve Against Empire: The Anti-Imperialists, 1898–1900*. New York: McGraw Hill, 1968.

Bell, Susan Groag and Karen M. Offen, eds. *Women, the Family, and Freedom: The Debate in Documents*. 2 vols. Stanford: Stanford University Press, 1983.

Benedict, Philip. "Religion and Politics in the European Struggle for Stability." In *Early Modern Europe: From Crisis to Stability*, edited by Benedict and Myron P. Gutmann, 120–137. Newark: University of Delaware Press, 2003.

Berdyaev, Nikolai. "Church Discord and Freedom of Conscience." Translated by Alvian N. Smirensky. *The Wheel* 21/22 (Spring/Summer, 2020): 6–18.

Berg, Thomas C., Carl H. Esbeck, Douglas Laycock, and Robin Fretwell Wilson. "Letter in Support of Fairness for All." *Alliance for Lasting Liberty*. December 6, 2019. https://fairnessforall.org/letter-in-support-of-fairness-for-all/.

Berlin, Isaiah. *The Hedgehog and the Fox: An Essay on Tolstoy's View of History*. Edited by Henry Hardy. 2nd edition. Princeton: Princeton University Press, 2013.

Bernstein, David E. "A History of 'Substantive' Due Process: It's Complicated." *Texas Law Review* 95, no. 1 (2016): 1–11. https://papers.ssrn.com/sol3/papers.cfn?abstract_id=2908130.

Berry, Jonathan with Rob Wood. *Satisfaction Guaranteed: A Future and A Hope for Same-Sex Attracted Christians*. London: Inter-Varsity Press, 2016.

Berzonsky, Margarita. "Organizing Business Women to Serve the Church." *Parish Development* 1 (1983). https://oca.org/parish-ministry/parishdevelopment/organizing-business-women-to-serve-the-church.

Bickel, Alexander M. *The Supreme Court and the Idea of Progress.* New Haven, CT: Yale University Press, 1978.

Birkle, Carmen. "Multiculturalism and the new Woman in Early Twentieth-Century America." In *Feminist Forerunners: New Womanism and Feminism in the Early Twentieth Century*, edited by Ann Heilmann, 58–75. London: Pandora, 2003.

Black, Allida et al., eds. *The Eleanor Roosevelt papers: Vol. I The Human Rights Years, 1945–1948.* Detroit: Thomason Gale, 2007.

Black, Lydia. *The Round the World Voyage of Hieromonk Gideon.* Kingston, ON: Limestone Press, 1989.

Blackstone, William. *Commentaries on the Laws of England: A Facsimile of the First Edition of 1765–1769.* Introduction by Stanley N. Katz, 4 vols. Chicago: University of Chicago Press, 1979.

Bloomfield, Paul and Bradley J. Strawser. "A Review of James Griffin's *On Human Rights.*" *Analysis* 71, no. 1 (January 2011): 195–197. https://doi.org/10.1093/analys/anq093

Boersma, Hans. *Seeing God: The Beatific Vision in Christian Tradition.* Grand Rapids, MI: William B. Eerdmans Publishing Co., 2018.

Bomboy, Scott. "Constitutional Powers and Issues during a Quarantine Situation." https://constitutioncenter.org/blog/constitutional-powers-and-issues -during-a-quarantine-situation.

Bon Tempo, Carl J. *Americans at the Gate: The United States and Refugees during the Cold War.* Princeton: Princeton University Press, 2008.

Bordeianu, Radu. "Primacies and Primacy According to John Zizioulas." *St. Vladimir's Theological Quarterly* 58 (2014): 5–24.

———. "Orthodox Observers at the Second Vatican Council and Intra-Orthodox Dynamics." *Theological Studies* 79, no. 1 (2018): 86–106.

Borgwardt, Elizabeth. *A New Deal for the World: America's Vision for Human Rights.* Cambridge, MA: Harvard University Press, 2005.

Boswell, John. *Same-Sex Unions in Pre-Modern Europe.* New York: Vintage Books, 1995.

Bouteneff, Peter C. *Beginnings: Ancient Christian Readings of the Biblical Creation Narratives.* Grand Rapids, MI: Baker Academic, 2008.

Bradshaw, David. *Aristotle East and West: Metaphysics and the Division of Christendom.* Cambridge: Cambridge University Press, 2004.

Brady, Joel. "Transnational Conversions: Greek Catholic Migrants and Russky Orthodox Conversion Movements in Austria-Hungary, Russia, and the Americas (1890–1914)." PhD dissertation, University of Pittsburgh, 2012.

Branch, Taylor. *At Canaan's Edge: America in the King Years 1965–68.* New York: Simon & Schuster, 2006.

Breck, John. *God with Us: Critical Issues in Christian Life and Faith*. Crestwood, NY: St. Vladimir's Seminary Press, 2003.

———. *Scripture in Tradition: The Bible and its Interpretation in the Orthodox Church*. Crestwood, NY: St. Vladimir's Seminary Press, 2001.

Broyde, Michael J. "Human Rights in Judaism Reviewed and Renewed." In *Human v. Religious Rights? German and U.S. Exchanges and their Global Implications*, edited by A.G. Roeber, 59–75. Göttingen: Vandenhoeck & Ruprecht, 2020.

Brüning, Alfons, "'Freedom' vs. 'Morality'"—On Orthodox Anti-Westernism and Human Rights." In *Orthodox Christianity and Human Rights*, edited by Alfons Brüning and Evert van der Zweerde, 125–152. Leuven, Paris, Walpole, MA: Peeters, 2012.

Brewer, Holly. *By Birth or Consent: Children, Law, and the Anglo-American Revolution in Authority*. Chapel Hill: University of North Carolina Press, 2005.

Burns, Timothy W. "John Courtney Murray, Religious Liberty, and Modernity: Part I: Inalienable Natural Rights." *Logos: A Journal of Catholic Thought and Culture* 17, no. 2 (Spring, 2014): 13–38.

———. "John Courtney Murray, Religious Liberty, and Modernity: Part II: Modern Constitutional Democracy." *Logos: A Journal of Catholic Thought and Culture* 17, no. 3 (Summer, 2014): 49–65.

Butcher, Brian A. "Gender and Orthodox Theology: Vistas and Vantage Points. In *Orthodox Christianity and Gender: Dynamics of Tradition, Culture and Lived Practice*. Edited by Helena Kupari and Elina Vuola, 25–46. London and New York: Routledge, 2021.

Calhoun, Samuel W. "Grounding Normative Assertions: Arthur Leff's Still Irrefutable, But Incomplete, 'Sez Who?' Critique" *Journal of Law and Religion* 20, no. 1 (2004–2005): 31–96.

Camosy, Charles C. *Losing Our Dignity: How Secularized Medicine Is Undermining Fundamental Human Equality*. Hyde Park: New City Press, 2021.

———. "'Orthodox Social Ethos' aims to put Eastern Church spin on social issues," *Crux: Taking the Catholic Pulse*. May 16, 2020. https://cruxnow.com /interviews/2020/05/orthodox-social-ethos-aims-to-put-eastern-church-spin -on-social-issues/.

Cargas, Sarita. "Questioning Samuel Moyn's Revisionist History of Human Rights." *Human Rights Quarterly* 38 (2016): 411–425.

Case, Mary Anne. "Why 'Live-And-Let-Live' Is Not A Viable Solution To The Difficult Problems of Religious Accommodation in the Age of Sexual Civil Rights." In "Religious Accommodation in the Age of Civil Rights Symposium," special issue, *Southern California Law Review* 88, no. 3 (March, 2015): 463–492.

Cases, Laurent. "Remaking Provincial Administration: Dioceses, Vicarii and Social Change in Late Antiquity (283–395)." PhD dissertation, The Pennsylvania State University, 2016.

Casey, Damien. "The Spiritual Valency of Gender in Byzantine Society." In *Questions of Gender in Byzantine Society*, edited by Bronwen Neil and Lynda Garland, 167–81. Farnham, UK: Ashgate Publishing, 2013.

Casper, Jayson. "'Thou Shalt Not Kill,' Ukrainian Orthodox Church Ruptures Relations with Russia." https://www.christianitytoday.com/news/2022/may/ukrainian-orthodox-church-condemns-war-moscow-kirill-uoc-mp.html.

Chalmers, David M. *Hooded Americanisms: The First Century of the Ku Klux Klan 1865–1965*. New York: Doubleday & Company, 1965.

Cherniak, Misha, Olga Gerassimenko, Michael Brinkschröder, eds. *"For I am Wonderfully Made": Texts on Eastern Orthodoxy and LGBT Inclusion*. Nieuwegein, Netherlands: Esuberanza Publishing, 2017.

Chryssavgis, John, et al., eds. *Deaconesses: A Tradition for Today and Tomorrow*. Brookline, Massachusetts: Holy Cross Orthodox Press, 2023.

Clapsis, Emmanuel, ed. *The Orthodox Churches in a Pluralistic World: An Ecumenical Conversation*. Geneva: World Council of Churches, 2004.

———. "An Orthodox Encounter with Liberal Democracy." In *Christianity, Democracy, and the Shadow of Constantine*, edited by George E. Demacopoulos and Aristotle Papanikolaou, 111–126. New York: Fordham University Press, 2017.

Cline, Wendy. *Building a Better Race: Gender, Sexuality and Eugenics from the Turn of the Century to the Baby Boom*. Berkeley: University of California Press, 2005.

Cogdell, Christina. *Eugenic Design: Streamlining America in the 1930s*. Philadelphia: University of Pennsylvania Press, 2004.

Coleman, Heather. "History, Faith, and Regional Identity in Nineteenth-Century Kyiv: Father Petro Lebedyntsev as Priest and Scholar." *Harvard Ukrainian Studies* 34, nos. 1–4 (2015–16): 343–372.

Colley, Linda. *The Gun, The Ship, and The Pen: Warfare, Constitutions, and the Making of the Modern World*. New York and London: Liveright Publishing Corporation, 2021.

Collins, Nate. *All But Invisible: Exploring Identity Questions at the Intersection of Faith, Gender, and Sexuality*. Grand Rapids. MI: Zondervan, 2017.

Congregation for Catholic Education. *Male and Female He Created Them: For a Path of Dialogue on the Issue of Gender in Education*. Vatican City: Congregation for Catholic Education, 2019. https://zenit.org/articles/new-vatican-document-provides-schools-with-guidance-on-gender-issues/.

Conrad, Sebastian. "Enlightenment in Global History: A Historiographical Critique." *American Historical Review* 117, no. 4 (October, 2012): 999–1027.

Conser, Jr., Walter H. *Church and Confession: Conservative Theologians in Germany, England, and America, 1815–1866*. Macon, GA: Mercer University Press, 1984.

Copenhaver, Brian. "Giovanni Pico della Mirandola." *The Stanford Encyclopedia of Philosophy* (Fall 2016). http://plato.stanford.edu/entries/pico-della -mirandola/.

Corwin, Edward S. *The 'Higher Law' Background of American Constitutional Law*. Ithaca: Cornell University Press, 1955.

Costache, Doru, Darren Cranshaw and James Harrison, eds. *Wellbeing, Personal Wholeness and the Social Fabric*. Newcastle on Tyne: Cambridge Scholars Publishing, 2017.

"Council of the Metropolia Issues a Statement on the Ongoing War in Ukraine." February 24, 2022. https://uocofusa.org/news_220304_2.

Cowie, Jefferson. *Stayin' Alive': The 1970s and the Last Days of the Working Class*. New York: The New Press, 2010.

Cross, Gary. *Kid's Stuff: Toys and the Changing World of American Childhood*. Cambridge, MA: Harvard University Press, 1999.

———. *Men to Boys: The Making of Modern Immaturity*. New York: Columbia University Press, 2010.

Curran, William J. "An Historical Perspective on the Law of Personality and Status with Special Regard to the Human Fetus and the Rights of Women." *Milbank Memorial Fund Quarterly/Health and Society* 61, no. 1 (1983): 58–75.

Currie, Elliott. *A Peculiar Indifference: The Neglected Toll of Violence on Black America*. New York: Metropolitan Books, 2020.

Curti, Merle. *Human Nature in American Thought: A History*. Madison: The University of Wisconsin Press, 1980.

Curtis, Daniel E. "Judicial Intervention in Church Property Disputes—Some Constitutional Considerations." *Yale Law Journal* 74 (1964–1965): 1113–1139. https://digitalcommons.law.yale.edu/fss_papers/1594.

Daley, S.J., Brian E. "The Meaning and Exercise of 'Primacies of Honor' in the Early Church." In *Primacy in the Church: The Office of Primate and the Authority of Councils*, edited by John Chryssavgis, 35–50. Yonkers, NY: St. Vladimir's Seminary Press, 2016.

———. "Universal Love and Local Structure: Augustine, the Papacy, and The Church in Africa." *The Jurist* 64 (2004): 39–63.

Dauenhauer, Richard. "Conflicting Visions in Alaskan Education." Occasional Paper #3. Fairbanks: Center for Cross-Cultural Studies, University of Alaska - Fairbanks, 1980.

———. "Two Missions to Alaska." *The Pacific Historian* 25, no. 1 (1982): 29–41.

Davis, Stephen J. *The Early Coptic Papacy: The Egyptian Church and its Leadership in Late Antiquity*. Cairo: The American University in Cairo Press, 2017.

"A Declaration on the 'Russian world' (Russki Mir) Teaching," March 13, 2022. https://publicorthodoxy.org/2022/03/13/a-declaration-on-the-russian-world-russkii-mir-teaching.

Demacopoulos. George E. "Ecclesiastical Jurisdiction, the Nation-State, and the Specter of Byzantium." *The Wheel* 17/18 (Spring/Summer, 2019): 12–17.

Denysenko, Nicholas E. *The Orthodox Church in Ukraine: A Century of Separation*. DeKalb: Northern Illinois University Press, 2018.

Deringil, Selim. *Conversion and Apostasy in the Late Ottoman Empire*. Cambridge: Cambridge University Press, 2012.

Destivelle, O.P., Hyacinthe. *The Moscow Council (1917–1918): The Creation of the Conciliar Institutions of the Russian Orthodox Church*. Notre Dame, IN: University of Notre Dame Press, 2015.

Devereux, Robert. *The First Ottoman Constitutional Period: A Study of the Midhat Constitution and Parliament*. Baltimore: The Johns Hopkins University Press, 1963.

Dias, Elizabeth and Ruth Graham, "White Evangelical Resistance Is Obstacle in Vaccination Effort." *New York Times*. April 5, 2021. https://www.nytimes.com/2021/04/05/us/covid-vaccine-evangelicals.html.

Doe, Norman. *Christian Law: Contemporary Principles*. Cambridge: Cambridge University Press, 2013.

Domingo, Rafael. *God and the Secular Legal System*. Cambridge: Cambridge University Press, 2016.

Donahue, Jr., Charles. "*Ius* in the subjective sense in Roman law. Reflections on Villey and Tierney." In *A Ennio Cortese*, edited by Domenico Maffei et al., 3 volumes, I:506–535. Rome: Il Cigno Galileo Galilei, 2001.

Doughtery, M.V. "Three Precursors to Pico della Mirandola's Roman Disputation and the Question of Human Nature in the *Oratio*." In *Pico della Mirandola: New Essays,* edited by M.V. Doughtery, 114–151. Cambridge: Cambridge University Press, 2008.

Dowland, Seth. "'Family Values' and the Formation of a Christian Right Agenda." *Church History* 78, no. 3 (September, 2009): 606–631.

Dreher, Rod. *The Benedict Option: A Strategy for Christians in a Post-Christian Nation*. New York: Sentinel, 2017.

Dulle, Colleen. "Explainer: What Pope Francis actually said about civil unions—and why it matters." *America Magazine*. October 22, 2020. https://www.americamagazine.org/faith/2020/10/22/pope-francis-gay-civil-union-lgtb-context-media-documentary.

Durham, Jr., W. Cole and Robert T. Smith. "Religion and the State in the United States at the Turn of the Twenty-first Century." In *Law and Religion in the 21ˢᵗ Century: Relations between States and Religious Communities*, edited by Silvio Ferrari and Rinaldo Cristofori, 79–110. Burlington, VT: Ashgate, 2010.

Eckel, Jan and Samuel Moyn, eds. *The Breakthrough: Human Rights in the 1970s*. Philadelphia: University of Pennsylvania Press, 2014.

Ecumenical Patriarchate of Constantinople, Special Commission on Social Doctrine. *For the Life of the World: Toward a Social Ethos of the Orthodox Church*. John Chryssavgis, David Bentley Hart, George Demacopoulos, Carrie Frederick Frost, Grandon Gallaher, Perry Hamalis, Nicolas Kazarian, Aristotle Papanikolaou, James Skedros, Gayle Woloschak, et al. Istanbul: Ecumenical Patriarchate of Constantinople, 2020. http://www.goarch.org /social-ethos.

Eichenberg, Julia. "Sammelrez: Geschichte der Menschenrechte." h-soz-u -kult@h-net.msu.edu. December 22, 2016. http://hsozkult.geschichte.hu -berlin.de/index.asp?id=20869&view=pdf&pn=rezensionen&type =rezbuecher.

Eire, Carlos N.N. *Reformations: The Early Modern World, 1450–1650*. New Haven, CT: Yale University Press, 2016.

Epp, Charles R. *The Rights Revolution: Lawyers, Activists, and Supreme Courts in Comparative Perspective*. Chicago: University of Chicago Press, 1998.

Erickson, John H. "Autocephaly in Orthodox Canonical Literature to the Thirteenth Century." *St. Vladimir's Theological Quarterly*, 15 nos.1and 2 (1971), 28–41.

———. "Canon 28 de Calcedonia: Su permanente significado para el debate del primado en la Iglesia." In *Communio et Sacramentum: En el 70 cumpleaños del Prof. Dr. Pedro Rodriguez*, edited by Jose R. Villar, 733–53. Pamplona: Universidad de Navarra, 2003.

———. "Chalcedon Canon 28: Its Continuing Significance for Discussion of Primacy in the Church." Orthodox Synaxis. Accessed June 1, 2019. https:// orthodoxsynaxis.files.wordpress.com/2018/10/erickson-chalcedon-canon-28 .pdf.

———. "Eastern Orthodox Christianity in America." In *The Cambridge History of Religion in America, Vol II: 1790 to 1945*, edited by Stephen J. Stein, 324–343. Cambridge: Cambridge University Press, 2012.

———. *Orthodox Christian in America: A Short History*. New York: Oxford University Press, 2008.

Esbeck, Carl H. and Jonathan J. Den Hartog, editors. *Disestablishment and Religious Dissent: Church-State Relations in the New American States, 1776–1833*. Columbia, MO: University of Missouri Press, 2019.

"Facts about Suicide." *The Trevor Project*. Accessed June 29, 2019. https://www .thetrevorproject.org/resources/article/facts-about-lgbtq-youth-suicide/.

"Common Questions" St. Phoebe Center for the Deaconess. Accessed October 20, 2017. https://orthodoxdeaconess.org/mission-vision/faqs/.

Fea, John. "Evangelical Fear Elected Trump." *The Atlantic*. June 24, 2018. https://www.theatlantic.com/ideas/archive/2018/06/a-history-of-evangelical-fear/563558/.

Felice, William F. *The Global New Deal: Economic and Social Human Rights in World Politics*. Lanham, MD: Rowman & Littlefield, 2003.

Ferencz, Nicholas. *American Orthodoxy and Parish Congregationalism*. Piscataway, NJ: Gorgias Press, 2006.

Fisher, David Hackett. *Growing Old in America*. New York: Oxford University Press, 1977.

Fitzgerald, Kyriaki Karidoyanes. *Women Deacons in the Orthodox Church: Called to Holiness and Ministry*. Brookline, MA: Holy Cross Orthodox Press, 1998.

Fitzgerald, Thomas. *The Orthodox Church*. Westport, CT: Greenwood Press, 1995.

Flexner, Eleanor and Ellen Fitzpatrick. *Century of Struggle: The Women's Rights Movement in the United States*. Enlarged ed. 1959; repr., Cambridge, MA: Bellknap Press of Harvard University Press, 1996. Citations are from the 1996 edition.

Florensky, Pavel. *The Pillar and Ground of Truth: An Essay in Orthodox Theodicy in Twelve Letters*. Translated by Boris Jakim, introduction by Richard F. Gustafson. Princeton, NJ: Princeton University Press, 2004.

Foner, Eric. *The Second Founding: How the Civil War and Reconstruction Remade the Constitution*. New York: Norton, 2019.

Foster, Gaines. *Moral Reconstruction: Christian Lobbyists and the Federal Legislation of Morality, 1865–1920*. Chapel Hill, NC: University of North Carolina Press, 2002.

Frangouli-Argyris, Justine. *The Lonely Path of Integrity: Archbishop Spyridon of America, 1996–1999*. Athens: Exandas Publishers, 2002.

Franklin, John Hope. *Racial Equality in America*. Chicago: University of Chicago Press, 1976.

Free, Lloyd A. and Hadley Cantril. *The Political Beliefs of Americans: A Study of Public Opinion*. Camden, NJ: Rutgers University Press, 1967.

Friendly, Henry J. "Some Kind of Hearing." *University of Pennsylvania Law Review* 123 (1975): 1267–1317. https://scholarship.law.upenn.edu/cgi/viewcontent.cgi?article=5317&context=penn_law_review

Frost, Carrie Frederick. *Church of Our Granddaughters*. Eugene, Oregon: Cascade Books, 2023.

Fuller, Lon. *The Morality of Law: Revised Edition*. New Haven: Yale University Press, 1964.

Gabriel, Antony. "A Retrospective: One Hundred years of Antiochian Orthodoxy in North America." In *The First One Hundred Years: A Centennial Anthology Celebrating Antiochian Orthodoxy in North America*, foreword by The Most Reverend Metropolitan Philip, edited by George S. Corey, 243–291. Englewood, NJ: Antakya Press, 1995.

Gallagher, Sally K. "The Marginalization of Evangelical Feminism." *Sociology of Religion* 65:3 (Autumn, 2004): 215–237.

Gallaher, Brandon. "Tangling with Orthodox Tradition in the Modern West: Natural Law, Homosexuality and Living Tradition." 50–63. *The Wheel* 13/14: (Spring/Summer, 2018),

Galli, Mark. "Revoice's Founder Answers the LGBT Conference's Critics." *Christianity Today.* July 25, 2018. https://www.christianitytoday.com/ct/2018/july-web-only/revoices-founder-answers-lgbt-conferences-critics.html.

Garnett, Richard W. "'Things That Are Not Caesar's': The Story of Kedroff v. St. Nicholas Cathedral." In *First Amendment Stories,* edited by Richard W. Garnett and Andrew Koppelman, 171–191. New York: Thomson Reuters/Foundation Press, 2012.

Garreau, Joel. *The Nine Nations of North America.* New York: Avon Books, 1981.

Gates, Jr., Henry Louis. *Stony the Road: Reconstruction, White Supremacy, and the Rise of Jim Crow.* New York: Penguin Press, 2019.

Gattrell, Peter. *The Making of the Modern Refugee.* Oxford: Oxford University Press, 2013.

Gillquist, Peter E. *Becoming Orthodox: A Journey to the Ancient Christian Faith.* Ben Lomond, CA: Conciliar Press, 1989.

———. *Metropolitan Philip: His Life and His Times.* Nashville, TN: Thomas Nelson Publishers, 1991.

Glendon, Mary Ann. *A World Made New: Eleanor Roosevelt and the Universal Declaration of Human Rights.* New York: Random House, 2001.

———. *Rights Talk: The Impoverishment of Political Discourse.* New York: The Free Press, 1991.

———. *The Forum and the Tower: How Scholars and politicians Have Imagined the World, From Plato to Eleanor Roosevelt.* Oxford: Oxford University Press, 2011.

Goodman, Lenn E. *Religious Pluralism and Values in the Public Sphere.* New York: Cambridge University Press, 2014.

Goodstein, Laurie. "How the Willow Creek Church Scandal Has Stunned the Evangelical World." *New York Times.* August 9, 2018. https://www.nytimes.com/2018/08/09/us/evangelicals-willow-creek-scandal.html.

Goodstein, Laurie and Sharon Otterman. "He Preyed on Men Who Wanted to Be Priests. Then He Became a Cardinal." *New York Times.* July 16, 2018. https://www.nytimes.com/2018/07/16/us/cardinal-mccarrick-abuse-priest.html.

Gordon, David C. *Lebanon: The Fragmented Nation*. London: Croom Helm, 1980.

Gordon, Sarah Barringer. *The Mormon Question: Polygamy and Constitutional Conflict in Nineteenth Century America*. Chapel Hill: University of North Carolina Press, 2002.

Goria, Wade R. *Sovereignty and Leadership in Lebanon 1943–1976*. London: Ithaca Press, 1985.

Gray, Mark M., Mary L. Goutier, and Melissa A. Cidade. *The Changing Face of U.S. Catholic Parishes: Emerging Models of Pastoral Leadership Project*. Washington, D.C.: National Association for Lay Ministries, 2011.

"The Greek Church." *The Liberator*. April 24, 1863. http://www.theliberatorfiles .com/wp-content/uploads/2015/10/The-Liberator-1863-04-24-Page-2.png.

Greek Orthodox Archdiocese of America. "Official Charter of the Archdiocese." January 18, 2003. https://www.goarch.org/documents/charter.

Greek Orthodox Stewards of America. "Affidavit of George Chelpon filed in Court by Archdiocese in Suit Brought by Simos C. Dimas." June 10, 1999. http://www.archbishopspyridon.gr/spyridon_1999/gosa_chelpon_10jun99 .html.

Green, Steven K. *Inventing a Christian America: The Myth of the Religious Founding*. Oxford: Oxford University Press, 2015.

———. *The Second Disestablishment: Church and State in Nineteenth-Century America*. New York: Oxford University Press, 2010.

Gregory, Brad. *The Unintended Reformation: How a Religious Revolution Secularized Society*. Cambridge, MA: Harvard University Press, 2012.

Griffin, James. *On Human Rights*. New York: Oxford University Press, 2008.

Grossman, Joan Delaney. "Krushchev's Anti-Religious Policy and the Campaign of 1954." *Soviet Studies* 24, no. 3 (January, 1973): 374–86.

Grote, Simon. "Review-Essay: Religion and Enlightenment." *Journal of the History of Ideas* 75, no. 1 (January, 2014): 137–160.

Gudziak, Borys. *Crisis and Reform: The Kyivan Metropolitinate, the Patriarch of Constantinople, and the Genesis of the Union of Brest*. Cambridge, MA: Harvard University Press, 1998.

Guroian, Vigen. "Godless Theosis." *First Things*. April, 2014. http://www.first things.com/article/2014/04/godless-theosis.

———. "The Problem of a Social Ethic: Diaspora Reflections." In *Incarnate Love: Essays in Orthodox Ethics*, edited by Vigen Guroian, 117–139. Notre Dame: University of Notre Dame Press, 1989.

———. *Ethics after Christendom: Toward an Ecclesial Christian Ethic*. Grand Rapids. MI: William B. Eerdmans Publishing Company, 1994.

———. *Rallying the Really Human Things: The Moral Imagination in Politics, Literature, and Everyday Life*. Wilmington, DE: ISS Books, 2005.

———. *The Orthodox Reality: Culture, Theology, and Ethics in the Modern World*. Grand Rapids, Michigan: Baker Academic, 2018.

Haiduc-Dale, Noah. *Arab Christians in British Mandate Palestine: Communalism and Nationalism, 1917–1948*. Edinburgh: Edinburgh University Press, 2013.

Hamalis, Perry T. "Just Peacemaking and Christian Realism." In *Orthodox Christian Perspectives on War*, edited by Perry T. Hamalis and Valerie A. Karras, 335–359. Notre Dame, IN: University of Notre Dame Press, 2018.

———. and Valerie A. Karras, editors. *Orthodox Christian Perspectives on War*. Notre Dame: University of Notre Dame Press, 2018.

Hamburger, Philip. *Is Administrative Law Unlawful?* Chicago: University of Chicago Press, 2014.

———. *Separation of Church and State*. Cambridge, MA: Harvard University Press, 2002.

Hand, Learned. *The Bill of Rights*. Cambridge, MA: Harvard University Press, 1958.

Hanley, Mark Y. *Beyond a Christian Commonwealth: The Protestant Quarrel with the American Republic, 1830–1860*. Chapel Hill: University of North Carolina Press, 1994.

Harakas, Stanley. "Orthodox Christianity in American Public Life: The Challenges and Opportunities of Religious Pluralism in the Twenty-First Century." *Greek Orthodox Theological Review* 56, nos. 1–4 (Spring-Winter 2011): 377–397.

Harcourt, Felix. *Ku Klux Kulture: American and the Klan in the 1920s*. Chicago: The University of Chicago Press, 2017.

Hardenbrook, Fr. John Weldon. "Fr. John Weldon Hardenbrook's Defense." Ben Lomond Tragedy: Opposing the blacking out of history. May 26, 1998. https://benlomond.wordpress.com/1998/05/26/fr-john-weldon-hardenbrooks-defense/.

Harper, Kyle. "Christianity and the Roots of Human Dignity in Late Antiquity." In *Christianity and Freedom: Vol. I: Historical Perspectives*, ed. T. Shah and A. Hertzke, 123–148. Cambridge: Cambridge University Press, 2016.

Hart, David Bentley. "Foreward." In *Encounter between Eastern Orthodoxy and Radical Orthodoxy: Transfiguring the World through the Word*, edited by Adrian Pabst and Christoph Schneider, xi–xiii. London: Routledge, 2016.

———. "Is, Ought, and Nature's Laws." *First Things*. March, 2013. http://www.firstthings.com/article/2013/03/is-ought-and-natures-laws.

Hart, H.L.A. "Positivism and the Separation of Law and Morals." *Harvard Law Review* 71 (1958): 593–629.

Hawaweeny, Raphael. "Letter to Evdokim Meschersky," December 17, 1914. *Orthodox Church in America Archives*, https://www.oca.org/history-archives/commemorating-saint-raphael-bishop-brooklyn.

―――. *An Historical Glance at the Brotherhood of the Holy Sepulcher.* Translated by Archpriest Michel Najim. Torrance, CA: Oakwood Publications, 1996.

Haycox, Stephen W. "Sheldon Jackson in Historical Perspective: Alaska Native Schools and Mission Contracts, 1885–1895." *The Pacific Historian* 28, no. 1 (1984): 18–28.

Herbel, D. Oliver. *Turning to Tradition: Converts and the Making of an American Orthodox Church.* New York: Oxford University Press, 2013.

Herrin, Judith. *Byzantium: The Surprising Life of a Medieval Empire.* Princeton, NJ: Princeton University Press, 2009.

Hertz, Karl H. *Two Kingdoms and One World.* Minneapolis: Augsburg Publishing House, 1976.

Hieromonk Dionysius. "The main Problems and the Character of the Russian Orthodox Foreign Mission work . . ." In *Alaskan Missionary Spirituality,* edited by Michael Oleksa, 279–284. New York: Paulist Press, 1987.

Hill, Harvey. "History and Heresy: Religious Authority and the Trial of Charles Augustus Briggs." *U.S. Catholic Historian* 20, no. 3 (Summer, 2002): 1–21.

Hill, Kashmir. "Your Face is Not Your Own / What Happens When Our Faces Are Tracked Everywhere We Go?" *New York Times.* March 18, 2021. https://www.nytimes.com/interactive/2021/03/18/magazine/facial -recognition-clearview-ai.html.

Hill, Wesley. *Spiritual Friendship: Finding Love in the Church as a Celibate Gay Christian.* Ada, MI: Brazos Press, 2015.

―――. *Washed and Waiting: Reflections on Christian Faithfulness and Homosexuality.* Grand Rapids, MI: Zondervan, 2016.

Hinka, John Paul. *Religion and Nationality in Western Ukraine: The Greek Catholic Church and the Ruthenian National Movement in Galicia, 1867–1900.* Montreal: McGill-Queen's University Press, 1998.

Hirsch, Arnold R. *Making the Second Ghetto: Race and Housing in Chicago, 1940–1960.* Cambridge: Cambridge University Press, 1983.

Hirschmann, Albert O. *The Passions and the Interests: Political Arguments for Capitalism Before its Triumph.* Princeton, NJ: Princeton University Press, 1977.

Hitti, Philip K. *The Syrians in America.* New York: George H. Doran Company, 1924.

Hoffer, Peter C. *Law and People in Colonial America.* Baltimore: Johns Hopkins University Press, 1998.

Hoffmann, Stefan-Ludwig, ed. *Moralpolitik. Geschichte der Menschenrechte im 20. Jahrhundert.* Göttingen: Van den Hoeck & Ruprecht, 2010.

Holifield, E. Brooks. *Theology in America: Christian Thought from the Age of the Puritans to the Civil War.* New Haven, CT: Yale University Press, 2003.

Holland, Tom. *Dominion: How the Christian Revolution Remade the World*. New York: Basic Books, 2019.

Hollinger, David A. *Protestants Abroad: How Missionaries Tried to Change the World but Changed America*. Princeton: Princeton University Press, 2017.

Holy Synod of the Orthodox Church in America. "Resolution of the Holy Synod on Canonical Procedures for Church Courts," October 21, 2015. https://oca.org/holy-synod/statements/holy-synod/resolution-of-the-holy -synod-of-the-orthodox-church-in-america.

———. "Statement from the Holy Synod Regarding the Resignation of Metropolitan Jonah." July 16, 2012. https://wdcoca.org/files/letters/2012 /2012-Holy-Synod-statement-Archdiocese-of-Washington.pdf.

Honore, Tony. *Ulpian: Pioneer of Human Rights*. 2nd edition. Oxford: Oxford University Press, 2002.

Hoover, Brett C. *The Shared Parish: Latinos, Anglos, and the Future of U.S. Catholicism*. New York: New York University Press, 2014.

Hopko, Thomas. *Christian Faith and Same Sex Attraction: Eastern Orthodox Reflections*. Ben Lomond, CA: Conciliar Press, 2006.

Horwitz, Morton J. "Natural Law and Natural Rights." In *Rights: Concepts and Contexts*, edited by Brian H. Bix and Horacio Spector, 3–16. London: Routledge, 2012.

"How much authority do state and local officials have during a health emergency, such as the COVID-19 pandemic?" https://www.americanbar.org/news /abanews/publications/youraba/2020/youraba-may-2020/state-local-authority -during-covid/#:~:text=While%20state%20governors%20and%20 local,will%20have%20the%20last%20word.

Hudson, Jr., David L. "Social Media" *The First Amendment Encyclopedia*. 2017. https://mtsu.edu/first-amendment/article/1561/social-media.

Humfress, Caroline. *Orthodoxy and the Courts in Late Antiquity*. Oxford: Oxford University Press, 2007.

Hunter, James Davison. *Culture Wars: The Struggle to Define America: Making Sense of the Battles over the Family, Art, Education, Law and Politics*. New York: Basic Books, 1991.

Hutson, James H. "The Emergence of the Modern Concept of a Right in America: The Contribution of Michel Villey." *The American Journal of Jurisprudence* 39 (1994): 185–224.

———. "The Emergence of the Modern Concept of a Right in America: The Contribution of Michel Villey." In *The Nature of Rights at the American Founding and Beyond,* edited by Barry Alan Shain, 25–63. Charlottesville: University of Virginia Press, 2007.

Hyland, Drew A. and John Panteleimon Manoussakis, editors. *Heidegger and the Greeks: Interpretive Essays*. Bloomington: Indiana University Press, 2006.

Iftimiu, Aurelian. "Theodoros of Alexandria performs first consecration of deaconesses." Basilica.ro. February 22, 2017. https://basilica.ro/en/patriarch-theodoros-of-alexandria-performs-first-consecration-of-deaconesses/.

Ignatieff, Michael. *The Rights Revolution (CBC Massey Lecture).* 2nd edition Toronto: House of Anansi Press, 2007.

Inazu, John D. "The Freedom of the Church (New Revised Standard Version)." *Journal of Contemporary Legal Issues* 21 (2013): 335–367.

———. *Confident Pluralism: Surviving and Thriving through Deep Difference.* Chicago: University of Chicago Press, 2016.

———. *Liberty's Refuge: The Forgotten Freedom of Assembly.* New Haven, CT: Yale University Press, 2012.

Jackson, Thomas F. *From Civil Rights to Human Rights: Martin Luther King, Jr., and the Struggle for Economic Justice.* Philadelphia: University of Pennsylvania Press, 2007.

James, David. "Subjective Freedom and Necessity in Hegel's *Philosophy of Right.*" *Theoria: A Journal of Social and Political Theory* 59, no. 131 (June, 2012): 41–63.

Jensen, Steven L. B. *The Making of International Human Rights: The 1960s, Decolonization and the Reconstruction of Global Values.* New York: Cambridge University Press, 2016.

Jillions, John A. "The *Amerikansii Pravoslavnyi Vestnik (The Russian Orthodox American Messenger)* 1917–18: In the Aftermath of Revolutions in Russia." *St. Vladimir's Theological Quarterly* 61, no. 2 (2017): 195–229.

———. "*Obergefell* v. *Hodges*: Questions for Orthodox Christians." 117–128.

———. "The Tomos of Autocephaly: Forty-Six Years Later." Orthodox Church in America. April 7, 2016. https://oca.org/news/headline-news/the-tomos-of-autocephaly-forty-six-years-later.

Josephson-Storm, Jason A. *The Myth of Disenchantment: Magic, Modernity, and the Birth of the Human Sciences.* Chicago: University of Chicago Press, 2017.

Jovcic-Sas, Nik. "The Tradition of Homophobia: Responses to Same-Sex Relationships in Serbian Orthodoxy from the Nineteenth Century to the Present Day." In *New Approaches in History and Theology to Same-Sex Love and Desire,* edited by Mark D. Chapman and Dominic Janes, 55–77. Cham, Switzerland: Palgrave MacMillan, 2018.

Joyce, Helen. *Trans: When Ideology Meets Reality.* New York: Oneworld, 2022.

Kabala, James S. *Church-State Relations in the Early American Republic, 1787–1846.* London: Pickering & Chatto, 2013.

Kalaitzidis, Pantelis. "The Discovery of Greekness and Theological Antiwesternism in the Theological Generation of the '60s." In *Turmoil in Postwar Theology: The Theology of the '60s,* edited by P. Kalaitzidis, Ath. N.

Papathansiou and Th. Abatzidis, 429–514. Athens: Indiktos Publications, 2009.

Kalkandjieva, Daniela. *The Russian Orthodox Church, 1917–1948: From Decline to Resurrection*. Oxford: Routledge, 2015.

Kalmoukos, Theodoros. "Election of Metropolitan of Chicago Canceled." *Orthodox Christian Laity*, July 13, 2017. https://ocl.org/election-metropolitan-chicago-canceled/.

Karpov, Vyacheslav, and Manfred Svensoon, eds. *Secularization, Desecularization, and Toleration: Cross-Disciplinary Challenges to a Modern Myth*. Cham, Switzerland: Palgrave MacMillan, 2020.

Karras, Valerie A. "Patristic Views on the Ontology of Gender." In *Personhood: Orthodox Christianity and the Connection between Body, Mind, and Soul*. Edited by John T. Chirban, 113–19. Westport: Bergin & Garvey, 1996.

Kattan, Assaad E. "The Ways of Polemic Literature: Vatican I in *al-Hadiyya*." *Ostkirchliche Studien* 62, no. 1 (2013): 136–142.

Kattan, Assaad E. and Fadi A. Georgi, editors. *Thinking Modernity: Towards a Reconfiguration of the Relationship between Orthodox Theology and Modern Culture*. Tripoli, Leb.: St. John of Damascus Institute of Theology University of Balamand, 2010.

Kawtharani, Wajih. "The Ottoman *Tanzimat* and the Constitution (Research Paper)" *Tabayyun* 3 (Winter, 2013): 7–22.

Kelaidis, Katherine. "The Russian Exarchate: A Eulogy." *The Wheel* 20 (Winter, 2020): 6–9.

Keleher, Serge. "Orthodox Rivalry in the Twentieth Century: Moscow versus Constantinople." *Religion, State & Society* 25, no. 2 (1997): 125–137.

Kelly, Alfred H., Winfred A. Harbison, and Herman Belz. *The American Constitution Its Origins and Development*. 6th ed. New York: W.W. Norton & Company, 1983.

Kenworthy, Scott M. *The Heart of Russia: Trinity-Sergius, Monasticism, and Society after 1825*. Washington. D.C.: Oxford University Press for Woodrow Wilson Center Press, 2010.

Kerber, Linda. "U.S. Women's History as the History of Human Rights." *Travail, genre et sociétés* 28, no. 2 (2012): 25–44. https://doi.org/10.3917/tgs.028.0025.

Keynes, Edward. *Liberty, Property, and Privacy: Toward a Jurisprudence of Substantive Due Process*. University Park, PA: Penn State University Press, 1996.

Khalaf, Samir. *Civil and Uncivil Violence in Lebanon: A History of the Internationalization of Communal Conflict*. New York: Columbia University Press, 2002.

Khodarkovsky, Michael. *Russia's 20th Century: A Journey in 100 Histories*. London: Bloomsbury Academic, 2019.

Kitroeff, Alexander. *The Greek Orthodox Church in America: A Modern History*. Ithaca: Cornell University Press, 2020.

Kivelson, Valerie A. and Ronald Grigor Suny. *Russia's Empires*. New York: Oxford University Press, 2017.

Klarman, Michael J. "*Windsor* and *Brown*: Marriage Equality and Racial Equality." *Harvard Law Review* 127, no. 1 (November, 2013): 127–160.

Klepp, Susan E. *Revolutionary Conceptions: Women, Fertility, & Family Limitation in America, 1760–1820*. Chapel Hill: University of North Carolina Press, 2009.

Kloehn, Steve. "Feud Forces Out America's Greek Orthodox Leader." *Chicago Tribune*. August 20, 1999. https://www.chicagotribune.com/news/ct-xpm -1999-08-20-9908200104-story.html.

Kluger, Richard. *Simple Justice: The History of Brown v. Board of Education and Black America's Struggle for Equality*. Revised and expanded edition. New York: Alfred A. Knopf, 2008.

Knott, Sarah. "Female Liberty? Sentimental Gallantry, Republican Womanhood, and Rights Feminism in the Age of Revolutions." *William and Mary Quarterly* 71, no. 3 (July, 2014): 425–456.

Kolko, Gabriel. *The Triumph of Conservatism: A Reinterpretation of American History*. New York: Quadrangle Books, 1967.

Konig, David. "Natural Rights, Bills of Rights, and the People's Rights in Virginian Constitutional Discourse, 1787–1791." In *The South's Role in the Creation of the Bill of Rights*, edited by Robert Haws, 33–50. Jackson: University Press of Mississippi, 1991.

———. "Regionalism and Early American Law." In *The Cambridge History of American Law, Vol 1: Early America (1580–1815)*, edited by Michael Grossberg and Christopher Tomlins, 144–177. Cambridge: Cambridge University Press, 2008.

———. "Thomas Jefferson and the Search for an American Natural Law Tradition." Paper presented at the American Society of Legal History, Princeton University, Princeton, NJ, 2000.

Koppelman, Andrew. "Gay Rights, Religious Accommodations, and the Purposes of Antidiscrimination Law." *Southern California Law Review* 88, no. 3 (March, 2015): 619–659.

Kornblatt, Judith Deutsch and Richard F. Gustafson. *Russian Religious Thought*. Madison: The University of Wisconsin Press, 1996.

Koskenniemi, Martii. "Rights, History, Critique." In *Human Rights: Moral or Political?*, edited by Adam Etison, 41–60. Oxford: Oxford University Press, 2018.

Kostryukov, Andrey. "Granting of Autocephaly to Orthodox Church in America in the Light of the Documents of Church Archives." *St. Tikhons*

University Review 70, no. 3 (June 2016): 93–103. https://www.researchgate
.net/publication/304583171.

Krauth, Charles Porterfield. *The Conservative Reformation and Its Theology: As
Represented in the Augsburg Confession, and in the History and Literature of the
Evangelical Lutheran Church.* Philadelphia: J.B. Lippincott Company, 1888.

Krindatch, Alexei D. *The Orthodox Church Today: A National Study of
Parishioners and the Realities of Orthodox Parish Life in the USA.* Berkley,
CA: Patriarch Athenagoras Orthodox Institute, 2010. http://www
.hartfordinstitute.org/research/OrthChurchFullReport.pdf.

Krivonosov, Alexander. "When East Meets West: A Landscape of Familiar
Strangers—Missionary Alaska, 1794–1898." PhD dissertation, The Pennsylvania State University, 2008.

Kulikowski, Michael. "The *Notitia Dignitatum* as a Historical Source." *Historia*
49, no. 3 (2000): 358–377.

Kupari, Helena and Elina Vuola, "Introduction." In *Orthodox Christianity and
Gender: Dynamics of Tradition, Culture and Lived Practice*, edited by Helena
Kupari and Elina Vuola, 1–21. London and New York: Routledge, 2020.

L'Huillier, Peter. *The Church of the Ancient Councils: The Disciplinary Work of
the First Four Ecumenical Councils.* Crestwood, NY: St. Vladimir's Seminary
Press, 1996.

La Bat, Sean J. "The Holy Catholic and Apostolic Church in North America,
1927–1934, A Case Study in North American Missions." M.Div. Thesis,
St. Vladimir's Orthodox Theological Seminary, 1995.

Lambrianidis, Elpidophoros. "Greek Orthodoxy, the Ecumenical Patriarchate,
and the Church in the USA." *St. Vladimir's Theological Quarterly* 54, nos.
3–4 (2010): 421–440.

Larin, Vassa. T*he Byzantine Hierarchical Divine Liturgy in Arsenij Suxanov's
Proskinitarij.* Rome, Italy: Pontificio Instituto Orientalem Orientalia
Christiana Analecta 286, 2010.

———. "The Hierarchal Liturgy in Late Byzantium and After: Toward a
Liturgical Ecclesiology." *St. Vladimir's Theological Quarterly* 55, no. 1 (2011):
5–26.

Larson, John L. *Laid Waste! The Culture of Exploitation in Early America.*
Philadelphia: University of Pennsylvania Press, 2020.

———. *The Market Revolution in America: Liberty, Ambition, and the Eclipse of
the Common Good.* New York: Cambridge University Press, 2011.

Lasch, Christopher. *The True and Only Heaven: Progress and its Critics.* New York:
Norton, 1991.

Lauren, Paul Gordon. "A Human Rights Lens on U.S. History: Human Rights
at Home and Human Rights Abroad." In *Bringing Human Rights Home: A
History of Human Rights in the United States (Abridged Edition)*, edited by

Cynthia Soohoo, Catherine Albisa, and Martha F. Davis, 7–39. Philadelphia: University of Pennsylvania Press, 2009.

Laycock, Douglas. *Religious Liberty.* 5 vols. Grand Rapids, MI: W.B. Eerdmans, 2010–2018.

Leber, George J. *The History of the Order of AHEPA.* Washington, D.C.: The Order of AHEPA, 1972.

Lee, Justin. "The Great Debate: Justin's View." *Geeky Justin.* 2003. Accessed April 6, 2021. http://geekyjustin.com/great-debate/.

Leff, Arthur Allen. "Unspeakable Ethics, Unnatural Law." *Duke Law Journal* 6 (1979): 1229–1249.

Lehmann, Hartmut. "Die Entdeckung Luthers im Amerika des frühen 19. Jahrhunderts." In *Luthergedächtnis 1817 bis 2017,* Hartmut Lehmann, 78–93. Göttingen: Vandenhoeck Ruprecht, 2012.

———. "Die Lutherjubiläen 1883 und 1917 in Amerika." In *Luthergedächtnis 1817 bis 2017,* Hartmut Lehmann, 35–43. Göttingen: Vandenhoeck Ruprecht, 2012.

LeMasters, Philip. "Guroian and Papanikolaou: Reflections on Orthodoxy, Western Democracy, and Postmodernity." Paper presented at the annual meeting of the Orthodox Theological Society in America, Holy Cross Greek Orthodox School of Theology, Brookline, MA, October 2014.

———. Review of *The Mystical as Political: Democracy and Non-Radical Orthodoxy,* by Papanikolaou Guroian. *St. Vladimir's Theological Quarterly* 58, no. 1 (2014): 235–39.

Leo XIII, Pope. *"In Plurimis."* Papal Encyclicals Online. May 5, 1888. www.papalencyclicals.net/Leo13/l13abl.htm.

Levine, Joseph. *Purple Haze: The Puzzle of Consciousness.* Oxford: Oxford University Press, 2011.

Lewis, Andrew. *The Rights Turn in Conservative Christian Politics: How Abortion Transformed the Culture Wars.* Cambridge: Cambridge University Press, 2017.

Lewis, Anthony. *Gideon's Trumpet: How One Man, a Poor Prisoner, Took His Case to the Supreme Court and Changed the Law of the United States.* New York: Vintage Books, 1964.

Lewis, Hope. "'New' Human Rights? U.S. Ambivalence toward the International Economic and Social Rights Framework." In *Bringing Human Rights Home: A History of Human Rights in the United States (Abridged Edition),* edited by Cynthia Soohoo, Catherine Albisa, and Martha F. Davis, 100–141. Philadelphia: University of Pennsylvania Press, 2009.

Library of Congress Archives Division. *Charles Malik Papers, Correspondence.* Boxes 1–75.

Library of Congress. *The Treaty Concerning the Cession of the Russian Possessions in North America by his Majesty the Emperor of all the Russias to the United*

States of America. Washington, D.C.: March 30, 1867. https://memory.loc
.gov/cgi-bin/ampage?collId=llsl&fileName=015/llsl015.db&recNum=572.

Livanos, Christopher. *Greek Tradition and Latin Influence in the Work of George
Scholarios: 'Alone against All of Europe'.* Piscataway, NJ: Gorgias Press, 2006.

Lively, Kit. "Faculty Firings Throw a Greek Orthodox College Into Turmoil."
Chronicle of Higher Education, July 18, 1997.

Liveris, Leonie B. *Ancient Taboos and Gender Prejudice: Challenges for Orthodox
Women and the Church.* New York: Ashgate, 2005.

Louth, Andrew. *Modern Orthodox Thinkers: From the Philokalia to the Present.*
Downers Grove, IL: Inter-Varsity Press, 2015.

Lowrie, Donald A. and William C. Fletcher. "Krushchev's Religious Policy,
1959–1964." In *Aspects of Religion in the Soviet Union, 1917–67,* edited by
Richard H. Marshall, Jr., 132–137. Chicago: University of Chicago Press,
1971.

Lucas, Joseph S. "Conquering the Passions: Indians, Europeans, and the Idea of
Cultural Change in Early American Social Thought, 1580–1830." PhD
dissertation, Pennsylvania State University, 1999.

Lupu, Ira C. and Robert W. Tuttle. *Secular Government, Religious People.*
Grand Rapids, MI: William B. Eerdmans Publishing Company, 2014.

MacFarquhar, Neil. "Ukrainian Orthodox Church Breaks with Moscow Over
War." https://www.nytimes.com/2022/05/28/world/europe/ukraine
-orthodox-church-moscow.html.

MacIntyre, Alasdair. *After Virtue: A Study in Moral Theory.* Notre Dame, IN:
University of Notre Dame Press, 1984.

Maclean, Nancy. *Behind the Mask of Chivalry: The Making of the Second Ku Klux
Klan.* New York: Oxford University Press, 1994.

MacPherson, C.B. *The Political Theory of Possessive Individualism.* Oxford:
Oxford University Press, 1962.

Magocsi, Paul Robert. *A History of Ukraine: The Land and Its Peoples* 2nd rev. ed.
(Toronto: University of Toronto Press, 2010).

Maican, Petre. "Overcoming Exclusion in Eastern Orthodoxy: Human Dignity
and Disability from a Christological Perspective." *Studies in Christian Ethics*
34, no. 4 (June, 2019): 1–14. https://doi.org/10.1177/0953946819859512.

Mailer, Gideon. *John Witherspoon's American Revolution.* Chapel Hill:
University of North Carolina Press, 2017.

Makrides, Vasilios N., Jennifer Wasmuth, and Stefan Kube, eds. *Christentum
und Menschenrechte in Europa: Perspektiven und Debatten in Ost und West.*
Frankfurt-am-Main: Peter Lang, 2016.

Malik, Charles. "The Near East." In *The Prospects of Christianity throughout the
World,* edited by M. Searle Bates and Wilhelm Pauck, 83–104. New York:
Charles Scribner's Sons, 1964.

————. *A Christian Critique of the University.* Downers Grove, IL: InterVarsity Press, 1982.

————. *Christ and Crisis.* Grand Rapids, MI: William B. Eerdmans Publishing Co., 1962.

————. *Man in the Struggle for Peace.* New York: Harper and Rowe, 1963.

————. *The Wonder of Being.* Waco, TX: Word Books, 1974.

Malik, Kenan. *Man, Beast and Zombie: What Science Can and Cannot Tell Us About Human Nature.* New Brunswick, NJ: Rutgers University Press, 2002.

Mancini, Susanna and Michel Rosenfeld, eds. *The Conscience Wars: Rethinking the Balance between Religion, Identity, and Equality.* Cambridge: Cambridge University Press, 2018.

Mancini, Susanna and Kristina Stoeckl. "Transatlantic Conversations: The Emergence of Society-Protective Antiabortion Arguments in the United States, Europe, and Russia." 220–257.

Marsden, George M. *The Evangelical Mind and the New School Presbyterian Experience: A Case Study of Thought and Theology in Nineteenth-Century America.* New Haven: Yale University Press, 1970; Eugene, OR: Wipf and tock Publishers, 2003. Page references are to the Wipf and Stock edition.

————. *The Twilight of the American Enlightenment: The 1950s and the Crisis of Liberal Belief.* New York: Basic Books, 2014.

Marsh, Christopher and Daniel Payne. "Religiosity, Tolerance and Respect for Human Rights in the Orthodox World." In *Orthodox Christianity and Human Rights*, edited by Alfons Brüning and Evert van der Zweerde, 201–214. Leuven: Peeters, 2012.

Mashaw, Jerry L. *Creating the Administrative Constitution: The Lost One Hundred Years of Administrative Law.* New Haven, CT: Yale University Press, 2012.

Matthews, John F. *Laying Down the Law: A Study of the Theodosian Code.* New Haven: Yale University Press, 2000.

Mattox, Mickey L. and A.G. Roeber. *Changing Churches: An Orthodox, Catholic, and Lutheran Theological Conversation.* Grand Rapids, MI: William B. Eerdmans Publishing Company, 2012.

Mautner, Thomas. "How Rights Became 'Subjective.'" *Ratio Juris* 26, no. 1 (March 2013): 111–132.

McCall-Smith, Kasey, Andrea Birdsall, and Elisenda Casanas Adam, eds. *Human Rights in Times of Transition: Liberal Democracies and Challenges of National Security* Cheltenham, UK: Edward Elgar Publishing, 2020.

McConnell, Michael W. "Accommodation of Religion." *The Supreme Court Review* 1985 (1985): 1–59.

———. "On Religion, the Supreme Court Protects the Right to Be Different." *New York Times.* July 9, 2020. https://www.nytimes.com/2020/07/09 /opinion/supreme-court-religion.html.

McCormack, John. "A Liberal Law Professor Explains Why the Equality Act Would 'Crush' Religious Dissenters." *National Review.* May 17, 2019. https://www.nationalreview.com/2019/05/law-professor-explains-why-the -equality-act-would-crush-religious-dissenters.

McCrudden, Christopher. "Human Dignity and Judicial Interpretation of Human Rights. *The European Journal of International Law* 19, no. 4 (2008): 655–724

———. "In Pursuit of Human Dignity: An Introduction to Current Debates." In *Understanding Human Dignity*, edited by Christopher McCrudden, 1–58. Oxford: Oxford University Press/The British Academy, 2013.

McElwee, Joshua J. "Francis institutes commission to study female deacons, appointing gender-balanced membership." National Catholic Reporter. August 2, 2016. https://www.ncronline.org/news/vatican/francis-institutes -commission-study-female-deacons-appointing-gender-balanced.

McGifferet, Michael, ed. "Constructing Race: Differentiating Peoples in the Early Modern World." Special issue, *The William and Mary Quarterly* 3rd Ser., 54, no. 1 (January 1997).

McGuckin, John A. *The Ascent of Christian Law: Patristic and Byzantine Formulations of a New Civilization.* Yonkers, NY: St. Vladimir's Seminary Press, 2012.

———. *The Path of Christianity: The First Thousand Years.* Downer's Grove, IL: IVP Press, 2017.

———. *The Eastern Orthodox Church: A New History.* New Haven, CT: Yale University Press, 2020.

McLoughlin, William G. *Cherokees and Missionaries, 1789–1839.* New Haven, CT: Yale University Press, 1984.

———. *Revivals, Awakenings, and Reform: An Essay on Religion and Social Change in America, 1607–1977.* Chicago: University of Chicago Press, 1978.

McMurtrie, Beth. "Hellenic College Reinstates 4 Professors in Wake of Archbishop's Resignation." *Chronicle of Higher Education.* September 10, 1999.

Melnick, R. Shep. *The Transformation of Title IX: Regulating Gender Equality in Education.* Washington, D.C.: Brookings Institution Press, 2018.

Merched, Aksam J. "People of Bterram: Dr. Charles Malek." Last modified April 10, 2012. http://people.bterram.com/CharlesMalek.

Merritt, Jane T. *At the Crossroads: Indians and Empires on a Mid-Atlantic Frontier, 1700–1763.* Chapel Hill: The Omohundro Institute of Early

American History and Culture and University of North Carolina Press, 2003.

Messer, Peter C. *Stories of Independence: Identity, Ideology, and History in Eighteenth-Century America*. DeKalb: Northern Illinois University Press, 2005.

Meyendorff, John. *Living Tradition: Orthodox Witness in the Contemporary World*. Crestwood, NY: St. Vladimir's Seminary Press, 1978.

Meyendorff, Paul. "A Response to Archimandrite Elpidophoros Lambriniadis." *St. Vladimir's Theological Quarterly* 54, nos. 3–4 (2010): 441–448.

———. "Fr. John Meyendorff and the Autocephaly of the Orthodox Church in America." *St. Vladimir's Theological Quarterly* 56, no. 3 (2012): 335–352. https://churchmotherofgod.org/salvation-history/new-life-church-history /6308-fr-john-meyendorff-and-the-autocephaly-of-the-oca.html.

Michalopoulos, George C. and Herb Ham. *The American Orthodox Church: A History of Its Beginnings*. Salisbury, MA: Regina Orthodox Press, 2003.

Milbank, John. *Theology & Social Theory: Beyond Secular Reason*. 2nd edition. Maiden, MA: Blackwell Publishing, 2006.

"Minutes of the General Assembly of the XXVI Annual Convention of the Antiochian Orthodox Christian Archdiocese of New York and All North America" and "The Metropolitan's Charge." *The Word Magazine* 39, no. 9 (November, 1971): 3–8.

Mitscherlich, Alexander. *Society Without Father: a Contribution to Social Psychology*. New York: Harper Perennial, 1992.

Moore, H.J. "Antinomism in Twentieth-Century Philosophy: The Case of Pavel Florensky." *Studies in East European Thought* 73 (2021): 53–76. https://doi .org/10.1007/s11212-020-09378-y.

Morris, Stephen. *'When Brothers Dwell in Unity': Byzantine Christianity and Homosexuality*. Jefferson, NC: McFarland & Company, 2016.

Morsink, Johannes. *The Universal Declaration of Human Rights: Origins, Drafting, and Intent*. Philadelphia: University of Pennsylvania Press, 1999.

Moschos, Dimitrios. "The Churches of the East and the Enlightenment." In *The Oxford Handbook to Early Modern Theology,* edited by Ulrich Lehner, Richard Muller, and A.G. Roeber, 499–516. Oxford: Oxford University Press, 2016.

Moskos, Peter C. and Charles C. Moskos. *Greek Americans: Struggle and Success*. 3rd ed. Cambridge, MA: Harvard University Press, 1995.

Movsesian, Mark L. "Of Human Dignities." *Notre Dame Law Review* 91, no. 4 (2016): 1517–1551.

———. "Religious Rights." Review of *Christian Human Rights*, by Samuel Moyn. *First Things*. January, 2016. https://firstthings.com/article/2016/01 /religious-rights.

Moyn, Samuel. *Christian Human Rights*. Philadelphia: University of Pennsylvania Press, 2015.

Murphy, Teresa Anne. *Citizenship and the Origins of Women's History in the United States*. Philadelphia: University of Pennsylvania Press, 2013.

Murray, Melissa. "Accommodating Nonmarriage." In "Religious Accommodation in the Age of Civil Rights Symposium," special issue, *Southern California Law Review* 88, no. 3 (March, 2015): 661–702.

Murrin, John M. and A.G. Roeber. "Trial by Jury: The Virginia Paradox." In *The Bill of Rights: A Lively Heritage*, edited by Jon Kukla, 109–130. Richmond: The Virginia State Library, 1987.

Namee, Matthew. "Ecumenical Patriarch Opposes American Slavery in 1862." Orthodox History. April 27, 2015. https://orthodoxhistory.org/2015/04/27 /ecumenical-patriarch-opposes-american-slavery-in-1862/.

———. "The Dionisije Conundrum and why Deference Doesn't Work." Orthodox History. Orthodox History. June 14, 2011. https://orthodoxhistory .org/2011/06/14/the-dionisije-conundrum-and-why-deference-doesnt-work/.

Nasr, Constantine. *Antony Bashir: Metropolitan & Missionary*. Yonkers, NY: St. Vladimir's Seminary Press, 2012.

Nasrallah, Tony E. "A Lebanese Role in the UN: Charles Malik." In *The Quest for Peace: A Decade of Politics in the Middle East; Proceedings of Selected Conferences and Papers 2006–2016*, edited by Georges Yahchouchi, 93–102. Kaslik, Lebanon: Holy Spirit University of Kaslik Press, 2016.

Neary, Timothy B. *Crossing Parish Boundaries: Race, Sports, and Catholic Youth in Chicago, 1914–1954*. Chicago: University of Chicago Press, 2016.

Neely, Mark. *Lincoln and the Triumph of the Nation: Constitutional Conflict in the American Civil War*. Chapel Hill: University of North Carolina Press, 2011.

Nejaime, Douglas and Reva B. Siegel. "Conscience Wars: Complicity-Based Conscience Claims in Religion and Politics." *Yale Law Journal* 124, no. 7 (May, 2015): 2516–2591.

———. "Conscience Wars in Transnational Perspective: Religious Liberty, Third-Party Harm, and Pluralism." In *The Conscience Wars: Rethinking the Balance Between Religion, Identity, and Equality*. Edited by Susanna Mancini and Michel Rosenfeld, 187–219. Cambridge. Cambridge University Press, 2018.

Newman, Jay Scott. "The End of the Imperial Episcopate." *First Things*. August 20, 2018. https://www.firstthings.com/web-exclusives/2018/08/the -end-of-the-imperial-episcopate.

Niarchos, Sophia A. "Patriarchate-Granted Charter and New Regulations Among Issues at Clergy-Laity Congress." *Greek News*, July 26, 2004.

Nicholas of Cusa. *The Catholic Concordance*. Edited by Paul E. Sigmund. Cambridge: Cambridge University Press, 2003.

Nichols, O.P., Aidan. *Rome and the Eastern Churches: A Study in Schism.* Collegeville, MN: The Liturgical Press, 1992.

Niebuhr, H. Richard. *Christ and Culture.* New York: Harper and Row, 1951.

Niederberger, Andreas. "Are Human Rights Moral Rights?" In *Human Rights, Human Dignity, and Cosmopolitan Ideals: Essays on Critical Theory and Human Rights,* edited by Matthias Lutz-Bachmann and Amos Nascimento, 75–92. Burlington, VT: Ashgate, 2014.

Noll, Mark A. "Reconsidering Christendom." In *The Future of Christian Learning: An Evangelical and Catholic Dialogue,* edited by Thomas Albert Howard, 23–70. Grand Rapids, MI: Brazos Press, 2008.

———. *A History of Christianity in the United States and Canada.* Grand Rapids, MI: William B. Eerdmans Publishing Company, 1992.

———. *America's God: From Jonathan Edwards to Abraham Lincoln.* New York: Oxford University Press, 2002.

———. *God and Race in American Politics.* Princeton, NJ: Princeton University Press, 2008.

———. *The Civil War as a Theological Crisis.* Chapel Hill: University of North Carolina Press, 2006.

———. *The Scandal of the Evangelical Mind.* Grand Rapids, MI: William B. Eerdmans, 1994.

Nolt, Steven M. *Foreigners in Their Own Land: Pennsylvania Germans in the Early Republic.* University Park: The Pennsylvania State University Press, 2002.

Noonan, Jr., John T. *A Church That Can and Cannot Change: The Development of Catholic Moral Teaching.* Notre Dame, IN: University of Notre Dame Press, 2005.

Novak, Michael. "Public Arguments: Murray After 26 Years." *Crisis Magazine* (May 1, 1993). https://www.crisismagazine.com/1993/public-arguments-murray-after-26-years.

O'Donovan, Oliver. *Church in Crisis: The Gay Controversy and the Anglican Communion.* Eugene, OR: Cascade Books, 2008.

Oakes, James. *The Crooked Path to Abolition: Abraham Lincoln and the Antislavery Constitution.* New York: W.W. Norton & Co., 2020.

Oakley, Francis. "The Conciliar Heritage and the Politics of Oblivion." In *The Church, the Councils, & Reform: The Legacy of the Fifteenth Century,* edited by Gerald Christianson, Thomas M. Izbicki, and Christopher M. Bellitto, 82–97. Washington, D.C.: The Catholic University of America Press, 2008.

———. "Throne & Altar: *Liberty in the Things of God.*" *Commonweal Magazine* 31 (July 2019). http://commonwealmagazine.org/throne-altar.

Oghlukian, Abel. *The Deaconess in the Armenian Church: A Brief Survey.* New Rochelle, NY: St. Nersess Armenian Seminary, 1994.

Ogilvie, Brian W. "Natural History, Ethics, and Physico-Theology." In *"Historia": Empiricism and Erudition in Early Modern Europe*, edited by Gianna Pomata and Nancy G. Sirensi, 75–103. Cambridge: MIT Press, 2015.

"Ohio." *Protestantische Kirchenzeitung für das evangelische Deutschland* 10 Nr 32 (Aug. 10, 1861): 763–4

Okrent, Daniel. *Last Call: The Rise and Fall of Prohibition*. New York: Scribner, 2010.

Oleksa, Michael, ed. *Alaskan Missionary Spirituality*. New York: Paulist Press, 1987.

———. *Orthodox Alaska: A Theology of Mission*. Crestwood, NY: St. Vladimir's Seminary Press, 1992.

"An Open Letter to the Hierarchy of ROCOR." 2006. https://www .rocorstudies.org/2021/02/22/an-open-letter-to-the-hierarchy-of-rocor/.

"Opinions from 2020." *Justia US Supreme Court Center*. Accessed April 7, 2021, https://supreme.justia.com/cases/federal/us/year/2020.html.

Orfanos, Spyros D., ed. *Reading Greek America: Studies in the Experience of Greeks in the United States*. New York: Pella Publishing Company, 2002.

Fygetakis, Leah M. "Greek American Lesbians: Identity Odysseys of Honorable Good Girls." 291–325.

Georgakas, Dan. "Greek American Radicalism: The Twentieth Century." 63–84.

Moskos, Jr., Charles C. "The Greek Orthodox Church in America." 85–97.

Papanikolas, Helen. "Greek Immigrant Women in the Intermountain West." 99–114.

Orthodox Church in America. "His Grace Bishop Jonah Addresses Questions and Concerns." November 11, 2008. https://oca.org/holy-synod/statements /metropolitan-jonah/jonah-15aac-qna.

———. "The Statute of the Orthodox Church in America: Article XV, Ecclesiastical Courts." Accessed July 25, 2016. https://oca.org/statute/article -xv.

Owens, Kenneth N. and Alexander Yu. Petrov. *Empire Maker: Aleksander Baranov and Russian Colonial Expansion into Alaska and Northern California*. Seattle: University of Washington Press, 2017.

Pabst, Adrian. *Metaphysics: The Creation of Hierarchy*. Grand Rapids, MI: William B. Eerdmans Publishing Co., 2012.

Palassis, Fr. Neketas S. *A History of the Russian Church Abroad and The Events Leading to the American Metropolia's Autocephaly*. Brookline, MA: Holy Transfiguration Monastery, 1972.

Panchenko, Constantine A. *Arab Orthodox Christians Under the Ottomans 1516–1831*. Translated by Brittany Pheiffer Noble and Samuel Noble. Jordanville, NY: Holy Trinity Seminary Press, 2016.

Papanikolaou, Aristotle and George Demacopoulos, eds. *Christianity, Democracy, and the Shadow of Constantine*. New York: Fordham University Press, 2017.

Papanikolaou, Aristotle. *The Mystical as Political: Democracy and Non-Radical Orthodoxy*. Notre Dame, IN: University of Notre Dame Press, 2012.

———. "A Theology of Sex." In *Orthodox Tradition and Human Sexuality*, edited by Thomas Arentzen, Ashley Purpura, Aristotle Papanikolaou. New York: Fordham University Press, 2022.

"Patriarch Alexander III (Tahan)." *Canadian Orthodox History Project*, February 27, 2021. https://orthodoxcanada.ca/Patriarch_Alexander_III _(Tahan).

Patriarchate of Moscow. *The Basis of the Social Concept of the Russian Orthodox Church*. Metropolitan Kirill of Smolensk and Kaliningrad et al. Moscow: Patriarchate of Moscow, 2001. http://mospatusa.com/files/the-basis-of-the -social-concept.pdf.

Patsavos, Lewis J. *A Noble Task: Entry into the Clergy in the First Five Centuries*. Translated by Norman Russell. Brookline, MA: Holy Cross Orthodox Press, 2007.

———. "The Primacy of the See of Constantinople in Theory and Practice." *Panorthodox Synod*. September 13, 2018. https://panorthodoxcemes.blogspot .com/2018/09/the-primacy-of-see-of-constantinople-in.html.

Paul, Michael C. "Episcopal Election in Novgorod, Russia 1156–1478." *Church History* 72, no. 2 (June, 2003): 251–275.

Pennington, Kenneth. ""Review Essay: The History of Rights in Western Thought." *Emory Law Journal* 47 (1998): 237–252.

Pentin, Edward. "Widespread Orthodox Church Backlash Unleased Against Russia's Aggression in Ukraine," *National Catholic Register* (March 11, 2022). https://www.ncregister.com/news/widespread-orthodox-church-backlash -unleashed-against-russia-s-aggression-in-ukraine.

Pentiuc, Eugen J. *The Old Testament in Eastern Orthodox Tradition*. New York: Oxford University Press, 2014.

Peppard, Michael. *The World's Oldest Church: Bible, Art, and Ritual at Dura-Europos, Syria*. New Haven, CT: Yale University Press, 2016.

Perman, Michael. *Struggle for Mastery: Disenfranchisement in the South, 1888–1908*. Chapel Hill: University of North Carolina Press, 2001.

Perry, Michael J. *A Global Political Morality: Human Rights, Democracy, and Constitutionalism*. Cambridge: Cambridge University Press, 2017.

———. *Human Rights in the Constitutional Law of the United States*. New York: Cambridge University Press, 2013.

———. *Toward a Theory of Human Rights: Religion, Law, Courts*. New York: Cambridge University Press, 2007.

Petra, Basilio. "Christos Yannaras and the Idea of 'Dysis.'" In *Orthodox Constructions of the West,* edited by George E. Demacopoulos and Aristotle Papanikolaou, 161–180. New York: Fordham University Press, 2013.

Pew Research Center: Religion & Public Life. "America's Changing Religious Landscape." May 12, 2015. www.pewforum.org/2015/05/12/americas -changing-religious-landscape.

Pfau, Thomas. "History without Hermeneutics: Brad Gregory's Unintended Modernity." *The Immanent Frame: Secularism, Religion and the Public Sphere.* November 6, 2013. https://tif.ssrc.org/2013/11/06/history-without -hermeneutics-brad-gregorys-unintended-modernity/.

Phares, Walīd. *Lebanese Christian Nationalism: The Rise & Fall of an Ethnic Resistance.* Boulder, CO: Lynne Rienner Publishers, 1995.

Pietersma, Albert and Benjamin G. Wright, editors. *A New English Translation of the Septuagint and the other Greek Translations traditionally included under that Title.* Oxford: Oxford University Press, 2007.

Piketty, Thomas. *Capital in the Twenty-First Century.* Cambridge, MA: Harvard University Press, 2014.

Plested, Marcus. "Between Rigorism and Relativism: The Givenness of Tradition," Public Orthodoxy May 25, 2017; https://publicorthodoxy.org /2017/05/25/between-rigorism-and-relativism.

———. *Orthodox Readings of Aquinas.* Oxford: Oxford University Press, 2012.

Pocock, J.G. A. *The Ancient Constitution and the Feudal Law: a Study of English Historical Thought in the Seventeenth Century.* Cambridge: Cambridge University Press, 1987.

Porter, Jean. *Ministers of the Law: A Natural Law Theory of Legal Authority.* Grand Rapids, MI: William B. Eerdmans Publishing Company, 2010.

Porter, Roy. *Flesh in the Age of Reason: The Modern Foundations of Body and Soul.* New York: W.W. Norton and Co., 2003.

Pospielovsky, Dimitry. *The Russian Church under the Soviet Regime 1917–1982.* 2 vols. Crestwood, NY: St. Vladimir Seminary Press, 1984.

Pravoslavyi amerikanskii viestnik [Russian Orthodox American Messenger]

December, 1896, 111–112.
February 13, 1897, 196; 204–05.
February 27, 1897, 242–246.
May 15, 1897, 367.
August, 1897, 395–6.
July 6, 1922
July 19, 1922
January 1, 1924
April 2, 1924

Post, Robert. "The Politics of Religion Democracy and *The Conscience Wars*." In *The Conscience Wars: Rethinking the Balance between Religion, Identity, and Equality*. Edited by Susanna Mancini and Michel Rosenfeld, 473–484. Cambridge: Cambridge University Press, 2018.

Presbyterian Historical Society. *Sheldon Jackson Papers, 1855–1909 (RG 239) Series I: Correspondence, 1856–1908*. Philadelphia.

Prevelakis, Nicholas. "Eastern Christian Conceptions of Personhood and their Political Significance." In *Personhood in the Byzantine Christian Tradition: Early, Medieval, and Modern Perspectives*, edited by Alexis Torrance and Symeon Paschalidis, 173–181. London: Routledge, 2018.

Primus, Richard. "An Introduction to the Nature of American Rights." In *The Nature of Rights at the American Founding and Beyond*, edited by Barry Alan Shain, 15–24. Charlottesville: University of Virginia Press, 2007.

Prodromou, Elizabeth. "Christianity and Democracy: The Ambivalent Orthodox." *Journal of Democracy* 15, no. 2 (2004): 62–75.

———. "Orthodox Christianity and Pluralism: Moving Beyond Ambivalence?" In *The Orthodox Churches in a Pluralistic World: An Ecumenical Conversation*, edited by Emmanuel Clapsis, 22–46. Geneva: WCC Publications, 2004 / Brookline, MA: Holy Cross Orthodox Press, 2004.

———. "Human Rights and the Orthodox Church in a Global World." *Theology and the Political: Theo-Political Reflections on Contemporary Politics in Ecumenical Conversation*, edited by Alexei Bodrov and Stephen M. Garrett, 51–69. Leiden: Brill, 2020.

"Proposed Limits on Public Health Authority: Dangerous for Public Health." The Network for Public Health Law (National Association of County & City Health Officials. https://www.naccho.org/uploads/downloadable -resources/Proposed-Limits-on-Public-Health-Authority-Dangerous-for -Public-Health-final-5.24.21pm.pdf.

Prucha, Francis Paul. *American Indian Policy in Crisis: Christian Reformers and the Indian, 1865–1900*. Norman: University of Oklahoma Press, 1975.

———. *The Churches and the Indian Schools, 1888–1912*. Lincoln: University of Nebraska Press, 1979.

———. *The Great Father: The United States Government and the American Indian*. 2 vols. Lincoln: University of Nebraska Press, 1984.

Puhalo, Lazar. *On the Neurobiology of Sin*. Dewdney, B.C.: The Monastery of All Saints of North America, 2016.

Purvis, Zachary. "Transatlantic Textbooks: Karl Hagenbach, Shared Interests, and German Academic Theology in Nineteenth-Century America." *Church History* 83, no. 3 (September, 2014): 650–683.

Quammen, David. *The Tangled Tree: A Radical New History of Life*. New York: Simon & Schuster, 2018.

Rabb, Theodore K. *The Struggle for Stability in Early Modern Europe*. New York: Oxford University Press, 1976.

Raboteau, Albert Jordy. "In the World, not of the World, for the Sake of the World: Orthodoxy and American Culture." *Orthodoxy in America Lecture Series*. New York: Fordham University Office of Development and Human Relations, 2007. https://publicorthodoxy.org/wp-content/uploads/2017/01/raboteau2006.pdf.

Rakove, Jack N. *Beyond Belief, Beyond Conscience: The Radical Significance of the Free Exercise of Religion*. New York: Oxford University Press, 2020.

Rapp, Claudia. *Holy Bishops in Late Antiquity: The Nature of Christian Leadership in an Age of Transition*. Berkeley: University of California Press, 2003.

Rauch, Jonathan. "The Constitution of Knowledge." *National Affairs* 37 (Fall, 2018). https://nationalaffairs.com/publications/detail/the-constitution-of-knowledge.

———. *The Constitution of Knowledge: A Defense of Truth*. New York: Brookings Institution Press, 2021.

Rawson, Albert, et al. *What the World Believes, The False and the True, embracing the People of All Races and Nations, their Peculiar Teachings, Rites, Ceremonies, from the Earliest Pagan Times to the Present, to which is added an Account of What the World Believes Today, by Countries*. New York: Gay Brothers & Co., 1884.

Regan, Ethna. *Theology and the Boundary Discourse of Human Rights*. Washington, D.C.: Georgetown University Press, 2010.

Reid, Jr., Charles J. "Thirteenth-Century Canon Law and Rights: The Word *ius* and Its Range of Subjective Meanings." *Studia canonica* 30 (1996): 295–342.

Rentel, Alexander. "Autocephaly with a Canonical Perspective," (lecture, St. Tikhon's Seminary, 29 October, 2019). https://www.stots.edu/news_191105_2.

———. "The Relationship between Bishops, Synods, and the Metropolitan-Bishop in the Orthodox Canonical Tradition." In *Power and Authority in Eastern Christian Tradition*, edited by John A. McGuckin and F. K. Soumakis, 83–90. New York: Theotokos Press, 2011.

Retter, Mark. "The Road Not Taken: On MacIntyre's Human Rights Scepticism." *American Journal of Jurisprudence* 63, no. 2 (December, 2018): 189–219.

Riccardi-Swartz, Sarah. *Between Heaven and Russia: Religious Conversion and Political Apostasy in Appalachia*. New York: Fordham University Press, 2022.

Rich, Bryce E. *Gender Essentialism and Orthodoxy: Beyond Male and Female*. New York: Fordham University Press, 2022.

Robinson, Jonathan. *William of Ockham's Early Theory of Property Rights in Context*. Leiden: Brill, 2013.

Rode, Christian. *Zugänge zum Selbst: Innere Erfahrung in spätmittelalter und früher Neuzeit*. Münster: Aschendorff Verlag, 2016.

Rodes, Jr., Robert E. *Law and Modernization in the Church of England: Charles II to the Welfare State*. Notre Dame: The University of Notre Dame Press, 1991.

Rodopoulos, Panteleimon. *An Overview of Orthodox Canon Law*. Rollinsford, NH: Orthodox Research Institutie, 2007.

Roeber, A. G. "'What the Law Requires Is Written on Their Hearts': Noachic and Natural Law among German-Speakers in Early Modern North America." *William and Mary Quarterly* 3rd Series 58, no. 4 (October, 2001): 883–912.

————. "Das Problem der Zwei-Reiche-Lehre in den USA." In *Angewandtes Luthertum? Die Zwei-Reiche-Lehre als theologische Konstruktion in den politischen Kontexten des 20. Jhts.*, edited by Hans Otte and J. Kampmann, 348–64. Gütersloh: Gütersloher Verlagshaus, 2017.

————. "Orthodox Christians, Human Rights and the Dignity of the Person: Reflections on Charles Malik (1907–1987)." *Journal of Eastern Christian Studies* 70, nos. 3–4 (2018): 285–306.

————. "Orthodox Theological Influences on Early Modern Western Theologies." In *The Oxford Handbook to Early Modern Theology*, edited by Ulrich Lehner, Richard Muller, and A.G. Roeber, 517–530. Oxford: Oxford University Press, 2015.

————. "Review of *Christentum und Menschenrechte in Europa: Perspektiven und Debatten in Ost und West*." *Theologische Revue* 112, no. 6 (December, 2016): 502–04.

————. "The Limited Horizons of Whig Religious Rights." In *The Nature of Rights at the American Founding and Beyond*, edited by Barry Alan Shain, 198–229. Charlottesville: University of Virginia Press, 2007.

————. "The Long Road to *Vidal*: Charity Law and State Formation in Early America." In *The Many Legalities of Early America*, edited by Christopher L. Tomlins and Bruce H. Mann, 414–47. Chapel Hill: University of North Carolina Press, 2001.

————. "The Orthodox Christians and the Bible." In *The Oxford Handbook of the Bible in America*, edited by Paul Gutjahr, 531–545. New York: Oxford University Press, 2017.

————. *Faithful Magistrates and Republican Lawyers: Creators of Virginia Legal Culture, 1680–1810*. Chapel Hill: University of North Carolina Press, 1981.

————. *Hopes for Better Spouses: Protestant Marriage and Church Renewal in Early Modern Europe, India, and North America*. Grand Rapids, MI: William B. Eerdmans Publishing Company, 2013.

———. *Mixed Marriages: An Orthodox History.* Yonkers, NY: St. Vladimir's Seminary Press, 2018.

———. *Palatines, Liberty, and Property: German Lutherans in Colonial British America.* Baltimore: Johns Hopkins University Press, 1993.

———. "No Bishop, No King, No Millennial Republic." *Reviews in American History* 23, no. 2 (June, 1995): 202–205.

———. "Orthodox Christians and Biblical Studies: A Historian's Perspective." *Greek Orthodox Theological Review* 63, 1/2 (2018): 61–95.

———, ed. *Ethnographies and Exchanges: Native Americans, Moravians, and Catholics in Early North America.* University Park: The Pennsylvania State University Press, 2008.

———, ed. *Human v. Religious Rights? German and U.S. Exchanges and the Global Implications.* Göttingen: Vandenhoeck & Ruprecht, 2020.

Finke, Roger and Dane R. Mataic. "Recent Findings on Religious Freedoms: A Global Assessment and American Update." 127–152.

Roeber, Sister Margarete. "Wherefore Man and Woman? Exploring the Discussion of a Theology of Sex and its Implications for the Ordination of Women to the Priesthood Among Contemporary Orthodox Christian Scholars." MA Thesis, Antiochian House of Studies, Balamand University, 2013.

———. "Wherefore Man and Woman?" Paper, Holy Assumption Monastery, Calistoga, CA, December 8, 2013.

Roosevelt, Eleanor. *On My Own.* New York: Harper & Brothers, 1959.

Ross, Richard J. and Philip J. Stern. "Reconstructing Early Modern Notions of Legal Pluralism." In *Legal Pluralism and Empires, 1500–1850*, edited by Lauren Benton and Richard J. Ross, 109–141. New York: New York University Press, 2013.

Rubin, Joan Shelley and Scott E. Casper, eds. *The Oxford Encyclopedia of American Cultural and Intellectual History.* 2 vols. New York: Oxford University Press, 2013.

Rudalevige, Andrew. *The New Imperial Presidency: Renewing Presidential Power after Watergate.* Ann Arbor: University of Michigan Press, 2006.

Russian Autocephaly and Orthodoxy in America: An Appraisal with Decisions and Formal Opinions. New York: Orthodox Observer Press, 1972.

Sabra, George. "Two Ways of Being a Christian in the Muslim Context of the Middle East." *Islam & Christian Muslim Relations* 17, no. 1 (2006): 43–53.

Said, Edward. *Out of Place.* New York: Vintage Books, 1999.

Saliba, Archbishop Philip and Najib E. Saliba. *Broken Promises and White House Meetings.* Englewood, NJ: Antakya Press, 2015.

Saliba, Metropolitan Philip. "Orthodoxy in America: Success and Failure." Homily delivered at St. George Cathedral, Worcester, MA, Sunday of Orthodoxy, 1984. http://ww1.antiochian.org/node/17372.

Sarkisian, Aram G. "Orthodox American Has a Lost Cause Problem." https://
publicorthodoxy.org/2021/12/03/orthodox-lost-cause/.

Schlesinger, Jr., Arthur. *The Imperial Presidency.* New York: Houghton-Mifflin,
1973.

Schmemann, Alexander, ed. "Autocephaly in the Orthodox Church in America."
Special issue, *St. Vladimir' Theological Quarterly* 15, nos.1–2 (1971).

Schmoeckel, Mathias. "Procedure, proof, and evidence." In *Christianity and
Law: An Introduction,* edited by John Witte, Jr., and Frank S. Alexander,
143–62. Cambridge: Cambridge University Press, 2008.

Schmucker, Samuel S. *Elements of Popular Theology, with special reference to the
Doctrines of the Reformation, as avowed before the Diet at Augsburg, in
MDCCC.* Second edition. New York: Leavitt, Lord, Co., 1834.

———. *The American Lutheran Church, Historically, Doctrinally, and Practically
Delineated in Several Occasional Discourses.* Springfield: Harbaugh & Butler,
1851; New York: The Arno Press, 1969. Citations refer to the Arno Press
edition.

———. *Letters of Rev. Dr. Schmucker and Gerrit Smith, Esq.* n.p. 1838? U.S.
[electronic resource], Penn State University. https://searchworks.stanford.edu
/view/9676286

Scholl, Sarah. "Freedom in the Congregation? Culture Wars, Individual Rights,
and National Churches in Switzerland (1848–1907)." *Church History* 89,
no. 2 (June, 2020): 333–349.

Shain, Barry. *Man, God and Society: An Interpretive History of Individualism.*
London: University of London Institute of United States Studies, 2000.

———. *The Myth of American Individualism: The Protestant Origins of American
Political Thought.* Princeton, NJ: Princeton University Press, 1996.

———, ed. *The Nature of Rights at the American Founding and Beyond.*
Charlottesville: University of Virginia Press, 2007.

Slesinski, Robert. "S. L. Frank's Intuition of Pan-Unity." 199–212.

"Reflections of Metropolitan Tikhon." https://www.oca.org/reflections
/metropolitan-tikhon/message-to-ecumenical-gathering-on-peace-in
-ukraine.

Reid, John Phillip. "The Authority of Rights at the American Founding."
67–115.

Rodgers, Daniel T. "Rights Consciousness in American History." 258–279.

Roeber, A.G. "The Limited Horizons of Whig Religious Rights." 198–229.

Smith, Rogers M. "The Politics of Rights Talk, Then and Now." 303–323.

Shammas, Carol. *A History of Household Government in America.*
Charlottesville: University of Virginia Press, 2002.

Shapin, Steven. *The Scientific Revolution.* Chicago: University of Chicago Press,
1996.

Shapiro, Adam R. *Trying Biology: The Scopes Trial, Textbooks, and the Antievolution Movement in American Schools.* Chicago: University of Chicago Press, 2013.

Shapiro, Barbara. *Probability and Certainty in Seventeenth-Century England: A Study of the Relationships between Natural Science, Religion, History, Law, and Literature.* Princeton, NJ: Princeton University Press, 1983.

Shapiro, Ian. *The Evolution of Rights in Liberal Theory.* Cambridge: Cambridge University Press, 1986.

Sheehan, Bernard W. *Seeds of Extinction: Jeffersonian Philanthropy and the American Indian.* Chapel Hill: The Omohundro Institute of Early American History and Culture and University of North Carolina Press, 1973.

Shevzov, Vera. "Letting the People into Church: Reflections on Orthodoxy and Community in Late Imperial Russia." *In Orthodox Russia: Belief and Practice under the Tsars,* edited by Valerie A. Kivelson and Robert H. Greene, 59–77. University Park: The Pennsylvania State University Press, 2003.

———. "The Burdens of Tradition: Orthodox Constructions of the West in Russia (Late 19th-Early 20th CC.)." In *Orthodox Constructions of the West,* edited by George E. Demacopoulos and Aristotle Papanikolaou, 83–101. New York: Fordham University Press, 2013.

———. *Russian Orthodoxy on the Eve of Revolution.* Oxford: Oxford University Press, 2004.

Shishkov, Andrey. "Two Ecumenisms: Conservative Christian Alliances as a New Form of Ecumenical Cooperation." Translated by April L. French. *State, Religion and Church* 4, no. 2 (2017): 58–87.

"Side A/Side B Theology Primer." Coming Out for Christians. Accessed April 19, 2019. www.comingout4christians.net/side-a-side-b-primer.html.

"Significant Supreme Court Rulings." Pew Research Center: Religion & Public Life. March 31, 2011. https://www.pewforum.org/2011/03/31/churches-in -courts8/.

Sikkink, Kathryn. "'Human Rights, Responsibilities, and Democracy,' Sikkink Comments on Tasioulas and Moyn Papers: 'Symposium on the Future of International Human Rights Law." *Vanderbilt Journal of Transnational Law* 52, no. 5 (November 2019): 1315–1330.

———. *Evidence for Hope: Making Human Rights Work in the 21st Century* Princeton: Princeton University Press, 2017.

Silk, Mark. "The Other Russian Collusion Story." Religion News Service. March 25, 2019. https://religionnews.com/2019/03/25/the-other-russian -collusion-story/.

Slagle, Amy. *The Eastern Church in the Spiritual Marketplace: American Conversions to Orthodox Christianity.* Dekalb: Northern Illinois University Press, 2011.

Smith, Steven B. "What is "Right" in Hegel's Philosophy of Right." *American Political Science Review* 83, no. 1 (March, 1989): 3–18.

Smith, Steven D. "Die and Let Live? The Asymmetry of Accommodation." *Southern California Law Review* 88, no. 3 (March 2015): 703–725.

Snyder, Christina. *Great Crossings: Indians, Settlers, and Slaves in the Age of Jackson.* New York: Oxford University Press, 2017.

Sobrino, Jon. "Human Rights and Oppressed Peoples: Historical-Theological Reflections." In *Truth and Memory: The Church and Human Rights in El Salvador and Guatemala,* edited by M.A. Hayes and D. Tombs. 134–58. Herefordshire, UK: Gracewing, 2001.

———. *The Principle of Mercy: Taking the Crucified People from the Cross.* Maryknoll, NY: Orbis Books, 1994.

Soper, J. Christopher, Kevin R. den Dulk, and Stephen V. Monsma, eds. *The Challenge of Pluralism: Church and State in Six Democracies.* 3rd ed. New York: Rowman and Littlefield, 2017.

Soroka, George. "International Relations by Proxy? The Kremlin and the Russian Orthodox Church," *Religions* 13: 3 (March, 2022). https://www.mdpl.com/2077–1444/13/3/208/htm.

Stamatopoulos, Dimitris. "Holy Canons or General Regulations? The Ecumenical Patriarchate *vis-à-vis* the Challenge of Secularization in the Nineteenth Century." In *Innovation in the Orthodox Christian Tradition? The Question of Change in Greek Orthodox Thought and Practice,* edited by Trine Stauning Willert and Lina Molokotos-Liederman, 143–162. Farnham, UK: Ashgate Publishing, 2012.

"A Statement from His Eminence Metropolitan JOSEPH Regarding Ukraine." https://antiochian.org/regulararticle/1159.

Steiner, Michael and Clarence Mondale, eds. *Region and Regionalism in the United States: A Source Book for the Humanities and Social Sciences.* New York: Garland, 1988.

Stephens, Christopher W.B. *Canon Law and Episcopal Authority: The Canons of Antioch and Serdica.* Oxford: Oxford University Press, 2015.

Sterk, Andrea. *Renouncing the World Yet Leading the Church: The Monk-Bishop in Late Antiquity.* Cambridge, MA: Harvard University Press, 2004.

Stoeckl, Kristina. *The Russian Orthodox Church and Human Rights.* London: Routledge, 2014.

Stokoe, Mark and Leonid Kishkovsky. *Orthodox Christians in North America 1794–1994.* N.p.: Orthodox Christian Publications Center, 1995.

"The Story of the White Russian Refugees in Tubabao Island, Guiuan Eastern Samar Philippines, 1949–1953." Accessed 30 March 2019. https://www.visiteasternsamar.com/2018/11/the-story-of-white-russian-refugees-in.html.

Stout, Harry S. *Upon the Altar of the Nation: A Moral History of the American Civil War.* New York: Viking, 2006.

Strode, Tom. "Christian Persecution Focus of Global Summit." *Baptist Press.* May 12, 2017. http://www.bpnews.net/48862/christian-persecution-focus-of -global-summit.

Subcommittee on Amendments to the Displaced Persons Act. Displaced Persons, HRG-1949-SJS-0016 (1950). https://congressional.proquest.com /congressional/docview/t29.d30.hrg-1949-sjs-0016.

Sullivan, Winnifred Fallers. *The Impossibility of Religious Freedom.* Princeton: Princeton University Press, 2005.

Sussman, Robert Wald. *The Myth of Race: The Troubling Persistence of an Unscientific Idea.* Cambridge, MA: Harvard University Press, 2014.

Sword, Kirsten. *Wives Not Slaves: Patriarchy and Modernity in the Age of Revolutions* (Chicago and London: University of Chicago Press, 2021.

Taft, S.J., Robert F. "Perceptions and Realities in Orthodox-Catholic Relations Today: Reflections on the Past, Prospects for the Future." In *Orthodox Constructions of the West,* edited by George E. Demacopoulos and Aristotle Papanikolaou, 23–44. New York: Fordham University Press, 2013.

Tarazi, Paul Nadim. *Galatians: A Commentary.* Crestwood, NY: St. Vladimir's Seminary Press, 1999.

Tasioulas, John. "Exiting the Hall of Mirrors: Morality and Law in Human Rights." *King's College London Law School Research Paper No. 2017–19,* February 10, 2017. http://dx.doi.org/10.2139/ssrn.2915307.

———. "On the Foundations of Human Rights." In *Philosophical Foundations of Human Rights,* edited by Rowan Cruft, S. Matthew Liao, and Massimo Renzo, 45–70. Oxford: Oxford University Press, 2015.

———. "Towards a Philosophy of Human Rights." *Current Legal Problems 65* (2012): 1–30.

Taylor, Leonard Francis. *Catholic Cosmopolitanism and Human Rights.* Cambridge: Cambridge University Press, 2020.

Ten Napel, Hans-Martien. "A Natural Basis for Human Rights?" *Canopy Forum on the Interaction of Law & Religion.* January 6, 2020. https:// canopyforum.org/2020/01/06/a-natural-law-basis-for-human-rights.

———. *Constitutionalism, Democracy, and Religious Freedom: To Be Fully Human.* Abingdon-on-Thames: Routledge, 2017.

Tharoor, Ishaan. "The Christian Nationalism behind Putin's War." *The Washington Post* (April 19, 2022). https://www.washingtonpost.com/world /2022/04/19/patriarch-kirill-orthodox-church-russia-ukraine/.

The Orthodox Christian Studies Center of Fordham University. "The Coronavirus (COVID-19) and Communion Practice in the Orthodox Church." YouTube video, 2:12:32, recording of a webinar hosted by the

Orthodox Theological Society in America. August 22, 2020. https://
otsamerica.net/the-coronavirus-covid-19-and-communion-practice-in-the
-orthodox-church/.

Theodorou, Evangelos. Prologue to *Women Deacons in the Orthodox Church:
Called to Holiness and Ministry*, by Kyriaki Karidoyanes FitzGerald, xxi–
xxviii. Brookline, MA: Holy Cross Orthodox Press, 1998.

———. *Sexual Orientation and Gender Identity. Answers and . . . People.*
Vasileios Tsangalos, transl. Athens: EN PLO Editions. 2019.

———. "The Orthodox Church, Sexual Orientation, and Gender Identity:
From Embarrassment to Calling." 83–90.

Thermos, Vasileios. *Thirst for Love and Truth: Encounters of Orthodox Theology
and Psychological Science*. Montreal: Alexander Press, 2010.

Thomas, John L. *The Liberator: William Lloyd Garrison: A Biography*. New York:
Little, Brown, 1963.

Tierney, Brian. *The Idea of Natural Rights: Studies on Natural Rights, Natural
Law and Church Law 1150–1625*. Atlanta: Scholars Press, 1997.

Torrance, Alexis and Johannes Zachhuber, editors. *Individuality in Late Antiquity.*
Farnham, UK: Ashgate, 2014.

Torrance, Alexis. "Precedents for Palamas' Essence-Energies Theology in the
Cappadocian Fathers." *Vigiliae Christianae* 63 (2009): 47–70.

Trempelas, Panagiotes N. *The Autocephaly of the Metropolia in America.*
Translated and edited by George S. Bebis, Robert G. Stephanopoulos, and
N.M. Vaporis. Brookline, MA: Holy Cross Theological School Press, 1974.

Abbot Tryphon. "Same Sex Attraction: The Homosexual Person in Light of the
Orthodox Faith." Ancient Faith. September 7, 2017. https://blogs
.ancientfaith.com/morningoffering/2021/same-sex-attraction

Tucker, Gregory and Brandon Gallaher, editors. *Orthodox Christianity, Sexual
Diversity & Public Policy*. British Council Bridging Voices Project, 2017–
2020. https://www.fordham.edu/download/downloads/id/14882/orthodox
_christianity_sexual_diversity_and_public_policy.pdf.

Tudorie, Ionut-Alexandru. *The Time Has Come: Debates over the OCA
Autocephaly Reflected in St. Vladimir's Quarterly*. Yonkers, NY: St. Vladimir's
Seminary Press, 2020.

Turner, Ronald. "On Neutral and Preferred Principles of Constitutional Law."
University of Pittsburgh Law Review 74 (Spring 2013): 433–489. https://doi
.org/10.5195/lawreview.2013.261.

Tusan, Michelle. "'Crimes against Humanity': Human Rights, the British
Empire, and the Origins of the Response to the Armenian Genocide."
American Historical Review 119, no. 1 (February, 2014): 47–77.

Tushnet, Eve. *Gay and Catholic: Accepting My Sexuality, Finding Community,
Living My Faith*. Notre Dame, IN: Ave Maria Press, 2014.

Tushnet, Mark. "Accommodation of Religion Thirty Years On." *Harvard Journal of Law and Gender* 38 (2015): 1–33.

U.S. Central Intelligence Agency. *The Study of Foreign Political Developments in the United States*. CIA-RDP89-01258R000100010004-2. Washington, D.C.: CIA, 1944. https://www.cia.gov/readingroom/docs/CIA-RDP89 -01258R000100010004-2.pdf.

Uhalde, Kevin. *Expectations of Justice in the Age of Augustine*. Philadelphia: University of Pennsylvania Press, 2007.

Valliere, Paul. *Conciliarism: A History of Decision-Making in the Church*. Cambridge: Cambridge University Press, 2012.

———. *Modern Russian Theology: Bukharev, Soloview, Bulgakov: Orthodox Theology in a New Key*. Grand Rapids, MI: William B. Eerdmans Publishing Company, 2000.

———. "Sophiology as the Dialogue of Orthodoxy with Modern Civilization." 176–192.

Van Drunen, David. *Natural Law and the Two Kingdoms: A Study in the Development of Reformed Social Thought*. Grand Rapids, MI: William B. Eerdmans Publishing Company, 2010.

Van Duffel, Siegfried. "From Objective Right to Subjective Rights: The Franciscans and the Interest and Will Conceptions of Rights." In *The Nature of Rights: Moral and Political Rights in Late Medieval and Early Modern Philosophy*, edited by Virpi Mäkinen, 63–92. Helsinki: The Philosophical Society of Finland, 2010.

Vasilevich, Natallia. "Sexual Orientation and Gender Identity in the Social Doctrine of the Russian Orthodox Church and Anthropological Challenges." 66–70. In *"For I Am Wonderfully Made": Texts on Eastern Orthodoxy and LGBT Inclusion*. Edited by Misha Cherniak et al. n.p. :Esubernanza, 2016.

Vedder, Ben. *Heidegger's Philosophy of Religion: From God to the Gods*. Pittsburgh, PA: Duquesne University Press, 2007.

Viscuso, Patrick. *A Quest for Reform of the Orthodox Church: The 1923 Pan-Orthodox Congress An Analysis and Translation of Its Acts and Decisions*. Berkeley, CA: InterOrthodox Press, 2006.

Voogt, Gerrit. "Primacy of Individual Conscience or Primacy of the State? The Clash between Dirck Volckertsz, Coornhert and Justus Lipsius." *Sixteenth Century Journal* 28, no. 4 (1997): 1231–1249.

Vrame, Anton C. "Four Types of 'Orthopraxy' among Orthodox Christians in America." In *Thinking through Faith: New Perspectives from Orthodox Christian Scholars*, edited by Aristotle Papanikolaou and Elizabeth H. Prodromou, 279–308. Crestwood, NY: St. Vladimir's Seminary Press, 2008.

Wagschal, David F. *Law and Legality in the Greek East: The Byzantine Canonical Tradition, 381–881.* Oxford: Oxford University Press, 2015.

Walsh, Andrew. "Those Revolting Greeks." *Religion in the News* 2, no. 3 (September 1, 1999). http://www2.trincoll.edu/csrpl/RINVol2No3 /Revolting%20Greeks.htm.

———. "Unexpected Consequences: The Revolt Against Archbishop Spyridon in the Greek Orthodox Archdiocese of America, 1996–1999." In *One Calling in Christ: The Laity in the Orthodox Church,* edited by Anton Vrame, 57–74. Berkeley, CA: InterOrthodox Press, 2005.

Wanner, Catherine. *Burden of Dreams: History and Identity in Post-Soviet Ukraine.* University Park, PA: Penn State University Press, 1998.

Weiner, James F. *Tree Leaf Talk: A Heideggerian Anthropology.* Oxford: Berg, 2001.

Weitz, Eric D. "Self-Determination: How a German Enlightenment Idea Became the Slogan of National Liberation and a Human Right." *American Historical Review* 120, no. 2 (April, 2015): 462–496.

Welch, Jr., Richard E. *Response to Imperialism: The United States and the Philippine-American War, 1899–1902.* Chapel Hill: University of North Carolina Press, 1978.

Wellenreuther, Hermann and Carola Wessel, eds. *Moravian Mission among the Delaware during the American Revolution: The Diaries of David Zeisberger 1772 to 1781.* Translated by Julia Weber. University Park: The Pennsylvania State University Press, 2005.

Werth, Paul W. *The Tsar's Foreign Faiths: Toleration and the Fate of Religious Freedom in Imperial Russia.* Oxford: Oxford University Press, 2014.

Westerman, Pauline C. *The Disintegration of Natural Law Theory Aquinas to Finnis.* Leiden: Brill, 1998.

White, G. Edward. *Law in American History.* 3 vols. New York: Oxford University Press, 2006.

Wicker, Christine. *The Simple Faith of Franklin Delano Roosevelt: Religion's Role in the FDR Presidency.* Washington, D.C.: Smithsonian Books, 2017.

Wilentz, Sean. *No Property in Man: Slavery and Antislavery at the Nation's Founding.* Cambridge, MA: Harvard University Press, 2018.

Wilkins, David E. and K. Tsianima Lomawaima. *Uneven Ground: American Indian Sovereignty and Federal Law.* Norman: University of Oklahoma Press, 2001.

Wilken, Robert Louis. *Liberty in the Things of God: The Christian Origins of Religious Freedom.* New Haven: Yale University Press, 2019.

Williams, A. N. *The Ground of Union: Deification in Aquinas and Palamas.* New York: Oxford University Press, 1999.

Williams, Daniel K. "Jerry Falwell's Sunbelt Politics: The Regional Origins of the Moral Majority." *Journal of Policy History* 22, no. 2 (April, 2010): 125–47.

Willrich, Michael. *Pox: An American History*, New York: Penguin Books, 2012.

Wilson, Sarah Hinlicky. "Tradition, Priesthood and Personhood in the Trinitarian Theology of Elisabeth Behr-Sigel." *Pro Ecclesia* 19, no. 2 (Spring, 2010): 129–150.

Witte, Jr., John. "The Long History of Human Rights: Assessing an Influential Revisionist Account." Review of *Christian Human Rights*, by Samuel Moyn. *Books and Culture*. November/December, 2016. https://www.booksand culture.com/articles/2016/marapr/long-history-of-human-rights.html.

———. *Church, State, and Family: Reconciling Traditional Teachings and Modern Liberties*. Cambridge: Cambridge University Press, 2019.

Witte, Jr., John and Frank S. Alexander, eds. *The Teachings of Modern Christianity on Law, Politics, and Human Nature*. 2 vols. New York: Columbia University Press, 2006.

Witte, Jr., John and Joel A. Nichols. "The Frontiers of Marital Pluralism." In *Marriage and Divorce in a Multi-Cultural Context: Multi-Tiered Marriage and the Boundaries of Civil Law and Religion*, edited by Joel A. Nichols, 357–378. Cambridge: Cambridge University Press, 2011.

Witte, Jr., John and Justin J. Latterell. "Christianity and Human Rights: Past Contributions and Future Challenges." *Journal of Law and Religion* 30 (2015): 353–385.

Wittreck, Fabian. *Christentum und Menshenrechte*. Tübingen: Mohr Siebeck, 2013.

Wollstonecraft, Mary. *A Vindication of the Rights of Women with Strictures on Political and Moral Subjects*. First American edition. Boston: Peter Edes for Thomas and Andrews, 1792.

Woloschak, Gayle E. *Faith, Science, Mystery*. Edited by Bishop Maxim Vasiljevic. Alhambra, CA: Sebastian Press, 2018.

Wolterstorff, Nicholas. *Justice in Love*. Grand Rapids, MI: William B. Eerdmans Publishing Co., 2015.

———. *Justice: Rights and Wrongs*. Princeton, NJ: Princeton University Press, 2008).

———. *Thomas Reid and the Story of Epistemology*. Cambridge: Cambridge University Press, 2004.

Wood, Gordon S. *The Creation of the American Republic, 1776–1787*. Chapel Hill: University of North Carolina Press, 1969.

———. "The History of Rights in Early America." 233–257. In *The Nature of Rights at the American Founding and Beyond*. Edited by Barry Alan Shain. Charlottesville and London: University of Virginia Press, 2007.

Woodard, Colin. *American Nations: A History of the Eleven Regional Cultures of North America*. New York: Viking, 2011.

Woodcock, Andrew. "Jacques Maritain, Natural Law and the Universal Declaration of Human Rights." *Journal of the History of International Law* 8 (2006): 245–66.

Woodhouse, C.M. *The Struggle for Greece 1941–1949*. With an introduction by Richard Clogg. London: Hurst & Co., 1976; Chicago: Ivan R. Dee, 2002. Citations refer to the Ivan R. Dee edition.

Woodward, C. Vann. *The Strange Career of Jim Crow: A Commemorative Edition*. Afterword by William S. McFeely. New York: Oxford University Press, 1955; Oxford: Oxford University Press, 2001. Citations from the 2001 edition.

Wright, J. Skelly. "Professor Bickel, the Scholarly Tradition, and the Supreme Court." *Harvard Law Review* 84, no. 4 (Feb., 1971): 769–805.

Wybraniac, John and Roger Finke. "Religious Regulation and the Courts: The Judiciary's Changing Role in Protecting Minority Religions from Majoritarian Rule." *Journal for the Scientific Study of Religion* 40, no. 3 (September, 2001): 427–444.

Wyler, William, dir. *Friendly Persuasion*. 1956; Los Angeles: Allied Artists Pictures.

Yannaras, Christos. *On the Absence and Unknowability of God: Heidegger and the Areopagite*. Edited with an introduction by Andrew Louth. Translated by Haralambos Ventis. London: T&T Clark International, 2005.

Yannaras, Christos and Norman Russell. *Metaphysics as a Personal Adventure: Christos Yannaras in Conversation with Norman Russell*. Yonkers, NY: St. Vladimir's Seminary Press, 2017.

Yarhouse, Mark. *Understanding Gender Dysphoria: Navigating Transgender Issues in a Changing Culture*. Downers Grove, IL: IVP Academic, 2015.

Yarhouse, Mark and Julia Sadusky. *Emerging Gender Identities: Understanding the Diverse Experiences of Today's Youth*. Grand Rapids, MI: Brazos Press, 2020.

Zablonsky, Nina. *Living Color: The Biological and Social meaning of Skin Color*. Berkeley: University of California Press, 2012.

Zagarri, Rosemarie. "American Women's Rights before Seneca Falls." In *Women, Gender and Enlightenment*, edited by Sarah Knott and Barbara Taylor, 667–691. Houndsmills, UK: Palgrave MacMillan, 2005.

———. *Revolutionary Backlash: Women and Politics in the Early American Republic*. Philadelphia: University of Pennsylvania Press, 2007.

Zherebyatyev, Mikhail. "The Russian Orthodox Church's Interpretation of European Legal Values (1990–2011)." In *Eastern Orthodox Encounters of Identity and Otherness: Values, Self-Reflection, Dialogue*, edited by Andrii

Krawchuk and Thomas Bremer, 207–217. New York: Palgrave MacMillan, 2014.

Ziegler, Mary. "Eugenic Feminism: Mental Hygiene, The Women's Movement and the Campaign for Eugenic Legal Reform, 1900–1935." *Harvard Journal of Law & Gender* 31 (2008): 211–235.

———. *Beyond Abortion: Roe v. Wade and the Battle for Privacy*. Cambridge, MA: Harvard University Press, 2018.

Zizioulas, John D. *Being as Communion: Studies in Personhood and the Church*. London: Darton, Longman & Todd, 1985.

———. "Law and Personhood in Orthodox Theology." In *The One and the Many: Studies on God, Man, the Church, and the World Today*, by John Zizioulas, edited by Fr Gregory Edwards, 402–413. Alhambra, CA: Sebastian Press, 2010.

Zollmann, Carl. *American Civil Church Law*. New York: Columbia University, 1917; New York: AMS Press, 1969. Citations refer to the AMS Press edition.

Zuboff, Shoshana. *The Age of Surveillance Capitalism: The Fight for a Human Future at the New Frontier of Power*. New York: Public Affairs, 2019.

Zymaris, Philip. "Tonsure and Cursus Honorum up to the Photian Era." *Greek Orthodox Theological Review* 56, nos. 1–4 (2011): 321–345.

INDEX

Abo-Hatab, Emmanuel, 151
abolition of slavery. *See* slavery and abolitionism
abortion, 94, 173–77, 184, 188, 231, 234
Abou-Assaley, Victor, 152
Adams, John, 37, 47, 54
adelphopoiia, 218n25
Afghanistan, Russian war in (1979–89), 129
African Americans: Civil Rights movement, 96,
   109–15, 121, 185, 205; colonization of freed-
   men, 59; evangelical defense of traditional
   values and hostility to racial integration, 187;
   Jim Crow laws, 112; prejudice against Orthodox in America compared to, 103–6, 111,
   116–17; racism in U.S. after rebirth of Ku Klux
   Klan, 103; women's rights movement and,
   182, 184. *See also* slavery and abolitionism
Agnew, Spiro T., 93, 115n62
AIDS epidemic, 185
Ajalat, Charles R., 162, 165
Aktines, 198
Alaska, Orthodox and Presbyterian missions
   in, 24, 25, 63, 67–75, 83, 84, 193–95, 282
alcohol: First Peoples and problem of alcohol
   addiction, 68, 72–73, 74–75; Prohibition, 106
Alexander, Frank S., 23, 27, 28, 89, 239
Alexander, Nicholas, 118, 119
Alexander II (tsar), 75, 101, 292
Alexander III (Patriarch of Antioch). *See* Bashir,
   Antony
Alexandria, Patriarchate of, 81–82, 126, 130,
   131n27, 138, 154, 155, 166, 202
Alexandria, VA, prevention of incorporation of
   Episcopal Church in, 55
Alexii I (Patriarch of Moscow), 130–32, 134–35

Alfeyev, Hilarion, 93, 144
Alivizatos, Amilkas, 134
All American Council of OCA, 143, 144, 145
All We're Meant to Be (Scarponi and Hardesty),
   191
Allen, Joseph, 164
Ambrosius of Helsinki, 216
American Colonization Society, 59
American concept of rights. *See* North America,
   rights in
American Hellenic Educational Progressive
   Association (AHEPA), 104–5, 115n62
American Indians. *See* First Peoples
American Orthodox Church, self-government
   by. *See* self-government
Amnesty International, 280
Amphilocius of Iconium, 15
Anatolikos Aster (Star of Anatolia), 77
Anatolius (priest-monastic in Alaska), 74–75
Angelis, John, 148
Anglicans, 49, 50, 51, 122
Anthimus VI (Ecumenical Patriarch), 76n18
Anthony (Bishop of Alaska), 124
Antiochan Orthodox. *See* Arabic-origin/
   Antiochan Orthodox
Arab Nationalism, 248, 257
Arabic-origin/Antiochan Orthodox, 256, 260n61,
   294, 296; autocephaly of OCA and self-
   determination of American Orthodox Church,
   120, 123, 126, 128, 131n27, 138, 139, 144, 145,
   152–59; "autonomous" or "self-ruled" arch-
   diocese, controversy over, 168–70; auxiliary/
   diocesan bishops of, 167–70; constitution,
   issues related to, 167, 168; Damascus, Synod

Arabic-origin/Antiochan Orthodox (*continued*)
of, 152, 153, 155, 159, 167–70, 201; episcopal
authority, crisis over, 144; Greek Orthodox in
America and, 151–61, 164, 166–70; Hawaweeny
and Patriarchate of, 83; Charles Malik,
Lebanese Christian origins of, 243, 245
(*see also* Malik, Charles); in Ottoman Empire,
81–84; Palestinians immigrating to U.S.,
117–19; split in/unification of, 152–54, 158–59,
160, 167; Ukraine, on Russian invasion of,
294, 296; women, sex, gender, and marriage
amongst, 201, 203, 223n29
Aristotle and Aristotelianism, 4, 278, 300, 304
Armenian genocide, 82
Armenians, 19, 34, 82, 102, 142, 203, 210, 265
assembly, freedom of: COVID-19 pandemic
and, 29, 287–88; expressive association, right
of, 285; as political right, 20n50
Assembly of Canonical Orthodox Bishops of
the United States of America, 92–93
association, freedom of. *See* assembly, freedom of
asylum, right to, 119
Athenagoras I (Aristocles Sperou; Ecumenical
Patriarch), 131, 132, 135n34, 136–39, 198–99,
201
Attraction and Passion (Thermos), 220
Augustine of Hippo, 4, 216, 255, 268
Aune, Kristin, 215
autocephaly. *See* self-government

Baathism, 248, 257
Bacon, Sir Francis, 303
Bacon, Hannah, 209–10
Badeen, John, 160–62
Bader-Saye, Scott, 226n46
Bale, Naef, 256
Balmer, Randall, 187
Baptists in North America, 42, 52–53, 55, 60
Baranov, Alexander Andreevich, 194
Baroody, Jamil, 245, 260, 283
Barth, Karl, 209, 255
Bartholet, Elizabeth, 223
Bartholomew (Ecumenical Patriarch), 149,
165, 295
Bashara, Sophronios, 151
Bashir, Antony (Alexander III of Antioch),
152–55, 256
Basil of Caesarea, 15, 78, 255
Behr-Sigel, Elisabeth, 199
Being and Time (Heidegger), 250
Belgau, Ron, 208n5
Bellah, Robert, 210
Bellavin, Tikhon (Patriarch of Moscow), 123,
133, 134, 195, 296

Ben Lomond, CA parish crisis, 159–64, 167
Berdyaev, Nikolai, 98–99, 130, 249
Berlin, Isaiah, 22–23
Bill of Rights, 39, 40, 106, 176, 311
Billy Graham Evangelistic Association, 93
birth control, 184, 231, 234n61
bishops, rights of. *See* episcopal rights, privileges,
and authority
Blackstone, William, 8–9
body, theology of the, 205
Bolshevik Revolution, 27, 98, 100, 116, 124,
127, 195
Bowell, John, 218n25
Boyle, Robert, 300, 301
Breck, John, 221–22
Brezhnev, Leonid, 129, 130
Bridegroom of the Church, Christ as, 210
Briggs, Charles Augustus, heresy trial of, 85
Brotherhood of the Holy Sepulcher, 82–83
"brother-making" (*adelphopoiia*), 218n25
Brown, Charles Brockden, 180
Brown, John, 116
Brown v. Board of Education (1954), 109–10, 185
Brüning, Alfons, 264–65
Bukharev, Aleksandr, 249
Bulgakov, Makarii, 102
Bulgakov, Sergei/Sergius, 101, 249, 250n25
Bulgarian Orthodox, 76, 138
Burstyn v. Wilson (1952), 107
Butcher, Brian, 215

Calvert family of Maryland, 51
Camosy, Charles, 173–74
canons in Orthodox Church, 10–11
Carpatho-Rusyns, 117, 166, 129132
Cassin, René, 244
Catholic Concordance (Nicholas of Cusa), 50
Catholicism. *See* Roman Catholicism
celibacy/virginity, 212, 218
Center for the Social Education of the Greek
Woman, 198
Chalcedon, Council of (451), 13, 19, 126, 166
Chamoun, Camile, 248
Chang, Peng-chun, 243
Chapnin, Sergei, 291
Charles I (king of England), 54
Charlottesville, VA, white supremacist rally in, 92
Chelpon, George, 149
Chicago Tribune, 148
Children's Relief Fund, 280
China: on U.N. Declaration of Human Rights,
243; White Russians fleeing via, 118
Christian Legal Society, Hastings College of
Law, 234–35

Christian realism, 309

Christian Union of Scientists, 198

Christianity: episcopal rights, privileges, and authority, 10–20; North American concepts of rights and, 38; religious liberty, origins of concept of, 50; rights, origins and development of, 2, 3–7, 11, 14; rights revolution and, 21. *See also specific denominations*

Chronicle of Higher Education, 147

Chuhovits, Arseny, 152

Church of England. *See* Anglicans; Episcopalians

Church of Jesus Christ of Latter-Day Saints (Mormons), polygamy practiced by, 52, 55, 60–62, 80, 182

Cicero, 2

civil rights, 20n50; early twentieth-century Supreme Court rulings on, 106–7; for First Peoples, 56–57, 68, 72–75; gender issues as, 224–25, 234, 235; in North America, 56–61; women, civil and political rights for, 180–86, 191, 195, 197–98

Civil Rights movement, 96, 109–15, 121, 185, 205

civil unions, 224, 225n40

Civil War, British, 299

Civil War, Greece, 114, 136–37, 197

Civil War, Lebanon, 248, 259

Civil War, U.S.: concepts of rights in North America and, 40, 41, 52, 53, 54, 59, 61; Joachim II on, 76–78; women's civil rights and, 182

Clapsis, Emmanuel, 95–96

Clearview AI, 307–8

Codex Theodosianus, 14

Cold War, 27, 128, 248, 280

Collins, Nate, 213

Columbian College (Baptist foundation), incorporation of, 55

Commentaries on the Laws of England (Blackstone), 8–9

communism: Athenagoras I (Ecumenical Patriarch), anti-communism of, 137; Balkans, communist insurgencies in, 136; end of Cold War and collapse of statist forms of, 280; feminism and, 198; Greece, civil war in, 114, 136–37; labor and socialist movements, Greek Orthodox involvement with, 114; U.S. anti-communist sentiment, 114; White Russians fleeing Soviet Russia and communist China, 118–19

Community Party-USA, 114

Conference on the Human Environment, United Nations, Stockholm Declaration, 242n6

Confucianism, 243

Congregationalism in North America, 42

Constantine (emperor), 14, 15

Constantinople, Patriarchate of. *See* Ecumenical Patriarchate

Constitution, U.S., 39, 52, 57, 62–63, 163, 183, 195, 197, 242. *See also specific amendments*

Constitutional Convention, 34

constitutional rights, 20n50

Consultation of Orthodox Women, 200

Continental Congress, 38

contraception, 184, 231, 234n61

contract and property rights of religious bodies, 80–82, 86–87, 107–8, 117, 140–42, 159–64

Convention Relating to the Status of Refugees, United Nations, 118

Copts, 19, 82, 146

Corpus Juris Civilis, 14

COVID-19 pandemic, 29, 287–90

Crimea, Russian seizure of, 294

Crimean War, 75

cursus honorum, 13

Czech revolution (1968), 129

Daly, Mary, 209

Damascus, Synod of, 152, 153, 155, 159, 167–70, 201

Darwin, Charles, 226n44

David, Samuel, 152–54

Dawes Act (1887), 71

deacons, women as, 177, 196–97, 202–3

Declaration of Independence, 22, 39, 51, 53, 105, 244

"A Declaration on the 'Russian World' (Russki Mir) Teaching," 295

Defense of Marriage Act (DOMA), 185

Democratic Party, Orthodox shift away from, 93–94

Demoglou, Alexandros, 134

Descartes, René, 9, 300, 304

diaconate, admission of women to, 177, 196–97, 202–3

Dickinson, Emily, 54

Dickinson, John, 34

Dignitatis Humanae, 90

dignity of the human person, 28, 80, 174, 175, 193, 210–11, 224, 244

Dionysius (hieromonk), 46–47

Displaced Persons Act (1948) and displaced persons after WWII, 118–19

dissent, right of, 94, 175–76, 178–79, 190, 222–23, 225, 227, 230–38, 311

Dobbs v. Jackson Women's Health Organization (2022), 175

Doctors without Borders, 280

Dogmengeschichte (Harnack), 84

Domingo, Rafael, 277
Donahue, Charles, 3, 5
Douglas, Justice, 107
Duane, James, 38
due process, 18, 57, 85, 106, 122, 144, 171, 176, 177, 185, 306, 309
Dura-Europos, Christian church at, 210
Dusky v. United States (1960), 185n26
Dworkin, Ronald, 272, 282n135
Dyophysite Christians, 19

ecclesial constitutionalism, 48–51
ecclesial self-government. *See* self-government
Ecumenical Patriarchate: on autocephaly, 126; "Charter of the Greek Orthodox Archdiocese of America," controversies over, 150; Ligonier proposal for united Orthodox Church of North America and, 164–65, 166–67; phyletism, condemnation of, 76; Russian exarchate in Europe, abolition of, 127; Russian invasion of Ukraine, condemnation of, 295; social justice document, 35; Soviet campaign against, 128, 130–32, 137–40; on women's ministry, 197
ecumenism and ecumenical movement, 198–99, 236, 249, 255
education. *See* schools
Edwards, Jonathan, 255
Efsevia (sisterhood organization), 197–98
Eighteenth Amendment, 106
Ekaterinovsky, Peter, 194–95
El Zaher (Mamluk sultan), 83
Elias IV of Aleppo (Patriarch of Antioch), 155–57
Elpidophoros (Greek Orthodox Metropolitan), 295
Elshtain, Jean Bethke, 309
Ely, Ezra Stile, 58
Emerson, Ralph Waldo, 37
Employment Division, Department of Human Resources of Oregon v. Smith (1990), 231–32
England: Civil War in, 299; rights law in, 7–9; Royal Society, 301, 303
Englishmen, rights of, in North America, 8, 9, 34, 37, 38
Enlightenment: North American rights concepts and, 40–41, 43, 45, 47; Orthodox Church and, 25, 45–46; scientific revolution and problem of knowledge, 298–305; Scottish Common Sense philosophers, 39, 41–45, 270, 275, 303, 304
Ephraim (abbot of St. Anthony's Monastery, AZ), 160
Ephrem of Antioch, 15, 19
Ephrem the Syrian, 255

Epiphanias (Ukrainian Orthodox Metropolitan), 295, 297
episcopal rights, privileges, and authority, 10–20, 142–45, 159–64, 309–10
Episcopalians, 48, 55, 94, 115n62, 243n7
equal protection claims, 109, 189, 312
Equal Rights Amendment, 189, 197
Equality Act (proposed), 311
Erastianism, 49
Establishment Clause, 108n45, 236
ethnic nationalism: Arab Nationalism, 248, 257; Orthodox churches and problem of, 297–98; in Ottoman Empire, 76, 79; Russian national identity, quest for, 291–93; Soviet efforts to curb, 129; in Ukraine, 129
eugenic feminism, 184
European Court of Human Rights, 290–91
Evangelical Protestant Orthodox Church, 158, 159, 160, 163–64
evangelical Protestantism, 93, 94, 185–91, 227–28, 288
Evdokimov, Paul, 215
expression, freedom of. *See* pluralism and freedom of speech/expression

facial recognition technology, 307–8
Faisal (king of Saudi Arabia), 156
Falwell, Jerry, 188
Fea, John, 186–87
feminism. *See* women, sexuality, gender, and marriage
Ferencz, Nicholas, 124, 310
Fifth Amendment, 57n54, 185
First Amendment, 62, 106, 141, 232, 308
First Peoples: Alaska, Orthodox and Presbyterian missionaries in, 24, 25, 63, 67–75, 83, 84, 193–95; alcohol addiction, problem of, 68, 72–73, 74–75; civil/citizenship rights for, 56–57, 68, 72–75; Dawes Act (1887) ending tribal collective rights and identity, 71; federal funding for Protestant missionary efforts among, 55; peyote, religious use of, 231; private property and "civilization" of, 68; protection of women and children, Orthodox concerns about, 68, 193–95; Social Gospel movement and, 85; women's rights movement and, 183, 184, 195
First Vatican Council, 84
First World War, 64, 102, 105
Fitzgerald, Kyriaki, 202
Flesh in the Age of Reason (Porter), 304
Flexner, Eleanor, 183
Florensky, Pavel, 249, 276
"four freedoms," 242n7

Fourteenth Amendment, 52, 57n54, 106, 109, 176
Francis (pope), 224
Franciscans, 4, 8
Frank, Semen Liudvigovich, 250
Franklin, Benjamin, 303
free choice and agency, right of, 188, 224, 228
Free Exercise Clause, 62, 108n45, 230, 231, 236
freedom of assembly. *See* assembly, freedom of
freedom of speech/expression. *See* pluralism and freedom of speech/expression
French Reformed Church, 199
French Revolution, 41–42, 46, 242n6
Friendly Persuasion (film), 308–9
Fuller, Lon, 20n50
Fundamental Law of the Sultanate (1876), 78
Fygetakis, Leah, 206

Galilei, Galileo, 300
Gamayel, Pierre, 248
Garrison, William Lloyd, 52
Gender Essentialism and Orthodoxy (Rich), 216
gender issues, 27, 205–38; Byzantine culture, ambiguity of gender in, 192; as civil rights, 224–25, 234, 235; civil unions, 224, 225n40; creation of humans as male and female, 11, 178, 192–93, 206–9, 215–16, 219n28; critiques of Orthodox received teaching on, 213–29; dissent, right of, 222–23, 225, 227, 230–38, 311; gender dysphoria, 219n28, 224, 227–29; God as Father, Son, and Holy Spirit, 209–10; historical shift from women's studies to gender studies, 179; LGBT community, 27, 92, 94, 175, 185–86, 204–6, 211–13, 218–27, 233–34, 240, 263, 311; Orthodox received teaching on, 206–13; before rights revolution, 178, 179, 192–93, 199; same-sex marriage, 92, 94, 175, 177, 189, 211–13, 218, 235, 240, 263; same-sex sexual practices, 211–13, 220; scientific views on, 225–26; Side A and Side B approaches to, 208n5, 211–12, 224; transgender individuals, 94, 175, 178, 210, 222–29, 226n46, 263. *See also* women, sexuality, gender, and marriage
Georgians, 146, 294
Gewirth, Alan, 272
Gibbons, James Cardinal, 183
Gideon (hieromonk in Alaska), 193–94
Gladden, Washington, 85
Glendon, Mary Ann, 244
God, humans made in image and likeness of *(imago Dei)*, 11, 11n27, 28, 92, 173, 228, 265, 270, 273, 276, 277
Goodman, Lenn, 91
Graham, Franklin, 93

Greek Catholics, 117, 134
Greek Orthodox American Leaders (GOAL), 147
Greek Orthodox in North America, 27, 146–72; AHEPA (American Hellenic Educational Progressive Association), 104–5, 115n62; autocephaly of OCA and self-governed American Orthodox Church, 128, 130, 131, 134–40, 152–59; "Charter of the Greek Orthodox Archdiocese of America," controversies over, 149–51; Civil Rights movement and, 111; Damascus, Synod of, 152, 153, 155, 159, 167–70, 201; defined, 146; ecumenical movement, 198; episcopal authority, ecclesiastical discipline, and property issues, 144, 159–64; Evangelical Protestant Orthodox Church and Hardenbrook/Ben Lomond controversy, 158, 159–64, 167; immigration of, 102–3, 134; labor and socialist movements, involvement with, 114; prejudice and discrimination against, 103–6, 111; Protestant American values and, 149; Russian invasion of Ukraine, condemnation of, 295, 296; Spiritual Courts, operating procedures for, 150, 160–62; Archbishop Spyridon, controversy and resignation of, 146–49, 165; united Orthodox Church of North America, Ligonier proposal for, 164–67; women, gender, sex, and marriage amongst, 196–99, 201, 202, 206. *See also* Arabic-origin/ Antiochan Orthodox; Iakovos
Greek Orthodox in Ottoman Empire: Patriarchate of Jerusalem taken over by Brotherhood of the Holy Sepulcher, 82–83; *Tanzimat* reforms, opposition to, 78–79
Greenland, Norse settlements in, 24
Gregorian Calendar, OCA adopting, 128, 141
Gregory VI Constantine (Ecumenical Patriarch), 76n18
Gregory XVI (pope), 80
Gregory Nazianzus, 15
Gregory of Nyssa, 15, 207, 215, 216
Griffin, James, 281–82
Griswold v. Connecticut (1965), 176, 185, 234
Grotius, Hugo, 268
Guroian, Vigen, 34, 210–11, 262–63

Haddad, Arsenius, 152
Haddad, Gregory, 152
Hadrian (emperor), 14
Hagenbach, Karl Rudolf, 84
Haitian Revolution, 42
Hamalis, Perry, 309
Hammarskjold, Dag, 257
Hand, Learned, 163

Hanna, Emile, 154
Harakas, Stanley, 96–97, 110
Hardenbrook, John Weldon, 159–60, 162, 163
Hardesty, Nancy A., 191
Harnack, Adolph von, 84
Harper, Kyle, 20n50
Hart, David Bentley, 278–79
Hart, H. L. A., 20n50
Hawaweeny, Raphael, 82–84, 123, 151, 156, 285
Hazim, Ignatius, 158
The Hedgehog and the Fox (Berlin), 22–23
Hegel, G. W. F., 3
Heidegger, Martin, 246, 247, 249–55
Hellenic College/Holy Cross Greek Orthodox School of Theology, MA, 147, 154
Heroines of Love (Theodorou), 196–97
Herron, George, 85
Hill, Wesley, 208n5
Hobbes, Thomas, 268, 300, 304
Hocking, William Ernest, 256–57
Hodge, Charles, 58
Holmes, Oliver Wendell, Jr., 54, 106–7
Holocaust, 198
Holy Cross Greek Orthodox School of Theology/Hellenic College, MA, 147, 154
Holy Trinity Business Women Group, 202
homeschooling, 223, 224n39
homosexuality. *See* gender issues; LGBT community; women, sexuality, gender, and marriage
Hopko, Thomas, 154, 215, 225n40
Hosanna-Tabor v. EEOC (2012), 232
Hovorun, Cyril, 291
human rights, 28–29, 239–85; Civil Rights movement and, 111, 112; defined, 239–41; dignity of human person and, 28; first generation of, 242–44; Malik and, 243–62 (*see also* Malik, Charles); moral rights and, 20n50; Orthodox thought since 1970s and, 262–70, 275–76, 278–79, 280–85; personhood, understanding of, 266–67, 285; Protestant scholarship on, 28, 241, 242, 267–76, 279, 283–84; Roman Catholic thought on, 28, 228, 241, 242, 244, 267, 268, 271, 276–79, 281, 283–84; secular human rights regimes, 240, 241, 242, 267, 270, 272, 279–85; slavery and abolitionism, 51–52; U.N. Universal Declaration of Human Rights, 118, 119, 242n6, 243–44, 256–57, 260n62, 280; Wolterstorff on, 269–76, 278, 284
humanism, 300
Humphrey, John P., 243
Hunter, James Davison, 21
Hutcheson, Francis, 42, 304

Iakovos (Demetrios Koukouzis; Archbishop of North and South America): Civil Rights movement and, 96, 110–12, 115, 205; Ecumenical Patriarchate, estrangement from, 147, 148; Greek Archdiocese charter, vision of, 151; self-government of American Orthodox Church and, 139–40, 154, 155; Archbishop Spyridon controversy and, 147–49; supposed plot to declare himself primate of autocephalous church, 166; united Orthodox Church of North America, Ligonier proposal for, 164
Ignatius (saint), 165
Ignatius IV (Antiochan Patriarch), 168, 169, 171, 260n61
Ilia II (Catholicos-Patriarch of All Georgia), 294
imago Dei (image and likeness of God), 11, 11n27, 28, 92, 173, 228, 265, 270, 273, 276, 277
immigration to U.S.: earliest Orthodox immigrants, 134; from Eastern, Central, and Southern Europe/Middle East, 62, 76, 83, 102–3, 116–19; Ku Klux Klan and American opposition to, 102–3, 106; role of immigrant Orthodox women in Church and society, 196–97
In plurimus (1888), 80
In supremo Apostolatus fastigio (1839), 80
Inazu, John, 91, 234, 235, 268, 269
Indians. *See* First Peoples
Indigenous peoples. *See* First Peoples
individual rights: Alaska, Orthodox Church and Presbyterian missionaries in, 69, 73–75; Berdyaev contrasting Orthodox freedom of conscience with, 99; confessional authority versus, 83–86; dignity of the human person and, 28, 29; Greek, Russian, and Slavonic terms for "just and right," 12; in Jewish legal tradition, 16n39; Malik and, 244–45; in North America, 36–73; origins and development of, 3, 5–6, 8; personhood, understanding of, 266–67; rights revolution and, 21, 22, 28
Innocent (Veniaminov, Archbishop of Alaska), 46, 69, 71n7, 181, 194
Islam: Malik on, 255, 260n62; Organization of Islamic Cooperation, 156; polygamy and, 60; Wahabism, 260n62. *See also* Ottoman Empire
Israeli-Palestinian conflict, 117, 119, 257, 283
Istanbul, Patriarchate in. *See* Ecumenical Patriarchate
IWW, 114

Jackson, Andrew, 37
Jackson, Justice, 108

Jackson, Sheldon, 67–68, 70–73, 85n35, 196
Jacobson v. Massachusetts (1905), 288
Jefferson, Thomas, 37, 54, 57, 105
Jerusalem, Patriarchate of, 82–83, 126, 130, 131n27, 138, 154, 155
Jews and Judaism: antisemitism in U.S. after rebirth of Ku Klux Klan, 103, 104; pluralism, support for, 91–92; Prohibition, opposition to, 106; rights in, 6–7, 16; Soviet Jews, concerns about, 283
Jillions, John, 225
Jim Crow laws, 112
Jimmy Swaggart Ministries v. Board of Equalization (1990), 230–31
Joachim II (Ecumenical Patriarch), 76n18, 77–78, 79–80
Joachim III (Ecumenical Patriarch), 135
John Chrysostom, 78, 255
John of Damascus, 255
John Paul II (pope), 205
Johnson, Elizabeth, 209
Jonah (OCA Metropolitan primate), 142–45, 146
Jones v. Wolf (1979), 141, 163
Joseph (Antiochan archbishop), 167–71
Josephson-Storn, Jason, 298
Judaism. *See* Jews and Judaism
Jumblat, Kamal, 248
Justinian (emperor), 14, 19

Kant, Immanuel, 272
Kattan, Assaad Elias, 260n61
Kavalah, Mehmet Ali Pasha, 78
Kedroff v. St. Nicholas Cathedral (1952), 108
Kelly, John W., 68
Kepler, Johannes, 300
KGB, 128, 138n41
Khodr, George, 158
Khomiakov, Aleksei, 102
Khouri, Ellis, 155
Khrapovitskii, Antonii, 124
Khrushchev, Nikita, 128n23, 129, 130
King, Martin Luther, Jr., 111
Kitroeff, Alexander, 148
Klarman, Michael, 185
Knapp, Lyman, 73
Knowland, William, 118
knowledge, problem of: epistemic crisis of twenty-first century and digital media threats, 305–8; scientific revolution and, 298–305
Konig, David, 36n4
Koory, Robert A., 165
Koppelman, Andrew, 179

Koskenniemi, Martti, 1
Kostryukov, Andrey, 140n47
Koukouzis, Demetrios. *See* Iakovos
Ku Klux Klan, 103–6
Kyrill (Russian Orthodox Patriarch), 290–91, 294–97

labor and socialist movements and Greek Orthodox in North America, 114
Ladies Philoptochos Society, 201
L'Anse aux Meadows, Newfoundland, Norse settlement in, 24
Latter-Day Saints. *See* Church of Jesus Christ of Latter-Day Saints
Laycock, Douglas, 175–76, 230, 236–37, 311
Lee, Justin, 208n5
Leff, Arthur Allen, 174
legal rights, concept of, 20n50
Legaspi, Michael, 217
Leo XIII (pope), 80, 90
LGBT community, 27, 92, 94, 175, 185–86, 204–6, 211–13, 218–27, 233–34, 240, 263, 311. *See also* gender issues; same-sex marriage
liberation theology, 276–77
The Liberator (abolitionist magazine), 52, 77n19
Ligonier proposal for united Orthodox Church of North America, 164–67
Linakis, Yorka, 148
Lincoln, Abraham, 37, 54
Liveris, Leonie, 199
Locke, John, 8, 40, 43, 274, 301, 304
Ludwell, Philip, 51
Lukin, Constantine, 194–95
Luther, Martin, 64
Lutheranism, 44n27, 59, 63–65, 96, 186n28, 224n39

MacIntyre, Alasdair, 271, 277–78
MacPherson, C. B., 6n14
Madison, James, 39, 42, 55
Magazine of the German Reformed Church, 58
Maidansky, Vsevolod, 166
Makarrii (hieromonk in Alaska), 193
Malik, Charles, 243–62; academic career, 246–49, 259; background and education, 243, 245–46; brothers, conversion and Catholic priesthood of, 244, 248, 259; on conflict in Middle East, 257, 258–59, 261–62; ecumenism of, 249, 255; on Islam, 255; Orthodox faith of, 244, 245–46, 249–50, 253–54, 255–56, 258–62; permanent minority, on Christian acceptance as, 97, 258–59; political and diplomatic career, 243, 246–47, 248, 259; rejection of Arab Nationalism and

Malik, Charles (*continued*)
   pan-Arabism, 248, 256, 257; reputation and
   legacy of, 244, 259–61; theological and
   philosophical thought of, 249–55; on U.N.
   Human Rights Commission and Declaration
   of Human Rights, 243–45, 256–57; Western
   thought, comfort with, 243, 246, 247,
   249–50, 252–53, 255–56, 259
Malik, Mikhail Nicolas (uncle), 245
Maritain, Jacques, 244, 249
Maronites, 249, 256
marriage. *See* civil unions; polygamy; same-sex
   marriage; women, sexuality, gender, and
   marriage
Marsden, George M., 42
Marshall, John, 37
The Mathematical Principles of Natural Philosophy
   (Newton), 301
Matthopoulos, Efsevia, 198
Maximos (Ecumenical Patriarch), 137
Maximus the Confessor, 215, 216, 219n28
McConnell, Michael, 231, 233, 234
McKinley, William, 73
Melnick, Shep, 188–89
Melville, Herman, 54
men's movement, 190
Meschersky, Evdokim, 285n143
Metaxakis, Meletios, 134–36
Methodists and Methodism, 42, 52–53, 60, 62
Meyendorff, John, 22, 91, 139, 154, 158
Meyendorff, Paul, 154
Miaphysite Christians, 19
Milbank, John, 28, 278
Milivojevich, Dionisije, 136
Mollard, Tikhon, 144
moral equality, right to, 240–41
Moral Majority, 188
moral rights, 20n50, 239–41, 257, 284
Morcos, Elias, 158
Mormons. *See* Church of Jesus Christ of
   Latter-Day Saints
Moscow Council of 1917–18, 100–1, 126–28,
   145, 200–1
Movsesian, Mark L., 265
Moyn, Samuel, 282–83
Murray, John Courtney, 90–91
Muslims. *See* Islam

Nasser, Gamal Abdel, 248, 257
National Association for the Advancement of
   Colored People (NAACP), 111
National Reform Association, 62
National Sisterhood of Presbyteres, 201
Native Americans. *See* First Peoples

natural rights: above, beyond, outside, and
   prior to institutions, 20n50; government
   police powers and, 106; Leo XIII's *Rerum
   Novarum* and, 90; MacIntyre on, 278;
   Malik and, 243; modern versus classical
   concepts of, 28, 268, 270, 278; in North
   America, 35, 37–40, 56, 57; origins and
   development of, 3, 6–9; Wolterstorff on,
   270, 271–72, 274
Nayden, Henry E., 73n12
NeJaime, Douglas, 175
Neo-Platonism, 278–79
neo-Thomism, 279
Netherlands, principled public pluralism in, 268
"neutral principles" doctrine, 22, 108n45, 141,
   163, 231, 236
New Christian Right, 188
New Deal, 191
New Jersey, voting rights for women in, 181
New Orleans claimed as oldest site of
   Orthodox presence, 134
New Smyrna, FL, early Greek Orthodox
   immigration to, 134
New Woman movement, 183
New York Observer, 58
Newton, Sir Isaac, 301, 303
Nicaea, First Council of, 82
Nicholas I (tsar), 101, 291–93
Nicholas (Metropolitan of Carpatho-Rusyn
   diocese), 166
Nicholas of Cusa, 50
Nicolas (bishop in Alaska), 73, 74
Niebuhr, Reinhold, 309
Niederberger, Andreas, 279
Nikodim (Metropolitan of Moscow), 128,
   138, 139
Nineteenth Amendment, 183, 195
nineteenth-century Orthodox confrontations
   with rights, 25–26, 67–88; Alaska, Orthodox
   Church and Presbyterian missionaries in,
   24, 25, 63, 67–75, 83, 84; Enlightenment,
   attacks on legacy of, 25, 45–46; European
   culture and civilization, American project of
   spreading, 46–47; immigration to U.S. and,
   62, 76, 83, 102–3; individual conscience versus
   confessional authority, 83–86; Philippines,
   lack of support for U.S. in, 73–74; pluralism
   and freedom of speech/expression, 98–103;
   property and contract rights of religious
   bodies, 80–82, 86–87; Protestant concept of
   Christian society and, 69; Russia, emancipation of serfs in, 75–76; Social Gospel
   movement and, 85–86. *See also* Ottoman
   Empire

Ninth Amendment, 176
Nixon, Richard, 93
Noachic law, 6–7
Noli, Fan, 136
Noll, Mark A., 42, 186, 187
North America, rights in, 34–66; civil rights, 56–61; conservative republicanism versus libertarianism, 45–48; ecclesial constitutionalism, 48–51; Englishmen, rights of, 8, 9, 34, 37, 38; Enlightenment and, 40–41, 43, 45, 47; experience-based nature of, 34–35; human rights, 280; immigrants from Eastern, Central, and Southern Europe/Middle East and, 62, 76, 83, 102–3, 116–19; individual rights, 36–73; late eighteenth century, competing visions in, 36–47; legal and constitutional tradition, 55–62; origins and development of, 9, 22, 36–41; polygamy debate, 52, 55, 60–62, 80; Protestant concept of Christian society and, 48–56, 59–65; Reformed Protestantism shaping, 26, 42–45, 52, 58, 60, 62–65; religious liberty, 50–51, 58–64; rights revolution and, 21–23; Scottish Common Sense philosophers, influence of, 39, 41–45, 303, 304; Second Great Awakening, 53–55; separation of church and state in, 53, 55–56, 63–64n67; slavery and abolitionism, 47, 51–52, 54, 55, 56–57, 60, 61. See also Orthodox Church and rights in North America
Notitia Dignitatum, 13

Oakley, Francis, 4
Obama, Barack, 222
Obergefell v. Hodges (2015), 92nn4–5, 177, 225
The Object of Knowledge (Frank), 250
Ofiesh, Aftimios, 151
oikonomia, 10–12, 13n30, 162
Omar Ibn al-Khatab (caliph), 83
Onufrij (Kyiv Metropolitan), 295–96
ordination of women, 197, 203
Organic Act, 73
Organization of Islamic Cooperation, 156
Origen, 207
Orthodox Christianity and Gender, 214, 215
Orthodox Church and rights in North America, 21–33, 287–312; Christian realism and just peacemaking, proper pursuit of, 308–12; COVID-19 pandemic and, 29, 287–90; ecclesial self-government, 27, 116–72 (See also self-government); episcopal rights, privileges, and authority, 10–20, 142–45, 159–64, 309–10; epistemic crisis of twenty-first century and digital media threats, 305–8;

ethnic nationalism, problem of, 297–98 (see also ethnic nationalism); history, composition, and numbers of Orthodox in America, 23–25; human rights and, 28–29, 239–85 (see also human rights); in nineteenth century, 25–26, 67–88 (see also nineteenth-century Orthodox confrontations with rights); North American rights concepts, 34–66 (see also North America, rights in); origins and development of concept of rights, 1–9; pluralism and, 26–27, 89–115 (see also pluralism and freedom of speech/expression); Reid's Scottish Common Sense philosophy and, 43–44; "right and just," Greek, Russian, and Slavonic terms for, 12; rights revolution and, 21–23, 185–86; Russian invasion of Ukraine and, 29, 128n22, 289–97; scientific revolution and problem of knowledge, 298–305; social justice tradition, Orthodox lack of, 34, 35–36; women, sexuality, gender, and marriage, 27, 173–238 (see also gender issues; women, sexuality, gender, and marriage)
Orthodox Church in America (OCA): autocephaly of, 125–33, 139–45, 149–59, 201, 203; Russian invasion of Ukraine, condemnation of, 295–96
Orthodox Indian Temperance and Mutual Aid Society, 74–75
Orthodox Tradition and Human Sexuality, 214, 215–16, 217
Orthodox Youth Movement, 158
Orthodox-Roman Catholic Theological Consultation, on abortion, 173–74
Otis, James, 39
Ottoman Empire: Arabic Christians, rights of, 81–84; Armenian genocide, 82; ethnic nationalism in, 76, 79; millet system in, 76, 77, 78, 79; Orthodox awareness of North American society in, 49; Patriarch Joachim II's condemnation of slavery, 76n18, 77–78, 79–80; Patriarchate of Jerusalem taken over by Greek Orthodox Brotherhood of the Holy Sepulcher, 82–83; Tanzimat reforms in, 78–79

Pabst, Adrian, 28, 278
Paffhausen, James, 142
Paine, Thomas, 37, 180
Palestinian-Israeli conflict, 117, 119, 257, 283
Palestinians immigrating to U.S., 117–19
pan-Arabic revolt (1936–39), 117
pan-Arabism, 256
Pan-Orthodox Synods/Congresses, 76, 130, 131n27, 164, 166

Pan-Slavic Brotherhood of Saints Cyril and Methodius, 292
Papadopoulos, Chrysostomos, 134
Papageorgiou, Spyridon. *See* Spyridon
Papanikolaou, Aristotle, 215–16, 218, 241, 262–63, 264, 266–67, 270, 275
Paris, Russian exarchate in, 127, 138–39
Paris, Thomas, 148
Parsenios, George, 217
Pascal, Blaise, 300
Paul (apostle), 6–7, 207–9
Paul VI (pope), 138
Pendleton, Edmund, 54
Pentiuc, Eugen, 217
Perry, Michael, 239–41, 309
personalism, 7n16, 216, 249, 251
personhood, Orthodox understanding of, 5n10, 7n16, 244, 247, 258, 262, 266–67, 277, 281, 284, 285
Peter I the Great (Russian emperor), 101, 292
Petra, Basilio, 251
Philip (Antiochan Metropolitan). *See* Saliba, Philip
Philippines: U.S. in, 73–74; White Russians fleeing to, 118
Phillipovsky, Adam, 152
Philo of Alexandria, 207
philotimo, 206
Photios II (Ecumenical Patriarch), 127
phyletism, 76
Pico della Mirandola, Giovanni, 4
Piketty, Thomas, 307
pluralism and freedom of speech/expression, 26–27, 89–115; challenges posed by, 90–98; Civil Rights movement, 96, 109–15, 121; dissent, right of, 94, 175–76, 178–79, 190, 222–23, 225, 227, 230–38, 311; First Amendment, 62, 106, 141, 232, 308; internalization by Orthodox, 119–21; interrelationship between, 89–90; Jewish commentators on, 91–92; Ku Klux Klan, Orthodox response to rebirth of, 103–6; nineteenth to mid-twentieth century Orthodox responses to, 98–108; polygamists' invocation of, 62; in pre-Revolutionary Russia, 98–102; Roman Catholicism and Vatican I, 90–91; Supreme Court and, 106–8; ten Napel on, 268
polygamy: Alaska First Peoples and, 68; Church of Jesus Christ of Latter-Day Saints (Mormons) and, 52, 55, 60–62, 80, 182; Islamic practice of, 60
Porter, Roy, 304
The Presbyterian and Theological Review, 77n19
Presbyterianism: Alaska, Presbyterian missionaries in, 24, 25, 63, 67–75, 83, 84, 282; Briggs

heresy trial, 85; National Reform Association and, 42, 53, 58, 60, 62; in North America, 42, 53, 58, 60, 62, 64; social justice tradition and, 58; traditional values movement and, 187; Walnut Street Presbyterian Church, Louisville, KY, and property rights of religious bodies, 80–81; Women's Executive Committee and Women's Board of the Home Missionary Society, 67
Presbytery of Beaver-Butler of United Presbyterian Church v. Middlesex Presbyterian Church (1985), 141
Prevelakis, Nicholas, 266–67
Prince v. Commonwealth of Massachusetts (1944), 288–89
privacy, right to, 22, 176–77, 184, 185, 189, 224, 234, 308
procedural due process, 57n54, 309
Prohibition, 106
Promise Keepers, 190
property and contract rights of religious bodies, 80–82, 86–87, 107–8, 117, 140–42, 159–64
Protestant Evangelical Orthodox Church, 158, 159, 160, 163–64
Protestant Reformation, 300
Protestantism: Christian society, concept of, 48–56, 59–65; Civil Rights movement and, 111; evangelicals, 93, 94, 185–91, 227–28, 288; First Peoples, federal funding to missionize, 55; freedom of speech/expression and, 27; Greek Orthodox in North America and values of, 149; human rights and, 28, 241, 242, 267–76, 279, 283–84; on individual conscience versus confessional authority, 83–86; Malik and, 255; North American rights concepts and, 40; Orthodox theology and Church life, awareness of, 49; Philippines, support for U.S. in, 74; Russian restrictions on proselytization by, 93; shaping of U.S. society and, 25–26; traditional values movement and, 185–91; Vatican I, response to, 83–84; women, sex, gender, and marriage issues, 185–91, 205, 209, 212, 213, 217, 219. *See also specific denominations*
pseudo-Dionysius the Areopagite, 250
public school policy, 94, 113, 178, 186–87, 222–23
Putin, Vladimir, 93, 294, 295

Quakers, 308–9
quarantine powers, 289
Queer Christian Fellowship, 208n5

race/racism. *See* African Americans; First Peoples; slavery and abolitionism
Rauch, Jonathan, 305–6

Rauschenbusch, Walter, 85
realism, Christian, 309
Reeb, James, 112
Reformed Protestantism: Christian society, Protestant concept of, 52, 60, 62–65, 69, 70; Dutch Reformed Church, 62; French Reformed Church, 199; German Reformed Church, 58, 62; human rights and, 267, 269, 270, 273n103, 281; National Reform Association and, 62; nineteenth-century Orthodox confrontation with rights and, 69, 70, 85n35; North American rights concepts shaped by, 26, 42–45, 52, 58, 60, 62–65; pluralism and freedom of speech/expression, 96; Southern Reformed theologians, 58; Swiss Reformed Church, 85n35; two kingdoms concept and, 186n28
Regan, Ethna, 276–77
Reid, Thomas, 42–45, 270, 275, 304
Religious Freedom Restoration Act (RFRA; 1994), 232, 311
religious liberty: internalization by Orthodox, 120–21; North American rights concepts and, 50–51, 58–64; origins of, 50; refugees making use of American commitments to, 119. See also pluralism and freedom of speech/expression
Religious News Service, 157
Renaissance humanism, 300
reproductive rights. See abortion
Republican Party, Orthodox shift toward from, 93–94
Rerum Novarum (1891), 90
Retter, Mark, 278
Revoice (LGBT group), 213
Reynolds v. United States (1878), 61–62
Rich, Bryce E., 213, 216
right to life. See abortion
rights, concept of, 1–20; episcopal rights, privileges, and authority in Orthodox Church, 10–20; in North America, 9, 22, 36–41; origins and development, 1–9; rights revolution, 21–23, 185–86. See also Orthodox Church and rights in North America; specific types of rights, e.g. civil rights
Rights of Man (Paine), 180
Riurik (Varangian prince), 292
Roe v. Wade (1973), 173, 175, 176, 184–85, 188
Roman Catholicism: anti-Catholicism in U.S. after rebirth of Ku Klux Klan, 103–4; Civil Rights movement and, 113, 114n60; diaconate, on admission of women to, 202; discipline and juridical enforcement in, 122; freedom of speech/expression and, 27; Greek Catholics, 117, 134; human rights and, 28,

241, 242, 244, 267, 268, 271, 276–79, 281, 283–84; on individual conscience versus confessional authority, 83–86; Malik's brothers, conversion and Catholic priesthood of, 244, 248, 259; Maronites, 249, 256; Orthodox theology and Church life, awareness of, 49; Orthodox-Roman Catholic Theological Consultation, on abortion, 173–74; Philippines, support for U.S. in, 74; pluralism and freedom of speech/expression, 90–91, 96; Prohibition, opposition to, 106; Ruthenian Catholics, 117; sex abuse scandals, 189; on slavery and abolitionism, 80; Social Gospel movement and, 85; social justice tradition of, 35, 80; Soviet concerns about Vatican power, 130, 132; trusteeism and charitable trusts in North America, 86n39; Vatican I, 84; Vatican II, 90–91, 138, 276; women, sex, gender, and marriage issues, 183, 191, 192, 202, 205, 209, 213, 217, 218, 219, 222, 224, 236, 237
Roman law, rights in, 2–3, 5, 11, 13–15, 25
Romans, Paul's letter to, 6–7
Rondos, Alexander, 165
Roosevelt, Eleanor, 197, 243, 244
Roosevelt, Franklin Delano, 242–43
Rousseau, Jean-Jacques, 180
Royal Society, 301, 303
Rozhdestvensky, Platon, 124, 134, 135
Ruether, Rosemary, 209
Russia, post-Cold War: Protestant proselytization, restrictions on, 93; traditional values in, 93, 94–95; Ukraine, invasion of, 29, 128n22, 289–97
Russia, pre-Revolutionary: freedom of conscience, Orthodox concepts of, 98–102; national identity, quest for, 291–93; Orthodox awareness of North American society in, 49; serfs, emancipation of, 75–76; U.S. purchase of Alaska from, 24, 69
Russian American Company, 194
Russian exarchate in Europe, 127–28, 138–39
Russian Orthodox American, 74
Russian Orthodox Church: on human rights, 263–65, 290–91; on invasion of Ukraine, 290–91, 294, 295; KGB infiltration of Moscow Patriarchate, 128, 138n41; Moscow Council of 1917–18, 100–1, 126–28, 145; Moscow Patriarchate, efforts to move center of global Orthodoxy to, 130–32, 140, 293; parish defection to Kyiv Patriarchate, 290–91
Russian Orthodox Church Outside Russia (ROCOR), 132, 133, 140, 141, 159, 200, 203

Russian Orthodox in America: in Alaska, 24, 25, 63, 67–75, 83, 84, 193–95; initial efforts to unite Orthodox in America under Russian diocese, 123–25; OCA (Orthodox Church in America), autocephaly claims of, 125–33, 159; "Rusyn" identity of most members of Metropolia, 132–33; St. Nicholas Cathedral, NYC, ownership of, 107–8, 133; women, gender, sex, and marriage amongst, 200–1, 202–3

Russian (Bolshevik) Revolution, 27, 98, 100, 116, 124, 127, 195

Russian Synod of Bishops in Serbia at Sremsky Karlovtsy, 152

Russian-American Orthodox Messenger, 124–25

Ruthenian Catholics, 117

Rutledge, John, 38

Sadusky, Julia, 229

Said, Edward, 259–60n61

Saliba, Philip (Antiochan Orthodox Patriarch), 120–21, 153–55, 157–60, 164, 167–71, 201, 256

same-sex marriage, 92, 94, 175, 177, 189, 211–13, 218, 235, 240, 263

same-sex sexual practices, 211–13

Sargent, Aaron A., 195

Saudi Arabia: King Faisal on Elias IV, 156; at United Nations, 245, 260, 260n62, 283; Wahabism and, 260n62

Scarponi, Letha Dawson, 191

Scheler, Max, 249

Schleiermacher, Friedrich, 209

Schmemann, Alexander, 110, 153, 154, 156, 158

Schmucker, Samuel Simon, 59, 63–64n67

Schneirla, Paul, 153

schools: for First Peoples in Alaska, 55, 71; gender and sexuality issues in, 94, 178, 222–23; homeschooling, 223, 224n39; public school policy, 94, 113, 178, 186–87, 222–23; racial integration of schools, 113, 187; religion in public schools, 186, 187; religious schools, 224n39, 234

scientific revolution and problem of knowledge, 298–305

Scott, Richard, 247

Scottish Common Sense philosophers, 39, 41–45, 270, 275, 303, 304

Second Great Awakening, 53–55

Second Vatican Council, 90–91, 138, 276

Second World War, 114, 119, 136, 198, 242n6

second-wave feminism, 190, 191, 205

secular human rights regimes, 240, 241, 242, 267, 270, 272, 279–85

self-government, 27, 116–72; Antiochan "autonomous" or "self-ruled" archdiocese,

controversy over, 168–70; autocephaly claims of OCA, 125–33, 139–45, 149–59, 201, 203; episcopal authority in, 142–45; Greek Orthodox in America and, 128, 130, 131, 134–40, 152–59; immigration of Orthodox to U.S., 116–19; internal disputes between individual hierarchs and groups of bishops, 121–25; internalization of values of freedom of speech/expression and, 119–21; property and contract rights of religious bodies, 117, 133, 140–42; Russian diocese, initial efforts to unite Orthodox in America under, 123–25; Russian Orthodox Church and, 125–33, 159; united Orthodox Church of North America, Ligonier proposal for, 164–67

Selma, march on, 111–12

Seneca Falls, NY, convention (1848), 182

separation of church and state: in North America, 53, 55–56, 63–64n67; in pre-Revolutionary Russian Church, 101

Serbian Eastern Orthodox Diocese v. Milivojevich (1976), 162, 163

Serbian Orthodox Church, 136, 294

serfs, Russian emancipation of, 75–76

Sevastianos of Zela, 150

sexuality. *See* gender issues; women, sexuality, gender, and marriage

Shaheen, Michael, 153, 167

Shapin, Steven, 299–300, 304

Shapiro, Barbara, 300–1, 303

Shapiro, Ian, 6n14

Sheldon, Lou, 187–88

Siegel, Reva B., 175–76

silent majority, 93

Sirmondian Constitutions, 14

Six Day War, 283

slavery and abolitionism: concepts of rights in North America and, 47, 51–52, 54, 55, 56–57, 60, 61; Patriarch Joachim II on, 77–78, 80; Roman Catholicism and, 80; serfs, Russian emancipation of, 75–76; Walnut Street Presbyterian Church, Louisville, KY, and property rights of religious bodies, 81; women's civil rights and, 182

Smith, Adam, 304

Smith, Gerrit, 59

sobornost, 100, 145, 310

Sobrino, Jon, 276–77

social justice: in North America, 58–59; Orthodox lack of tradition of, 34, 35–36; Presbyterianism and, 58; in Roman Catholicism, 35, 80; Social Gospel movement, 85–86

Social Teachings of the Christian Churches (Troeltsch), 96

socialist and labor movements and Greek Orthodox in North America, 114
Socialist Labor Party, 114
Society of Friends, 308–9
Soloviev, Vladimir, 101, 249
Sophiology, 250n25
Sophronios of Jerusalem, 83
Soviet Union: anti-religious campaign of 1958–64 in, 129; Cold War, 27, 128, 248, 280; Ecumenical Patriarchate, campaign against, 128, 130–32, 137–40; end of Cold War and collapse of, 280; Jews living in, 283; KGB, 128, 138n41; Moscow Patriarchate, efforts to move center of global Orthodoxy to, 130–32, 140, 293; Moscow Patriarchate, KGB infiltration of, 128, 138n41; OCA ([Russian] Orthodox Church in America), autocephaly claims of, 128–33; St. Nicholas Cathedral, NYC, ownership of, 107–8; U.N. Declaration of Human Rights and, 243, 244, 245; White Russians fleeing, 118–19
speech, freedom of. See pluralism and freedom of speech/expression
Sperou, Aristocles, 136. See also Athenagoras
Spinoza, Baruch, 9
Spyridon (Papageorgiou; Greek Orthodox Archbishop of North America), 146–49, 165
St. Basil, parish of, Simpson, PA, 140–41
St. John the Baptist Russian Orthodox Church, Mayfield, PA, 141
St. Nicholas Cathedral, NYC, ownership of, 107–8, 133
St. Phoebe Center for the Deaconess, 202, 203
St. Raphael Clergy Brotherhood of Wichita, KS, 169
St. Sergius Institute, Paris, 127, 138–39, 153, 154, 158
St. Vladimir's Orthodox Theological Seminary, 153, 154
Stalin, Josef, 130, 132, 136–37
Standing Conference of Orthodox Bishops (SCOBA), 153, 154, 164–67
Stephen II of Antioch, 19
Stewart, Chris, 233
Stockholm Declaration of the United Nations' Conference on the Human Environment, 242n6
Stoeckl, Kristina, 290
Stoics and stoicism, 1–2
Stromberg v. California (1931), 106
Stylianopoulos, Theodore, 217
subjective rights, 1, 3, 5, 6, 36, 37
substantive due process, 57, 176, 177, 185
Suez Crisis (1956), 248

Sullivan, Winnifred Fallers, 265
Supreme Court, U.S.: dissent, right of, 230–32, 234, 235; historical development of rights in North America and, 55, 61–62; nineteenth-century Orthodox confrontations with rights and, 80–81; pluralism and freedom of speech/expression, 92, 106–8; on religion in schools, 186; rights revolution and, 185–86; self-governed American Orthodox church and, 133, 141, 162–63; on vaccination mandates, 288; women, sexuality, gender, and marriage issues, 173–77, 185, 210–11, 225, 230–32, 234, 235. See also specific cases
surveillance capitalism, 306
Svoboda, 116
Sword, Kirsten, 181n18
Syrian Orthodox. See Arabic-origin/Antiochan Orthodox

Tahan, Alexander, 152
Tasioulas, John, 282n135, 284
Taylor, Charles, 28
The Teachings of Modern Christianity (Witte and Alexander), 23, 27, 28
Teller, Henry M., 72
ten Napel, Hans-Martien, 267–69
Teresa of Avila, 243, 244, 248, 255
The Word Magazine, 157
Theodoros (Patriarch of Alexandria), 202, 294
Theodorou, Evangelos, 196–97, 199, 202
Theodosian Code, 14
Theodosius VI (Patriarch of Antioch), 139, 152, 155–56
theology of the body, 205
Theophan (hieromonk in Alaska), 194
theosis, 11n27, 44n27, 228, 276
Thermos, Vasileios, 219–20, 226, 229
Thirteenth Amendment, 52
Thirty Years' War, 298, 304
Thomas Aquinas, 243, 244, 248, 255, 259, 268, 271, 278
Thornwall, James Henley, 58
Tierney, Brian, 4, 5–6, 278
Tikhon (Mollard; Metropolitan of OCA), 144
Tikhon (Patriarch of Moscow). See Bellavin, Tikhon
Title VII, 224
Title IX, 222n36, 223, 227
Tomos of Autocephaly. See Orthodox Church in America; self-government
Toth, Alexis, 117
tradition in Orthodox Church, 10n23

Traditional Values Coalition, 187–88
traditional values movement, 185–91
transgender individuals, 94, 175, 178, 210,
    222–29, 226n46, 263. *See also* gender issues;
    LGBT community; women, sexuality, gender,
    and marriage
Troeltsch, Ernest, 96
Truman, Harry, 114
Trump, Donald, 93
Tsalampouni, Ektarini, 217
Turkey's alliance with NATO, 137, 139
Turveich, Leonty, 152
Twain, Mark, 54
"two kingdoms" concept, 65, 186n28

Uhalde, Kevin, 17
Ukraine: anti-religious campaign of 1958–64
    in, 129; Crimea, Russian seizure of, 294; ethnic
    nationalism in, 129; independent nation-state,
    international recognition of, 294; Russian
    invasion of, 29, 128n22, 289–97; Russian
    quest for national identity and, 291–93
Ukrainian Orthodox Church: autocephaly of,
    295, 297; eparchate under Constantinople,
    166; Russian Orthodox parish defection to
    Kyiv Patriarchate, 290–91; of USA, 166, 295
ultra-Orthodox communities, 214
United Nations: Convention on Elimination of
    All Forms of Religious Intolerance, 283;
    Convention Relating to the Status of Refu-
    gees, 118; Malik and, 243–45, 246–47;
    Stockholm Declaration of the Conference on
    the Human Environment, 242n6; Universal
    Declaration of Human Rights, 118, 119,
    242n6, 243–44, 256–57, 260n62, 280
united Orthodox Church of North America,
    Ligonier proposal for, 164–67
United States. *See* North America, rights in
United States v. Windsor (2013), 185
Universal Declaration of Human Rights, United
    Nations, 118, 119, 242n6, 243–44, 256–57,
    260n62, 280

vaccination mandates, 288–89
Vadkovskii, Antonii, 100
Valliere, Paul, 249
Vasilevich, Natallia, 220
Vatican I, 84
Vatican II, 90–91, 138, 276
Venianimov, Ivan/John. *See* Innocent
Venizelos, Eleftherios, 136
Vestnik, 125
Vietnam War, 129
Villey, Michael, 5, 6
virginity/celibacy, 212, 218

Voitha, 147
Volodomyr of Kiev, 293

Wahabism, 260n62
Walnut Street Presbyterian Church, Louisville,
    KY, 80–81
Watson, John, 109
Watson v. Jones (1871), 81, 108, 162
Weber, Max, 298
Wechsler, Herbert, 163
The Wheel, 225–26
Whitehead, Alfred North, 246, 247
Wikipedia, 306
Wilkins, John, 303
William of Ockham, 5, 7–8
Witherspoon, John, 42, 45
Witte, John, Jr., 23, 27, 28, 31, 89, 238n67,
    239, 267
Woese, Carl, 226n44
Wollstonecraft, Mary, 180
Wolterstorff, Nicholas, 28, 43, 241, 269–76,
    278, 281, 284, 308, 309
women, sexuality, gender, and marriage, 27,
    173–204; abortion, right to life, and repro-
    ductive rights, 94, 173–77, 184, 188, 231,
    234; AIDS epidemic, 185; Alaska First
    Peoples, concerns about, 68, 193–95; birth
    control, 184, 231, 234n61; Bridegroom of the
    Church, Christ as, 210; civil and political
    rights for women, 180–86, 191, 195, 197–98;
    civil unions, 224, 225n40; clerical sex
    scandals, 189; contextual background,
    174–79; dissent, right of, 175–76, 178–79,
    190, 222–23, 225, 227, 230–38, 311; DOMA
    (Defense of Marriage Act), 185; equal partner
    marriage, 191; equal protection claims, 189,
    312; family structure and cohesion, 190, 191;
    free choice and agency, right of, 188, 224,
    228; historical shift from women's studies to
    gender studies, 179; legal accommodation of
    sexual liberty, 211; LGBT community, 27,
    92, 94, 175, 185–86, 204–6, 211–13, 218–27,
    233–34, 240, 263, 311; men's movement, 190;
    ministry, role for women in, 177, 196–97,
    199, 202–3; Moscow Council of 1917–18 on,
    100; Presbyterian Women's Executive Com-
    mittee and Women's Board of the Home
    Missionary Society, 67; priests and deacons,
    wives of, 201; privacy, constitutional right to,
    22, 176–77, 184, 185, 189, 224, 234; procre-
    ation as purpose of sex/marriage, 215–16;
    rights revolution and, 185–86; role of
    Orthodox women in Church and society,
    196–204; same-sex marriage, 92, 94, 175,
    177, 189, 211–13, 218, 235, 240, 263; same-sex

sexual practices, 211–13, 220; theological deliberations, participation of women in, 199, 200–1; traditional values movement and, 185–91; virginity/celibacy, 212, 218. *See also* gender issues
Women and Religiosity in Orthodox Christianity, 214–15
World Council of Churches (WCC), 198–99
World Summit in Defense of Persecuted Christians, 93
World War I, 64, 102, 105
World War II, 114, 119, 136, 198, 242n6

Yannaras, Christos, 198, 250–52, 262, 309
Yarhouse, Mark A., 227–29

Zain, Thomas, 162n26
Ziorov, Nikolai, 83
Zizioulas, John, 209–10, 251n32, 266
Zoe movement, 197–98
Zollmann, Carl, 86
Zorach v. Clausen (1952), 107
Zuboff, Shoshana, 306–7
Zucht v. King (1922), 288

The **Rev. Dr. A. G. Roeber** is Emeritus Professor of Early Modern History and Religious Studies at Penn State University, and Professor of Church History at St. Vladimir's Orthodox Theological Seminary. Author of many books, his *Palatines, Liberty, and Property: German Lutherans in Colonial British America* was the 1983 co-winner of the American Historical Association's John H. Dunning Prize. A past president of the Orthodox Theological Society in America, he is also co-author of *Changing Churches: An Orthodox, Catholic, and Lutheran Theological Conversation* (2012), author of *Mixed Marriages: An Orthodox History* (2018), and editor of *Human v. Religious Rights?: German and U.S. Exchanges and Their Global Implications* (2020).

ORTHODOX CHRISTIANITY AND CONTEMPORARY THOUGHT

SERIES EDITORS
Aristotle Papanikolaou and Ashley M. Purpura

A. G. Roeber, *Orthodox Christianity and the Rights Revolution in America*

Bryce E. Rich, *Gender Essentialism and Orthodoxy: Beyond Male and Female*

Kristina Stoeckl and Dmitry Uzlaner, *The Moralist International: Russia in the Global Culture Wars*

Sarah Riccardi-Swartz, *Between Heaven and Russia: Religious Conversion and Political Apostasy in Appalachia*

Thomas Arentzen, Ashley M. Purpura, and Aristotle Papanikolaou (eds.), *Orthodox Tradition and Human Sexuality*

Christina M. Gschwandtner, *Welcoming Finitude: Toward a Phenomenology of Orthodox Liturgy*

George E. Demacopoulos, *Colonizing Christianity: Greek and Latin Religious Identity in the Era of the Fourth Crusade.*

Pia Sophia Chaudhari, *Dynamis of Healing: Patristic Theology and the Psyche*

Brian A. Butcher, *Liturgical Theology after Schmemann: An Orthodox Reading of Paul Ricoeur.* Foreword by Andrew Louth.

Ashley M. Purpura, *God, Hierarchy, and Power: Orthodox Theologies of Authority from Byzantium.*

Aristotle and George E. Demacopoulos (eds.), *Faith, Reason, and Theosis*

Aristotle Papanikolaou and George E. Demacopoulos (eds.), *Fundamentalism or Tradition: Christianity after Secularism*

George E. Demacopoulos and Aristotle Papanikolaou (eds.), *Christianity, Democracy, and the Shadow of Constantine.*

George E. Demacopoulos and Aristotle Papanikolaou (eds.), *Orthodox Constructions of the West.*

George E. Demacopoulos and Aristotle Papanikolaou (eds.), *Orthodox Readings of Augustine* [available 2020]

John Chryssavgis and Bruce V. Foltz (eds.), *Toward an Ecology of Transfiguration: Orthodox Christian Perspectives on Environment, Nature, and Creation.* Foreword by Bill McKibben. Prefatory Letter by Ecumenical Patriarch Bartholomew.

Lucian N. Leustean (ed.), *Orthodox Christianity and Nationalism in Nineteenth-Century Southeastern Europe.*

Georgia Frank, Susan R. Holman, and Andrew S. Jacobs (eds.), *The Garb of Being: Embodiment and the Pursuit of Holiness in Late Ancient Christianity*

John Chryssavgis (ed.), *Dialogue of Love: Breaking the Silence of Centuries.* Contributions by Brian E. Daley, S.J., and Georges Florovsky

Ecumenical Patriarch Bartholomew, *In the World, Yet Not of the World: Social and Global Initiatives of Ecumenical Patriarch Bartholomew*. Edited by John Chryssavgis. Foreword by Jose Manuel Barroso

Ecumenical Patriarch Bartholomew, *Speaking the Truth in Love: Theological and Spiritual Exhortations of Ecumenical Patriarch Bartholomew*. Edited by John Chryssavgis. Foreword by Dr. Rowan Williams, Archbishop of Canterbury.

Ecumenical Patriarch Bartholomew, *On Earth as in Heaven: Ecological Vision and Initiatives of Ecumenical Patriarch Bartholomew*. Edited by John Chryssavgis. Foreword by His Royal Highness, the Duke of Edinburgh.